TRANSNATIONAL LAW

In this era of globalisation, different legal systems and structures no longer operate within their own jurisdictions. Decisions, policies and political developments are having an increasingly wide-reaching impact. Nowhere is this more keenly felt than in the sphere of European Union law. This collection of essays contributes to the cooperative search for interpretative and normative grids needed in charting the contemporary legal landscape. Written by leading lawyers and legal philosophers, they examine the effects of law's denationalisation by placing European law in the context of transnational law, demonstrate how it forces us to rethink our basic legal concepts and propose an approach to transnational law beyond the dichotomy of national and international law.

MIGUEL MADURO is Deputy Prime Minister and Minister for Regional Development in the Portuguese Government. He is also Professor of European Law and Director of the Global Governance programme at the European University Institute. From 2003–9 he was Advocate General at the Court of Justice of the European Union. He is the winner of several awards for scientific excellence including the Gulbenkian Science Prize and Obiettivo Europa.

KAARLO TUORI is Professor of Jurisprudence and Academy Professor at the University of Helsinki. He is also Vice-President of the Venice Commission of the Council of Europe and serves as a consulting expert on the Constitutional Law Committee at the Finnish Parliament.

SUVI SANKARI is Postdoctoral Researcher at the Centre of Excellence in the Foundations of European Law and Polity at the University of Helsinki.

TRANSNATIONAL LAW

Rethinking European Law and Legal Thinking

Edited by

MIGUEL MADURO

KAARLO TUORI

and

SUVI SANKARI

CAMBRIDGE
UNIVERSITY PRESS

CAMBRIDGE
UNIVERSITY PRESS

University Printing House, Cambridge CB2 8BS, United Kingdom

Cambridge University Press is part of the University of Cambridge.

It furthers the University's mission by disseminating knowledge in the pursuit of
education, learning and research at the highest international levels of excellence.

www.cambridge.org
Information on this title: www.cambridge.org/9781107028319

© Cambridge University Press 2014

First published 2014

Printed in the United Kingdom by Clays, St Ives plc

A catalogue record for this publication is available from the British Library

Library of Congress Cataloging in Publication data
Transnational law : rethinking European law and legal thinking / edited by Miguel Maduro,
Kaarlo Tuori, Suvi Sankari.
pages cm
"This volume presents a collection of contributions originally prepared for events convened by
the Centre of Excellence in the Foundations of European Law and Polity" – Introduction.
Includes bibliographical references and index.
ISBN 978-1-107-02831-9 (hardback)
1. Law – European Union countries – Congresses. 2. International and municipal law –
European Union countries – Congresses. 3. Conflict of laws – European Union countries –
Congresses. 4. Legal polycentricity – European Union countries – Congresses. I. Maduro,
Miguel Poiares, editor of compilation. II. Tuori, Kaarlo, editor of compilation. III. Sankari,
Suvi, editor of compilation.
KJE935   2014
341.242′2 – dc23   2014010129

ISBN 978-1-107-02831-9 Hardback

CONTENTS

v

CONTRIBUTORS

MARCO BASSINI is a Junior Associate at Baker & McKenzie, Milan and a PhD. candidate in Constitutional and European Law at the University of Verona.

JOXERRAMON BENGOETXEA is Professor (titular) in Jurisprudence and Sociology of Law at the University of the Basque Country (UPV/EHU).

SAMANTHA BESSON is Professor of Public International Law and European Law and Co-director of the European Law Institute at the University of Freiburg.

BEATRICE I. BONAFÈ is Associate Professor of International Law at the University of Rome, La Sapienza.

GIACINTO DELLA CANANEA is Visiting Professor of Law at Yale Law School and Professor of Law at the University of Rome.

ENZO CANNIZZARO is Professor of International and European Law at the University of Rome, La Sapienza.

SIONAIDH DOUGLAS-SCOTT is a Fellow of Lady Margaret Hall and Professor of European and Human Rights Law at the University of Oxford. She is also a barrister and a member of Gray's Inn.

H. PATRICK GLENN holds the Peter M. Laing Chair of the Faculty of Law at McGill University, Montreal.

CHRISTIAN JOERGES is Research Professor, Centre of European Law and Politics, University of Bremen and Professor of Law and Society at the Hertie School of Governance in Berlin.

MIGUEL MADURO is Deputy Prime Minister and Minister for Regional Development of the Portuguese Government. He is also Professor of European Law and Director of the Global Governance programme at the European University Institute.

RALF MICHAELS is Arthur Larson Professor of Law at Duke University School of Law, Durham, North Carolina.

HANS-W. MICKLITZ is Professor for Economic Law at the European University Institute, Florence.

ORESTE POLLICINO is Associate Professor in Comparative Public Law at the Bocconi University, Milan.

SUVI SANKARI is Postdoctoral Researcher at the Centre of Excellence in the Foundations of European Law and Polity, University of Helsinki.

ALEXANDER SOMEK holds the Charles E. Floete Chair in Law, University of Iowa, College of Law.

JAN M. SMITS holds the Chair of European Private Law at Maastricht University, is the Visiting Professor of Comparative Legal Studies at the University of Helsinki and the academic director of the Maastricht European Private Law Institute.

KAARLO TUORI is Professor of Jurisprudence and Academy Professor at the University of Helsinki. He is also Vice-President of the Venice Commission of the Council of Europe and serves as a consulting expert on the Constitutional Law Committee at the Finnish Parliament.

NEIL WALKER is Professor of Public Law and the Law of Nature and Nations at the University of Edinburgh.

~

Introduction

KAARLO TUORI AND SUVI SANKARI

This volume presents a collection of contributions originally prepared for events convened by the Centre of Excellence in the Foundations of European Law and Polity, funded by the Academy of Finland and directed by Kaarlo Tuori. One important aspect of the Centre's work is to rethink or reassess traditional legal-theoretical, conceptual and doctrinal starting points – 'traditionally' bound to the nation-state perspective – that are considered insufficient for discussing transnationalisation. As for lack of a viable option, nation-state bound vocabulary forms the starting point for examining transnational frameworks: it cannot simply be abandoned but must be reframed or reassessed. To take up this challenge, the Centre's work has brought together researchers from different substantive areas of law to address the challenge faced by both public and private law. The contributors to the present volume have joined forces with the Centre in this quest.

The book opens with Kaarlo Tuori's 'Transnational law: on legal hybrids and perspectivism' (Chapter 1), setting the scene for the chapters to come by seeking an interpretative and normative framework to make sense of transnational legal hybrids that escape the confines of the inherited conceptual frameworks of contemporary lawyers. The point of view is presented as criticism of the radical pluralist position, in order to draw attention to the challenge that legal hybridisation poses on the level of individual legal phenomena and concepts, of traditional systematisation of branches of law, and of legal orders and legal systems. Especially as to relations between legal orders, one should focus on interlegality instead of conflict, unlike radical pluralists. Moreover, approaching transnational law – 'the true El Dorado of legal hybrids' – from the perspective of global interlegality can serve as an exercise in sharpening one's view of the significance of inherent perspectivism and discursiveness in all law.

The rest of the volume is organised in three parts. Part I is devoted to fundamental questions related to transnational law and the legal-theoretical means to address these questions. European law is the most advanced example of transnational law, so it inevitably occupies a central place even in a discussion on the need to rethink legal thinking in the face of the law's increasing transnationalisation. In Part II, the focus is on two concepts, – 'pluralism' and 'justice' – the rethinking of which is central for a legal-theoretical analysis of how European law has changed our legal landscape. Illuminatingly enough, the authors are not unanimous in their definition of these concepts, nor do they necessarily agree with the conceptual proposals presented in the introductory chapter. Once again this testifies to the ongoing cooperative process of renewing our conceptual tools. The law's transnationalisation entails shaking its divisions and the emergence of new branches that, in the framework of traditional systematisation, epitomise legal hybridisation. Part III addresses the impact of transnationalisation on the established fields of municipal law and the need to rethink the law's divisions.

Each chapter in its own way pursues the task of rethinking legal thinking in order to address the consequences of the law's transnationalisation. But each chapter also manifests the state of fermentation in which legal theory finds itself. Proposals for rethinking are not uniform, indeed may even contradict one another, even at the level of basic concepts. Most, but not all, of the authors, use the term 'transnational law' in the sense defined by Tuori in the opening chapter. But in addition to or in lieu of 'transnational' some authors employ the term 'supranational'. No effort has been made to unify terms or concepts; any attempt to do this would have entailed injustice to at least some authors' substantive argument.

Part I on transnational law's fundamental questions and the legal-theoretical means to address them begins with H. Patrick Glenn's probe into the foundations of legal thinking. He claims that law has been in the grip of binary thinking, making an underlying assumption that the laws of identity, non-contradiction and the excluded middle are self-evident and have universal validity. He draws attention to the 'multi-valued turn' in contemporary logic and explores both existing examples – such as the margin-of-appreciation doctrine of the ECtHR and the *Solange* decisions of the German Constitutional Court – and future possibilities for multivalent logic in legal thinking. But more importantly, so Glenn argues, multivalent logic opens up a space for transnational law, an included middle, no longer shut out by the binary logic of national and international law.

In Chapter 3, Enzo Cannizzaro and Beatrice Bonafè start from the paradox that although monism and dualism never applied in practice, these archetypes based on the principle of legal solipsism are still used to conceptualise relations between legal orders – for lack of an alternative scheme. They propose that a way forward could be sought by focusing more on relations between legal rules contextualised in their original systems than on relations between legal orders as such. The assumption is that this approach could ultimately reveal more of how legal orders actually interact.

Cannizzaro and Bonafè demonstrate their approach by analysing examples of what they call 'techniques that judges tend to apply in order to avoid what they perceive as an improper implication of the doctrines of legal solipsism': the margin of appreciation, consistent interpretation and equivalent protection. This extensive analysis draws on material collected from national constitutional courts within and outside Europe and from the CJEU, the ECtHR and other international courts. Based on their analysis, Cannizzaro and Bonafè conclude that an emerging practice already seems to exist in which relations between legal orders are based on mutual recognition, tolerance and cooperation rather than on supremacy and subordination. However, they suggest that, at most, finding emerging patterns merely relativises the principles of legal solipsism or exclusivity. What has emerged is not ready to replace the classic archetypes of monism and dualism. In order to rethink these (normative) archetypes of modern legal thinking, Cannizzaro and Bonafè suggest that closer focus on the practice of consistent legal interaction between legal orders is especially promising from the point of view of legal theory and might even give rise, eventually, to a scheme to overcome the paradoxical archetypes.

Next, Alexander Somek proposes that the concept 'constitution' should be rethought. He introduces the notion of the cosmopolitan constitution. This, he supposes, might provide the solution to the dilemmas created by previous constitutionalism, which Somek reconstructs as three ideal types, taken from history. Constitutionalism 1.0 amounts to creating and sustaining limited government through jurisdictional constraints and negative rights. Under it, a constitution is conceived of as a document, written by 'the people' or the 'nation' and authoritatively interpreted by either the judiciary or a representative body. In constitutionalism 2.0, the constitution is supposed not only to limit but also to guide optimal government. What matters more than the authorship of the constitution is an understanding of it as an expression of practical reason. The Constitution of the United States is the epitome of constitutionalism 1.0, while the constitution of Germany, as applied by the Constitutional Court, provides the paradigm for constitutionalism 2.0. Constitutionalism 3.0 belongs to an era in which even constitutional authority is denationalised; it sees the national constitution entangled with transnational regulatory processes, as in the European Union, or observance of shared constitutional standards being monitored by a peer group. Typical of constitutionalism 3.0 is the growing importance of the executive branch, and the collapse of the distinction between norms and their application in risk management and crisis intervention.

Somek presents the cosmopolitan constitution as the type of constitutional law that emerges from the situation marked by constitutionalism 3.0, in particular from three currents of comparison and peer review that it contains: mobility and belonging; proportionality and pluralism; and issues of fundamental rights. He argues that the cosmopolitan constitution comes in two forms, one defensible and the other defective. Somek points to a revolution in 'belonging' that is most strongly epitomised by European citizenship. Together the rise of peer review and the revolution in belonging are unravelling the special tie between a constitution and national history. In turn, through proportionality the constitution is transformed from limits established by legal rules into standards for assessing the rationality and reasonableness of government action. This tends to result in a pluralism of constitutional authority and the allocation of jurisdiction becoming an issue of second-order rationality. The changes brought about by constitutionalism 3.0 necessitate a reconsidering of constitutional authority.

Somek argues for the cosmopolitan constitution as 'an attempt to rescue the universalistic ambition of modern constitutionalism from being suffocated by its particularistic mode of realisation'. The defensible form of cosmopolitan constitution combines political self-determination, which involves a deep commitment to a bounded form of life, with what Somek calls a mixed form of cosmopolitan self-determination.

In Chapter 5, Ralf Michaels discusses the compatibility of legal pluralism with liberalism. He argues that liberalism, in the sense of the order of a liberal state, presupposes political, cultural and religious pluralism. However, recognising such pluralism does not entail legal pluralism in the sense of giving autonomous law-making power to cultural or religious groups, i.e. recognition of separate legal orders. This would be strong legal pluralism, denoting a situation in which non-state law is not subordinated to state law. The argument seems to be that a liberal state must have the power to monitor the respect that non-state law accords the liberal order. By contrast, Michaels claims that liberalism is compatible with what he calls weak legal pluralism, while at the same time doubting whether this weak form is pluralism at all. In weak legal pluralism, non-state orders remain normatively inferior to state legal order. In addition, the validity of non-state law depends on its recognition by state law. At the end of his chapter, Michaels transfers his discussion beyond state boundaries. He argues that strong legal pluralism may well be compatible with liberalism beyond the state; neo-liberalism, as he calls it. Strong legal pluralism contends that no automatic superiority of state law to non-state law exists. Correspondingly, neo-liberalism, in the sense Michaels uses the term, sees the state merely as one among diverse legitimate orders.

Part II of the book, where the focus is on rethinking the concepts of 'pluralism' and 'justice', begins with Joxerramon Bengoetxea discussing the conceptual pairs legal and cultural plurality, and legal and cultural pluralism, with a specific focus on the European Union context. He proposes to use 'legal *plurality*' and 'cultural *plurality*' as empirical concepts; as ideas linked to sociological, cognitive or descriptive interest. By contrast, to his mind 'legal *pluralism*' and 'constitutional *pluralism*', or '*multiculturalism*', are better understood as normative concepts. Bengoetxea perceives pluralism as a solution to the tensions created by plurality. The chapter builds on Neil MacCormick's conception of law as an institutional normative order and locates law in a wider context of practical reasoning. With regard to legal and constitutional plurality in Europe, Bengoetxea calls for accommodation rather than confrontation as a response to cultural normative diversity and contested constitutional claims. Accommodation is facilitated by liberal cosmopolitan values, related to human rights and shared across the EU, which should be included as essential elements in the concept of (EU) law. Bengoetxea emphasises 'subsidiarity', 'primacy' – instead of 'supremacy' – and 'reasonable accommodation' as concepts contributing to the new lexicon and the new logic needed to rethink EU law and legal thinking.

In Chapter 7, Samantha Besson examines legal pluralism in Europe from the perspective of human rights law and human rights legal theory. She identifies a human rights plurality in the sense of a coexistence of multilevel human rights norms and judicial interpretations of these norms within international, European and domestic legal orders and institutions. But this plurality does not necessarily amount to human rights pluralism. This claim is linked to Besson's understanding of 'legal pluralism' as the idea that not all legal norms applicable in a given legal order ought to be regarded as validated by the same criteria and situated within a hierarchy, and that, hence, some normative conflicts may receive no legal answer. She criticises the literature on human rights pluralism for being mainly empirical and descriptive, and lacking the necessary normative arguments for pluralism. She points to the specific character of human rights norms as legitimating norms, which entails that their pluralism is bound to be very different from that of other legal norms. She concludes by contending that if there is a form of human rights pluralism at work in Europe, it is about mutual validation and legitimation, located at the very core of the democratic legitimation of European legal orders.

Sionaidh Douglas-Scott and Christian Joerges discuss the concept of justice in the context of the European Union but their approaches are very different. In Chapter 8, Douglas-Scott starts from, not justice, but absence of justice, that is, injustice. She analyses what she considers to be instances of injustice in the EU. She argues that perhaps more crucial than an elusive or utopian concept of justice is the diagnosis of *injustice*: it is in its absence that justice moves people. Her examples consist of measures taken in handling the Eurozone crisis that contradict the EU's avowal of social justice and infringe human rights; the incoherence and undue focus on security in establishing the EU area of freedom, security and justice; the subordination of social justice to free movement concerns; and the consequences of the specific legal pluralism of the EU in terms of, e.g., lack of accountability. Douglas-Scott also introduces what she names critical legal justice, in which adherence to the rule of law plays a central role. She maintains the importance of critical legal justice, invoking the centrality of legal integration for the development of the EU. But she also reminds us that justice is not confined to legal justice and concludes by suggesting that 'perhaps justice is best envisaged as a discourse of absence'.

In Chapter 9, Christian Joerges bases his search for a concept of justice for the EU on a reconstruction of Friedrich Carl von Savigny's conceptualisation of 'justice under private international law' (*internationalprivatrechtliche Gerechtigkeit*), and Hermann Heller's theory of the 'social state' (*Sozialstaat*). However Joerges contends, first, that justice as defined under private international law cannot serve as a model for governing the relations between the Member States of the EU and, second, that the social state as envisaged by Heller has eroded in the integration process. Joerges calls for a new synthesis related to the recent debate on justice and democracy in the EU between the political scientist Jürgen Neyer and the philosopher Rainer Forst. Joerges brings into the debate his own proposal for conflicts-law constitutionalism and Rudolf Wiethölter's concept of *Rechtfertigungsrecht* (law of justification). His conclusion is a turn to proceduralisation and an understanding of European law primarily as a *Recht-Fertigungs-Recht*, as a law of law production.

Part III of the book addresses how transnationalisation affects established fields of municipal law. In Chapter 10, Hans-W. Micklitz discusses the alleged vanishing of the public/private divide using the conceptual tools of legal hybrids and perspectivism. He looks at legal hybrids on the four levels identified above – individual legal cases, branches of law, legal orders or legal systems and legal spaces – and from the perspective of three fields of law – constitutional law, (private) administrative law and private law. Furthermore, within each of these fields he distinguishes between an inward- and an outward-looking perspective. His conclusion is that, in spite of a variety of legal hybrids at all four levels, the public/private distinction is still very much alive. In particular, it is cherished in the inward-looking perspective typical of constitutional law and traditional private law, which both try to shield the autonomy of their respective disciplines. However, the introduction of the notion of economic law and, later, regulatory private law signified the breakthrough of an outward-looking perspective, even in private law. A similar role in constitutional law has been played by, e.g., debates on many constitutions and constitutional pluralism.

At the end of his chapter, Micklitz briefly comments on the emergence of the private/public divide and subsequent hybridisation as a process and addresses the question whether what is at issue is a linear development or whether it should be understood as a loop. He proposes a link between the emergence of the public/private divide and the rise of the state nation in the seventeenth and eighteenth centuries, and between the beginning of hybridisation in its diverse variations and the nation state of the nineteenth and twentieth centuries. In turn, the twenty-first century will witness the full development of the market state, under which the fate of the public/private divide is uncertain, as it requires redefinition of the role of the state and the function of the private.

In Chapter 11, Jan M. Smits focuses on transformations within the field of private law. He claims that in actuality the main changes caused by transnationalisation and simultaneous technological progress do not concern the substance of private law but rather its role and function. State law is losing its power to govern relationships among private parties, who increasingly turn to other types of ordering. Smits characterises this as a development from *ex post* to *ex ante* governance of private relationships.

Thus, in rulemaking there is a turn towards private regulation and choice of law. If state law, because of its territorial limitations, can no longer meet the demand for legal certainty, then privately created orders take its place. In addition to large functional systems, such as *lex mercatoria* and *lex sportiva*, these include the use of general conditions in business-to-consumer transactions and private rulemaking in certain types of trade. Private regimes offer what a national legal system is not able to provide: a set of rules that is not territorially limited. If parties still make use of state law, they do not necessarily choose the law of their own jurisdiction but might submit some specific aspect of their activities to a foreign law.

A parallel development from state enforcement to self-enforcement exists. If state law cannot guarantee effective enforcement, parties will turn to other types of enforcement or to devices that allow them to avoid enforcement completely. One of the major mechanisms is *ex ante* reliance on reputation instead of *ex post* recourse to law. *Ex post* dispute resolution is increasingly replaced by *ex ante* avoidance of disputes through, e.g., reputational networks. Where dispute resolution still plays a role, private justice – in the shape of arbitration, mediation and other types of alternative dispute resolution – is pushing state courts aside. In online dispute resolution, the legal needs of globalising commerce and technological progress come together. In conclusion, Smits claims that the increasing delivery of 'legality' without law is much more important for understanding the denationalisation of law than the concrete efforts of European and supranational organisations to create rules fit for the European or global market.

In Chapter 12, Giacinto della Cananea discusses the impact of transnationalisation on the other side of the public/private divide, namely in administrative law. He uses as the vehicle for his analysis a particular institution of administrative law: *jus poenitendi* or the power to modify or cancel the effects of a previous administrative act. According to the traditional paradigm, administrative law is a national enclave, closely bound to the nation state. Cananea examines the transnationalisation of administrative law in two dimensions: in the vertical dimension leading from national administrative law(s) to European administrative law and in the horizontal relations between national administrative laws. In both dimensions, administrative-law principles common to different nation states (Member States) have had a major impact. He carries out his analysis through two legal cases involving *jus poenitendi*. *Algera*, decided by the ECJ in 1957, illustrates how European administrative-law principles were elaborated on the basis of principles common to Member States. In turn, the other case, decided by the Tribunale di giustizia amministrativa di Trento in 2009, illuminates the interpretation of the legislation of one Member State (Italy) in the light of the judicial doctrine of another (Germany). At issue is the use of the law of another municipal jurisdiction. However, the relevant normative model is not conflict of laws but *lex alius loci.*

In their contribution, Oreste Pollicino and Marco Bassini take up a new branch of law that is often regarded as a typical product of the hybridisation caused by transnationalisation and simultaneous technological progress: namely, Internet law. They address the question to what extent and especially at what level of governance a regulatory approach could play its role in cyberspace. The hypothesis they explore is that, although Internet law has been treated as an epitome of national law's limitations in an era of globalisation, it could turn out to be one of the few fields of law that are still encapsulated in national law.

Pollicino and Bassini analyse two phases in the scholarly and judicial treatment of Internet law. The first was dominated by what the authors call the cyber-anarchic approach, claiming the disintegration of state sovereignty over cyberspace, in which territorially defined jurisdictions were impotent. The authors argue that this approach overlooked three important arguments. First, it relied on a static notion of sovereignty, which was already outdated when the Internet acquired a commercial dimension. Second, its advocates mistook the direction of technological development in assuming, e.g., that a content provider or Internet service provider with a multijurisdictional presence cannot monitor or control the geographical flow of information on the Internet. Third, the cyber-anarchic approach ignored the distinction between prospective jurisdiction and enforcement jurisdiction. The authors contend that national law continues to play a crucial role, even where the content source is beyond the reach of a territorial government. They do not consider top-down harmonisation a feasible option in Internet law because of the nature of the state interests involved in transnational regulatory issues. These often touch upon hard-core values at the heart of national identity, as the authors show through their analysis of Internet-related case law in the fields of hate speech, gambling and privacy. The solution that the authors advocate, which they think takes into account both transnational and national aspects, is a case-by-case approach that takes place in the no-man's-land between municipal law and international law, on the common ground of shared values and in accordance with the discursive principles of a pluralistic vision of transnational law. Pollicino and Bassini conclude by making a call for what they term a new fundamental right in the new season of transnational law: the right of access to the Internet.

1

Transnational law

On legal hybrids and perspectivism

KAARLO TUORI

Legal theory is groping for conceptual tools to come to terms with new phenomena that seem to shatter the solid foundations of our inherited legal worldview. These are often called legal hybrids. This, as I shall argue, only demonstrates the inadequacy of our traditional legal distinctions. By the same token, the presence of new inhabitants in the legal universe calls for rethinking the mode of legal thinking we have received from an era the approaching demise of which they seem to herald. Many of the alleged hybrids are related to transnational law: law that does not fit into the dichotomy of municipal and international law. EU law is the most developed but not the only epitome of this type of law.

This chapter – and, indeed, this book as a whole – is intended to contribute to the co-operative search for new interpretative and normative grids needed in charting our contemporary legal landscape and expelling at least some of the hybrids now populating it. I shall address and try to clarify key concepts such as 'legal hybridity', 'transnational law', 'legal pluralism', 'interlegality' and 'legal perspectivism'. However, my aims are not confined to discussing individual concepts but extend to elaborating a more comprehensive interpretative and normative framework. I shall develop my own views by way of criticising what I call the radical pluralist position. This position appears in three main guises: the Kelsenian reading of fundamental conflicts of legal authority; the 'critical' account of the fragmentation of international law; and the systems-theoretical view of global, functionally differentiated social systems developing their own instances of transnational law. I agree with radical pluralists on the significance of perspectivism in law, but give this perspectivism a legal-cultural turn. This allows me to show a discursive way out of the enclosures erected by radical pluralists.

1. Traditional divisions of law

Our legal universe used to be so nicely organised, every legal phenomenon finding its 'natural' conceptual department; the legal universe was ordered in a quasi-Linnaean way into kingdoms, classes, orders, genera and species. In Continental Europe, the law's systematisation was brought into perfection by German *Begriffsjurisprudenz* in the nineteenth century, but had its origins in (the reception of) Roman law. The basic division between public and private law derived from Justinian's *Institutiones*. Classification of the law's objects into persons (*personae*), things (*res*) and actions (*actiones*) went back to Gaius (130–180CE), and the further division of things into material (*res corporales*) and immaterial (*res incorporales*) was also found in Roman sources. These divisions were reiterated in the five books of German nineteenth-century private law *Begriffsjurisprudenz* or Pandect law (*Pandektenrecht*): the general part, the law of obligations, property law (*Sachenrecht*), family law and the law of inheritance. Within public law, the nineteenth century brought about the differentiation of state law between constitutional and administrative law. This basic systematisation was conceived from a nation-state perspective; despite the legal-cultural transnationalism deriving from common Roman law roots, especially in private law, systematisation stemming from the efforts of nineteenth-century legal scholarship focused on the national legal order.

Two branches, which crossed state boundaries, complemented the basic systematisation of law: public and private international law. But these fields of law did not dispense with the nation-state perspective, either. Both private and public international law regulate relationships between nation states and their legal orders. International private law comprises the rules determining the choice of norms to apply to an issue bearing on more than one nation-state municipal legal order. Private international law itself is part of the municipal legal order of the nation state. And when sovereign states opt for either the monistic or the dualistic model in the relationship between municipal law and public international law, they also define the place of public international law in the overall system of law. What is important is that, in the traditional view, public international law does not interfere in the domestic legal order. This falls under the exclusive, sovereign jurisdiction of the state; no rival legal orders are supposed to exist, claiming authority within the space of the nation state.

The traditional mapping of our legal universe gives expression to a *state-sovereigntist* view of modern law. On the global scale, this view leads to what William Twining (2000) has fittingly termed the *black box model*.[1] This model is premised on the (co)existence of territorially differentiated state legal orders, each of them claiming exclusive jurisdiction within its respective territorially defined social space, and international law, confined to regulating external relations among sovereign states. In internal legal relations, sovereign states are expected to treat each other according to the principle of exclusivity, that is, as black boxes. Furthermore, within their respective territorial confines, states raise the claim of, and mutually acknowledge, the universal scope of their exclusive legal sovereignty. In this account, both national legal orders and international law are treated as self-contained and self-sufficient normative wholes.

In their respective versions of legal positivism, Hans Kelsen and H. L. A. Hart put forward perhaps the most sophisticated formulations of the black box view. As we recall, Kelsen conceives of law as a hierarchically organised whole, in which lower order norms derive their validity from higher ones: bylaws from laws, laws from the constitution and the constitution from a hypothetical, presupposed basic norm (*Grundnorm*). Kelsen's hierarchical normative structure, the *Stufenbau*, is, above all, tailored to depict a state legal order: the basic norm crowning the hierarchy commands obedience to the (historically first) constitution of the state, while the norms on the lower echelons are issued by state organs empowered by this constitution. It is true, though, that Kelsen's world of legal *Sollen* included international law, too. He advocated a monistic view in which both international and national law are subject to the same basic norm: either that of international law or that of the national legal order. Kelsen's monism with regard to international law does not question the state premises of his construction. International law merely regulates relationships between states. Even if the legal *Stufenbau* is construed starting from the basic norm of international law, international law only provides the national legal order with the basis for its validity, leaving the national legislator free to decide on the normative contents of that order in compliance with the (procedural) requirements of the state constitution.[2] So in the pure theory of law, relations between national and international law are analysed in terms of validity (authority) and against two monistic alternatives: either national law derives its validity from international law or vice versa.

---

[1] W. Twining, *Globalisation and Legal Theory* (Evanston, IL: Northwestern University Press, 2000).

[2] H. Kelsen, *The Pure Theory of Law*, trans. Knight (Berkeley: California University Press, 1989), p. 328ff.

Legal systematisation within the boxes of national legal orders did not stop at division of the law into distinct branches. Under the systematic ideal of nineteenth-century German legal scholarship, each branch of law was to be ordered through its specific general doctrines (*allgemeine Lehren*). Actually, it was general doctrines with their general legal concepts – such as 'contract' in the law of obligations or 'competence' and 'administrative act' in administrative law – that lent legal fields their identity and further systematised legal 'raw material'. In the division of labour between the three main actors of modern law – the legislator, judges and legal scholars – it was the legal scholars who produced the law's systematisation, hence playing an active role in the development of law. A strict, classifying, conceptual hierarchy or pyramid, often attributed to Georg Friedrich Puchta, is probably an invention of the critics of *Begriffsjurisprudenz* – as is the very term *Begriffsjurisprudenz*, too – but there is no doubt of the systematising and conceptualising urge so typical of nineteenth- and early twentieth-century continental legal scholarship. In the USA, this had its parallel development in the conceptualism of what has been called Classical Legal Thought, the main object of ridicule by American legal realists (as *Begriffsjurisprudenz* was an object of derision for German *Interessenjurisprudenz* and Scandinavian legal realism).[3]

2. Specimens of legal hybrid

Today, strange creatures, legal hybrids, threaten the traditional order of our legal universe. In biology, 'hybrid' is defined as an offspring resulting from crossbreeding. Biological hybrids break out of the nested hierarchy of Linnaean taxonomy. Correspondingly, legal hybrids defy the conceptual compartmentalising of traditional systematisation. To put it in the shape of a definition: legal hybrids are legal phenomena that our inherited conceptual framework is unable to capture and imprison in a determinate conceptual box.

Contemporary legal literature abounds with examples of legal hybrids. Legal concepts are organised in line with the law's division into distinct branches; each branch of law possesses its specific concepts, which are vital for its very identity. But because of the different temporality of the law and the society it regulates, it may well be that problems awaiting

---

[3] I have discussed the traditional divisions of law, as well as the realist criticism of conceptual jurisprudence, in my *Ratio and Voluntas: The Tension between Reason and Will in Law* (Farnham: Ashgate, 2011), especially pp 105–172.

legal translation do not respect but cut across the boundaries separating branches of law. In recent decades, public administration in all Western countries has been subject to extensive *privatisation*. Administrative tasks have been assigned to private law organisations, while the administrative management of society has had recourse to private law means, such as contracts. Traditional general doctrines of administrative law, premised on hierarchical power relations between the parties, are no longer able to catch all legally relevant problems in public administration's external or internal relationships. New concepts are needed to open channels between public and private law. 'Administrative contract' is a representative example of such a conceptual renewal; but, seen through the lenses of traditional legal systematisation, it is a typical legal hybrid, an offspring of crossbreeding private and public law concepts.

Privatising of administration manifests the characteristic late modern expansion of market mechanisms. This development has extended the relevance of *competition law* considerations. Competition law traverses almost the whole legal order, including domains previously reserved for administrative law. This, too, can be deemed hybridisation, incursion of foreign elements into the citadel of public law, shaking its traditional hierarchical model. But, viewed from the perspective of the law's traditional systematisation, even competition law as such is, in effect, a legal hybrid: it brings elements from both sides of the principal division into public and private law.

Thus, not only do legal hybrids exist at the level of individual legal phenomena and tentative concepts trying to come to grips with these – such as 'administrative contract' – but even entire branches of law can be examined as resulting from hybridisation. Present-day debates on the law's divisions have moved far from traditional systematisation. Interest in the law's differentiation into specific branches has not vanished nor even diminished. On the contrary, we are witnessing a revival of classification debates. The focus, however, has shifted, so that nineteenth-century disputants would have a hard time orienting themselves in present debates on such putative departments of law as social law, medical and bio-law, sports law, information law or communications law. Characteristic of recent contributions is that they are no longer concerned with the law's overall systematisation. When, some decades ago, labour law waged its battle for independence, at least on the Continent, commentators still assigned importance to pondering its place in the basic distinction between private and public law. Present debaters do not seem to be troubled by the location in the law's comprehensive system of the new fields (and disciplines) they are advocating. Instead of *total coherence* of the law, their aim is more modest: to bring *local coherence* to a particular body of law. It may even be argued that the local coherence sought in contemporary debates stands in contradiction of the aspiration for total coherence. As was earlier the case with labour law or environmental law, putative new branches of law typically combine normative material that would fall into several compartments within the traditional divisions.

In the dominant German systematisation of law in the last century, labour law and environmental law were treated as subfields of economic law or special private law, as it was also called. Economic law, and its counterpart on the side of public law, special administrative law, were latecomers in the law's divisions, introduced to address the consequences of welfare state regulation, in particular the increasing intrusion of public law elements into the domain of private law. But by the same token they also shook the premises of the system; neither economic law nor special administrative law could display the unifying general doctrines that, according to the basic idea of traditional systematisation, confer identity on relatively independent fields of law.

Yet as new residual categories economic law and special administrative law made continuity possible. As I have argued, the traditional divisions were meant to classify the legal order of the sovereign nation state, although they relied in part on the legal tradition predating the rise of nation states. The welfare state has been a political project of the nation state, and the regulations that were included in economic law and special administrative law were still attached to the monocentric perspective of the nation state legislator. Present pretenders to the status of an independent field of law throw down a more profound challenge to the traditional system. They are no longer tied to the nation state legislator but attest to the polycentrism of legal sources and the pluralism of legal orders, perhaps even legal systems. They also blur the sharp boundary between legal and other social norms that, in Max Weber's view, was indispensable for the law's formal rationality.[4] Environmental law, medical and bio-law, information law or sports law introduce breaches into the system based on the fundamental distinction between private and public law and gather together norms that, in traditional divisions, are dispersed across several fields. But this is not all. Alongside norms issued by the domestic

---

[4] M. Weber, *Economy and Society*, ed. Roth and Wittich, trans. Fischoff et al. (Berkeley: University of California Press, 1978), p. 657.

legislator, they include EU norms and other norms of international or transnational origin. Finally, *soft law* material, such as recommendations or codes of good practice adopted by international and national organisations, also plays an important role in the self-conception of would-be new branches of law. Thus, not only are new fields of law unsuitable for unequivocal insertion into the traditional system; they also renounce its nation-state premises and even question the very separateness of law from other social norms. Here we could perhaps speak of multiple hybridisation!

Our brief discussion of new branches of law points to a third level of legal hybridisation, complementing the first level, individual legal phenomena and concepts, and the second, branches of law. This is the level of legal orders and legal systems. The black box model of national legal orders and international law has proved incapable of mapping the present global legal landscape. This is largely owing to the rise of transnational law, the truc El Dorado of legal hybrids.

3. Transnational law

In effect, the very idea of transnational law is an epitome of legal hybridisation. Transnational law is law beyond the dichotomy of state law and international law, and as such it is a reaction to the spatial and temporal shortcomings of the black box model in face of the cultural and social changes often enough examined under the heading of *globalisation*. What is globalisation or – to use the less pretentious expression – *denationalisation* about? According to David Harvey's well-known, succinct definition, 'globalisation' connotes the compression of time and space.[5] Globalisation involves not only the spatial but also the temporal element in social relations; enlargement of the *locus* of social interaction is matched by its acceleration. Capital investors and currency dealers not only establish contacts that pay no heed to state borders and geographical distances, but thanks to computers and the Internet, complete their transactions in the blink of an eye. The restricted spatiality of modern state law does not allow it to regulate such global connections. Moreover, the temporality typical of modern law and its practices may also make the law unsuitable for regulating transactions in virtual time; for example, legal proceedings in state courts may simply be far too slow.

---

[5] D. Harvey, *The Conditions of Postmodernity: An Inquiry into the Origins of Cultural Change* (Cambridge, MA: Blackwell, 1989).

Many accounts of globalisation and its legal consequences privilege the perspective of the economy. But globalisation – or denationalisation – is not solely an economic process; it is not manifest only in production and exchange of goods, services and capital. Pollutants and other environmental risks, cultural influences or criminality and terrorism are none of them stopped by the border controls of nation states. The social space for which legal regulation is demanded has been identified, more or less self-evidently, with the legal and political space of the state.[6] The nation state's legal sovereignty met the regulatory needs of the time when economy was still largely identical with the national economy; when criminality, too, had its nationality and the consequences of crimes were felt in the place where they were committed; and when the polluting effects of industrial or agricultural production extended only to their immediate environment. The spatial presuppositions of the state legislator have lost their self-evident validity: the functioning of social systems – with the economy as the forerunner – pays increasingly less heed to state borders. Development has been from state societies towards a world society (*Weltgesellschaft*) composed of functionally differentiated global social subsystems.[7] State law loses its capacity to respond to regulatory needs when society undergoes denationalisation and when, as a consequence, the social space to be regulated is no longer identical with the political space of the state. State law is not able to provide solutions to disputes arising in the global economic marketplace or fence off social dumping, threatening the foundations of the national welfare state, nor can the environmental legislation of individual states prevent climate change and global warming. Legal regulation has to find new forms; otherwise, the law will be increasingly replaced by other means of solving problems. Even within nation states, law has never been the only instrument for the political management of society, and neither does it hold any exclusive privileges at the suprastate level. In global governance, legal regulation is only one option among others.

Traditionally, modern law has responded to crossboundary regulatory needs by means of international law. However, as noted above, international law has been firmly tied to the state in both its creation and its legal effects. The focus has been on relations among states, not on

---

[6] M. Zürn, *Regieren Jenseits des Nationalstaates* (Frankfurt: Suhrkamp, 1998), pp 54–5; M. Schroer, *Räume, Orte, Grenzen: Auf dem Weg zu einer Soziologie des Raums* (Frankfurt: Suhrkamp, 2006), p. 189ff.

[7] R. Stichweh, *Die Weltgesellschaft: Soziologische Analysen* (Frankfurt: Suhrkamp, 2000).

a crossboundary interaction involving mainly non-state actors as has set the stage for the current debate on globalisation and denationalisation.

The distinctive features of transnational law, escaping from the straitjacket of the black box model, can be attached to either the formation or the application of norms. Transnational norm-setting assumes forms other than bi- or multilateral treaties between states. In turn, norm-application that involves the establishing of dispute-solving or sanctioning bodies outside the control of nation states suggests that transnational law is emerging. But, of course, no impermeable boundary exists between the formation and the application of norms, despite the ingrained thought habits of (us) continental European lawyers. Through its case law, a court-like body established by an international treaty elaborates on and complements the treaty rules it is supposed to apply. Provisions of treaties applied by the international courts and other monitoring bodies are usually formulated in very general terms, and for an obvious reason, too. Political consensus among states is easier to reach the vaguer the provisions under negotiation are; hence, their specification is left to legal experts responsible for monitoring adherence to a treaty.

So the often rather equivocal provisions of the European Convention on Human Rights (ECHR) have only gained precision through the case law of the Strasbourg Court. To take an example, by itself the wording of Article 6 ECHR conveys but a pallid picture of the normative contents of a fair trial. European human rights law possesses a treaty basis – the Convention and the Protocols. Nonetheless, we may be warranted to speak of human rights as a transnational legal system, both the normative and the institutional structure of which have distanced themselves from the system's background in international law. Arguably, the case law of the European Court of Human Rights (ECtHR) is an instance of transnational lawmaking. The Court's (at least partial) breakout from (general) international law is also manifest in the qualifications it has imposed on the applicability of the Vienna Convention on the Law of Treaties.[8]

---

[8] For analysis, see F. Vanneste, *General International Law Before Human Rights Courts: Assessing the Specialty Claims of International Human Rights Law* (Antwerp: Intersentia, 2010) and J. Polakiewicz, 'Collective responsibility and reservations in a common European human rights area' in I. Ziemele (ed.), *Reservations to Human Rights Treaties and the Vienna Convention Regime: Conflict, Harmony or Reconciliation* (Leiden: Martinus Nijhoff, 2004), pp 95–132.

The Court has underlined the constitutional character of the Convention and inferred from this that the Vienna Convention's provisions on reservations and international legal succession are not applicable in this arena.[9]

Despite its tendency towards independence, European human rights law has retained its interaction with the domestic legal systems of the Signatory States. In line with the fundamental rights enshrined in national constitutions, the Convention creates justiciable individual rights. This explains the steps that national legal systems have taken to avoid conflicts between transnational and national law. Human rights norms have been accorded binding effect in most national legal orders;[10] even human rights sceptics might prefer national monitoring to the transnational jurisdiction of the Strasbourg Court. The central role national courts play in ensuring that not only domestic fundamental rights but also Convention rights are realised is further strengthened by the Strasbourg Court's margin of appreciation doctrine. This doctrine confirms that it falls primarily to national courts to assess whether the requirements that the Convention sets for limitations on rights are met in individual cases.[11]

EU law provides another example of a legal system that has largely disconnected itself from its international law foundation. Primary EU norms derive from international treaty law, but secondary norms, such as regulations and directives, cannot be classified under international law. Furthermore, if it falls under the principle of direct effect as defined and applied by the Court of Justice of the European Union (CJEU), EU treaty law treats even private persons as legal subjects, thus departing from the premises of international law. Ever since the 1960s, the ECJ has characterised EC law as an independent legal order, distinct both from the municipal legal orders of Member States and from international law.[12]

---

[9] See, e.g., *Belilos* v. *Switzerland* (1988) Series A No. 132, paras 47–9, *Loizidou* v. *Turkey* (Preliminary Objections) (1995) Series A No. 310, paras 93 and 96.

[10] See A. Drezewczewski, *European Human Rights Convention in Domestic Law: A Comparative Study* (Oxford: Oxford University Press, 1998); H. Keller and A. Stone Sweet (eds), *A Europe of Rights: The Impact of the ECHR on National Legal Systems* (Oxford: Oxford University Press, 2008).

[11] J. Viljanen, *European Court of Human Rights as a Developer of the General Doctrines of Human Rights Law: A study of the limitation clauses of the European Convention on Human Rights* (Tampere, Finland: Tampere University Press, 2003).

[12] The landmark rulings were the celebrated Case 26/62 *Van Gend en Loos* [1963] ECR 1 and Case 6/64 *Costa* v. *Enel* [1964] ECR 585.

Nevertheless, both normatively and institutionally, EU law remains inter-twined with the legal systems of Member States. With regard to relations between municipal and international law, the constitutional legislator of Finland has opted for the dualistic model. Nonetheless, following the prevailing conception, Finland's municipal legal order incorporates not only regulations, directives and framework decisions duly implemented by the national legislature, but also other EU law covered by the doctrine of direct effect. And when national courts apply EU norms, they act simultaneously as institutions of both municipal and EU legal systems. In the latter capacity, they are obliged to comply with preliminary rulings of the CJEU.

In spite of its basis in international treaty law, WTO law, too, has assumed features of a transnational legal system, resisting the dichotomy of international and municipal law. Its institutional structure includes dispute settlement panels, whose decisions may be appealed to the Appellate Body. The panels and the Appellate Body also produce normative material specifying and complementing treaty provisions. However, adhering to the traditional premises of international law, WTO law focuses on relations between states, and execution of decisions by dispute-resolving bodies is also left to the states themselves.[13] International environmental and maritime law, too, display signs of a corresponding movement away from international treaty law towards a transnational legal system.[14]

The examples of transnational law given above display a similar pattern: they all have their background in international law but have subsequently severed their international law moorings and, by the same token, largely elude the control of nation states. Notwithstanding, they still bear traces of their origin, as can be seen, for instance, from the debate on the dual nature of the foundational treaties of the EU. From the internal perspective of EU law, assumed by, e.g., the CJEU, they are considered embodiments of constitutional law, with legal effects analogous to those

---

[13] See Article IX:2 of the WTO Agreement and Articles 3.2, 3.7 and 3.9 of the Dispute Settlement Understanding (Annex 2 to the WTO Agreement). See also WTO Panel Report, *Argentina – Poultry*, WT/DS241/R, adopted 19 May 2003, DSR 2003:V, 1727, para. 7.12.

[14] The first issue of a journal focusing on environmental law and governance beyond the state (Transnational Environmental Law) was published by Cambridge University Press in 2012. On environmental law, see, e.g., N. Affolder, 'Transnational conservation contracts', 15 *Leiden Journal of International Law* (2012), 443–60; as for maritime law, see, e.g., J. D. Peppetti, 'Building the global maritime security network: a multinational legal structure to combat transnational threats', 55 *Naval Law Review* (2008), 73–156.

of nation-state constitutions. But they have also retained their character of international treaties, as have Member States their position of *Herren der Verträge.*[15] Here we have another instance of legal hybridity, so typical of contemporary law!

The hybrid nature of our examples relates them to recent debate among international lawyers. Indeed, from an international law perspective they can be examined as instances of *fragmentation* that, in the view of some observers, worryingly threatens its cogency. Particular court-like bodies that do not defer to the precedents of the International Court of Justice (ICJ) shake its status as the guarantor of international law's unity. The qualified approach of some special courts, including the ECtHR, to the Vienna Convention on the Law of Treaties has also been conceived as jeopardising the coherence of international law.[16]

But whether we conceive of the ongoing process as fragmentation of international law or as the dawn of transnational law, the growing plethora of legal sources, legal orders and even legal systems does not fit within the dichotomy of municipal and international law. The municipal legal order has lost its monopoly over determining legal relations involving private individuals. Even in states whose constitutional choice with regard to international law has been the dualistic model, transnational norms may be directly effective, regardless of a transformative act of the national legislator. This is the case in Finland, for instance. Article 95 of the Constitution lays down that international treaties and other international law obligations are incorporated into the domestic legal order through an Act of Parliament or a Presidential Decree. Nonetheless, this constitutional provision cannot prevent the direct effect of, for instance, EU law provisions, preliminary rulings of the European Court of Justice, or precedents of the European Court of Human Rights. Here no previous decision of the national legislator is needed.

---

[15] The position of Member States as 'Masters of the Treaties' is one that the German Constitutional Court (BVerfGE) does not tire of repeating. See e.g. para. 231 of the BVerfGE Lisbon ruling (2 BvE 2/08, 30 June 2009). In turn, the ECJ/CJEU has characterised the Treaties in constitutional terms ever since *Les Verts* (Case 294/83 [1986] ECR 1339).

[16] M. Koskenniemi and P. Leino, 'Fragmentation of international law? Postmodern anxieties', 15 *Leiden Journal of International Law* 3 (2002), 553–79; A. Pellet, '"Droits de l'hommisme" et droit international', Gilberto Amado Memorial Lecture, given on 18 July 2000, International Law Commission (United Nations, 2000) [published in English in the Italian Yearbook of International Law (2000), 3–16]; M. Scheinin, 'Human rights treaties and the Vienna Convention on the Law of Treaties – conflicts or harmony?' in Venice Commission (ed.), *The Status of International Treaties on Human Rights* (Strasbourg: Council of Europe Publishing, 2006), pp 43–55.

The deficiency of the black box model is even more conspicuous when we examine instances of transnational law that altogether lack a background in international treaty law and that – if we are to lend credence to Niklas Luhmann's disciples in autopoietic systems theory, whom I shall discuss below – have emerged from autonomous operation of denationalised social subsystems. The examples most often invoked are the *lex mercatoria* of international trade, the *lex sportiva* of international sports and the *lex digitalis* of the Internet. These legal orders have been subsumed by neither municipal nor international law, while disputes are settled and sanctions imposed by designated transnational bodies.[17]

4. Legal pluralism

Transnational law has not replaced law adhering to the state-sovereigntist premises of the black box model; that is, municipal law and international law, which both match the nation-state template. Rather, it has overlaid itself on the boxes of the traditional model. It is this constellation that theorists of (new) legal pluralism have tried to grasp. But, as is typical of the conceptual proposals with which legal theorists have attempted to cope with the new inhabitants of law's empire, 'legal pluralism' is a concept difficult to pin down. Let me present some suggestions aiming to increase conceptual clarity.

First, we should make at least a tentative distinction between normative and descriptive/explanatory use of the concept.[18] In normative terms, legal pluralism has been presented as a mediating option, supposedly able to avoid the pitfalls of the extremes of state-sovereigntist particularism and natural law-flavoured universalism. As a normative master principle expected to create order in the current disintegrated global law, it has been equipped with the virtues of discursiveness and mutual tolerance.[19]

---

[17] For succinct presentations of these transnational legal systems, see B. Zangl and M. Zürn (eds), *Verrechtlichung – Baustein für Global Governance* (Bonn: Dietz, 2004). See also Micklitz (*lex mercatoria*) and Pollicino and Bassini (*lex digitalis*) in Chapters 10 and 13 of this volume.

[18] Tentative, because of the inevitable, implicit, normative commitments of even descriptively oriented legal theory. For an analysis critical of embracing human rights plurality as a form of legal pluralism from a legal theoretical point of view, see Besson in Chapter 7 of this volume.

[19] P. Berman, 'Global legal pluralism', 80 *Southern California Law Review* (2007), 1155–1237; N. Krisch, *The Case for Pluralism in Postnational Law* (London: LSE Legal Studies Working Papers, 2009).

However, most commonly the term 'legal pluralism' is used in the latter, empirical sense. The origins of the concept lie in anthropological research,[20] and the 'new legal pluralism' of modern Western societies was first detected by legal sociologists.[21] But in legal theory, too, 'legal pluralism' usually has a primarily descriptive or explanatory connotation; it is introduced as an interpretative grid, which it is hoped will illuminate and make intelligible phenomena characterising our legal late modernity. The following discussion will also opt for non-normative use of the concept.

As a second step in my attempt at conceptual clarification, I propose a distinction between three types of legal pluralism: pluralisms of legal sources, of legal orders and of legal systems. The doctrine of legal sources determines who is allowed to participate in the continuous discourse specifying the contents of the legal order and what weight the respective contributions carry. *Pluralism of legal sources* is equivalent to what in Scandinavian debates has been called *polycentricity*. 'Polycentricity' connotes a multiplication of sources of law; the fact that new participants have been granted access to legal discourse, where the ever-changing content of the legal order is determined. Moreover, the weight of diverse contributions is no longer defined in such an unequivocal and hierarchical manner as has been previously assumed in, for instance, Scandinavian doctrine; formal authority has been forced to give way to substantive authority.[22]

This growing polycentricity questions the fiction of a unitary state will expressing itself in law and also creates difficulties for the hierarchical view of law adopted in the legal positivism of the Kelsenian or Hartian type. But it does not need to sever the bonds tying law to the state. The doctrine of legal sources always adopts the perspective of a particular legal actor, usually that of the judge. The judge epitomises the state's standpoint, and if the multiplication of legal sources disrupts the state's monopoly over lawmaking, such polycentricity does not necessarily entail undermining the state's monopoly over law enforcement.

---

[20] As an introduction see M. B. Hooker, *Legal Pluralism: An Introduction to Colonial and Neo-Colonial Laws* (Oxford: Oxford University Press, 1975).

[21] One of the ground-breaking contributions was J. Griffiths, 'What is legal pluralism?', 24 *Journal of Legal Pluralism* (1986), 1–55. See also the influential S. Falk Moore, *Law as Process: An Anthropological Approach* (London: Routledge & Kegan Paul, 1978).

[22] H. Zahle, 'The polycentricity of the law or the importance of legal pluralism for legal dogmatics', in H. Petersen and H. Zahle (eds), *Legal Polycentricity: Consequences of Pluralism in Law* (Aldershot: Ashgate, 1995), pp 185–200.

My understanding of the two remaining types of legal pluralism is built on the conceptual distinction between 'legal order' and 'legal system'. The law has two aspects. On one hand, it is a symbolic-normative phenomenon, a *legal order*. On the other, it consists of specific social practices – *legal practices* – in which the legal order is produced and reproduced and which take place in a particular institutional setting such as lawmaking in parliament and government, adjudication in courts and legal scholarship at law faculties. By '*legal system*', I refer to the whole formed by the law's two dimensions: the legal order and institutionally framed legal practices. The existence of a distinct legal order presupposes particular rules of recognition (a normative doctrine of legal sources), determining the criteria for membership in this order.[23] For the existence of a distinct legal system, such a recognisable and definable legal order will not suffice. What is required in addition is institutional independence that facilitates differentiation of the dimension of legal practices as well; first of all, establishment of court-like dispute-resolving or sanctioning bodies responsible for enforcement of the legal order. In the normative dimension – in the dimension of the legal order – rules of recognition must be complemented by other types of secondary rule.[24]

'*Pluralism of legal orders*' alludes to a situation in which more than one legal order claims authority within the same geographically delineated social space. Such a situation may challenge not only the Kelsenian-Hartian hierarchical view of law but also the exclusivity of state law. However, the challenge need not be fatal, and state law may still retain its dominance. This is the case when the conditions for the authority and applicability of non-state law are defined by state law,[25] and when enforcement of the latter, too, falls to state courts. This is how things are in what Twining has called a pluralist state system and in which state courts apply different normative orders to different groups of persons. Twining's example is the Tanzania of the 1960s where, in addition to English common law and statutes, state courts applied local legislation, Islamic law, Hindu law and local customary law. Tanzania's law was 'plural' only in the sense that the state recognised different rules for specific

---

[23] Here I am addressing the legal order as it appears at its surface level. Below, I shall extend the concept of legal order to include even 'subsurface', legal-cultural levels.

[24] I have developed my general view of law in my *Critical Legal Positivism* (Aldershot: Ashgate, 2002) and *Ratio and Voluntas*, note 3 above.

[25] See Michaels's discussion of the alternative ways for state law to acknowledge the significance of non-state law: R. Michaels, 'The re-state-ment of non-state law: the state, choice of law, and the challenge from global legal pluralism', 51 *Wayne Law Review* (2005), 1209–59.

categories of persons, especially in such matters as inheritance, family and some aspects of land tenure.[26] In turn, *pluralism of legal systems* contests the exclusivity of state law, not only in the normative dimension but in that of legal institutions and practices as well: non-state law, claiming authority in the territory of a state, possesses its own court-like, law-enforcing bodies. Evidently, this form of legal pluralism constitutes the gravest threat to the state-sovereigntist premises of the black box model.

Legal pluralist phenomena need not always have cross-boundary implications. Polycentricity of legal sources is possible without inclusion of any 'non-national' sources, and neither do Twining's pluralist systems traverse state boundaries. However, the most advanced type of legal pluralism – pluralism of legal systems – is intimately linked with the rise of transnational law. All the instances of transnational law evoked above display features of a legal system: in addition to a distinctive normative order, they possess court-like bodies for settling disputes or sanctioning.

5. From boundary disputes to fundamental conflicts of authority

As EU law – the most advanced epitome of transnational law – has taught us, under such a pluralism of legal systems clashes between transnational and municipal law are close to inevitable.

Conflicts between legal systems can also occur under the black box model of self-contained, territorially differentiated legal systems. But under the dominance of this model, the default assumption is that these are mere boundary disputes, few in number and manageable by private international law and the choice-of-law rules.[27] Similar boundary disputes can, of course, crop up in relations between transnational and national law, too. But here a much more momentous conflict, extending to the very foundations of legal authority, is continuously lurking.

In the black box model, legal systems and the reach of their respective claims of authority are differentiated using *territorial* criteria; within its territory, the claim to authority of the state legal system is universal and exclusive. It is *universal* in the sense of covering all substantive fields of regulation, and it is *exclusive* in the sense of not acknowledging any rival legal authority. By contrast, transnational law adopts not territorial but *functional* or substantive criteria for differentiation. Luhmann's disciples

---

[26] Twining, note 1 above, p. 83.
[27] See N. Walker, 'Beyond boundary disputes and basic grids: mapping the global disorder of normative orders', 6 *International Journal of Constitutional Law* 3–4 (2008), 373–96.

in legal theory relate the emergence of transnational law to a development towards a world society (*Weltgesellschaft*). According to this view, globalisation reiterates the functional divisions of modern nation-state society: global society is differentiated into relatively independent subsystems that produce their own transnational law.[28] Hence, not only is global law (*Weltrecht*) partitioned territorially into national legal systems, but the territorial criterion has been complemented and overlaid by new, functional grounds.

Whatever its merits in general, systems-theoretically oriented interpretation is correct in emphasising that transnational law's claim to authority is not universal in its scope but always limited to specific substantive fields. This is true even of EU law, which, in spite of its ever more conspicuous expansionist tendencies, is bound by the principle of conferral, explicitly enshrined in Article 5(2) TEU by the Lisbon Treaty. As a rule, transnational law's claim to authority is not exclusive, either. There are, though, exceptions to this rule, as is proved by Treaty provisions on exclusive EU legislative competence (Articles 2(1) and 3 TFEU). Transnational law challenges state law's claim to both exclusivity and universality. Clashes arising from contradictory principles for attributing legal authority seem inescapable: transnational law's functionally or substantively limited claim to authority contradicts state law's universal and exclusive claim. Now at issue are not mere border skirmishes, disputes over the exact course of the boundary separating two territorially defined jurisdictions. The battle has moved inland and involves a much more serious controversy. Rival legal orders, with diversely defined jurisdictions and enforced and ensured by at least partly different institutions, are competing for authority in the same territorial and social space: no longer at issue is the territorial demarcation of two legal systems, the supremacy of which – sovereignty – within the territorially defined social space is uncontested. We face what Paul Schiff Berman has called *hybrid legal spaces*;[29] a fourth instance of legal hybridity, we could say. In clashes between transnational and national law, the

---

[28] G. Teubner, 'Global Bukowina: legal pluralism in the world society' in Teubner (ed.), *Global Law without a State* (Aldershot: Ashgate, 1996); G. Teubner, 'Societal constitutionalism: alternatives to state-centred constitutional theory?', in C. Joerges, I-J. Sand and G. Teubner (eds), *Transnational Governance and Constitutionalism* (Oxford: Hart Publishing, 2004), pp 3–28; A. Fischer-Lescano and G. Teubner, 'Regime-collisions: the vain search for legal unity in the fragmentation of global law', 25 *Michigan Journal of International Law* 4 (2004), 999–1046; G. Teubner, *Constitutional Fragments: Societal Constitutionalism and Globalization*, trans. Norbury (Oxford: Oxford University Press, 2012).

[29] Berman, note 19 above.

battle is waged within the acknowledged territorial and social space of a nation state, and the competing claim to authority raised by transnational law challenges the very supremacy (sovereignty) of the legal system of that state. A particularly acute crisis erupts when transnational law's claims pertain to issues that in state law are reserved for the constitutional level.

EU law provides us with illuminating examples of such fundamental conflicts brewing in transnational law's relations with national law. In the 1960s, the ECJ defined Community law's relation to national legal orders in terms of independence, direct effect and primacy: community law constitutes an independent legal order, distinct from both (general) international law and the national legal orders of the Member States; it has, under certain conditions, direct effect in Member States insofar as it can be invoked by private litigants before national courts; and when, in a case pending before a national court, application of a directly effective EC/EU rule and a rule of municipal law cannot be reconciled but lead to contradictory results, the former must be accorded primacy over the latter.

From the perspective of private international law, the principle of primacy can be characterised as a conflict-of-laws rule resembling those pertaining to boundary disputes under the black box model. However, in contrast to border clashes familiar from the black box model, in relations between EC/EU law and Member State law the primacy issue may affect the very foundations of the constitutional order and legal authority.

The saga of how national courts – first ordinary and, subsequently, even constitutional courts – gradually accepted the bold claims to independence, direct effect and primacy raised by the ECJ has often been recounted and there is no need to reiterate it here.[30] What should, however, be emphasised is that acceptance by national constitutional courts of the principle of primacy, in particular, has never been wholly unequivocal. National courts have not had much problem in applying the principle to boundary disputes of the traditional character. But when national constitutional courts have experienced the principle of primacy as jeopardising the constitutional foundations of the national legal order, as well

---

[30] See, e.g., A-M. Slaughter, A. Stone Sweet and J. H. H. Weiler (eds), *The European Court and National Courts: Doctrine and Jurisprudence* (Oxford: Hart Publishing, 1998); K. Alter, *Establishing the Supremacy of European Law: The Making of an International Rule of Law* (Oxford: Oxford University Press, 2001); A. Stone Sweet, *The Judicial Construction of Europe* (Oxford: Oxford University Press, 2004).

as their own jurisdiction as the supreme guardian of these foundations, they have raised the banner of resistance. National constitutional courts, with the German one arguably the most prominent among them, have contested EU law's – and, at the institutional level, the ECJ/CJEU's – claim to authority in three interrelated issues: *Kompetenz-Kompetenz*; monitoring of fundamental rights; and (other) fundamental constitutional principles.

The *Kompetenz-Kompetenz* issue concerns the competence to decide the boundaries of the EU's functionally defined competence. Is this an issue of EU constitutional law where the exclusive jurisdiction falls to the CJEU? Or does it pertain to interpretation of the provisions of national constitutions on transferral of competence to the transnational level, and, hence, should Member State constitutional courts ultimately decide it? The German Constitutional Court has consistently defended its jurisdiction. Thus, it reiterated this position in its Lisbon judgment. It argued, with reference to the principle of conferral, that the EU can only exercise such power as Member States, in accordance with their respective constitutions, have transferred to it through the Treaties. Because of the derivative nature of its powers, the EU cannot possess *Kompetenz-Kompetenz* with regard to the Treaties.[31] The Member States remain Masters of the Treaties, and they possess ultimate jurisdiction over EU institutions remaining within the confines of the competence Member States have transferred to them. Consequently, the Constitutional Court declared its readiness to exert, when needed, *ultra vires* review of acts adopted by EU institutions. Analogously to fundamental rights review, *ultra vires* review is of *ultima ratio* nature, and will not be exercised *so lange* the EU's internal monitoring is able to prevent or correct excesses of competence.[32]

As has also been told many times, EC/EU law's fundamental rights dimension emerged as a reaction to national constitutional courts' insistence on their jurisdiction to submit even rules of Community origin to scrutiny in light of fundamental rights guaranteed in the national constitution, *pace* the principle of primacy. The German Constitutional Court replied to the ECJ's doctrine of fundamental rights as general principles of EC law with its *solange* rulings. The German Constitutional Court did

---

[31] According to the BVerfGE Lisbon ruling, 'the Basic Law does not authorise German state bodies to transfer sovereign powers in such a way that their exercise can independently establish other competences for the European Union. It prohibits the transfer of competence to decide on its own competence . . .' Note 15 above, para. 233.

[32] *Ibid.*, para. 240.

not renounce the claim of domestic constitutional law's ultimate authority nor, in institutional terms, its own jurisdiction, but professed its willingness to refrain from reasserting this authority with regard to Community law as long as (*so lange*) the Community's monitoring of fundamental rights works in a satisfactory way.[33] Subsequently, the requirement that the EU guarantee 'a level of protection of basic rights essentially comparable to that afforded by this Basic Law' was included in Article 23 of the Basic Law, which sets out the conditions for Germany's participation in the EU and which was amended in anticipation of the Maastricht Treaty. The normative basis of this monitoring has been further strengthened by adoption of the European Union Charter of Fundamental Rights and confirmation of its legal effect through the Lisbon Treaty (Article 6(1) TEU).

In its Maastricht and Lisbon rulings, the German Constitutional Court carved out an area of fundamental constitutional principles, crucial to the constitutional identity, which transfer of competence to the transnational level, facilitated by Article 23 of the Basic Law, cannot cover, and therefore lies outside, EU competence. The Court premised its argument on the reference in the third sentence of Article 23(1) to the so-called eternity clause in Article 79(3) of the Basic Law: this clause must be complied with even in constitutional amendments because Germany participates in the EU. Correspondingly, it also sets an absolute limit on transfer of powers to the EU and may not be exceeded by EU institutions when these exert their competences in adherence to the principle of conferral. In addition to the federal structure, the eternity clause declares the principles enshrined in Articles 1 and 20 of the Basic Law non-amendable. These, in turn, comprise the inviolability of human dignity, the inviolability and inalienability of human rights, and democratic, social, federal and rule-of-law principles.

The German Constitutional Court derived from the principle of democracy rather far-reaching and vague substantive limits to transfer of powers; it employed expressions such as 'democratic formative action' and 'the ability of a constitutional state to democratically shape itself'. It argued that European unification must leave sufficient space to the Member States for the political formation of economic, cultural and social living conditions. It stated that

---

[33] BVerfGE 37, 271 (*solange I*) and 73, 339 (*solange II*). On the emergence of the fundamental rights dimension in ECJ/CJEU case law and the dialogue between the ECJ and the German Constitutional Court see, e.g., Alter, note 30 above, especially p. 64ff.

this applies in particular to areas which shape the citizens' living conditions, in particular the private sphere of their own responsibility and of
political and social security, protected by fundamental rights, as well as to
political decisions that rely especially on cultural, historical and linguistic perceptions . . . [Thus,] essential areas of democratic formative action
comprise, *inter alia*, citizenship, the civil and the military monopoly on
the use of force, revenue and expenditure including external financing and
all elements of encroachment that are decisive for the realisation of fundamental rights, above all in major encroachments on fundamental rights
such as deprivation of liberty in the administration of criminal law or
placement in an institution . . . [They] also include cultural issues such as
the disposition of language, the shaping of circumstances concerning the
family and education, the ordering of the freedom of opinion, press and
of association and the dealing with the profession of faith or ideology.[34]

The Court also invoked the protection that Article 4(2) TEU (Lisbon)
offers to Member States' constitutional identity and added that constitutionally it is safeguarded by the possibility of 'identity review', provided
by the reference in the third sentence of Article 23(1) of the Basic Law to
the eternity clause in Article 79(3).[35] Thus, the German Constitutional
Court claims to possess three interrelated instruments with which, when
needed, it can contest the primacy claim of EU law: *ultra vires* review,
fundamental rights review and constitutional identity review.

Conflicts of authority are not specific to EU law's relation to Member State legal systems, but can – and are almost bound to –arise in other
areas, too, where the substantively limited claims of transnational law confront the universal and exclusive pretensions of national law, particularly
those endowed with the prestige of constitutional law. The monitoring of
human and fundamental rights touches upon the constitutional foundations of the national legal order. In Europe, overlaps between national and
transnational human rights regimes entail potential clashes of authority
in national constitutional courts' relations not only with the CJEU but
also with the ECtHR. At issue is a contest over the privilege of specifying
human rights law in Europe. According to Article 35(1) of the Convention,
the way to the Human Rights Court is open only after national remedies
have been exhausted. This implies a certain hierarchical superiority of the
transnational Strasbourg court over national courts, including constitutional ones. But constitutional courts are hesitant to acknowledge without
qualification the interpretative authority of the Human Rights Court both
at the level of single cases and at the level where case law guides future

---

[34] BVerfGE, note 15 above, para. 249.   [35] See *ibid.*, paras 240–41.

interpretation and the application of human and fundamental rights in national courts. Arguably, the German Constitutional Court's hesitancy again expresses a more general attitude among its counterparts in other Signatory States.[36]

Introduction of the EU's own fundamental rights regime, in which final jurisdiction lies with the CJEU, has led to an overlap with the claim to authority of the Human Rights Court, which holds itself competent to review legal acts of the Signatory States that relate to EU law. In Article 52(3) of the Charter, the EU has acknowledged the interpretative authority of the Convention, at a general level, in situations of normative overlap: the Convention is stipulated to define the bottom line of protection for EU law. However, this does not exclude conflicts of authority in single cases between the CJEU and the Human Rights Court. For its part, the Human Rights Court has assumed towards EU law a posture analogous to that of the German Constitutional Court. Thus, the judgment of the Human Rights Court in *Bosphorus* reads like a variant of the *solange* doctrine. The Human Rights Court announces the suspension – but mere suspension! – of its ultimate authority over application of the Convention to legal acts of the Member States that relate to EU law. Suspension is conditional on EU institutions providing equivalent protection, and the Court reserves to itself the right to revoke its authority.[37] If the EU accedes to the Convention, as laid down in Article 6(2) TEU, doctrines on respective responsibilities in monitoring human rights will obviously need reformulating for both the ECHR and the EU.

As we recall, international law, too, has had an acknowledged compartment in the traditional black box model. Transnational law may challenge the authority not only of nation-state law but also of (general) international law. A typical developmental path followed by instances of transnational law has been their gradual disconnection from their

---

[36] See the much-debated *Görgülü* judgment, BVerfGE 111, 307 and the comments in M. Hartwig, 'Much Ado About Human Rights: the Federal Constitutional Court confronts the European Court of Human Rights', 6 *German Law Review* 5 (2005), 869–94. Matti Pellonpää, a former Strasbourg judge, gives an overview of the discussion in several Member States, including the UK, Austria, Norway, Denmark and Sweden: 'Euroopan ihmisoikeussopimuksen tulkintaa koskevasta vuoropuhelusta' in T. Heinonen and J. Lavapuro (eds), *Oikeuskulttuurin eurooppalaistuminen: Ihmisoikeuksien murroksesta kansainväliseen vuoropuheluun* (Vantaa, Finland: Suomalainen Lakimiesyhdistys, 2012).

[37] *Bosphorus* v. *Ireland* (App. no. 45036/98) ECtHR 2005–VI, paras 155–6. Of the quite extensive literature, see S. Douglas-Scott, 'A Tale of Two Courts: Luxembourg, Strasbourg and the growing European human rights *acquis*', 43 *Common Market Law Review* (2006), 629–65.

original anchorage in international law. Thus, *Van Gend en Loos* and *Costa v. Enel* should be read as Community law's declaration of independence not only from the municipal law of the Member States but from (general) international law, as well. *Kadi* reaffirmed EU law's claim to independence in the field of the then Third Pillar. But, of course, separations do not necessarily entail subsequent hostilities or clashes of authority between either political entities or legal systems. *Kadi*'s significance for the definition of EU law's relation to general international law is not restricted to reaffirming EU law's distinctiveness but extends to questioning the superior authority of UN law. The ECJ asserted jurisdiction to review a Community act intended to give effect to a Security Council resolution in light of EU law's fundamental rights principles.[38]

The ICJ, with its general jurisdiction, has been the traditional guarantor of the unity of international law. A backdrop fundamental to debates on fragmentation of international law sees tribunals with a more restricted jurisdiction contesting the binding effect of ICJ precedents.[39] At least in some cases, this can be interpreted as testifying to a movement of a regime of international law towards an instance of transnational law. Contesting claims of authority between general international law, in the *Kadi* case represented by UN Security Council Resolutions and precedents of the ICJ, and transnational or international courts or tribunals with a restricted jurisdiction, bear some resemblance to the almost inevitable frictions that occur when the substantively limited claims of transnational law confront the universal pretentions of nation-state law.[40]

As overlaps in the human rights monitoring of the EU and the Human Rights Court prove, the substantive scopes of two instances of transnational law can collide as well, producing what I have called fundamental

---

[38] Joined cases C–402/05 P and C–415/05 P, *Kadi v. Council and Commission* [2008] ECR I–6351. See also G. de Búrca, 'The European Court of Justice and the international legal order after *Kadi*', 51 *Harvard International Law Journal* (2010), 1–49; and J. Kokott and C. Sobotta, 'The *Kadi* case: constitutional core values and international law – finding the balance?', 23 *European Journal of International Law* (2012), 1015–24.

[39] Koskenniemi and Leino, note 16 above.

[40] R. Y. Jennings, 'The proliferation of adjudicatory bodies: dangers and possible answers, implications of the proliferation of international adjudicatory bodies for dispute resolution', *ASIL Bulletin: Educational Resources on International Law* (1995) 2–7; B. Simma, 'Universality of international law from the perspective of a practitioner', 20 *European Journal of International Law* (2009) 265–97; see also special issue 'The proliferation of international tribunals: piecing together the puzzle', 31 *NYU Journal of International Law and Politics* 4 (1999); and Y. Shany, *The Competing Jurisdictions of International Courts and Tribunals* (Oxford: Oxford University Press, 2003).

conflicts of authority. Another example is provided by the refusal of the ECJ/CJEU to accept WTO law's claim of direct applicability within the EU.[41] In turn, in the fragmentation discussion, a favourite illustration is the contest between the WTO and the international environmental law regime concerning jurisdiction over the whale trade.[42]

6. Three versions of radical pluralism

Is there a solution to these conflicts involving new, transnational inhabitants of the legal universe? There is no shortage of proposals for new master principles that, according to their advocates, could create order in the (seemingly) global anarchy of legal authority and provide cross-boundary contests with a peaceful settlement. Below, I shall examine some of them and introduce my own account of the possibility of a global interlegality. But the scholarly field of transnational law and legal pluralism is crowded and contested. Let us call those who profess dialogue before antagonism and striving for coherence before the inevitability of fragmentation *legal dialogists*. They are confronted by *radical pluralists*; proponents of a position that, in principle, recognises no consensual way out of the controversies that have arisen from the downfall of the neatly organised, black box, legal world and where instances of transnational law are major protagonists. Radical pluralists wear three main guises: in personified terms, a Kelsenian one, a Koskenniemian one and a Luhmannian one.

The Kelsenian position claims to articulate the internal perspective of legal actors. Kelsen maintains that every legal actor is bound to assume the existence of a *Grundnorm* that constitutes the ultimate ground for validity and cognoscibility of the legal order she is applying. Multiple interpretations of the nature of the *Grundnorm* exist, and variation also exists in Kelsen's own accounts of its role. But a Kantian-transcendental aspect, at least, is crucial to an understanding of the function of the *Grundnorm* in the pure theory of law: for Kelsen, the (tacit) assumption of a *Grundnorm* is a necessary precondition of all legal cognition and all judgements of legal validity; or, to put it in Gadamerian terms, an integral element of the *Vorverständnis* of legal actors.

---

[41] See Case C–377/02 *Léon Van Parys NV* [2005] ECR I–1465.
[42] Koskenniemi and Leino, note 16 above; M. Koskenniemi, 'International law: constitutionalism, managerialism and the ethos of legal education', *European Journal of Legal Studies* 1 (2007), 1–18.

According to the Kelsenian account, in the clashes of legal authority, each of the conflicting legal orders is subjected to its specific *Grundnorm*, which establishes its normativity and crowns its hierarchical structure of authority (validity). Contests of authority are bound to arrive at different solutions in legal systems deferring to different *Grundnorms*. What we encounter is an alleged case of inescapable legal perspectivism: no neutral ground exists on which legal orders subordinated to diverse *Grundnorms* could meet, but the solution to the contested issue depends on the legal order from the perspective of which it is approached. Now, so Kelsenian radical pluralists argue, institutional legal actors such as judges or legislators are bound to adopt the perspective of the legal order under which the institution they serve has been established and its powers defined, and whose norms they are expected to apply and uphold. Following this line of argument, it is inevitable that – to take a familiar example – Member State constitutional courts assess EU law's claims of authority in light of the domestic constitution, whereas the CJEU treats EU law as an independent legal order and employs its inherent criteria of validity. Kelsenian premises do not admit of any (legal) principle that could bridge the gulf between the perspectives of self-contained legal orders; what we have here is the black box model revisited.[43]

Kelsenians and 'crits' might seem to be odd bedfellows. However, Koskenniemi cites with approval Kelsen's statement of the twin features *solipsism* and *imperialism*, characterising especially those nation-state legal orders that subscribe to the monist doctrine in relations between municipal and international law.[44] Still, this is perhaps not so surprising, considering that 'solipsism' and 'imperialism' are apt descriptions of Koskenniemi's portrayal of the antagonistic relations among international law regimes as well. But, of course, there is a vast distance – a diametrical opposition, we could even say – between Kelsen's and Koskenniemi's legal-theoretical starting points. The Kelsenian approach is an extreme version of the internal point of view. By contrast, Koskenniemi does not try to probe into or reconstruct the normative *Vorverständnis* of legal actors. On the contrary; he shuns discussion of the normative

---

[43] MacCormick's path-breaking articles from the 1990s, which in fact launched the still continuing debate on constitutional pluralism, largely adhered to the Kelsenian approach. See N. MacCormick, *Questioning Sovereignty* (Oxford: Oxford University Press, 1999). As a representative example of the approach, see also T. Schilling, 'Autonomy of the Community legal order: an analysis of possible foundations', 37 *Harvard International Law Journal* (1996), 389–410.

[44] Koskenniemi, note 42 above.

presuppositions or implications of legal speech acts; for him, the grand issues of normatively oriented legal theory – validity or authority and meaning – possess no intrinsic significance. Instead of legal speech acts' illocutionary dimension, where normative credentials are appraised, Koskenniemi focuses on the perlocutionary, strategic aspect; illocution is subordinated to the strategic, interest-driven aims of perlocution. Conflicts of jurisdiction are irresolvable, not because of divergent *Grundnorms*, but because of divergent institutional biases and the irreconcilability of the strategic interests that the institutional actors of different regimes are pursuing; say, the CJEU and national constitutional courts, or representatives of the WTO and the international environmental law regime, or EU law.

In addition to neo-Kelsenians and legal strategists of the Koskenniemi type, a third group of contemporary radical pluralists exists: theorists drawing from Niklas Luhmann's autopoietic systems theory. Autopoietic systems theorists deny Koskenniemi's interpretation of the intractability of inter-regime conflicts. Gunther Teubner and Andreas Fischer-Lescano argue that ultimately inter-regime conflicts do not derive from policy divergences and strategic interests of institutional actors but originate in the self-contained, autopoietic character of the global social subsystems that have given rise to transnational law. Nothing can be done to the very source of the problem: the evolutionary accomplishment of (global) social differentiation. Teubner's and Fischer-Lescano's favourite citation from the Master is the following: 'The sin of differentiation cannot be undone. Paradise is lost.'[45] At most, we are entitled to hope that some of the consequences of transnational legal fragmentation can be managed, through, for instance, conflict rules of a new type, focusing on the functional location of legal issues; mutual observation of systems of transnational law; and a striving for compatibility of the respective claims and criteria of validity. Yet instances of transnational law are tied to the particular rationality of a particular global social system – economy, health, sports, etc. – and each instance produces its own functionally oriented conflict rules and reactions to problems of compatibility. The source of the problem remains, and no guarantee exists that the separate treatment of inter-regime disputes in each legal subsystem will achieve congruence. Such is our third variant of radical pluralism.[46]

---

[45] Fischer-Lescano and Teubner, note 28 above, p. 1007. The citation is from N. Luhmann, *Die Wirtschaft der Gesellschaft* (Frankfurt: Suhrkamp, 1994), p. 344.

[46] Fischer-Lescano and Teubner, note 28 above.

In sum, the three varieties of radical pluralism condemn legal orders (Kelsenians), regimes (legal strategists) or systems (autopoietic systems theorists) to their solipsist perspective, with no prospect of boundary-breaking, cross-perspective contacts. They all end up advocating a new version of the black box model of the legal universe. The boxes are defined differently from the traditional model and the emergence of transnational law beyond the dichotomy of national and international law is acknowledged. But self-contained legal orders, regimes and systems remain shut in their respective boxes.

Radical pluralists point to a central lesson to be gained from theorising about transnational law: namely, the necessary perspectivism in law. But, as I will argue below, perspectivism does not necessarily condemn legal orders and systems to hermetic solipsism, but may imply resources for dialogue and co-operation. I shall present my own, culturally oriented interpretation of perspectivism after discussing some of the global meta-principles of order propounded in recent debates.

7. In search of a new global master principle

Radical pluralists recognise the rise of transnational law beyond the dichotomy of national and international law, but only end up with new versions of the black box model. They are content to register the new fragmentation and growing ground for fundamental conflicts of legal authority that I have traced down to contradictory and overlapping principles of legal differentiation. Radical pluralists' legal worldview is rather desolate; it does not offer much hope of reconciliation or overcoming the solipsism of legal orders subordinated to their distinct *Grundnorms*, legal regimes pursuing their particular interests or legal systems obeying their specific rationality and employing their distinct code of communication. They propose a global master principle of law but this principle does not bring order to the new disorder. On the contrary, radical pluralists deny the possibility of a principle that could bridge the gulf between particular legal orders, regimes or systems.

But, as I have already indicated, radical pluralists do not monopolise the debate. They have found a counterweight in scholars who put their emphasis not on fragmentation but on its counter-tendency, the increasing legal interconnectedness that has resulted from lowering the walls that previously separated states with their municipal legal systems and that the traditional black box model had registered. The search for a new, harmonising, global master principle capable of addressing legal transnationalisation has pursued both descriptive/explanatory and normative aims, often enough intertwined. Scholars have longed for both a basic grid of interpretation, rendering the new global constellation of law intelligible, and a normative paradigm that would facilitate the creation of coherence in the fragmented legal world and, by the same token, enhance the law's legitimacy. The meta-level order of orders aspired for displays both intellectual and normative features.

Under conditions of pre-modern law, that is, before the rise of the nation state with its claim to exclusive and universal legal sovereignty, more than one legal order or system claiming authority within the same territorially delineated social space was the rule rather than an exception: canon law, feudal law, manorial law, borough law, royal law, mercantile law and so on.[47] It does not come as a great surprise that, in the quest for a new frame of reference capable of rendering intelligible and/or normatively coherent legal phenomena that contradict state-sovereigntist premises, inspiration has been sought in pre- or early-modern concepts and principles. Reinhard Zimmermann is perhaps the best-known scholar who has seen in the Europeanisation of law, especially the expansion of EC/EU law, the emergence of a new *ius commune*.[48] In his theorising on the interrelations of legal orders, Patrick H. Glenn has taken a step further and treated 'common law' as a generic concept of which early-modern *ius commune* or the English common law only constitute particular instances. What, according to Glenn, is distinctive of common law is its relational character: it only exists in relation to *iura propria* and is subsidiary to them.[49] Another example of the re-enlivenment of a pre-modern legal figure is Jeremy Waldron's appeal to *ius gentium* as a justification for interjudicial dialogue and references to foreign court decisions in the rulings of US courts. For Waldron, *ius gentium* is a reservoir of juridical wisdom, common to mankind, comparable to scientific knowledge and applicable regardless of state or other boundaries. Court decisions apply, manifest and elaborate principles of not merely municipal law but, at least potentially, even worldwide *ius gentium*.[50]

---

[47] H. Berman, *Law and Revolution* (Cambridge, MA: Harvard University Press, 1983).

[48] See, e.g., R. Zimmermann, 'Roman law and European legal unity' in A. S. Hartkamp et al. (eds), *Towards a European Civil Code* (Nijmegen: Ars Aequi Libri, 1994), pp 65–81.

[49] H. P. Glenn, *Common Laws* (Oxford: Oxford University Press, 2005). See also Glenn in Chapter 2 of this volume.

[50] J. Waldron, 'Foreign law and the modern *ius gentium*', 119 *Harvard Law Review* 1 (2005), 129–47; J. Waldron, '*Ius gentium*: a defense of Gentili's equation of the law of nations and

Evidently, pre- or early-modern legal figures are not offered as comprehensive explanatory or normative paradigms for coming to terms with contemporary transnationalised and pluralised law; the ambition is more modest. In a normative respect, more is expected of the extension of constitutionalism beyond its nation-state confines. Proposals for *non-state constitutionalism* have appeared in two fundamentally different guises: as regime- or system-bound and as universal or global constitutionalism. The former aspires to constitutionalise particular transnational legal systems or regimes; again, the EU proffers an illuminating example. In effect, by enhancing the self-contained character of single instances of transnational law, such particularistic, non-state constitutionalism may well accentuate rather than alleviate global legal fragmentation. In contrast, global constitutionalism aims to establish overarching constitutional principles and values, and/or institutional and procedural devices. If we leave outright natural law talk aside, at least embryos of global constitutional principles have been discerned in the *ius cogens* of international law as well as in the common elements of treaty-based human rights instruments; indeed, here the distance to Waldron's revived *ius gentium* is not necessarily very great. A recurring theme in the critique of global constitutionalism is the accusation of Western-biased ethnocentricity and disregard or even suppression of cultural diversity. The critique may be overdriven: as I try to argue below, cultural diversity does not exclude congruence at a 'deep-cultural' level. Still, at least in the institutional respect, global constitutionalism seems to confront insurmountable problems: the idea of global constitutional review has not found convincing institutional specifications, nor does the more modest proposal of reinforcing the status of the ICJ in order to combat fragmentation of international law appear to have much chance of success.[51]

The utopianism of much of the constitutional debate has led some debaters to draw inspiration from the legal principles and concepts of another field of law, familiar from the systematisation of nation-state law: namely, administrative law. Advocates of *global administrative law* pursue more modest normative aims than global constitutionalists: the objective is to enhance the legitimacy of transnational law, not to achieve

the law of nature', *New York University Public Law and Legal Theory Working Papers*, paper 99 (2008). Available at: http://lsr.nellco.org/nyu_plltwp/99.

[51] See, e.g., Jennings, note 40 above, 2–7; P-M. Dupuy, 'The danger of fragmentation or unification of the international legal system and the International Court of Justice', 31 *NYU Journal of International Law and Politics* (1999), 791–807.

comprehensive normative coherence. The basic idea is to promote the application of such administrative law principles as *audiatur et altera pars* and access to information in the decision making of both international and transnational bureaucracies.[52]

As a normative paradigm, 'legal pluralism' has been alleged to be able to tack between the shoals of the particularism of old-time state sovereigntism, and utopian and difference-levelling universalism. The pluralist paradigm is supposed to respect diversity but also to promote the design of procedural and institutional mechanisms for managing 'hybrid legal spaces'; that is, social spaces inhabited by a plurality of legal orders or systems. Berman is able to point to several devices already in use; most of them, interestingly enough, in European legal space.[53] By contrast, Neil Walker seems to indicate that we are bound to live with a disorder of orders, in which no master principle provides explanatory or normative coherence but several candidates compete for dominance.[54] Some of the candidates Walker discusses lie closer to the pole of descriptive/explanatory grids of interpretation, others to that of normative paradigms. Both constitutionalism and global administrative law figure in Walker's inventory, as does pluralism, although in other guises than in the contributions of Berman or Nico Krisch.[55]

Walker lists the following, putative, global meta-principles of legal authority:

1. state sovereigntist (realism – liberal internationalism)
2. global hierarchical (world government – pyramid structure with some cosmopolitan norms/institutions)
3. unipolar (*Pax Americana* – global liberal hegemony)
4. regional (divided world order – new balance between different regional conceptions of constitutional/international order)
5. integrity (universalisability of norms across orders – coherence of conflict norms between orders)

---

[52] B. Kingsbury, N. Krisch and R. Stewart, 'The emergence of global administrative law', 68 *Law & Contemporary Problems* 15 (2005), 15–61; D. Esty, 'Good governance at the supranational scale: globalizing administrative law', 115 *Yale Law Journal* (2006), 1490–1562.
[53] Berman, note 19 above.   [54] Walker, note 27 above.
[55] Krisch, note 19 above; N. Krisch, *Beyond Constitutionalism: The Pluralist Structure of Postnational Law* (Oxford: Oxford University Press, 2011).

6. legal-field discursive (particular legal field as master discourse of law – extension and application of discourse of conceptualisation and imagination associated with a particular legal field to the global level) and

7. pluralist (new anarchy of legal forms and relations – 'bottom up' countervailing power model).

According to Walker, all of these meta-principles exist in both a strong and exclusive and a moderate and contributory application. He argues that, in their moderate forms, the principles are not necessarily mutually exclusive but may well overlap. They also possess a discursive potential, which enables them to enter into a dialogue with each other. Below, I shall relate my own normatively oriented discussion to this potential. By the same token, I shall address an objection that appears to deal a fatal blow to the very idea of a potential master principle that could bring order and coherence to our fragmented normative universe. We are already familiar with the debate. At issue is the argument from perspectivism, put forth by radical pluralists: all putative normative master principles are necessarily applied and interpreted from the hermetic point of view of each legal system, without any guarantee of the coherence or even compatibility of the respective applications and interpretations.

8. From conflict to interlegality

Evidently, radical pluralism with its new black box models conveys a one-sided and distorted picture of our contemporary legal landscape. True, hegemonistic turf wars occur among legal orders, systems and regimes; institutional and professional interests influence legal speech acts; legal actors are committed to their legal order of affiliation; and functionally differentiated legal orders follow their divergent rationalities. But this is not all there is; co-operative relations, cross-boundary dialogue, mutual learning, overlapping and interpenetration exist as well. Perspectivism in law is inevitable, but solipsism is not. What Boaventura de Sousa Santos has called *interlegality* offers an alternative to the solipsism of radical pluralisms. Instead of the either/or logic of dichotomisation, characteristic of radical pluralism, interlegality rather follows a both/and approach. In Sousa Santos's account, typical of interlegality are 'different legal spaces superimposed, interpenetrated and mixed in our minds, as much as in our actions'. He argues that 'we live in a time of porous legality or of legal porosity, multiple networks of legal orders forcing us to constant transitions and trespassing. Our legal life is constituted by an intersection of different legal orders, that is, by interlegality.'[56] Thus, in the mirror of interlegality, plural legal orders, systems or regimes do not appear as self-contained entities; they are seen as mutually overlapping and maintaining a dialogical relation with each other.

Koskenniemi's legal strategism cannot come to terms with such dialogical relations – and is not even interested in doing so. From Koskenniemi's external perspective, legal actors are moved by their particular interests and strategic aims; their primary objective is not to reach a consensus with their interlocutors in the illocutionary dimension of legal discourse, but to pursue their extra-discursive, perlocutionary aims. This produces a rather cynical picture of our global, transnationalised, legal landscape; a picture of conflicts and fights over jurisdiction – the right to state the law. Koskenniemi recognises merely one side of the coin. But there is a reverse side to this coin, too.

We must give credit to legal systems theorists of the Luhmannian school for many insightful observations of legal systems in general and of transnational law in particular. They quite rightly point to the difficulties of dialogical interaction between social subsystems; difficulties that they attribute to diverse rationalities and language. But they tend to shut their eyes before the fact that, in spite of such difficulties, dialogue and discourse do indeed occur across the boundaries of social subsystems and that even instances of transnational law seem to be able to engage in mutual communication. As autopoietic systems theorists condemn legal actors to the isolation of their legal subsystems, they themselves remain prisoners of their idiosyncratic conceptual apparatus. Their perennial but largely self-generated problem is how systems can still interact in spite of their supposed operative closure. Admittedly, the concept of structural coupling may produce fruitful results in,[57] for instance, illuminating how legal and political systems interact through the constitution. Still, mere structural coupling conveys but a deficient depiction of all the existing richness of dialogical relations across the borders of social systems or instances of law. In line with the legal strategists of the Koskenniemi template, Luhmannian systems theorists account more convincingly for

---

[56] B. de Sousa Santos, *Toward a New Legal Common Sense* (London: Butterworths, 2002), p. 347.
[57] N. Luhmann, *Law as a Social System*, trans. Ziegert (Oxford: Oxford University Press, 2004), p. 381ff.

conflicts than for consensus and for misunderstandings than for successful dialogue.

In recent debates, many scholars have examined forms of peaceful contact and adjustment between legal orders or systems. Out of many, let me
just briefly mention some examples. The first of these consists of the procedural and institutional mechanisms that Berman discusses as expressing
pluralism as a normative paradigm occupying the middle ground between
the particularism of state sovereigntism and the universalism of, e.g.,
world constitutionalism: such as 'dialectical legal interactions', margins
of appreciation, subsidiarity schemes and mutual recognition regimes,
all of them employed, in particular in European legal space.[58] Second, I
would like to refer to the forms of interaction between legal orders that,
according to Walker's analysis,[59] allow a 'host' legal order to take account
of a 'foreign' legal order's claim to authority: institutional incorporation,
system recognition, normative coordination, environmental overlap and
sympathetic consideration.

In turn, Ralf Michaels's focus is on relations between state and non-state
law. He distinguishes between three forms in which state law may recognise and 'restate' non-state law without renouncing its exclusive claim
to authority.[60] He argues that *incorporation* leads to transformation of
non-state law into state law; *deference* to its transformation into facts; and
delegation to its transformation into subordinated law. And, to conclude
my quick and selective survey of the rapidly expanding literature, Allan
Rosas's focus is still more restricted: he analyses forms of judicial dialogue
in the European context, from the point of view of the CJEU. The first
category covers hierarchical relationships between courts of one and the
same institutional order, e.g., between the CJEU and the General Court;
the second category the relationship between the CJEU and national
courts in the preliminary rulings procedure concerning the interpretation
or validity of EU law; the third category the 'semi-vertical' relationship
that, according to Rosas, the CJEU entertains with the ECtHR, the WTO
Appellate Body and, on points of general international law, the ICJ; the
fourth category instances of overlapping jurisdiction as may be the case
in relations between the ICJ and, e.g., the Law of the Sea Tribunal; and

---

[58] *In toto*, the devices examined by Berman, note 19 above, are: A. dialectical legal interactions; B. margins of appreciation; C. limited autonomy regimes; D. subsidiarity schemes;
E. jurisdictional redundancy; F. hybrid participation procedures; G. mutual recognition
regimes; H. 'safe harbor' agreements; and I. pluralist approach to conflict of laws.
[59] Walker, note 27 above.   [60] Michaels, note 25 above.

the fifth category horizontal dialogue between courts of more or less the same level, say, the CJEU and the EFTA Court.[61]

If the authors I have invoked are right in their observations, as I think they are, the relations between transnational and national law or among instances of the former are not marked merely by conflicting claims of authority and an unremitting contest over jurisdiction – the privilege to state the law; they also manifest overlap, interpenetration and dialogue, that is, features of interlegality. Existing interlegality warrants a new approach to the plurality and perspectivism of legal orders, systems and regimes. Instead of confining ourselves to conflicts of authority, hegemonistic turf wars or mutual misunderstandings – which do exist! – we should reformulate our problem. Given the inevitable perspectivism, how are cross-border co-operation and dialogue, as well as interlegality in general, possible?

I shall sketch my solution to the reformulated problem by giving the Kelsenian reading of perspectivism a legal-cultural twist. Kelsenian perspectivism revolves around the notion of *Grundnorm*. In Kelsen's pure theory of law, this notion is supposed to capture the fundamental presuppositions that make legal knowledge possible in the first place: legal cognition is premised on the general validity of the legal order, and this validity ultimately flows from a hypothetical, transcendental *Grundnorm*. Let us restate Kelsen's point in a way that allows for its immanent criticism and further development. Kelsen could perhaps have agreed with the following formulation: the normative claims of legal speech acts are always made with reference to a specific legal order. This is the backdrop to the perspectivism that Kelsenians have emphasised in the context of EU law: they have concluded that the multiplicity of alternative *referential legal orders* inevitably entails a multiplicity of views on the basis for the validity of European law.

In the debate on the allegedly irresolvable conflict of authority between EU law and the municipal law of the Member States, the perspective of EU law is institutionally attached to the CJEU and that of national legal orders to national courts. But that equation may be too simplistic and straightforward. Owing to the intertwining of transnational, European and Member State national legal systems, national courts fulfil a dual role. They are organs of not only the national but also the EU legal system. In cases involving both national and EU law, why should they necessarily

---

[61] A. Rosas, 'The European Court of Justice in context: forms and patterns of judicial dialogue', *European Journal of Legal Studies* 1 (2007) (online publication).

use the national legal order as the referential framework? Could they not instead adopt the perspective of EU law or of European law at large (comprising EU law, domestic legal orders and Council of Europe rule work)?

The answer depends on our answer to another question: what does it actually mean to adopt a particular legal order as one's normative framework and point of reference? For Kelsenians, this amounts to adherence to the *Grundnorm* of the legal order at issue, and this adherence accounts for the different views that the CJEU and national constitutional courts hold of the ultimate criteria for EU law's validity (authority). The courts have no choice, at least not legally speaking: a court is bound to take the perspective of the legal order under which it has been set up and the realisation of which is primarily expected to guarantee. Indeed, assumption of another *Grundnorm* would amount – again legally speaking – to a judicial revolution. Hence, the only option legally available to both national courts and the CJEU is the perspective and the *Grundnorm* of the legal order under which they have been established. A similar, Kelsenian, radical pluralist view is applicable to all conflicts of ultimate authority between legal orders: between state law and instances of transnational law or among the latter.

Another reformulation of Kelsen's position might help us to see its inherent flaws. Kelsen draws our attention to the significance of legal actors' implicit pre-understanding (*Vorverständnis*) of legal practices and legal discourse. But he tries to reconstruct this pre-understanding in transcendental, ahistorical terms: he contends that the assumption of a *Grundnorm* and the concomitant hierarchical understanding of the legal order are transcendental presuppositions necessarily involved in all legal cognition and reasoning. However, legal *Vorverständnis* is not transcendentally fixed for all times and places. Legal actors draw the pre-understanding – practical knowledge in Anthony Giddens's terms[62] – they need for engaging in legal reasoning and for tackling the legal problems confronting them from the temporally and spatially variable legal-cultural reservoir that is available to them.

Arguably, a legal order does not consist merely of such explicit norms as would be organisable in a Kelsenian hierarchical *Stufenbau* under the crowning apex of a *Grundnorm*. In the framework of Kelsenian positivism, a legal order is composed of posited (*gestellte*) norms, deriving their

---

[62] A. Giddens, *Central Problems in Social Theory: Action, Structure and Contradictions in Social Analysis* (Berkeley: University of California Press, 1979), pp 24–5.

validity (authority) from a pre-posited (*vor-gestellte*) *Grundnorm*. But, I claim, in addition to such explicit legal normative material, a legal order also includes legal-cultural elements, without which 'surface-level' norms could not be applied, interpreted or systematised. The legal-cultural layers provide legal actors' *Vorverständnis* with contents that reach far beyond anything compressible to a Kelsenian *Grundnorm*. Legal culture does include a doctrine of legal sources that determines what counts as valid law and what is accepted as a legal argument, but it also includes much else; for instance, legal concepts, principles and theories employed in legal interpretation, reasoning and decision making.[63] Furthermore, it is historically and culturally contingent whether the doctrine of legal sources adopts the hierarchical view implicit in both Kelsen's and Hart's version of legal positivism and related to the traditional black box model.

Legal actors assess the validity of legal norms in accordance with the doctrine of legal sources inherent in the legal culture of the referential legal order. In routine legal practice, this transpires in a quasi-automatic, unconscious way. The prevailing doctrine of legal sources is part of legal actors' tacitly functioning pre-understanding or – again in Giddens' term – practical knowledge. Only in hard cases do they experience the need to articulate this knowledge, to spell out the exact contents of the doctrine and to ponder its implications in the case at hand. This is how other legal-cultural elements of legal actors' pre-understanding function as well; elements such as legal concepts, principles and theories.

In sum, we should understand legal actors' dependence on a referential legal order in broader terms than merely as application of surface-level normative material or the doctrine of legal sources determining the legal validity of that material. We should also be aware of the general role of legal culture in legal practice, and of the functioning of legal concepts, principles and theories as a filter through which surface-level legal material is taken notice of and interpreted. Rejection of the Kelsenian reading of legal perspectivism does not imply a denial that national courts remain bound in an important way to their national legal order. Legal culture is internalised in the course of legal socialisation, during university studies and subsequent professional activities. Judges in national courts have received their legal education in national universities and have accumulated their professional experience in the national judiciary; consequently, their legal pre-understanding is imbued by the national

---

[63] I have presented my view of the multilayered nature of law in *Critical Legal Positivism*, note 24 above, and *Ratio and Voluntas*, note 3 above.

legal culture. Hence, we are entitled to assume, for instance, that judges in national courts approach and interpret EU law through their national legal culture: through the legal concepts, principles and theories inherent in that culture. And, recalling the thesis of legal culture as an integral part of the legal order, we can speak not only of divergent views on European law but also of different European laws, cast in different legal-cultural moulds.

On the specific issue of the ultimate basis for the validity of EU law, too, the Kelsenian, radical pluralist position is in need of revision. By no means is it a self-evident truth or an axiomatic fact that national courts are forever bound to a doctrine of legal sources that reserves ultimate and incontestable authority to the national constitution. We cannot exclude *a priori* the possibility that the doctrine of EU law's primacy is integrated in the legal culture not only of EU law but also of the national legal order, or that the national legal culture accords primacy to EU law even in hard cases in which clashes between EU law and Member State law touch on constitutional issues. Again, our conclusions are generalisable: they concern not merely relations between national law and EU law but also other instances in which actors from a particular legal system appraise claims of authority raised by a legal order other than the referential one.

It takes time for a budding legal order to manage to develop legal-cultural supports for explicit, surface-level norms. Nonetheless, legal practice is inconceivable without legal-cultural means of interpretation and argumentation. In emergent, transnational, legal systems, legal actors are likely to bring with them the *Vorverständnis* their national legal culture has equipped them with. This will, of course, lead to misunderstandings and problems of communication between actors from different, forma-tive, legal cultures. It is only through transnational legal practice that a transnational legal culture can develop. If we acknowledge law's mul-tilayered nature, we may argue that the independence of a legal order requires not only a rule of recognition capable of delineating its surface-level norms, but also development of legal-cultural supports for these norms. At least in its core areas of free movement and competition law, EU law has perhaps reached the stage at which a particular EU legal culture informs the pre-understanding of EU legal actors. And, consequently – to return to intractable perspectivism in EU law – to the versions of EU law, coloured by the particularities of Member States' legal cultures, should be added a distinct EU-law understanding of EU law!

An obvious perspectivist objection exists to my proposal for overcom-ing the solipsist perspectivism of radical pluralism. Has the reformulation and immanent criticism of the Kelsenian position been able to introduce openings to the enclosures of the new black box models? Have we not merely given Kelsenian perspectivism a wider twist, relating it to broader but culturally diverging contents of legal *Vorverständnis*? Arguably, more than that has been achieved: our restatement of the inevitable perspectivism in law also indicates the way out of Kelsenian solipsism.

If the idea of legal orders as self-contained normative entities with sharply definable contours – an idea implicit in Kelsen's pure theory as well as Hart's conception of law – is in general of any assistance in mapping our present legal landscape, its potential applicability is confined to the surface level of explicit norms. When we turn to the underpinning, legal-cultural layers, boundaries of legal orders turn out to be much more porous. No rule of recognition or *Grundnorm* exists that would allow us to draw exact borders between legal cultures. Ever since the reception of Roman law took off in Europe in the twelfth century, European legal culture has been a transnational affair, breaking the exclusiveness of *iura propria*. Medieval *ius commune* gave expression to transnational legal culture, shared and spread by a transnational, university-educated corps of learned lawyers, and this legal culture also influenced the application and interpretation of *leges propria*. Contemporary interlegality, too, is primarily about legal-cultural overlaps and interaction. Indeed, in a crucial sense, EU law is premised on this interlegality. Legal traditions common to Member States are an important source of general principles of EU law,[64] and Article 6(1) TEU explicitly refers to shared constitutional traditions as a basis of fundamental rights principles. And in spite of legal-culturally induced perspectivism, misunderstandings and problems of communication, EU law is still interpreted and applied in a sufficiently uniform manner across borders to guarantee, for instance, the functioning of the internal market. This would not be possible without similarities, interfaces and overlaps between national legal cultures and the legal *Vorverständnis* of the legal actors of different Member States.

In international law debates, opponents to Koskenniemi's radical pluralist view have pointed to the role general international law still plays in such 'fragmented' regimes as, say, human rights law, WTO law or international environmental law.[65] The argument perhaps gains in cogency when transferred to the legal-cultural level and detached from, say, the

---

[64] See, e.g., T. Tridimas, *The General Principles of EU Law* (Oxford: Oxford University Press, 2006), p. 5ff.

[65] See, e.g., P-M. Dupuy, 'A doctrinal debate in the globalisation era: on the "fragmentation" of international law', *European Journal of Legal Studies* 1 (2007).

jurisdiction of the ICJ and the reach of the precedent effect of its rulings. The perspectivism of semi-independent regimes – or, expressed in another conceptual framework, instances of transnational law – is tempered by affinities in the *Vorverständnis* of the jurists serving in them. Indeed, as Klaus Günther has remarked, much of transnational law – even when it has its origin in international-law treaties – is *Juristenrecht*, lawyers' law. And lawyers as primary legal actors seem to be in possession of a common language that enables them to engage in intersystemic dialogues; here, Günther introduces the notion of a *universal code of legality*.[66] Relations between legal systems do not consist merely of contests over jurisdiction, that is, the privilege to state the law; they also involve dialogue and co-operative strivings for normative coherence. All this is enabled by shared features in the legal culture informing legal actors' *Vorverständnis*, including the basics of a common legal language.

To sum up, our late-modern, denationalised, legal landscape displays not only signs of fragmentation and disputes of authority, but also counter-tendencies of consensus-oriented dialogue, overlapping and interpenetration, in particular at the legal-cultural level. Phenomena such as the spread of human rights talk and its incursion even into transnational legal systems that are not specialised in monitoring human rights even lend credence to the contention that the most fundamental processes of globalisation or denationalisation are occurring in the subsurface, legal-cultural layers of law. This does not equate to a universalist claim for a fundamental normative unity in all law. It is debatable whether in general it is meaningful to speak of a new master principle replacing state sovereigntism and creating an 'order of orders' in a legal world in which nation-state law is overlain by functionally delineated and mutually overlapping instances of transnational law. But if it were, such a meta-principle would be not of a substantive but of a *discursive* nature. It could not work, though, without sufficient congruence at legal-cultural level and without the existence of at least the foundations of a common legal language.

9. The perspectivism of legal roles and disciplines

So, I would paint the picture of the global legal landscape in quite different colours from those of radical pluralists. Which aspect of legal

---

[66] K. Günther, 'Rechtspluralismus und universaler Code der Legalität: Globalisierung als rechtstheoretischer Problem' in L. Wingert and K. Günther (eds), *Die Öffentlichkeit der Vernunft und die Vernunft der Öffentlichkeit* (Frankfurt: Suhrkamp, 2001), pp 539–67.

development dominates in one's account is obviously a matter of perspective as well. It is no coincidence that, from their external perspective, sociologically oriented observers have been prone to emphasise the fragmentation of law. Legal anthropologists and sociologists originally founded the very notion of legal pluralism, and in contemporary debates scholars drawing their inspiration from Niklas Luhmann's sociological theory of autopoietic social systems adhere to a radical pluralist position. As might be expected, among legal scholars the legal strategists in the critical camp have joined forces with sociologists in their depiction of relationships among legal systems and regimes; the 'crits', too, tend to ignore the internal point of view and, for instance, refuse doctrinal research the status of science. They extend their external, reductionist account from conflicts between legal regimes to other instances of perspectivism relating to law, indeed, to legal discourse in general. We are familiar with the narrative of international lawyers, constitutional lawyers and EU lawyers being engaged in a strategic contest over the vocabulary with which EU law should be depicted. No neutral linguistic ground exists but the conceptual apparatus disputants employ is unavoidably tainted by their positions in the (battle) field of law and academic scholarship, which provides the setting for the power game over the privilege of stating the law.

The dependence of legal actors' *Vorverständnis* on the legal culture of a referential legal order is not the only epitome of perspectivism in law. Here at least two other typical manifestations deserve mention: the perspectivism of legal roles and legal disciplines. The approaches to law adopted by legal actors such as the legislator, the judge, the counsellor (the practising lawyer) and the scholar display important differences. The legislator sees in law primarily a means of achieving politically defined social objectives, and the practising lawyer looks at it through the lens of her client's extra-legal interests, which she is supposed to promote. Both the legislator and the legal counsellor focus on the perlocutionary effects of legal speech acts, such as statutes and court decisions. Both of them participate in legal discourse and are players in the game of law, but the prizes they seek are of an extra-legal character. Consequently, they are prone to subordinate the illocutionary aspect of legal speech acts to the perlocutionary one.

Judges, by contrast, privilege the illocutionary dimension, in which criteria such as argumentative cogency and normative correctness hold sway. As Klaus Günther argued in his doctoral thesis, an aspiration towards normative coherence is inherent in judicial interpretation and decision-making.[67] Increasingly, in contemporary law, this aspiration is not confined merely to the national legal order – the referential legal order as defined above. It is here that mechanisms that enable a 'host' legal order to allow for the influence of a 'foreign' one show their potential; mechanisms that have been analysed by, e.g., Walker, Michaels and Berman. Of course, 'foreign' impacts are always filtered and translated through the legal-cultural perspectivism of the 'host' legal order. Still, as I have argued, this does not necessarily prevent the commensurability of the respective reconstructions of law.

What, then, about legal scholars? What is their typical perspective on law? Doctrinal scholars – 'legal dogmaticians' – assist other legal actors through recommending interpretations and proposing systematisation. Their focus is clearly on the illocutionary aspect; they appraise the normative credentials of the speech acts of other legal actors and claim normative correctness for their own contributions. Arguably, the perspective of a doctrinal scholar is close to that of a judge. By contrast, legal theory is a meta-level legal practice or discourse – and produces second-order observations, as a Luhmannian systems theorist would put it – that, consciously or unconsciously, relates to a particular first-order perspective and gives it a reflexive twist. The first-order perspective may be the normatively (illocutionarily) oriented perspective of a judge or a doctrinal scholar, as is the case both in Kelsenian and Hartian legal positivism and in the principle-oriented jurisprudence of, say, Ronald Dworkin or Robert Alexy.[68] But legal theory may also approach the law from a legislator- or counsellor-related meta-perspective. The former may not be so common, but it has animated contemporary endeavours in 'legisprudence' or *Gesetzgebungslehre*.[69] In turn, the point of view of a practising lawyer was the main gateway to law for American realists,[70] as it is for their successors in the CLS School, too. It is this perspective that leads legal strategists to

[67] K. Günther, *The Sense of Appropriateness* (Albany: State University of New York Press, 1993).

[68] Arguably, Dworkin's main legal-theoretical works remain *Taking Rights Seriously* (London: Duckworth, 1978) and *Law's Empire* (London: Fontana, 1986). Alexy develops his view on law and legal reasoning in *A Theory of Legal Argumentation*, trans. Adler and MacCormick (Oxford: Clarendon Press, 1989) and *A Theory of Constitutional Rights*, trans. Rivers (Oxford: Oxford University Press, 2002).

[69] As a representative example, see L. Wintgens, *Legisprudence: Practical Reason in Legislation* (Farnham: Ashgate 2012).

[70] See the perceptive analyses in B. Leiter, *Naturalizing Jurisprudence: Essays on American Legal Realism and Naturalism in Jurisprudence* (Oxford: Oxford University Press, 2007).

focus on institutional, professional and personal interests and biases, and to neglect the illocutionary aspect of law.

Finally, there is the perspectivism of distinct branches of law and corresponding academic disciplines: international law, constitutional law, criminal law, private law... Many debaters have noted that EU law as well as other instances of transnational law tend to ignore the traditional legal divisions that we are used to applying to municipal law. This is a major reason for legal hybridisation at the level of fields of law; the emergence of new putative fields of law that confuse the time-honoured systematisation. Nonetheless, this does not mean that the traditional divisions would have lost their significance in general or in the discourse on transnational law in particular. Most lawyers, including legal scholars, have developed their professional identity within a particular, established field and privilege the conceptual scheme and language of that field. This results in the seemingly never-ending succession of legal hybrids that legal scholarship parades before us and in the rival accounts that different legal disciplines produce of the same legal issues.

An external, sociological observer is prone to explain this variation by strategic disciplinary interests; by the stakes involved in the power game of the legal field.[71] A similar view, focusing on the perlocutionary aspect of legal discourse, is also cherished by the critical legal scholarship that Koskenniemi represents. An international lawyer favours the language of international law and, consequently, stresses the international law qualities of EU law, such as the power of Member States over the Treaties. Correspondingly, a scholar of constitutional law defends the institutional and academic status of her discipline, and depicts European law in constitutional terms.

Again, focusing on legal actors' strategic, perlocutionary aims has its justification. But, again, such an emphasis catches but one side of the coin. Participants in, say, EU law discourse make normative claims, too, and the illocutionary purport of their speech acts is affected by their legal-cultural pre-understanding. Not only is there variation in the legal cultures of the Member States, but legal culture is also differentiated in accordance with the divisions of law. Different branches of law and corresponding legal disciplines possess their particular concepts, principles and theories; what in German legal scholarship is called *allgemeine Lehren*, general doctrines. A distinct disciplinary perspective entails employment of the

---

[71] An already classic model is provided by P. Bourdieu, 'The force of law: toward a sociology of the juridical field', trans. and introd. Terdiman, 38 *The Hastings Law Journal* (1987), 805–53.

concepts, principles and theories of the discipline at issue. And, to return to EU law as an epitome of transnational law, we are confronted by a new variety of EU laws: a variety produced by divergent disciplinary approaches. If we can already speak of a specific EU legal culture, with its specific conceptual, normative and methodological elements, one of these disciplinarily differentiated EU laws consists of the EU law of EU lawyers.

The perspectivism of branches of law and corresponding academic disciplines is likely to affect one's view of the interrelations among legal orders, regimes and systems. Arguably, Koskenniemi's stress on adversarialism, the role of particular institutional and professional strategic interests and the ensuing fragmentation, is associated with his disciplinary identity as an international lawyer. International law is intimately linked with politics, which makes it particularly conflictual by nature and confers a more obviously strategic label upon its argumentation than is usual in other fields of law. In international law, court procedures are still quite underdeveloped, and as a rule the jurisdiction of courts or other dispute-resolving bodies depends on the consent of the parties. These distinct features probably impregnate the *Vorverständnis* of international lawyers and leave an imprint on their legal-theoretical views.

But as important as it is to note how one's legal role or discipline influences one's view on law, the effects of this kind of perspectivism should not be exaggerated, either. Again, solipsist generalisations would overstate their case. Legislators, judges, practising lawyers and scholars adopt divergent perspectives on law but usually they get each other's point and are able to engage in joint legal argument. The same goes for representatives of diverse branches of law. Private and public lawyers or international and constitutional lawyers may offer different conceptualisations of, say, regulatory private law or the EU Treaties. Still, they are ready to acknowledge that the interlocutor, too, is talking law and, often enough, even that something might be learned from her. Branch-specific idioms exist, but the foundations of a common legal language – such fundamental concepts as the vocabulary of law and the basic patterns of legal argumentation as its grammar – are shared across disciplinary boundaries.

10. The need to rethink legal thinking

In my discussion of legal pluralism caused by the emergence of transnational law, I have defended a discursive view that rejects both old and new variants of black box thinking. The latter include Kelsenian hierarchical normativism, Koskenniemi's portrayal of self-contained and mutually hostile legal regimes and the Luhmann-inspired account of global social systems creating their own transnational, autopoietically closed, legal (sub)systems. My view has both descriptive and normative pretensions. In a descriptive regard, it points to existing phenomena of interlegality – overlap, interpenetration and dialogue – that refute all versions of black box theorising and show these to be, at best, one-sided generalisations. In a normative respect, it advocates discursive treatment of conflicts of authority, a search for compatible solutions to those conflicts, mutual learning processes and inclusion of the perspective of relevant 'foreign' legal orders in coherence-seeking reconstructions of law. It embraces a horizontal rather than a vertical notion of coherence-creating relations and rejects hierarchical meta-principles, which remain stuck to state-sovereigntist *Stufenbau* models, no matter whether they appear in the guise of a putative global norm hierarchy topped by global constitutional law, a global, hierarchically structured, judiciary, or a World Government.

Such a discursive position is not an oddity in contemporary debates. It comes close to, say, Berman's understanding of legal pluralism, as well as to what Walker has termed moderate and contributory applications of putative, global, master principles of legal authority. In the context of EU law, it evidently neighbours both Miguel Poiares Maduro's contrapunctual law,[72] and Mattias Kumm's version of Constitutionalism Beyond the State.[73]

Despite being open to criticism, black box thinking, in particular its Kelsenian variant, draws our attention to an important attribute of law: the perspectivism inherent in law, manifest in and functioning through the *Vorverständnis* of legal actors. However, this perspectivism should be detached from its linkage to a hierarchical conception of legal validity, which leads to treating legal orders as mutually closed entities, and given a broader legal-cultural twist. This enables us to discern dialogue-facilitating overlaps and affinities in the perspectivist *Vorverständnis* of legal actors.

---

[72] M. Poiares Maduro, 'Contrapunctual law: Europe's constitutional pluralism in action' in N. Walker (ed.), *Sovereignty in Transition* (Oxford: Hart Publishing, 2003), pp 501–38.

[73] M. Kumm, 'The jurisprudence of constitutional conflict: constitutional supremacy in Europe before and after the Constitutional Treaty', 11 *European Law Journal* 3 (2005), 262–307. See also the contributions in M. Avbelj and J. Komárek (eds), *Constitutional Pluralism in the European Union and Beyond* (Oxford: Hart Publishing, 2011).

Perspectivism and discursiveness are particularly conspicuous in the setting of transnational law and the concomitant legal pluralism. But they are pertinent features even in the context of one and the same legal order or legal system. Perspectivism arises not only from the varying referential legal order but also from varying legal roles and disciplines: a judge views the law through different legal-cultural lenses to a legislator or a legal counsellor, and private- and public-law perspectives give rise to differing accounts of, say, post-welfare state law. Even when bracketing cross-boundary influences or the impact of non-state law, perspectivism and discursiveness should be granted a much more prominent role in the examination of nation-state law than is usual in Kelsenian or Hartian positivism. So, transnational law may sharpen our view of the significance of perspectivism and discursiveness in all law.

This is not the only generalisable lesson to be drawn from the study of transnational law. Transnational law enhances our sensitivity to the spatial and temporal qualities of law; multifaceted qualities, which mainstream legal theory of the twentieth century, with its universalist pretensions, tended to ignore or understood in narrow, positivist terms. In his inaugural lecture at Edinburgh, Neil Walker suggested complementing authority and meaning as the central issues of modern legal theory with a third grand topic, namely the situatedness of law.[74] But as our preceding discussion of transnational law has at least hinted, temporal and spatial relations should be conceived in broader terms. At issue is not only law's temporal and spatial location, but also conceptions of time and space, implicit in law, as well as durations and rhythms, boundaries and cross-boundary connections, typical of law at its various levels and in its two dimensions as a legal order and as legal practice.[75]

The difficulties legal theory faces in coming to terms with transnational law demonstrate how intimately linked to nation-state law are many of the supposedly universal concepts of our legal language. The field is open for new conceptual innovations, which perhaps, in due course of time, will establish themselves in the vocabulary in which global, cross-boundary, legal discourse is conducted. Probably 'transnational law', 'legal pluralism', 'interlegality', 'legal perspectivism' and, perhaps, 'legal hybrid' will belong to the lexis of the new legal Esperanto.

[74] N. Walker, 'Out of place and out of time: law's fading co-ordinates', *Edinburgh Law Review* 14 (2010), 13–46.

[75] Law's temporal and spatial qualities in this wider sense are two of the central topics in my *Ratio and Voluntas*, note 3 above.

However, these are meta-level, 'second-order' concepts that do not yet carry out the conceptualisation and systematisation needed to bring order and coherence to our legal universe. The traditional, comprehensive, systematisation of the national legal order and the complementary black box model have proved incapable of achieving this objective. There are no legal hybrids as such, but only those seen from the perspective of a particular conceptual and systematising framework. What we today call legal hybridity is a sign of our conceptual confusion: new conceptual and systematising grids are needed, but our legal mindset is still in many respects attached to the state-sovereigntism of the black box model and the distinctions of traditional systematisation.

Nonetheless, the conceptual and systematising frameworks erected in the nation state context are often enough the only available starting point for examining what we – temporarily – call legal hybrids. Thus, to revert to the example of constitutional analysis of the EU, we cannot simply abandon concepts attached to modern nation states; rather, the task is to assign them a meaning suited to an examination of the transnational polity of the EU and its transnational legal order. They must be detached from their 'nation-state logic', so that they can capture the interaction between the transnational and the national, so typical of the EU and its law (and a major source of present hybridity).

However, not only are new conceptual and systematic frameworks needed, but the very point of legal conceptualisation and systematisation must be redefined. For both scholarly and practical reasons, coherence of normative legal material is still a pertinent objective. But total coherence presupposing a gapless conceptual compartmentalisation of all legal phenomena is a chimera and as such can no longer constitute a viable regulative ideal for legal scholarship. Instead of comprehensive, total coherence, we have to be content with *local coherence*, which has been the central promise of recent proposals for new fields of law, such as bio or medical law, information or communication law, or – why not? – European regulatory private law.[76]

For their part, these new proposals, which dispense with traditional systematisation, help us to perceive the inevitable perspectivism in law. Along with the objective of total coherence, we have to abandon the idea of the one and only 'correct' way of conceptualising and systematising law. New branches of law or legal transnationalisation do not necessarily

---

[76] Here I refer to Hans-W. Micklitz's ongoing research project; see Micklitz in Chapter 10 of this volume.

render traditional systematisation completely obsolete. This may still be instrumental for specific purposes, but it has certainly lost its exclusive validity, as has the domestic legal order within the nation state. Alternative, mutually non-exclusive ways exist to conceptualise and systematise legal phenomena and to define and tackle legal problems. This too might be called legal pluralism; a fourth variant of legal pluralism, as it were, to be added to the three variants discussed above. It is legal pluralism that does not reject but acknowledges the objective of coherence.

Finally, the enterprise of rethinking legal thinking should address the very role of legal concepts in legal scholarship and practice. Now as before, concepts constitute an integral and indispensable element of our legal *Vorverständnis*. But we should accentuate their *heuristic* function. Concepts are necessary for identifying, defining and organising legal issues. But their mutual relations should be seen in terms of clusters and networks rather than as amounting to conceptual pyramids or trees. Emphasis on the heuristic function makes it clear that concepts as such cannot be expected to provide a basis for normative conclusions or derivation of new legal rules. But perhaps such legal constructivism, along with the ideal of a conceptual pyramid, only exists in the travesty of *Begriffs-jurisprudenz*, a travesty concocted by the 'late' Jhering and his intellectual heirs, as well as in the complementary caricatures of conceptualism drawn by the American and Scandinavian realist soulmates of German *Interessenjurisprudenz*.[77]

---

[77] See the discussion of anti-conceptualist criticism in its three versions of German *Interessenjurisprudenz* and American and Scandinavian realism in my *Ratio and Voluntas*, note 3 above, p. 105ff.

PART I

Law Beyond the State(s)

2

Transnational legal thought

Plato, Europe and beyond

H. PATRICK GLENN

1. Introduction

In preliminary discussions of this volume, participants were invited to 'rethink legal thinking' from a transnational perspective. This is an ambitious and impressive idea, since it implies not simply rethinking law, which has often been attempted, but rethinking legal thought itself, much less frequently attempted. What does it mean to rethink legal thought? It appears to imply more than simply thinking again and possibly reaching different conclusions, but a still larger process of questioning the thought processes that have yielded present concepts of law. Are there really inescapable 'laws of thought',[1] or can these too be rethought? Do the national and the international logically exclude the transnational? I will argue both that it is possible to rethink thought, in law as in all else, though it is extremely difficult to do so successfully with broad effect in society. There may not be inescapable 'laws of thought', but there are very deeply entrenched social attitudes and beliefs about thought, in all societies. They have had a profound effect on our thinking of the national and the international, an obviously binary conception, and they continue to profoundly affect our ability to think of the transnational.

2. Plato

Plato is known for many things in the western world, but he is perhaps least well known for his most successful idea. That is the idea that human knowledge is best advanced by dividing all the world and its knowledge into two parts, and each of those two parts into two further parts, and so

---

[1] The expression appears to have been created by George Boole (of Boolean algebra) in his 1854 *An Investigation of the Laws of Thought*.

on endlessly.[2] In Greek this was known as the principle of *diairesis,* which became in Latin *divisio,* and it has given to the modern world the process of dichotomous or binary thinking. Profoundly influential thinkers followed the Platonic principle of *divisio.* Aristotle, not a Platonist, nevertheless divided animals into blooded and bloodless, then the blooded into quadrupeds and non-quadrupeds, then the quadrupeds into mammals and reptiles.[3] The Roman lawyers divided law into the *ius civile* and the *ius gentium;* Christians divided the world into the secular and the spiritual, the flesh and the spirit; Descartes distinguished mind from matter, a *divisio* given new vigor by contemporary neuroscience. Closer to home, many modern lawyers hold ferociously to a distinction between law and ethics, or law and custom, or law and religion, and the state was recently described in Germany as a 'dichotomischer Fixbegriff'.[4] Law is still taught today according to the *summa divisio* (known as such) of public or private law, and each of these in turn yields further binary distinctions of the patrimonial or non-patrimonial, the contractual or non-contractual, the constitutional or the administrative.

Transnational law is profoundly hampered by the dichotomy, even though recent, between the national and the international and in his introductory paper in this volume Kaarlo Tuori speaks of the transnational as 'beyond' the dichotomy, still controlling in some measure.[5] In all of this, western lawyers would be adhering in some cases strictly to the pattern of 'hierarchical dualisms' that have been operative since Plato and that might well require centuries to overcome,[6] if that is

---

[2] Plato, *The Statesman,* 258e, 261b: 'it's not at all difficult to separate into two all of those things that come into being', 'divide all cases of knowledge in this way, calling the one sort practical knowledge, the other purely theoretical'; *The Sophist,* 219a: 'expertise falls pretty much into two types'. For reception and continuation in medieval law, A. Errera, 'The role of logic in the legal science of the Glossators and Commentators. Distinction, dialectical syllogism, and apodictic syllogism: an investigation into the epistemological roots of legal science in the late Middle Ages' in E. Pattaro (ed.), *A Treatise of Legal Philosophy and General Jurisprudence* (Dordrecht: Springer, 2007), Vol. VII, p. 79, at 81–4 ('The Dichotomous Technique').

[3] L. Schiebinger, *Nature's Body* (Piscataway, NJ: Rutgers University Press, 2004), p. 43.

[4] C. Möllers, *Staat als Argument* (Munich: C. H. Beck, 2000), p. 424. The state could not exist in degrees, therefore, in spite of the reality of failing states in the world. On the tendency of legal philosophers to 'cling dogmatically to classificatory ideas', rejecting analysis of legal systems as matters of degree, K. Füsser, 'Farewell to "legal positivism": the separation thesis unravelling' in R. P. George (ed.), *The Autonomy of Law: Essays on Legal Positivism* (Oxford: Clarendon Press, 1996), pp 124–55, with references (Dworkin opposing Fuller's non-classificatory proposals).

[5] See Tuori in Chapter 1 of this volume.

[6] D. Haraway, *Simians, Cyborgs, and Women: The Reinvention of Nature* (New York: Routledge, 1991), p. 163.

possible at all. How is the transnational hampered by binary thought and logic and how might such a profoundly anchored manner of thought be overcome?

The grip of binary thinking in law is itself based on an underlying 'law of identity' expressed usually in the form of 'A is A'. This is far from a tautological statement, in spite of its appearance, since it implicitly accepts a notion of radical separation of A from all of that which is not-A. It accepts a notion of conceptual and physical autonomy, however questionable this might be in the world of contemporary science (notably in quantum physics) and thought. From the law of identity are logically drawn the two further 'laws of thought' that are the law of non-contradiction and the law of the excluded middle. Given A, which is radically distinct from not-A, the two cannot be affirmed at the same time, or overlap, so we cannot have A *and* not-A, since this would be contradictory, affirming at the same time a proposition and its negation. What we therefore must have, which is where the current legal problems arise, is A *or* not-A, which is the law of the excluded middle. This is depressing news for lawyers in search of a middle ground, or law between the national and the international. Why *must* we have a logical rule of A *or* not-A, which excludes any middle ground between them? Why must a univalent choice be imposed upon us, given an initial binary distinction? It flows from the principle of radical separation or identity. Since A exists, independently of that which is not-A, the boundary of not-A begins precisely where the boundary of A stops and there can be no middle ground between them. Not-A is galactic in character and devours any possible middle ground. There is no space for the transnational between the national and the international, and the boundaries between them have been taken to be as crisp as those between A and not-A.

The rooted character of binary logic in contemporary legal thought has not been derived simply and directly, however, from Plato's notion of *divisio*. The fundamental character of *divisio* has been accepted, but its role has been reinforced over the last five centuries by much of the renaissance thought that has produced the contemporary state and defined the relations between national legal orders. Since the time of Bodin in the sixteenth century, there has been much discussion of the necessary consequences of sovereignty, sovereignty considered necessary both to overcome the violence of European social relations and to free national lawmakers from the grip of both church and custom. Sovereignty was said to be by nature absolute, as a necessary condition of its objectives, and absolute sovereignty required the construction of borders or national boundaries, since it was impossible to be sovereign *everywhere.*[7] The borders once established on the ground (a process that has taken centuries and that is not complete in much of the world), the dichotomy between the domestic and the foreign, the national and the international, became irresistible. By the time of Huber in the late seventeenth century, it had become possible to announce a principle of the *territoriality* of laws, a radical novelty at the time and one that constituted 'a complete change in theory', but which has since become accepted doctrine.[8] An era of transnational laws, whether civil, canon, commercial or even public, would have come to an end.

Given the thinking that produced autonomous, national legal orders from the seventeenth through the nineteenth centuries, it then became necessary to define their relations. The same thinking is evident in this process as had been operative in the defining of sovereign states. Hegel is perhaps the most significant figure, seeing the modern state as the ultimate realization of human society. Hegel drew the necessary conclusion from the principle of national sovereignty, that each state is a being 'exclusively' for itself (the law of identity)[9] and that each state therefore reaches its ultimate realization in external relations (the law of the excluded middle, A *or* not-A) and even war.[10] This remarkably belligerent manner of thinking human relations inevitably had its reflection in law. The dichotomy national/international was reinforced, public international law became inevitably rooted in the consent of states and Huber's neologism the 'conflict of laws' became accepted terminology, adding a completely conceptual and even fictional conflict of norms to that which might exist between parties in transnational private legal relations.[11] This general,

[7] See H. Krüger, *Allgemeine Staatslehre* (Stuttgart: Kohlammer, 1966), p. 22, on national borders both creating the possibility of sovereignty and defining at the same time its limits.
[8] For Huber in English translation, E. Lorenzen, 'Huber's *De Conflictu Legum*' in Lorenzen, *Selected Essays on the Conflict of Laws* (New Haven, CT: Yale University Press, 1947), p. 136; and for the complete change of theory, S. Thorne, 'Sovereignty and the conflict of laws' in Thorne, *Essays in English Legal History* (London: Hambledon Press, 1985), p. 181.
[9] G. Hegel, *Philosophy of Right* (New York: Cosmos, 2008), para. 322.
[10] *Ibid.*, notably paras 330 and 334 on international law's dependence on distinct and sovereign will of state – state as 'embodiment of freedom' – and on resolving conflicts by war in absence of agreement, respectively; C. Taylor, *Hegel* (Cambridge: Cambridge University Press, 1975), p. 448, for the view that 'as a reflection of an essential moment of the state, according to Hegel's ontological principles, war has necessarily to occur'; and J. Bartelson, *A Genealogy of Sovereignty* (Cambridge: Cambridge University Press, 1995), pp 215–16, on 'dialectic of conflict' and states in relation of 'mutual exclusion'.
[11] For the non-existence of 'conflicts of laws', as in private international law existing to prevent the existence of conflicts of laws rather than to resolve them, see H. P. Glenn, *La conciliation*

binary manner of thought unquestionably contributed to the belligerent nature of international relations and ensuing violence,[12] not only between states but amongst the empires that largely dominated the territory of the world from the seventeenth through twentieth centuries. The empires having disappeared, however, the problem is happily the lesser one of the relations of states, and contemporary developments themselves represent a challenge to binary and belligerent legal thought.

Since the end of empires in the mid-twentieth century, the number of states in the world has approximately tripled, and is now approaching two hundred. There has been a large movement towards state construction and the autonomy of peoples. With two hundred states in the world, however, the accent can no longer be on their creation and construction but on their collaboration. The growth of regional and international structures is the most evident proof of this, with the number of international institutions growing from 123 in 1951 to 395 in 1984 and many more today (there are problems of counting).[13] The contemporary state, therefore, is necessarily one of collaboration and its role in international relations is even in decline, with the multiplication of other fora of activity.[14] The state therefore integrates itself into more and more intense networks, and the language of networks or *réseaux* is beginning to replace that of systems and sovereignty.[15] Sovereign isolation has thus become incompatible with the well-being of national populations.[16] It has, moreover,

---

des lois, General Course in Private International Law, Hague Academy of International Law (forthcoming in *Receuil des cours*, 2013).

[12] M. van Creveld, *The Rise and Decline of the State* (Cambridge: Cambridge University Press, 1999), p. 197: 'the one way for states to play out their historical destiny was to pit themselves against other states by means of war . . . – . . . each state had to be made as strong as possible. – All this helped fuel the kind of interstate rivalry that was . . . – . . . a prominent feature of the period from 1848 to 1945.'

[13] *Ibid.*, p. 382; and for a historical perspective on the slow growth of interstate institutions and relations even during the period of state construction, E. Rosenberg (ed.), *A World Connecting, 1870–1940* (Cambridge, MA: Harvard University Press and C. H. Beck Verlag, 2012).

[14] J. Guillaumé, *L'affaiblissement de l'État-Nation et le droit international privé*, (Paris: LGDJ, 2011), p. 228.

[15] F. Ost and M. van de Kerchove, *De la pyramide au réseau?* (Brussels: Publications des Facultés universitaires Saint-Louis, 2000); H. Buxbaum, 'Transnational regulatory litigation', 46 *Virginia Journal of International Law* (2006), 252–317 at 306, on 'deterritorialization' of sovereign authority, disaggregation of its elements into networks, and emphasis on *participation* in transnational regimes.

[16] For the state as necessarily a 'trading state', given the impossibility of autonomously satisfying the needs of a population, R. Rosecrance, *The Rise of the Trading State: Commerce and Conquest in the Modern World* (New York: Basic Books, 1986), pp 15 and 140, on

become impossible, as national borders become increasingly porous in the face of the flow of goods, people and information made possible by modern technology.[17] There is contemporary language of '*Entgrenzung*' or debordering,[18] 'despatialization',[19] 'deterritorialising'[20] and 'a-territoriality'.[21] Even war would have become 'post-territorial',[22] while land would have become an 'old factor',[23] no longer of great interest to states overburdened with existing populations. Borders have to be 'smart', providing security but not complicated to cross.

These developments are challenging not only on the ground but to the formal or classical logic that has been so influential in modern legal thinking. The role of formal logic in law is admittedly debatable. Some have been of the view that the life of the law has not been logic but experience,[24] and there is much to be said for the view that lawyers have not systematically followed Aristotelian forms of syllogism. This is only one logical form, however, and it remains the case that much of what has been known as 'experience' has been largely conditioned by binary forms of thought, in law and beyond.[25] It therefore appears significant that the historical 'laws of thought' are being challenged within logic itself. The so-called laws of the excluded middle and non-contradiction are challenged notably by various forms of 'paraconsistent',

interdependence growing with decline in geographic size of state, given their multiplication.

[17] For the impossibility of national control of information, P. Bobbitt, *The Shield of Achilles: War, Peace and the Course of History* (New York: Knopf, 2002), p. 221, on circulation in near-instantaneous manner of financial and other information; van Creveld, note 12 above, pp 392–3, on electronic media as another step in retreat of the state.

[18] U. Beck and C. Lau, *Entgrenzung und Entscheidung: Was ist neu an der Theorie reflexiver Modernisierung?* (Frankfurt: Suhrkamp, 2004).

[19] J-B. Auby, *La globalisation, le droit et l'État* (Paris: Montchrestien, 2003).

[20] R. Michaels, 'Welche Globalisierung fur das Recht? Welches Recht für die Globalisierung?', 69 *The Rabel Journal of Comparative and International Private Law* (2005), 525–44 at 541.

[21] G. Agamben, *Means without End: Notes on Politics*, trans. Binetti and Casarino (Minneapolis, MN: University of Minneapolis Press, 2000), p. 23.

[22] W. Opello and S. Rosow, *The Nation-State and Global Order: A Historical Introduction to Contemporary Politics* (Boulder, CO: Lynne Rienner, 2004), p. 252.

[23] R. Cooper, *The Breaking of Nations: Order and Chaos in the 21st Century* (Toronto: McClelland & Steward, 2005), pp 17 and 33: 'governing people, especially potentially hostile people, is a burden' and 'acquiring territory is no longer of interest'.

[24] The phrase is that of Oliver Wendell Holmes, Jr in *The Common Law* (Boston: Little, Brown & Co., 1881), p. 1; see also S. Haack, 'On logic in the law: something, but not all', 20 *Ratio Juris* 1 (2007), 1–31.

[25] For further binaries – self/other, mind/body, culture/nature, male/female, civilized/primitive (long operative to exclude many peoples from the domain of public international law), reality/appearance, whole/part, agent/resource, maker/made, active/passive, right/wrong, truth/illusion, total/partial and God/man – see Haraway, note 6 above, p. 177.

'inconsistency tolerant' or 'dialethetic' logic. There would notably be a 'many valued turn' in contemporary logic that would replace bivalence with multivalence.[26] These newer forms of logic have perhaps most in common a rejection of the original dichotomy. They value the old Jewish joke that if you are in prison, and the prison keeper asks you to open one of two doors, always choose the third way. *Anything* is better than an initial dichotomy, and the Platonic *divisio* is a crude instrument that should not exclude a wider range of logical and empirical choice. Non-binary thought is also present in the physical sciences now, and a Nobel laureate has explicitly rejected the law of non-contradiction in the world of quantum physics, concluding that 'we can eat our quarks and have them too'.[27]

It should also be stated that binary logic has not been entirely controlling in contemporary law. Authors have written on the existence of 'antinomies' in national legal systems,[28] and Kelsen's insistence on the law of non-contradiction as an essential element of a national legal system would be here departed from.[29] The common law tradition is perhaps less attached to this form of logic and more attached to its own particular history, so it knows categories such as 'chattels real' (both moveable and immoveable), to say nothing of the trust and its two simultaneous forms of ownership (the choice is not the binary one of owner or non-owner, but the trivalent one of legal owner, equitable owner and non-owner). There

---

[26] D. Gabbay and J. Woods (eds), *The Many Valued and Nonmonotonic Turn in Logic* (Amsterdam: North- Holland, 2007); and see J. C. Beall and G. Restall, *Logical Pluralism* (Oxford: Oxford University Press, 2006); G. Malinowski, *Many-Valued Logics* (Oxford: Clarendon Press, 1993); G. Priest, *In Contradiction: A Study of the Transconsistent* (Oxford: Oxford University Press, 2006).

[27] F. Wilczek, *The Lightness of Being: Mass, Ether and the Unification of Forces* (New York: Basic Books, 2010), p. 43.

[28] D. Turpin, 'Le traitement des antinomies des droits de l'homme par le Conseil Constitutionnel', 2 Droits (1985), 85–97; L. Gannagé, *La Hiérarchie des Normes et les Méthodes du Droit International Privé: Étude de Droit International Privé de la Famille* (Paris: Montchrestien, 2001), pp 2 and 81; and earlier C. Perelman (ed.), *Les Antinomies en Droit* (Brussels: Établissements Émile Bruylant, 1965).

[29] H. Kelsen, *Pure Theory of Law*, trans. Knight (Gloucester, MA: Peter Smith, 1989), p. 206: 'the Principle of the Exclusion of Contradictions . . . – To say that *a* ought to be and at the same time ought not to be is just as meaningless as to say that *a* is and at the same time that it is not'. In the case of contradictory norms, 'only one of the two can be regarded as objectively valid'. In his later writing, however, Kelsen acknowledged the possibility of conflicting norms both being valid, a contradiction that could not be solved by logic and that required the intervention of an act of will of legal authority or 'customary non-observance'. H. Kelsen, *Essays in Legal and Moral Philosophy*, selected by Weinberger, trans. Heath (Dordrecht: D. Reidel Publishing, 1973), p. 235: 'that two mutually conflicting norms should both be valid, is possible'.

has therefore been a non-binary tradition in legal thought, in some measure at least, though binary logic has exercised a major and controlling influence. The question therefore arises of the relations between binary (or univalent) and multivalent forms of logic.

It is happily the case that multivalent forms of logic do not require a bivalent choice between themselves and bivalence. This can be put either in terms of multivalence including bivalence (the polar opposites are preserved but do not exclude the middle ground between them) or in terms of logical pluralism.[30] Choice of logic is possible. This opens up interesting possibilities in the middle ground between logic and 'experience' or between the logical and the 'realist' or between the national and the international. Multivalent logic can be used where it is appropriate to do so, without entailing abandonment of historically useful binary distinctions in domestic law. Europe appears to offer great potential for this. There would still be room for the right side of the brain, with its 'balanced creativity'.[31]

3. Europe

Europe may be proceeding towards a type of federalism but the nature of this federalism is not yet clear. So we are faced with multiple sets of laws, as has always been the case, to which is now added the law of the European Union and the law of the European Convention on Human Rights. This changes the legal perspective. Instead of viewing law from within a unified nation state, with diversity either relegated to its borders or confined to an exception within the existing unity, we are now faced with alternative unities, a genuinely diverse field of legal thought. These diverse unities have their own legitimacy – that of the nation states, that of European instruments – and the multiple unities must therefore be recognized, with their multiple values.[32] A world of multiple values appears to require a multivalent logic tolerant of what might initially appear as contradiction, and necessarily including a middle ground. This is now being described as

---

[30] See Beall and Restall, note 26 above, p. 31, arguing that logical pluralism 'does more justice to the mix of insight and perplexity found in many of the debates in logic in the last century'.

[31] I. McGilchrist, *The Master and His Emissary: The Divided Brain and the Making of the Western World* (New Haven, CT: Yale University Press, 2010).

[32] On conciliation of multiple legal unities, and their recognition, H. P. Glenn, 'Accommodating unity' in S. Muller and S. Richards (eds), *Highest Courts and Globalisation* (The Hague: Hague Academic Press, 2010), pp 85–98.

a 'both/and' logic, which encompasses any initial binary contrast, accepts both poles of the contrast, and opens a large included middle as a field of choice. Detail is what counts; not large binary contradictions. Multivalent logic, or fuzzy logic, as it is sometimes called, is not fuzzy nor imprecise but highly detailed. Only the false precision of binary logic is rejected.

There are examples of multivalent logic in existing European legal practice, in both public and private law. The margin of appreciation of the European Courts is perhaps the best example, by virtue of which a univocal interpretation of a European instrument is rejected in order to allow multiple and varied state interpretations of it. Neither national sovereignty nor a single European standard necessarily prevails. A continuum of alternatives is opened up, which may be seen as more or less compatible with European objectives.[33] In its *Solange* decisions the German Constitutional Court appears to have found an included middle between EU norms and the German constitution.[34] In European private law, the example I have used is that of the Rome Convention (now Regulation) on contractual obligations in private international law, which does not impose a binary choice between party autonomy and the most geographically proximate state law, but allows party choice subject to 'overriding mandatory' state law, with the category of 'overriding mandatory' representing a fuzzy standard (how imperative, for what types of case, with what geographic connection, etc.).[35] Other examples can no doubt be given.

Yet there is ongoing great attachment to binary concepts in the European legal world. Some of this binary construction is without prejudice

---

[33] For the vast jurisprudence of the ECtHR, see Y. Arai-Takahashi, *The Margin of Appreciation Doctrine and the Principle of Proportionality in the Jurisprudence of the ECHR* (Antwerp: Intersentia, 2002); and more particularly on 'ethical de-centralisation or subsidiarity' see J. Sweeney, 'Margins of appreciation: cultural relativity and the European Court of Human Rights in the post-Cold War era', 54 *International and Comparative Law Quarterly* 2 (2005), 459–74, notably at 467. The same concept has been used at least on one occasion by the ECJ in Case C–244/06 *Dynamic Medien Vertriebs* v. *Avides Media* [2008] ECR I–505, para. 44, and its extension to the CJEU is urged in J. Gerards, 'Pluralism, deference and the margin of appreciation doctrine', 17 *European Law Journal* 1 (2011), 80–120. For the ECJ/CJEU's proceeding according to a 'contrapunctual' notion of law, M. Maduro, 'Contrapunctual law: Europe's constitutional pluralism in action' in N. Walker (ed.), *Sovereignty in Transition* (Oxford: Hart Publishing, 2003), p. 502.

[34] See N. Barber, 'Legal pluralism and the European Union', 12 *European Law Journal* 3 (2006), 306–29 for the absence of a law of non-contradiction in the *Solange* jurisprudence and the EU generally.

[35] H. P. Glenn 'Multivalent logic and the Rome Convention' in K. Boele-Woelki and F. W. Grosheide (eds), *The Future of European Contract Law: Essays in Honour of Ewoud Hondius* (Alphen aan den Rijn: Kluwer Law International, 2007), pp 283–90.

to the conciliation of European laws and this appears to be the case for much internal private or public law, unchallenged at the international or European level. As noted above, multivalent logic in any event is not in contradiction with bivalent logic, but inclusive of it. Some continental laws, however, are unremittingly binary in their conception. Arguably the best, or worst, example is the rule of a number of jurisdictions that would require *application d'office* by a judge of rules of private international law in any transborder case. This amounts to a presumption of conflict of national laws, requiring choice between them even absent a plea or proof of a difference in national laws that would actually affect the outcome of the case. National laws are binary opposites, in constant contradiction, and the laws of non-contradiction and the excluded middle must be adhered to. The perspective would be one of radical pluralism, perlocutionary in the language of Kaarlo Tuori as opposed to illocutionary.[36] The common market of North America avoids this presumption of conflict through the happy coincidence of reception of the historically derived, common law rule that parties must plead foreign law before conflict is presumed. North America has received a presumption of harmony, useful in a common market.[37]

Mention of North America reminds us, however, that there is a world beyond Europe.

4. Beyond

I think it is the case that lawyers in the rest of the world are very ambivalent about the emergence of pan-European law. How will such European law fit in a possible world of transnational law? Will it constitute a type of Fortress Europe, impervious to outside influence and incapable of use and reception abroad? A historical note is perhaps useful. Law in Europe is thought to have been nationalized in the nineteenth century, with codification and a national concept of *stare decisis* limiting the sources of law to purely national and formal ones. This may have happened to some extent in Europe itself, largely overcoming a freer circulation of legal authority that was known under the rubric of common law. There were many such common laws in Europe.[38] With European nationalization of law

---

[36] See Tuori in Chapter 1 of this volume.
[37] See H. P. Glenn, 'Conciliation of laws in the NAFTA countries', 60 *Louisiana Law Review* 4 (2000), 1103–12.
[38] H. P. Glenn, *On Common Laws* (Oxford: Oxford University Press, 2005).

the operation of European common laws did not cease, however, since it was beyond the authority of any European state to nationalize law that was territorially beyond itself. So European common laws, or *droits communs*, or *iura communia*, continued to be used abroad, in at least English, French, Spanish, Dutch and German languages, and this throughout the world. The nationalized laws of Europe simply became elements in the ongoing common laws of the world. In my jurisdiction of Quebec, there has historically been great use of French law and the codification of law in France simply provided a more convenient form of reference to French law as an ongoing element of '*le droit commun français*'. Such common laws remain today, in a contemporary and ongoing manner, the largest and most widespread form of transnational law, though often invisible from within Europe. They are laws of influence, not binding authority. Logically they must be thought of not as binding or not, but as more or less persuasive, depending on local circumstance and potential relevance. The logic is non-binary and multivalent. Foreign persuasive law continues to be considered legitimate, as is local domestic law. An included middle is opened between them, an interpretative space, and the spread of European laws in the world has been largely the result of endless decisions made in this interpretative space on questions of 'suitability', just as the spread of the common laws within Europe was the result of a vast interpretative process of reconciling the common laws with the respective *iura propria* or particular laws.[39]

EU law does not have much resonance beyond the seas and is therefore a perturbing element in the operation of the world's common laws. It may well acquire such resonance, however, and we are perhaps seeing this most clearly with respect to the judgments of the European Court of Human Rights, as opposed to the judgments of the European Court of Justice.[40] European law can therefore acknowledge transnational sources of law and be acknowledged by transnational sources of law. In this process a multivalent type of logic seems as necessary as it is within Europe itself,

---

[39] For the extent of the process within Europe, S. Vogenauer, *Die Auslegung von Gesetzen in England und auf dem Kontinent: Eine Vergleichende Untersuchung der Rechtsprechung und ihrer Historischen Grundlagen* (Tübingen: Mohr Siebeck, 2001); and for the literature on only the reception of the English common law, and outside of the USA, the immense bibliography of J. Dupont, *The Common Law Abroad: Constitutional and Legal Legacy of the British Empire* (Littleton, CO: Fred B. Rothman Publications, 2001).

[40] For world-wide influence or 'rayonnement' of the case law of the ECtHR, G. Cohen-Jonathan and J. Flauss (eds), *Le Rayonnement International de la Jurisprudence de la Cour Européenne des Droits de l'Homme* (Brussels: Établissements Émile Bruylant, 2005).

since beyond Europe the values multiply beyond those of Europe, and in a transnational world it is difficult in the extreme to categorically exclude the possibility of a middle ground.[41]

How can the development of transnational law in the world be facilitated by multivalent forms of logic? Multivalent logic opens up a space for transnational law, an included middle. Both private international law and public international law have been constructed in ways that faithfully track the classic 'laws of thought'. There is a law of identity that means that France is France, an autonomous and sovereign entity, with its own block of laws. There is a law of non-contradiction, so French law would be, as a national and coherent legal system, free of internal contradictions, and it would not be possible, in a transnational contract case, to choose both the law of France and the law of Germany.[42] There is a law of the excluded middle, so in a transnational private law case the choice is only between the law of France and the law of another state connected to the case, and the choice is largely, in Europe at least, directed by geographic circumstances. Recently, however, the European Union rejected a proposal, which came close to being adopted, that parties to a contract should be able to choose a non-state law, such as the UNIDROIT Principles of International Commercial Contracts or the Lando Principles of European Contract Law.[43] The law of the excluded middle prevailed, for the moment. It does not prevail in the vast majority of international contract disputes that are subject to arbitration, since arbitrators prefer to work in an included middle of transnational commercial law. The Hague Conference Working Group on international contracts is now contemplating the possibility of party choice of non-state law. It is a logical option, given multivalent forms of

---

[41] For the diverse processes of 'denationalization' of law, state complicity in the overall process, and legal practice in large measure driving theoretical legal development, H. P. Glenn, 'A transnational concept of law' in P. Cane and M. V. Tushnet (eds), *The Oxford Handbook of Legal Studies* (Oxford: Oxford University Press, 2003), pp 839–62.

[42] Compare, however, the choice-of-law clause used for arbitrations in the construction of the Channel Tunnel between France and England, which provided that '[t]he construction, validity and performance of the contract shall in all respects be governed by and interpreted in accordance with the principles common to both English law and French law'; C. Schütz, 'The effects of general principles of law' in D. Campbell (ed.), *International Dispute Resolution* (Alphen aan den Rijn: Kluwer Law International, 2010), p. 45.

[43] The proposal was made in the context of converting the Rome Convention on the Law Applicable to Contractual Obligations to a European Directive; see R. Plender and M. Wilderspin, *The European Private International Law of Obligations* (London: Sweet and Maxwell, 2009), p. 137.

logic suitable to the complexity of the present world. Private international law is more generally witnessing a turn to considerations of material justice that would control the geographic choice-of-law process, instead of being driven by it.[44]

In public international law there is an equally important binary distinction, not between different states, but between national and international law. At the international or non-internal level, international law prevails, as a block of law. It consecrates the principle of what Amartya Sen has described as 'transcendental institutionalism', which precludes consideration of material justice.[45] A space or included middle is now opening up in public international law, however, with the so-called 'humanization' of public international law in matters of human rights,[46] as well as the recognition of aboriginal peoples and law, as seen recently with the adoption of the UN Declaration on the Rights of Indigenous Peoples.[47] The engagement of public international law with material justice, in a space between the national and the international, becomes possible once one recognizes the normative character of public international law itself and the possibility of renouncing its exclusive and formal application.[48] This is becoming increasingly evident with the growth of 'informal' international agreements. These now proliferate like mushrooms on the ground, as they say in Germany, but they represent a qualitative as well as a quantitative change in public international law and national law.[49] National law must

[44] S. Symeonides, 'Result-selectivism in private international law', *Romanian Journal of Private International Law & Comparative Private Law* (2008), 1–30; and for a process of conciliation of laws, as opposed to their conflict, Glenn, note 11 above.

[45] A. Sen, *The Idea of Justice* (Cambridge, MA: Harvard University Press, 2009), pp 5–6 (on the search for 'perfect justice' as opposed to relative comparisons of justice and injustice, combined with 'getting the institutions right' as opposed to focusing on the 'actual societies' that would emerge).

[46] T. Meron, *The Humanization of International Law* (Leiden: Martinus Nijhoff, 2006); and see R. McCorquodale, 'An inclusive international legal system', 17 *Leiden Journal of International Law* 3 (2004), 477–504.

[47] S. Allen and A. Xanthaki (eds), *Reflections on the UN Declaration on the Rights of Indigenous Peoples* (Oxford: Hart Publishing, 2011), notably H. P. Glenn, 'The three ironies of the UN Declaration on the Rights of Indigenous Peoples', pp 171–82.

[48] H. P. Glenn, 'The ethic of international law' in D. E. Childress III (ed.), *The Role of Ethics in International Law* (Cambridge: Cambridge University Press, 2011), pp 246–70.

[49] See J. Pauwelyn, R. Wessel and J. Wouters (eds) *Informal International Lawmaking* (Oxford: Oxford University Press, 2012), notably Ch. 6 by J. Pauwelyn, 'Is it international law or not and does it even matter?'; P. Dubinsky, 'International law in the legal system of the United States', 58 *American Journal of Comparative Law* 1 (2010), 455–78, on increase in USA of both 'congressional-executive' international agreements and 'sole executive' international

accommodate an expanded, executive, law-making function over a wide area of law, and international law must be more inclusive in accepting non-diplomatic sources of international obligations. It is part of the process, which Anne-Marie Slaughter describes as 'transgovernmentalism', that sees all government actors as competent to deal with their foreign counterparts on transnational problems.[50] There is no longer an exclusivity of foreign relations concentrated in a ministry of foreign affairs. The state thus becomes fuzzier in its dimensions and considerations of material justice come to overshadow preoccupation with jurisdiction and boundaries. A and not-A becomes possible with wider forms of collaboration. The process recalls the cosmopolitan character of state organization prior to the general adoption of ministries of foreign affairs and binary forms of logic during the period from the sixteenth to the nineteenth centuries.[51] There is therefore a space for transnational law, but it requires rethinking the binary manner of legal thinking that has played such an important role in the construction of transnational relations in the recent past.[52]

The space for transnational law has also become more evident and more occupied with the resurgence of earlier forms of transnational law, notably that of the *lex mercatoria*,[53] now accompanied by various contemporary

agreements, latter not requiring Congressional approval, at 468; not used, however, for interpretation of domestic law.
[50] A-M. Slaughter, *A New World Order* (Princeton, NJ: Princeton University Press, 2004), p. 41; B. Kingsbury, 'The international legal order', in Cane and Tushnet, note 41 above, p. 282, for 'functional' and not 'categorical' view of sovereignty.
[51] Until the sixteenth century, 'comparatively late in the day', 'provincial governors' were responsible for relations with neighbors; see Van Creveld, note 12 above, p. 133.
[52] For such renunciation of binary thinking within the International Court of Justice see the Declaration of Justice Simma in the *Kosovo* decision, available at www.icj-cij.org/docket/files/141/15993pdf, in which he speaks at paras 2, 8 and 9 of an 'old, tired view of international law' that would see permission in the absence of prohibition, a binary view that 'ignores the possible degrees of non-prohibition, ranging from "tolerated" to "permissible" to "desirable"'. The possibility of degrees of non-prohibition is seen as 'something which breaks from the binary understanding of permissive prohibition and which allows for a range of non-prohibited options'. I am grateful to Morag Goodwin of Tilburg Law School for this reference.
[53] Sources are found in the Transnational Law Database, at www.trans-lex.org; but for criticism of philosophical justifications for being 'overly ambitious, irrealistic and naïve' and attacked by developing countries, see F. De Ly, '*Lex mercatoria* (new law merchant): globalisation and international self-regulation' in R. P. Abbelbaum, W. L. F. Felstiner and V. Gessner (eds), *Rules and Networks: The Legal Culture of Global Business Transactions* (Oxford: Hart Publishing, 2001), pp 159–88.

derivatives such as a *lex sportiva*[54] and a *lex electronica*.[55] There is now an immense literature on these subjects, and one of their most vigorous proponents does not hesitate to qualify the exclusivist functions of public and private international law of recent centuries as an 'aberration'.[56] Less visible but perhaps even more significant is the development of what has become known as transnational private regulation (TPR), a form of non-state law that has become widespread where the state is unable to intervene, or chooses not to do so.

It is the product of a growing number of private, transnational organizations, including both businesses and non-profit NGOs, the latter playing a growing role in both making and monitoring rules.[57] State actors may participate in its formulation, though the state plays no particular role in its adoption. The TPR that is developed may be drafted by experts or by stakeholders and it already covers a wide field of activity, from accounting standards to food safety to forest stewardship.[58] TPR may intervene where the state has failed, or allegedly failed, and its legitimacy then flows from the lack of a viable alternative.[59] Legitimacy also flows, however, from state law renouncing its mandatory character or affirming its tolerance

---

[54] J. Nafziger and S. Ross (eds), *Handbook on International Sports Law* (Northampton, MA: Edward Elgar Publishing, 2001); S. Gardiner, *Sports Law* (London: Cavendish Publishing, 2006), pp 91–2 on 'The emergence of a *lex sportiva*'.

[55] M. Delmas-Marty, *Le relatif et l'universel* (Paris: Seuil, 2004), p. 103.

[56] J. Dalhuisen, *International Commercial, Financial and Trade Law* (Oxford: Hart Publishing, 2000), p. vii.

[57] On states being correspondingly more often rule-takers than rule-makers, F. Cafaggi, 'Private regulation in European private law' in A. Hartkamp, M. Hesselink, E. Hondiua, C. Mak and C. E. du Perron (eds), *Towards a European Civil Code* (The Hague: Kluwer Law International, 2011), p. 95; on states now meeting *competition* of new actors, J. Chevalier, 'L'État post-moderne: retour sur une hypothèse', 39 *Droits* (2004), 107–20 at 108; on 'emancipation' of social actors from state, S. Hobe, *Der offene Verfassungsstaat zwischen Souveränität und Interdependenz* (Berlin: Duncker & Humblot, 1998), p. 27; and for NGOs being 'everywhere' now also including Chinese GONGOs, government-organized NGOs, A. Cranston, *The Sovereignty Revolution* (Stanford, CA: Stanford University Press, 2004), p. 38.

[58] For the range of subjects (banking, tax, accounting, pharmaceuticals, etc.), T. Hale and D. Held, *Handbook of Transnational Governance: Institutions and Innovations* (Cambridge: Polity Press, 2011); for accounting, food safety and different models, F. Cafaggi, 'New foundations of transnational private regulation', 38 *Journal of Law & Society* 1 (2011), 20–49 at 33–4.

[59] On failure of states in matters of reforestation, Cafaggi, *ibid.*, at 26; also on reforestation, E. Meidinger, 'Beyond Westphalia: competitive legalization in emerging transnational regulatory systems' in C. Brütsch and D. Lehmkuhl (eds), *Law and Legalization in Transnational Relations* (New York: Routledge, 2007), p. 122.

of private initiatives.[60] In the result, in the language of Fabrizio Cafaggi, there is a type of 'institutional complementarity' (A and not-A).[61]

These recent developments in transnational forms of law are indicative both of the possibility of logical pluralism in law, and of the importance of legal practice as a testing ground of legal logic. Stephen Toulmin decades ago criticized formal or classical (binary) logic for its artificiality and 'field invariance'.[62] He suggested that classical binary forms of logic were crude and unsophisticated in comparison with the actual logic used notably in law and that '[c]omplete logical candour' would thus require employment of 'a pattern of argument no less sophisticated than is required in the law'.[63] If legal theory in the modern period has therefore been largely captured by modern or classical forms of logic, legal practice would have remained more logically subtle and would now be reasserting itself, given the inflexibility of classical logic before the complexity of the world. These are not novel conclusions. Roy Goode wrote more than a decade ago that in matters of transnational law it is 'practising lawyers who are making the running'[64] and the remark parallels a much larger apparent consensus that all theory is dependent on prior forms of practice.[65] Plato was seen

---

[60] That state will often 'leave space', even in case of mandatory state rules, e.g. in providing minimum standards, Cafaggi, note 57 above, p. 107; and for the relations between contract (in mass form) and statute even being 'turned upside down', D. Wielsch, 'Global law's toolbox: private regulation by standards', 60 *American Journal of Comparative Law* 4 (2012), 1075–104 at 1082–3.

[61] Cafaggi, note 57 above, p. 100, on complementarity through choice of state law or TPR, but also 'different combinations between the two'.

[62] Logicians restricting notions of soundness, validity, cogency, or strength of arguments and attempting to define them in field-invariant terms, S. Toulmin, *The Uses of Argument* (Cambridge: Cambridge University Press, 1958), p. 147.

[63] *Ibid.*, p. 89.

[64] R. Goode, 'International restatements and national law' in W. Swadling and G. Jones (eds), *The Search for Principle: Essays in Honour of Lord Goff of Chieveley* (Oxford: Oxford University Press, 1999), p. 56.

[65] For the priority of practice over theory, J. Strayer, *On the Medieval Origins of the Modern State* (Princeton, NJ: Princeton University Press, 1970), p. 9; on primacy of practice of law, all theory built on previous practice, W. Krawietz, 'Recht ohne Staat? Spielregeln des Rechts und Rechtssystem in normen- und systemtheoretischer Perspektive', 24 *Rechtstheorie* (1993), 81–133 at 105; for theory following practice in notion of continuity of state, E. Kantorowicz, *The King's Two Bodies: A Study in Mediaeval Political Theology* (Princeton, NJ: Princeton University Press, 1957), p. 301; C. Peirce, *Selected Writings (Values in a Universe of Chance)* (New York: Dover Publications, 1958), p. 336: '[u]nfortunately practice generally precedes theory, and it is the usual fate of mankind to get things done in some boggling way first, and find out afterwards how they could have done them much more easily and perfectly'; and for a recent trenchant critique of 'ideal' theoretical writing, insisting on the need to constantly situate it 'within the rest of human life';

as controlling when there were apparent reasons for viewing the world in a binary and inflexible, even belligerent, manner. The world today is different, and it is unlikely to come to a halt because of a decline in the role of binary logic, the law of the excluded middle and the law of non-contradiction. As the French philosophers Deleuze and Guattari have put it, 'no one has ever died from contradictions'.[66]

R. Geuss, *Philosophy and Real Politics* (Princeton, NJ: Princeton University Press, 2008), pp 7–9, on the need to comprehend 'the way social, economic, political, etc., institutions actually operate in some society at some given time, and what really does move human beings to act in given circumstances'. For a reciprocal relationship, however, P. Riesenberg, *Inalienability of Sovereignty in Medieval Political Thought* (New York: AMS Press, 1970), p. 83: 'incipient fact forms theory which in turn acts back upon original reality'.

[66] '*Jamais personne n'est mort de contradictions*', G. Deleuze and F. Guattari, *Anti-Oedipus* (trans. Hurley, Seem and Lane) (London: Continuum, 2004), p. 166.

3

Beyond the archetypes of modern legal thought

Appraising old and new forms of interaction between legal orders

ENZO CANNIZZARO AND BEATRICE I. BONAFÈ

1. Monism and dualism in contemporary legal experience

For more than a century, the landscape of relations between legal orders has been dominated by monism and dualism. From the beginning, these two doctrines have tended to assert themselves as comprehensive and mutually exclusive: antithetical paradigms of legal thought. Ever since, their confrontation has featured the evolution of legal thinking and still echoes in legal literature. In the course of the decades, many voices have recurrently been raised, invoking against this theological dispute and calling for abandonment of theoretical schemes regarded as relics of a different era.[1] Nonetheless, monism and dualism still resist and defy every attempt to construct alternative legal doctrines.

In our view, the reason for their enduring success consists in an apparent paradox.

On one hand, monism and dualism as such have never been applied in practice. No contemporary legal order can be defined as fully monist or fully dualist. Good reasons exist to believe that their integral application would create more problems than they could solve. Recurrently, voices have been raised that the time is ripe to abandon them. In other words,

---

This chapter as a whole is the product of cooperation between the two co-authors. However, it is possible to determine the sections that ought to be attributed to each of them: Enzo Cannizzaro is the author of sections 1, 2 and 3, and Beatrice I. Bonafè is the author of sections 4, 5 and 6.

[1] See e.g. I. Brownlie, *Principles of Public International Law* (Oxford: Oxford University Press, 2008), p. 33; more bluntly, A. von Bogdandy, 'Pluralism, direct effect, and the ultimate say: on the relationship between international and domestic constitutional law', 6 *International Journal of Constitutional Law* (2008), 397–413 at 400.

it seems that these conceptions are inapplicable in practice and only exist as purely ideal schemes.

On the other, monism and dualism are constantly referred to as the conceptual basis of legal discourse in relations between legal orders. Every endeavour to demonstrate their obsolescence clashes with the objection that no alternative scheme has been satisfactorily devised.

The reason for their persistence in legal discourse lies in the fact that monism and dualism do not have normative value. They do not establish rules, nor do they produce obligations. They are legal archetypes that we use to materialise our conception of legal orders and in which we channel the ways we conceptualise the relations between legal orders.[2] In other words, we use the term monism to indicate the universality of legal experience and the unity of political power. We use the term dualism to indicate that the existence of a plurality of legal orders is perfectly conceivable and established in practice.

Even from a practical viewpoint, the two terms depict mental archetypes of modern legal and political thought. Monism expresses a tendency towards extroversion and the idea that beyond the parochial values of each state legal order exist universal values constituting the common axiological turf of mankind. Dualism tends rather to express a tendency towards introversion, and the idea that the superior values of modern state orders, based on well-developed standards – the rule of law and democracy – are to be protected against threats from the barbarian, external legal experience.

However, to see in the struggle between monism and dualism a mere logical or theological dispute conceals the very point at stake in this centennial controversy. This dispute essentially concerns the degree of openness of a particular legal and political order and its propensity to accept values originating from the outer world: *Völkerrechtfreundlichkeit* v. *Völkerrechtfeindlichkeit*. In this regard, monism and dualism correspond to two rhetorical figures that fill the imagination with historical and cultural suggestions: a virtuous dualism seen as a barrier erected

---

[2] A major misconception that surrounds these two notions is that they are immutable concepts that accompany the evolution of legal thought without being significantly touched upon by it. This is largely a commonplace. A glance at history proves abundantly not only that each of these notions has changed over time, but also that their respective roles *vis-à-vis* the other have changed in a sort of a never-ending game of hide and seek. For more details of this development, see E. Cannizzaro, *Diritto internazionale* (Turin: Giappichelli, 2012), p. 449.

by democratic orders against intrusion from outside barbarians, on one hand; a virtuous monism seen as a door open to the universal application of common values, on the other. This also explains why most, if not all, modern legal orders are based on a blend of monism and dualism, both in their normative and in their jurisprudential dimensions.

2. A minimum denominator: legal orders as legal monads

In spite of these antithetical implications, in their traditional version, these two doctrines rest on the same logical premise, namely the principle of exclusivity of legal orders;[3] what Kaarlo Tuori terms the black box theory.[4]

According to the dualist version of that theory, contemporary legal experience reveals the existence of a plurality of legal systems, each claiming sole authority to determine the legal nature of its rules. The monist version does not contest the premise of the exclusivity of legal orders. It simply contends that, in contemporary legal experience, the various territorial communities of the globe only constitute the component parts of a unique global community. While the legality of the rules of each component part is determined on the bases of states' legal orders, the ultimate authority to determine the legal nature of the universal legal order rests with international law.

Not only, therefore, are monism and dualism far from being irreconcilable but they also constitute two conceptual variants of the same, positivist theory. Furthermore, they also constitute the indispensable corollary of that theory, in the sense that one who accepts that legal orders are necessarily exclusive can hardly escape this choice of alternatives: either each legal order is legally self-contained and autonomously determines its relations with other legal orders, or each legal order forms part of a wider, possibly universal, legal order that possesses the ultimate authority to determine relations between its component parts.

Thus, in spite of their apparently antithetical vision of the legal experience, monism and dualism share a common premise. Being based on the principle of exclusivity, both doctrines are totalitarian, in the sense

---

[3] See C. Grzegorczyk, F. Michaut and M. Troper (eds), *Le positivisme juridique* (Paris: LGDJ, 1992), p. 34.
[4] K. Tuori, *Critical Legal Positivism* (Farnham: Ashgate, 2002).

that they both accept the premise that a legal order is either completely dependent or completely independent.[5]

However, this scheme, underlying the entire doctrine of legal positivism, is under severe challenge in contemporary law. A plethora of scholarly writings warns us that no contemporary legal order is fully dependent or fully independent.[6] Increasingly, the very premise of legal positivism – namely, the principle of exclusivity of legal orders – is challenged. Increasingly, too, practice reveals that this principle does not correspond to the needs of the contemporary world, which are rather based on constant interrelations between different legal orders. And increasingly it appears as little more than a *fictio iuris*, useful perhaps to conceptualise legal relations based on the notion of sovereignty, but certainly not depicting the reality. Legal orders are deemed to be interdependent, interconnected, permeable with each other or even porous.

However, behind this shared perception has emerged no legal doctrine that proves capable of replacing the traditional conceptual paradigm. Nor is there any merit in the view that no legal doctrine is needed and, instead, a case-by-case determination should be resorted to for the solution of practical problems deriving from the coexistence of legal orders. This recurrent exhortation undoubtedly advocates a practical approach, which appears the most opportune after decades of theoretical intoxication. However, it falls short of providing guidance to theorists and practitioners. In the absence of an objective conceptual framework, a pragmatic approach cannot but rely on personal preference, thus creating uncertainty and multiplying legal conflicts.

Hence, in spite of the many developments in legal theory, dualism and monism still stand as almost insurmountable mental paradigms defying every attempt to set them aside. We know much about the many ways in which legal orders relate to each other,[7] but still we are incapable

---

[5] For an analysis of the principle of exclusivity of legal orders and the relationship between international and municipal law, see B. I. Bonafè, 'International law in domestic and supranational settings' in J. d'Aspremont and J. Kammerhofer (eds), *International Legal Positivism in a Post-Modern World* (Cambridge: Cambridge University Press, 2014, forthcoming).

[6] See in general J. Nijman and A. Nollkaemper, 'Introduction' in Nijman and Nollkaemper (eds), *New Perspectives on the Divide between National and International Law* (Oxford: Oxford University Press, 2007), p. 2.

[7] For the relevant practice of states see P. Eisemann (ed.), *The Integration of International and European Community Law into the National Legal Order* (The Hague: Springer, 1996); D. Sloss (ed.), *The Role of Domestic Courts in Treaty Enforcement. A Comparative Study* (Cambridge: Cambridge University Press, 2009); D. Shelton (ed.), *International Law and*

of answering the fundamental question about the ultimate authority to determine these interrelations.[8] Speaking in cosmological terms, we know much about the universe in which we live but we are still incapable of determining whether there is only one universe, albeit split into a finite or infinite number of subparts, or rather whether we have more than one universe and whether they are closed or open. At the current stage of conceptual development, this incapacity may make monism and dualism in a sense 'indispensable doctrines' and, ultimately, account for their astonishing success. Alternatively, more attention should be drawn to the way in which legal orders actually interact.

3. A methodological premise: relations between rules or relations between orders?

In this chapter, we do not intend to propose a new doctrine on the relationship between legal orders. Our attempt is more modest by far. We intend to explore some practical arrangements by which contemporary legal orders, without necessarily abjuring their ultimate authority, tend to refer to each other and, by so doing, to limit the paralysing effects of the principle of exclusivity.

Observing this practice of mutual recognition may thus sketch the contours of an emerging scheme, in which legal orders are not mutually exclusive but rather establish unilateral forms of coordination. This perspective tends to de-potentiate the perennial theoretical dispute between monism and dualism. It also seems more apt to accommodate the complex interrelations occurring within the thick network of rules of various origins, international, supranational, and national.

This scheme is based on the obvious premise that the contemporary legal environment is composed of a variety of legal rules of different origin and functions. This is the effect of a process of constant reference from one order to another, which might sometimes give the idea of a sort of transitional law. For the purposes of this study, it is unnecessary to determine the theoretical implications of this phenomenon and, in particular, the nature of this constant cross-reference.

Domestic Legal Systems. Incorporation, Transformation, and Persuasion (Oxford: Oxford University Press, 2011).

[8] See e.g. A. Nollkaemper, *National Courts and the International Rule of Law* (Oxford: Oxford University Press, 2011), p. 301.

If we accept the premise that legal orders tend constantly to refer to each other, the question arises as to how to determine and to apply the law that apparently derives from a legal order different from that in which it is applied. Our point is that this is a complex operation, which ought to take into account, for example, the origin and the function assigned to single rules within the system from which it emanates. In other words, it is necessary not to consider single rules in isolation, as pure normative propositions; rather, law must first be examined in the context of its original system, in the light of its own set of fundamental values, its normative dynamics and its own set of instrumental rules. This hypothesis therefore tends to take into account rules not so much at their abstract legal value but rather as the final product of a process of making and determining laws that takes place in another legal system. It is this final product, and not legal provisions considered as abstract sources of law, that must be implemented and enforced through internal remedies.[9]

In the following paragraphs, we propose to demonstrate the existence of a practice of cross-reference between legal orders. For this purpose, we will consider the functioning of some of the techniques that judges tend to apply in order to avoid what they perceive as an improper implication of the doctrines of legal solipsism. Obviously, we do not intend to demonstrate that these techniques apply in every possible situation and that a new conceptual model has emerged and replaced the classic schemes. What we intend to do is only to identify the possible direction of a conceptual development the contours of which have yet to take definite shape.

Some techniques will be analysed that seem to have reached a sufficient stage of elaboration: namely the margin of appreciation, consistent interpretation and equivalent protection. Although very different from one another, these techniques are based on analogous theoretical premises.

---

[9] The idea that international rules must be considered within domestic legal orders, not so much in terms of abstract normative value but rather as part of the international legal system, was the origin of considerable misconception in the past. In particular, it inspired the assumption that these rules are exclusively enforced through international legal enforcement mechanisms; and, in consequence, that international rules should not be enforced through the system of remedies in the domestic legal order. For a preliminary assessment of the use and misuse of this perspective, see E. Cannizzaro, 'The neo-monism of the European legal order' in Cannizzaro, P. Palchetti and R. A. Wessel (eds), *International Law as Law of the European Union* (Leiden: Brill, 2012), pp 35–58.

4. The margin of appreciation doctrine

Elaboration of the margin of appreciation doctrine is commonly attributed to the European Court of Human Rights,[10] but it has a much wider scope of application.[11] It has been and still is applied by other European and international courts, notably the International Court of Justice. This doctrine combines recognition of the normative competence of domestic legal orders with limited international review.[12]

The most interesting aspect of the margin of appreciation doctrine is that it ensures a degree of flexibility in the application of international obligations by acknowledging that, in certain areas, domestic legal orders are better placed than international courts to set normative standards.[13] Thus, when international obligations do not require strict uniformity of national law provisions, a variety of national measures – which take into

---

[10] See *Belgian Linguistic* case (App. Nos 1474/62, 1677/62, 1691/62, 1769/63, 1994/63, 2126/64) [1968] 1 EHRR 252, and previously the Report of the ECommHR in the *Lawless* case (App. No. 332/57), 19 December 1959.

[11] According to Y. Shany, 'Toward a general margin of appreciation doctrine in international law?', 16 *European Journal of International Law* 5 (2006), 907–40 at 909: 'the same considerations which have led to the creation of "margin of appreciation type" doctrines in the domestic law of many states (especially in the field of administrative law) and in the context of specific international regimes (most notably under the European Convention on Human Rights), also support the introduction of the doctrine into general international law'. The extensive body of literature regarding the margin of appreciation includes S. Greer, *The Margin of Appreciation: Interpretation and Discretion under the European Convention on Human Rights* (Strasbourg: Council of Europe, 2000); Y. Arai-Takamashi, *The Margin of Appreciation Doctrine and the Principle of Proportionality in the Jurisprudence of the European Court of Human Rights* (Antwerp: Intersentia, 2001); A. Legg, *The Margin of Appreciation in International Human Rights Law: Deference and Proportionality* (Oxford: Oxford University Press, 2012).

[12] For this reason the doctrine of a margin of appreciation has also been criticised. According to J. Brauch, 'The margin of appreciation and the jurisprudence of the European Court of Human Rights: threat to the rule of law', 11 *Columbia Journal of European Law* (2005), 113–50 at 115, it should be abandoned because it endangers protection of fundamental rights to some degree. See also E. Benvenisti, 'Margin of appreciation, consensus, and universal standards', 31 *New York University Journal of International Law and Politics* (1999), 843–54. For a supportive view see R. MacDonald, 'The margin of appreciation' in MacDonald, F. Matscher and H. Petzold (eds), *The European System for the Protection of Human Rights* (Dordrecht: Springer, 1993), p. 63; E. Kastanas, *Unité et diversité. Notions autonomes et marge d'appréciation des Etats dans la jurisprudence de la Cour européenne des droits de l'homme* (Brussels: Établissements Émile Bruylant, 1996), p. 331.

[13] See e.g. H. Yourow, *The Margin of Appreciation Doctrine in the Dynamics of European Human Rights Jurisprudence* (Dordrecht: Martinus Nijhoff, 1996); E. Brems, *Human Rights: Universality and Diversity* (The Hague: Brill, 2001).

account the specific features and needs of national communities and at the same time pursue the purpose dictated by international law – can be said to be compatible with international law. In such cases, international law accepts a certain margin of discretion within national legal orders and even recognises their primary role in moulding the content of international obligations. Accordingly, the margin of appreciation doctrine can be described as recognition of a certain discretion at the disposal of state legal orders to determine conformity to international obligations.[14]

The doctrine is consistently applied in order to recognise the normative competence of domestic legal orders to regulate the exercise of rights conferred on individuals by international law.

This scheme, also well known in less recent practice, was recently applied by the ICJ in the *Case concerning the dispute relating to navigational and related rights*.[15] A treaty concluded in 1858 established Nicaragua's sovereignty over the San Juan River, but affirmed Costa Rica's navigational rights 'for commercial purposes' on the lower course of that river. The Court was asked to review domestic legislation adopted by Nicaragua which, according to Costa Rica, contravened its right of free navigation. The Court held that 'Nicaragua has the power to regulate the exercise by Costa Rica of its right of freedom of navigation under the 1858 Treaty', provided that domestic legislation is compatible with the general principles set out therein (namely, Costa Rica's right of free navigation).[16] In particular, the measures adopted by Nicaragua had to pursue a legitimate purpose and not be discriminatory or unreasonable. Consistently with this approach, some measures adopted by Nicaragua were found to be incompatible with Costa Rica's right to free navigation because they could not be justified on the ground of a legitimate purpose or were excessive.[17] An analogous approach was also adopted by the International Tribunal for the Law of the Sea (ITLOS) in a 2011 Advisory Opinion.[18] When asked to indicate the measures that a sponsoring state should adopt in

---

[14] M. Hutchinson, 'The margin of appreciation doctrine in the European Court of Human Rights', 48 *International and Comparative Law Quarterly* 3 (1999), 638–50 at 649; T. O'Donnell, 'The margin of appreciation doctrine: standards in the jurisprudence of the European Court of Human Rights', 4 *Human Rights Quarterly* 4 (1982), 474–96 at 495.

[15] *Case concerning the Dispute regarding Navigational and Related rights*, Judgment, ICJ Reports 2009, para. 213.

[16] *Ibid.*, para. 87.   [17] *Ibid.*, paras 119 (legitimate purpose) and 123 (excessive).

[18] *Responsibilities and Obligations of States Sponsoring Persons and Entities with Respect to Activities in the Area*, ITLOS Seabed Dispute Chamber (2011).

order to discharge its duties under Articles 139(2), 153(4) and Annex III, Article 4(4) of the Convention, the Seabed Dispute Chamber recognised that 'policy choices on such matters must be made by the sponsoring State'.[19] However, while determination of specific measures is left to the 'discretion' of states, in order to be compatible with the Convention those measures should be 'reasonably appropriate'.[20]

Even more telling is the application of this doctrine in integrated international systems such as that established by the founding treaties of the EU and by the ECHR.

The search for a balance between the need to safeguard the effectiveness of Convention rights and the need to leave a significant margin of discretion to states features the entire case law of the ECtHR. It may suffice to recall, by way of example, the jurisprudence concerning Article 6 of the ECHR. In a recent case relating to compatibility of the institution of the lay jury with Article 6, the Court reaffirmed that it is not its task to standardise the variety of European legal systems: 'A State's choice of a particular criminal justice system is in principle outside the scope of the supervision carried out by the Court'.[21] Accordingly, the 'Contracting States enjoy considerable freedom in the choice of the means calculated to ensure that their judicial systems are in compliance with the requirements of Article 6'.[22] It follows that the Court will limit its review to respect for general principles set out in the Convention.[23]

On a similar conceptual scheme is based the doctrine of the procedural autonomy of the Member States of the EU. In the absence of specific EU law remedies, 'it is for the domestic legal system of each Member State to designate the courts having jurisdiction and to determine the procedural conditions governing actions at law intended to ensure the protection of the rights that citizens have from the direct effect of Community law',[24] provided that domestic remedies are consistent with the requirement of effectiveness and proportionality.[25]

The doctrine of the margin of appreciation has been paradigmatically applied in order to strike a fair balance between the international obligations and public policy objectives of states.

---

[19] *Ibid.*, para. 227.   [20] *Ibid.*, paras 228–30.

[21] *Taxquet* v. *Belgium* (App. No. 926/05) [2010] ECHR 1806, para. 83.

[22] *Ibid.*, para. 84.   [23] *Ibid.*, paras 85–92.

[24] Case 33/76 *Rewe* [1976] ECR 1989, para. 5; see also Case 45/76 *Comet* [1976] ECR 2043, para. 13.

[25] Today those general principles are enshrined in Article 19 TEU.

An example in international judicial practice is provided by the *Fisheries* case decided by the ICJ in 1951.[26] The Court held that even 'in the absence of rules having [a] technically precise character', the Norwegian delimitation remained nonetheless 'subject to certain principles which make it possible to judge as to its validity under international law'.[27] The recognition that 'the act of delimitation is necessarily a unilateral act, because only the coastal State is competent to undertake it', inevitably led the Court to accept that national measures could be subject to limited review only concerning their consistency with general principles of international law.[28]

An analogous conceptual scheme underlies some of the most famous trends in the case law of the ECJ/CJEU and of the ECtHR.

It is common knowledge that the ECtHR has applied the margin of appreciation doctrine to confer a large, albeit not unlimited, discretion on States party to the Convention to determine the level of protection of collective interests that can lawfully interfere with the human rights equally protected by the Convention.[29] The Court has recognised in general terms that 'State authorities are in principle in a better position than the international judge to give an opinion on the exact content of these

---

[26] *Fisheries* case *(United Kingdom* v. *Norway)*, Judgment, ICJ Reports 1951, p. 116.

[27] *Ibid.*, p. 132.

[28] See *Case concerning the Gabcikovo-Nagymaros Project*, Judgment, ICJ Reports 1997, p. 7, para. 40.

[29] The breadth of the margin of appreciation seems to depend on a number of factors: the relative importance of public policy objectives as opposed to the fundamental character of the individual interest at stake. The existence or inexistence of a consensus among states can contribute to the fundamental character of a public policy objective and to the level of protection that can reasonably be claimed. See G. Letsas, 'Two concepts of the margin of appreciation', 26 *Oxford Journal of Legal Studies* 4 (2006), 705–32; I. de la Rasilla del Moral, 'The increasingly marginal appreciation of the margin-of-appreciation doctrine', 6 *German Law Journal* 7 (2006), 611–24. In *Evans*, the ECtHR held: 'Where a particularly important facet of an individual's existence or identity is at stake, the margin allowed to the State will be restricted . . . Where, however, there is no consensus within the Member States of the Council of Europe, either as to the relative importance of the interest at stake or as to the best means of protecting it, particularly where the case raises sensitive moral or ethical issues, the margin will be wider' (*Evans* v. *United Kingdom* (App. No. 6339/05) ECtHR 2007–I, para. 77). In a recent case, the ECtHR held that notwithstanding the existence of a '*clear trend* in the legislation of Member States', the '*emerging* consensus is not, however, based on settled and long-standing principles established in the law of the member States but rather reflects a stage of development within a particularly dynamic field of law and does not decisively narrow the margin of appreciation of the State' (*SH et al.* v. *Austria* (App. No. 57813/00) [2011] ECtHR, para. 96, emphasis added). In any case, the precise threshold to be met to demonstrate a 'consensus' can hardly be regarded as well settled and the very notion of 'consensus' is still undergoing a process of gradual refinement.

requirements'.[30] Accordingly, the scope of judicial review was limited to the proportionality of states' measures.[31]

In a similar vein, in what is universally known as the doctrine of mandatory requirements,[32] the ECJ/CJEU has recognised a broad, but not unlimited, discretion for Member States to determine the level of protection of public policy objectives that can justify interference with free movement in the internal market.[33]

Impressively, international courts apply the margin of appreciation doctrine in a consistent manner. When discretion is accorded to domestic legal orders, the national measure is subjected to a limited international review concerning the legitimate aim pursued by the measure and applying a necessity/proportionality/reasonableness test. The domestic measure is never put into question *per se*; it is its compatibility with the purposes of the international regime that is tested.

The ultimate objective of the doctrine is to reconcile a plurality of divergent interests.[34] This goal is achieved by limiting review by international courts of domestic measures and considering this review as subsidiary to domestic normative intervention. The margin of appreciation doctrine is based on the acceptance that in certain cases priority should be accorded to the normative competence of domestic legal orders. Therefore, the basic assumption of the doctrine is the explicit or implicit recognition of the normative competence of domestic legal orders in certain areas of law.[35] International supervision is not excluded but it is significantly circumscribed and never puts into question the normative competence of domestic legal orders. Thus, the doctrine, which is built on the fundamental, assumed acceptance of 'external' normativity, ensures a certain degree of unity between different legal orders pursuing common goals.

---

[30] *Handyside* v. *UK* (App. No. 5493/72) Series A (1976) No. 24 ECtHR, para. 48; see also more recently *Otto Preminger Institut* v. *Austria* (App. No. 13470/87) Series A (1994) No. 295–A ECtHR, para. 50.

[31] For some recent decisions see *A, B, C* v. *Ireland* (App. No. 25579/05) [2010] ECtHR 2032, on abortion; *Schalk and Kopf* v. *Austria* (App. No. 30141/04) [2010] ECtHR, on same-sex marriage; *Lautsi* v. *Italy* (App. No. 30814/06) [2010] ECtHR, on religion.

[32] Case C–83/94 *Leifer* [1995] ECR I–3231, paras 35–6; see also Case C–273/97 *Sirdar* [1999] ECR I–7403, paras 27–8.

[33] J. Gerards, 'Pluralism, deference and the margin of appreciation doctrine', 17 *European Law Journal* 1 (2011), 80–120.

[34] See MacDonald, note 12 above, pp 123–4; Kastanas, note 12 above, pp 223 and 439.

[35] See e.g. Letsas, note 29 above, in whose view both the structural and the substantial concept of the margin of appreciation imply a recognition of the normative competence of the State parties in fostering collective interests to the detriment of protecting individual rights.

5. The canon of consistent interpretation

Consistent interpretation presents us with a logically reversed situation. The margin of appreciation doctrine is based on recognition of the competence of the domestic legal order to contribute in determining the content to be given to some indeterminate international notions. The doctrine of consistent interpretation seems to entail acknowledgement by domestic legal orders of the existence of an external normativity to which some sort of priority is granted in determining internal law.

The situations that will be taken into account are essentially those in which domestic courts rely upon a technique of consistent interpretation in order to apply domestic law in harmony with international law.

Practice of reliance on consistent interpretation by domestic courts is so abundant that an exhaustive account can hardly be given.[36] This technique is used to interpret the implemention of domestic legislation whether the implementing purpose is explicit[37] or implicit.[38] It is used to interpret domestic law in harmony with general international law[39] or treaties,[40] be they duly incorporated or not.[41] It is even used to solve cases that are not governed by binding international obligations.[42] In spite of the different legal grounds adduced to justify its application,[43] the

---

[36] According to G. Betlem and A. Nollkaemper, 'Giving effect to public international law and European Community law before domestic courts. A comparative analysis of the practice of consistent interpretation', 14 *European Journal of International Law* 3 (2003), 569–89, the spontaneous practice of states coupled with the required *opinio iuris* could give rise to a customary duty of consistent interpretation.

[37] See for example German Constitutional Court, *Görgülü*, Judgment No. 1481/04 (2004); Peru, Supreme Court, *Callao Bar Association* v. *Congress of the Republic*, ILDC 961 (2007).

[38] See in particular US Supreme Court, *Murray* v. *Schooner Charming Betsy*, [1804] 6 US (2 Cranch) 64; Supreme Court of the Netherlands, NJ 1992, 107, para. 3.2.3; Kenya, High Court of Nairobi, *RM and Cradle* v. *Attorney-General*, (2008) 1 KLR (G&F) 601.

[39] See for instance Supreme Court of Canada, *Mugesera* [2005] 2 SCR 100, para. 126.

[40] See e.g. Supreme Court of Canada, *Suresh* v. *Canada* [2002] 1 SCR 3, paras 96–8; Israeli Supreme Court, *Kav La'oved* v. *Israel* [2006] HCJ 4542/02.

[41] See e.g. High Court of Australia, *Minister of State for Immigration and Ethnic Affairs* v. *Ah Hin Teoh*, [1995] HCA 20, 128 ALR 358, paras 26–7; Supreme Court of Canada, *Baker* v. *Canada* [1999] 2 SCR 817, para. 69.

[42] See in particular South Africa, Constitutional Court, *S* v. *Makwanyane*, 3 SA 391 (1995); US Supreme Court, *Lawrence* v. *Texas*, 539 US 558 (2003).

[43] The legal basis of the duty of consistent interpretation is commonly to be found in domestic law. It is no longer exceptional to find specific national provisions (either in the constitution or in national legislation) laying down an express duty to interpret internal law consistently with international law. See e.g. Art. 16(2) of the Portuguese Constitution; Art. 18(3) of the Serbian Constitution; Art. 10(2) of the Spanish Constitution; Art. 233 of the South African Constitution; s. 2 of the UK Human Rights Act 1998. More often

doctrine of consistent interpretation is certainly one of the favourite tools for ensuring implementation of international obligations at the municipal level.[44]

In particular, consistent interpretation can be a very effective instrument to prevent normative conflicts.[45] The idea is frequently accepted that conflicts between international and municipal law should be prevented from arising by using interpretation techniques.[46] In a further development, the doctrine can also entail the need to interpret domestic law instrumentally, in order to secure the objectives and the full effect of international law.[47]

In a sense, connected with the doctrine of consistent interpretation is the tendency of domestic courts to rely on judicial determination of international rules by international courts and tribunals. For example, when applying or interpreting national law domestic judges tend to rely on the interpretation of the ECHR adopted by the European Court of Human Rights, even where such interpretations have no formal binding effect.[48] By so doing, they tend to recognise that the provisions of the ECHR should be understood in the light of the object and purpose of the Convention, conceived as a living instrument, and, therefore, carry the

consistent interpretation is a judge-made canon based on a presumed intention of the legislature to act in conformity with international law. Less frequently, domestic courts affirm that consistent interpretation is directly grounded in international law. This is for example the case with the duty of consistent interpretation with (and under) EU law.

[44] See e.g. UKHL *Ex parte Brind* [1991] 2 WLR 588; Italian Constitutional Court, judgments 348 and 349/2007.

[45] With respect to EU law see G. Betlem, 'The doctrine of consistent interpretation. Managing legal uncertainty', 22 *Oxford Journal of Legal Studies* 3 (2002), 397–418.

[46] See with respect to international law Betlem and Nollkaemper, note 36 above; and, with respect to EU law, F. Casolari, 'Giving indirect effect to international law within the EU legal order. The doctrine of consistent interpretation' in Cannizzaro, Palchetti and Wessel (eds), note 9 above, pp 395–415.

[47] According to Betlem and Nollkaemper, note 36 above at 588, '[t]he impact of the principle of construing domestic law consistently with supranational law in both legal systems further mitigates the clear distinction between Community law and public international law. In both situations, the courts recognize that there is a binding rule of law, higher in the hierarchy, and that the domestic law is to be construed so as to give effect to that rule of international law.'

[48] For an analysis of consistent interpretation in a different legal framework see T. Cottier and K. Schefer, 'The relationship between World Trade Organization law, national and regional law', 1 *Journal of International Economic Law* (1998), 83–122; G. Iorio Fiorelli, 'WTO as a parameter for the EC legislation through the "consistent interpretation" doctrine' in C. Dordi (ed.), *The Absence of Direct Effect of WTO in the EC and in Other Countries* (Turin: Giappichelli, 2010), p. 121; G. Gattinara, 'Consistent interpretation of WTO rulings in the EU legal order?' in Cannizzaro, Palchetti, and Wessel (eds), note 9 above, pp 269–87.

meaning given to them by the jurisprudence of the ECtHR.[49] Most interestingly, this approach seems based on the recognition of a particular competence with which international courts are entrusted under international law.[50]

More generally, consistent interpretation is a special form of judicial deference that domestic courts exercise with respect to international law. It allows the latter to permeate the domestic legal order and hence to ensure a certain coordination between international and municipal law. This doctrine is premised on the recognition that certain areas of law are better governed by 'external' rules that should somehow be allowed to mould the 'internal' legal order.[51]

6. The doctrine of equivalent protection

The doctrine of equivalent protection provides a particularly interesting example of a technique devised to coordinate legal orders. The doctrine is premised on the mutual recognition that every legal order has the competence to determine the conditions under which its rules are valid, even where they are to produce effects in another legal order. This is

---

[49] In *Dorigo* the Italian Court of Cassation assented to giving effect to a decision of the ECtHR concerning Italy because, among other reasons, the European Court is 'the body institutionally authorized to interpret and apply the provisions of the Convention' (Judgment No. 2800 [2007], para. 6).

[50] See, for example, Italian Constitutional Court, decision 348/2007, para. 4.6. Another example of judicial deference to the case law of an international court is provided by the German Constitutional Court decision in the *Consular Notification* case, Judgment No. 2115/2006. The Court held that 'für Staaten, die nicht an einem Verfahren beteiligt sind, haben die Urteile des Internationalen Gerichtshofs Orientierungswirkung, da die darin vertretene Auslegung Autorität bei der Auslegung der Konvention entfaltet', para. 61. This duty of consistent interpretation is derived from the nature of the Court, which is the principal judicial organ of the United Nations, and the specific interpretative competence it has under the Protocol to the Vienna Convention on Consular Relations. Since Germany has accepted the competence of the Court, its entire case law should provide guidance in the interpretation of domestic legislation: 'Voraussetzung hierfür ist, dass die Bundesrepublik Deutschland Partei des einschlägigen, die in Rede stehenden materiell-rechtlichen Vorgaben enthaltenen völkerrechtlichen Vertrags ist und sich – sei es, wie im Falle des Fakultativprotokolls zum Konsularrechtsübereinkommen, vertraglich, sei es durch einseitige Erklärung – der Gerichtsbarkeit des Internationalen Gerichtshofs unterworfen hat', para. 62.

[51] In this regard, it can be noted that the limits of consistent interpretation can all be understood as a priority accorded to 'internal' normativity. Consistent interpretation is typically inapplicable when normative competence has already been or can only be exercised at the domestic level, that is, when international law is in blatant contrast with municipal provisions, national fundamental principles or domestic final-judicial decisions.

possible when the conditions for validity established in the two legal orders involved – the one in which the rules are drawn up, and the one in which they are designed to produce effect – are homogeneous.

Although designed to solve a practical problem – namely, how to secure for fundamental human rights satisfactory protection *vis-à-vis* external rules without imposing respect for internal standards – the doctrine has a broad field of application and can theoretically apply to various situations in which the problem arises of which standard must be applied to determine the validity of external rules. Thus, equivalent protection can ensure coordination between legal orders in a wide spectrum of cases.

In its 'vertical' dimension, the doctrine ensures an orderly interaction between domestic legal orders and international law. Indeed, the doctrine has been elaborated in the courts of a number of EU Member States in order to avoid scrutiny of EU measures with human rights, provided that the EU offered 'equivalent protection' in that particular field of law. This is, notoriously, the case with the ruling of the German Federal Constitutional Court in *Solange II*[52] and of the Italian Constitutional Court in *Frontini*.[53] In these cases, the two Courts adopted an analogous scheme, that consists in the recognition that, under certain conditions, the existence of 'external' normativity (the EU legal order) can replace internal normativity. Where these conditions are absent, the classic scheme re-emerges, the internal system is reinsulated and it overrules external normativity.

In broader terms, the doctrine was recently relied upon by the French Conseil d'État in *Arcelor*. The Conseil d'État recognised in principle that the domestic judge will assess the conformity of a measure with French constitutional rules or principles only where EU law does not sufficiently ensure effective protection of such domestic rules or principles.[54]

Thus, the equivalent protection doctrine is not solely relied upon with the purpose of recognising the competence of another legal order and

---

[52] BvG, *Solange II* 73, 339 (1986).

[53] Corte Costituzionale, *Frontini*, judgment n. 183 of 27 December 1973.

[54] Conseil d'État, Assemblée, *Arcelor*, n. 287110 (2007): the 'juge administratif, saisi d'un moyen tiré de la méconnaissance d'une disposition ou d'un principe de valeur constitutionnelle, *(doit) rechercher s'il existe une règle ou un principe général du droit communautaire qui*, eu égard à sa nature et à sa portée, tel qu'il est interprété en l'état actuel de la jurisprudence du juge communautaire, *garantit par son application l'effectivité du respect de la disposition ou du principe constitutionnel invoqué*, ... s'il n'existe pas de règle ou de principe général du droit communautaire garantissant l'effectivité du respect de la disposition ou du principe constitutionnel invoqué, il revient au juge administratif d'examiner directement la constitutionnalité des dispositions réglementaires contestées' (emphasis added).

accepting that its provisions providing for equivalent protection can be applied to the detriment of national law. It also has an internal impact. Equivalent protection directs the domestic judge in the choice between application of national law and an equivalent, 'external' rule.

In its 'horizontal' dimension, the equivalent protection doctrine ensures an orderly interaction either between different international convention regimes or between different domestic legal orders. In the first situation, the doctrine was originally applied by the ECtHR with respect to EU law and subsequently extended to other international organisations.

A frequently mentioned example comes from the relationship between the system of the ECHR and the EU legal order. In *Bosphorus*,[55] the ECtHR upheld, although through quite a tortuous line of argument, that the legal system of the EU would be exempt from scrutiny if equivalent protection for human rights were provided within it. Accordingly, judicial review of EU law has been restricted to situations in which EU protection of human rights was manifestly deficient. In the presence of a system to protect human rights equivalent to, even if not necessarily identical with,[56] that offered by the Convention, the ECtHR was ready to grant primary competence to that 'external' system.[57] That primary competence, however, could be reversed, and full scrutiny of consistency with the Convention could be reinstated, if the protection secured by that external system fell below the level of equivalence.[58]

The features of the doctrine are twofold. First, it is based on a structural homogeneity among legal orders. Second, it is based on a high level of mutual trust, to admit that the fundamental functions of one might be delegated to the other. It is unlikely that the doctrine could apply in relations

---

[55] *Bosphorus* v. *Ireland* (App. No. 45036/98) ECHR 2005–VI. See more recently, *Kokkelvisserij* v. *The Netherlands*, Admissibility Decision (App. No. 13645/05) [2009] ECtHR.

[56] *Ibid.*, para. 143: 'it is primarily for the national authorities, notably the courts, to interpret and apply domestic law even when that law refers to international law or agreements. Equally, the Community judicial organs are better placed to interpret and apply EC law.'

[57] *Ibid.*, para. 155.

[58] *Ibid.*, para. 156:

> If such equivalent protection is considered to be provided by the organisation, the presumption will be that a State has not departed from the requirements of the Convention when it does no more than implement legal obligations flowing from its membership of the organisation. However, any such presumption can be rebutted if, in the circumstances of a particular case, it is considered that the protection of Convention rights was manifestly deficient. In such cases, the interest of international co-operation would be outweighed by the Convention's role as a 'constitutional instrument of European public order' in the field of human rights.

among legal orders inspired by different values. However, the doctrine can also be used to promote the evolution of legal orders. In *Kadi*,[59] the ECJ seemed to point out that full review of EU acts implementing Security Council Resolutions in the light of EU fundamental rights could be attenuated to correspond with development of a system to protect human rights within the UN system.[60] The promotional nature of the doctrine – together with the mutual recognition that every legal order controls the validity of its own rules – is fraught with far-reaching implications and reveals the tendency of modern legal orders to overcome the absolute version of the exclusivity principle through a reciprocal acceptance of exclusivity.

This assumption is proved by the further expansion of the doctrine well beyond its original scope. In *Gasparini* the ECtHR applied the doctrine of equivalent protection to the NATO Claims Commission.[61] The same logic lies behind the 'alternative remedies' doctrine applied in the Court's case law relating to Article 6 ECHR in order to ensure its protection even in situations in which the international rules on immunity apply.[62]

More recently, the doctrine has been applied to the relationship between different domestic legal orders. In *Larix*,[63] the CJEU upheld the consistency with EU law of Austrian legislation that prohibits the promotion of gambling organised legally in another state where the legal order of the foreign state does not afford a level of protection for gamblers at least comparable to the level provided in Austria.[64] Interestingly, the CJEU made it clear that clauses unilaterally imposing domestic standards on foreign states would be inconsistent with EU law.[65] In other words, requiring that foreign protection be 'identical' to the domestic level of protection would frustrate the purpose of the equivalent protection doctrine.

The doctrine of equivalent protection as developed in the case law discussed suggests a few general remarks. The doctrine relies on the basic

---

[59] Joined cases C–402/05P and C–415/05P *Kadi and Al Barakaat* [2008] ECR I–6351.

[60] *Ibid.*, para. 256.

[61] *Gasparini* (App. No. 10750/03), [2009] Admissibility Decision, ECtHR: 'les Etats membres ont l'obligation, au moment où ils transfèrent une partie de leurs pouvoirs souverains à une organisation internationale à laquelle ils adhèrent, de veiller à ce que les droits garantis par la Convention reçoivent au sein de cette organisation une "protection équivalente" à celle assurée par le mécanisme de la Convention'.

[62] See B. I. Bonafè, 'The ECHR and the immunities provided by international law', 20 *Italian Yearbook of International Law* (2010), 55–71.

[63] Case C–176/11 *Larix*, nyr.

[64] Art. 56 of the Austrian Federal Law on Gambling of 28 November 1989 (BGBl. I, 620/1989, in the version published in BGBl. I, 54/2010).

[65] *Larix*, note 63 above, para. 32.

assumption that concurrent normative competence will be recognised by separate legal orders. In both its vertical and horizontal dimensions, the final decision on the application of 'external' equivalent rules rests on the legal order of the forum. Nonetheless, the doctrine of equivalent protection ensures unilateral coordination between legal orders because it allows entire sets of 'external' normativity to be applied internally. This mechanism is profoundly different from the traditional tool of *renvoi* that allows only specific external provisions to be applied internally. In particular, coordination between different and separate legal orders is essentially possible because both the 'internal' and the 'external' legal orders *share* common (even though not identical) standards in discharging analogous functions. Accordingly, 'internal' control over the exercise of 'external' competence is very limited, and basically rests on the criterion of 'manifest unlawfulness'.[66] Thus, the equivalent protection doctrine ensures unity and diversity at the same time, because it relies on pursuit of common goals, on one hand, and accepts flexibility in the application of equivalent means of protection in different legal orders, on the other.

7. Attenuating legal solipsism?

The foregoing analysis has focused on a selection of techniques that aim at coordinating different legal orders. They are all premised on recognition of a sphere of external normativity that makes a legal order feel less alone in the universe.

In spite of its technical character, the practice referred to above seems thus to reveal the emergence of relations between legal orders that escape the alternative between supremacy and subordination, and are rather based on mutual recognition and cooperation. This observation should not prompt the facile but simplistic conclusion that a new model has already emerged, replacing the old monist and dualist schemes, and capable of providing a coherent and comprehensive explanation encompassing all the possible relations among legal orders. Reality seems still very far from this hasty conclusion. In their normal intercourse, legal orders still exhibit their enduring claim to exclusivity; still retain their pretence to be the only source of normativity.

---

[66] K. Kuhnert, '*Bosphorus* – double standards in European human rights protection?', 2 *Utrecht Law Review* 2 (2006), 177–89; F. Hoffmeister, '*Bosphorus Hava Yollari Turizm v. Ireland*, App. No. 45036/98', 100 *American Journal of International Law* 2 (2006), 442–8.

Our analysis has thus produced a modest result, if any. It has demonstrated that the absolute version of the principle of legal solipsism, around which the classic archetypes of modern legal thought are still hinged, is not a necessary postulate and can be challenged. In fact, it is questioned by some apparently minor events that, however, as a whole seem to show that a different legal scheme is well possible and that such archetypes might be overcome.

The thrust towards this possible development is that contemporary legal orders – be they considered autonomous and fully fledged or rather as subparts of a unitary order – tend to refer to each other and to delegate certain normative functions to one another. This observation, albeit of limited scope, is promising from a theoretical viewpoint.

Recognition of the primary competence of a certain legal order to discharge its own functions – with the corollary that the results of this process are assumed as such in another legal order – entails the relativisation of the principle of exclusivity. The claim to uniqueness, which stands at the basis of the modern concept of legal orders, may then be gradually replaced by a scheme in which mutual recognition and tolerance take their place.

Nonetheless, this does not entail disappearance of the claim by any legal order to the ultimate power to determine, unilaterally, the conditions under which its own rules are valid, as well as the conditions upon which mutual recognition is accorded. However, the myth of the ultimate power will be excluded from applying to particular fields of normative competence (through mutual recognition) and balanced with gradual emergence of a consistent practice of legal interactions among legal orders.

4

The cosmopolitan constitution

ALEXANDER SOMEK

1. Constitutionalism 3.0

During the late twentieth and early twenty-first century, the authority of constitutional law has undergone significant transformations. By and large, these transformations are manifest in greater international inter-dependence and in democratic processes having a diminishing capability to control social life within their political bounds. Constitutional law needs to recognise now that it is addressed to 'market-embedded states',[1] over which their real power of action is narrowly circumscribed unless they 'pool' their sovereign powers to address common concerns. When it comes to such combinations, administrative problem-solving is likely to predominate.

I posit, by way of introduction, that these three developments can be accurately accounted for by constructing three ideal types of constitution-alism taken from history. They provide useful guideposts in a seemingly endless ocean of perplexity.

Constitutionalism 1.0 stands for the old-fashioned project to create and to sustain limited government. The basic means thereto are jurisdic-tional constraints and negative rights. The constitution is understood as a written document, which has ideally been authored by 'the people' or 'the nation'. Its proper application is informed by constitutional interpreta-tion. It remains an open question whether the meaning of the constitution is to be authoritatively divined by the judiciary or by a representative body that most closely resembles the people themselves, in its composition and orientation. Interestingly, constitutionalism 1.0 appears to be incapable of arriving at a conclusive answer to this question.

Constitutionalism 2.0 assigns to the constitution an even more impor-tant role. Its norms are supposed to guide the creation of *optimal*

---

[1] See W. Streeck, *Competitive Solidarity: Rethinking the 'European Social Model'* (Cologne: Max Planck Institute for the Study of Societies Working Papers, 1999).

government. Therefore, it becomes itself a matter of constitutional law whether and how governments ought to be either more restrained or more active. Consequently, state authority may be found guilty not only of active interference but also of not having done enough to live up to its constitutional commitments. The constitution is taken not only as limiting, but also as a guide. The body adjudicating constitutional questions looms large, for it is taken for granted that representative bodies provide no panacea for the ills of high-energy politics. Indeed, constitutionalism 2.0 is an attempt to deal with certain shortcomings of 1.0, such as the power of the people to abandon constitutional government by constitutional means. The fact that the constitution is a written document is of merely peripheral concern. It does not even matter that this document might have an author, for it is basically understood to be an expression of practical reason. What is more, it is understood to be a blueprint of the good society. Owing to its relevance to every legal question, the constitution becomes 'total'.[2]

It is obvious that this ideal–typical contrast is formulated with an eye to paradigmatic examples. While the Constitution of the United States is the epitome of constitutionalism 1.0, the constitution of Germany, as applied by the Federal Constitutional Court, provides the paradigm for constitutionalism 2.0.[3] The authority of the constitution is strong under version 1.0; it is even greater under version 2.0, even though it is not so easy to pin down what its authority really is.

Constitutionalism 3.0, by contrast, is at first glance manifest in a gradual *de iure* and *de facto* loss of national constitutional authority. The constitution is perceived to be 'in the process of denationalization'.[4] In addition, the core values of constitutionalism no longer seem to be firmly in place. In this context, several strands of development can be distinguished.

First, the national constitution becomes strongly entangled with transnational regulatory processes, as is the case in the European Union, or linked with monitoring systems, the point of which is to secure observance of a standard shared by members of a peer group. The relationship between and among the relevant levels remains gloriously unclear. Even if claims to supremacy originating from one level are frequently met

---

[2] See M. Kumm, 'Who is afraid of the total constitution? Constitutional rights as principles and the constitutionalization of private law', 7 *German Law Journal* 4 (2006), 341–69.

[3] For an exposition, see T. Rensmann, *Wertordnung und Verfassung: Das Grundgesetz im Kontext Grenzüberschreitender Konstitutionalisierung* (Tübingen: Mohr Siebeck, 2004).

[4] See D. Grimm, 'The constitution in the process of denationalization', 12 *Constellations* 4 (2005), 447–63.

with counterclaims by others, pluralism and the skilful avoidance of open conflict sustain the integrity of complex arrangements.[5]

Second, related to transnational entanglement is the growing importance of the executive branch. The increasing importance of co-ordination by 'leaders' and problem solving within administrative networks adds a new dimension to the age-old problem of 'taming the prince'.[6] Viewed from a certain angle, at any rate since *Rex* v. *Hampden* (the Ship Money case), constitutionalism has always been about constraining executive discretion (or, for that matter, delimiting 'prerogative').[7] That attempt was not implausible as long as it made sense to see deliberative bodies – parliaments – invested with the authority and power to assert themselves against leaders. Controlling an agent that by virtue of his or her role is capable of claiming, with larger or smaller measure of credibility, to pursue the common weal is not a hopeless endeavour when, as is the case for the judiciary, the controlling branch by its very nature does not prima facie owe much deference to the political departments. Arguably, it also presupposes a type of normativity that is capable of being expressed in terms of 'legality', which means that norms are first laid down and then, subsequently, followed or applied. Such an understanding of normativity no longer predominates.[8] In the context of a global society, various processes are seen to be threatened with 'crisis' or 'acute risk'. All action becomes intervention. The distinction between norms and their application collapses as norms are perceived as needing constant reinvention and adjustment in the face of a constant flow of 'unprecedented' challenges. The normativity of legality becomes replaced with a normativity of distress. In an age of widespread social acceleration,[9] such development works in favour of the executive branch. Out of necessity, informally co-ordinated management and crisis intervention begin to occupy the

---

[5] For a perceptive sketch of 'constitutional pluralism', see D. Halberstam, 'Constitutional heterarchy: the centrality of conflict in the European Union and the United States' in J. L. Dunoff and J. P. Trachtman (eds), *Ruling the World? Constitutionalism, International Law, and Global Governance* (Cambridge: Cambridge University Press, 2009), pp 326–55.

[6] See H. Mansfield, *Taming the Prince: The Ambivalence of Modern Executive Power* (Baltimore, MD: Johns Hopkins University Press, 1989).

[7] See *Rex* v. *Hampden (Ship Money)*, paras 1637–8, reported in J. P. Kenyon (ed.), *The Stuart Constitution 1608–1688* (Cambridge: Cambridge University Press, 1986), pp 98–103.

[8] See my *Individualism: An Essay on the Authority of the European Union* (Oxford: Oxford University Press, 2008), pp 235–6.

[9] See W. Scheuerman, 'Citizenship and speed' in W. Scheuerman and H. Rosa (eds), *High-Speed Society: Social Acceleration, Power, and Modernity* (University Park, PA: Pennsylvania State University Press, 2009), pp 287–306.

place once taken by legislation. The rationality of public law changes from determining the exercise of powers ('discretion') or compliance with principles of rational action ('proportionality') to an open-ended assessment of the rationality of the system.[10] The focus rests on the performance of societal functions the point of which is expressed as problem-solving capacity. The backbone of system-rationality is the distinction between systems and their environment.

Legislation by representative bodies begins to lose relevance in step with the disappearing of large-scale political choices. It makes much sense, therefore, to defer to administrative authority in a world where nothing more is at stake than facilitating and stabilising the flows of persons, commodities, services and money.

Third, outside of the so-called 'Western world' the downfall of the political is manifest in a new form of constitutionalism.[11] It emerged after nationalism and socialism had lost their ideological grip on the developing world. This constitutionalism is firmly linked to an established religion having basic teachings and norms that are taken to be superior to constitutional law. Consequently, as an act of mere human will, the constitution is always overridden by the will of God. This development is ambivalent, nonetheless, as the constitutionalisation of theocracy appears to foster secular values, such as toleration, and to have the power to curb ardent fanaticism. Undoubtedly, however, once the constitution is fused with religion it also becomes dissociated from a program of emancipation.

2. The core idea

It is against the background of the challenges posed by constitutionalism 3.0 that the authority of constitutional law needs to be reconstructed.

In order to be continuous with constitutionalism proper, such a reconstruction of constitutional authority must not break with the fundamental ideas of 1648, 1776, 1787, 1791 or 1848; however, it will have to arrive at a contemporary rendering of what we have come to associate with political modernity.

As a concept, the *cosmopolitan constitution* is an attempt to identify a type of constitutional law that *emerges* from the situation marked by

---

[10] See N. Luhmann, *Zweckbegriff und Systemrationalität: Über die Funktion von Zwecken in Sozialen Systemen* (Frankfurt: Suhrkamp, 1977), pp 262–4.

[11] For a succinct analysis, see R. Hirschl, *Constitutional Theocracy* (Cambridge, MA: Harvard University Press, 2010).

constitutionalism 3.0. It is, however, not co-extensive with that type of constitutionalism; rather, it is a manner of lending shape to an otherwise fluid and loosely connected set of phenomena. More precisely, it is an attempt to identify those transformations that are commendable and to distinguish them from others that in fact appear to sound the death knell of constitutional law. Nonetheless, they are part of the same situation. Hence, it is assumed that the cosmopolitan constitution comes in two forms. In its *defensible* form, the cosmopolitan constitution is based on the recognition of political self-determination and represents an attractive re-articulation of received constitutional ideas. It focuses on the international embedding of constitutional law. In its *defective* form, its quality as law becomes dissolved into mere practical rationality owing to the ascendancy of diffuse administrative authority.

Lest I be misunderstood, I hasten to add that the cosmopolitan consti-tution, in its defensible form, signifies a *type* of constitutional law and *not* some, perhaps unwritten, constitution of the world. Any country can have a cosmopolitan constitution so long as its practice exhibits certain fea-tures. The cosmopolitan constitution, therefore, should not be mistaken for some blueprint of a unitary constitution beyond the nation state. Rather, it stands for how national constitutional law, confronted with the post-national constellation,[12] is capable of realising its aspiration by reaching out beyond itself.

What follows provides a rough sketch of an idea, the elaboration of which would require a much more extensive analysis.

3. Transformations

The cosmopolitan constitution emerges from three currents that are prevalent within constitutionalism 3.0. The first is the increasing rele-vance, within the constitutional adjudication of fundamental rights ques-tions, of *comparison and peer review*. The second concerns *mobility and belonging*. The third can be summed up as *proportionality and pluralism*.

3.1. Comparison and peer review

Comparison and peer review are essential to the internationalisation of fundamental rights adjudication. In the meantime, comparison and occa-sional borrowings can be observed on a world-wide scale, even though

---

[12] See J. Habermas, *The Post-National Constellation*, trans. Pensky (Cambridge, MA: Mas-sachusetts Institute of Technology Press, 2001).

there is a patent lack of reciprocity among jurisdictions.[13] More importantly, peer review is what explains the – regionally limited – relevance of
international multilevel systems of fundamental rights protection, such
as, in particular, the European Convention system. At the same time,
conditional deference to peers is a preferred strategy for avoiding potential conflict in the context of a multilevel setting. As is well known, the
core idea goes back to the German Federal Constitutional Court's *Solange*
judgments.[14] The European Court of Human Rights has adopted this idea
to position itself *vis-à-vis* European Union law.[15]

The rise to prominence of comparison, peer review and conditional
deference cannot be understood without taking into account that the
ascent of human rights marks the advent of a *post-utopian* vision of human
well-being.[16] The emergence of the cosmopolitan constitution, therefore,
appears to be concomitant with the depletion of utopian energies and
the widespread intellectual fatigue with which societies converge on some
attractive features of liberalism.

Through both comparison and peer review the authority of national
constitutional law becomes relativised. Its contingent character becomes
obvious against the background of sibling constitutions. The perspective
that is brought to bear on the latter is not merely external, for the constitutional practice of others is deemed to be *somehow* internally relevant.
In a sense, then, the external perspective is applied from within. This
has a defamiliarising effect on one's own constitution. Citizens look at
their own constitutional law as though they were uninvolved and wonder
whether it could be right for them. As a consequence, national constitutional authority becomes defamiliarised along a horizontal as well as
a vertical, potentially supranational, axis. Its authority is no longer simply taken for granted on the ground of its origin in the nation's history.
Rather, it needs to be somehow *earned* in the course of peer review and
critical comparison, even though the relevant threshold may be very low.

---

[13] See, for example, S. Choudhry, 'Migration as a new metaphor in comparative constitutional
law' in Choudhry (ed.), *The Migration of Constitutional Ideas* (Cambridge: Cambridge
University Press, 2006), pp 1–35.

[14] See *Internationale HandelsGesellschaft mBH* v. *Einfuhr- und Vorratsstelle für Getreide und
Futtermittel* (*Solange I*), 2 CMLR (1974), 540–69; *Wünsche Handelsgesellschaft* (*Solange
II*), 3 CMLR (1987), 263–5.

[15] See *Matthews* v. *United Kingdom* (App. No. 24833/94) ECtHR 1999–I.

[16] See S. Moyn, *The Last Utopia: Human Rights in History* (Cambridge, MA: Harvard University Press, 2010). I think that 'post-utopian' captures the development sketched by Moyn
better than the idea of a final utopia.

3.2. Mobility and belonging

Intriguingly, the developments in the field of *mobility and belonging* can be read as though they were in fact interpretations of this relativisation of national constitutional authority. They draw out the spatial implications of what it means to sever one's allegiance to the law of one's polity through defamiliarisation.

The most notable development of our overall attitude towards international migration is the growing belief that everyone has a strong prima facie right to move anywhere, at any rate as long as the *market* in the host state provides a reasonable livelihood. This is a quite remarkable conviction, the rise of which puts everyone who is against free migration into the uncomfortable position of adhering to parochial, unsympathetic and rearguard ideas. The conviction is matched with the perhaps even more extraordinary expectation that whoever has become somehow 'integrated' into a host society, paradigmatically as a worker, should also be able to benefit fully from its social or educational programs on equal terms.[17] Both beliefs in juxtaposition imply that the right to move freely subject to market demand opens the door to social citizenship. The political dimension of citizenship evidently plays a remarkably subordinate role.

What underpins these developments normatively is the principle of prohibiting discrimination on the ground of nationality. In principle, non-nationals also have a prima facie claim to residence, even though the claim on the part of nationals may eventually turn out to be stronger for very good reasons. In principle, the state must not treat nationals with more concern than non-nationals, particularly not when the latter have become somehow 'integrated' into their society.

Obviously, European citizenship epitomises most strongly this revolution of belonging.[18] Yet one merely needs to follow public debates on immigration in order to realise that the revolution is by no means restricted to this domain.[19]

Its full significance is revealed, however, when it is perceived from the perspective of citizens who no longer, or only in exceptional cases, are able to benefit from privileges exclusively on the ground of nationality. This

---

[17] See, for example, Case C–209/03 *Bidar* [2005] ECR I–2119, para. 57.
[18] See my 'Solidarity decomposed: being and time in European citizenship', 32 *European Law Review* (2007), 787–818.
[19] See, for example, P. Spiro, *Beyond Citizenship: American Identity after Globalization* (Oxford: Oxford University Press, 2008).

alters their relationship to their polity profoundly. Political participation aside, they find themselves in the same position as foreigners. Indeed, given the need to anticipate ending up as equals they have inadvertently to take the interests of foreigners into account. Foreigners are thereby represented *virtually*.

In juxtaposition, the rise of peer review and the revolution of belonging work to unravel the special tie between a constitution and national history. The internationalisation of constitutional law invites critical assessments of whether citizens at home should enjoy a lower level of protection under a particular right than others (a position for which there may be good reasons). It is no longer taken for granted that political communities are historically path-dependent and for that reason *alone* legitimately different. At the same time, the historical association with one 'community of fate' is no longer perceived to provide sufficient support for preferential treatment. Allegiance to national laws can no longer be garnered through benefiting nationals. In both cases, citizens experience themselves *simultaneously* as an integral part of, *and* like foreigners in, their own country.

3.3. Proportionality and pluralism

The last bundle of transformations concerns the manner in which constitutional law is considered to be binding. The prominence of *proportionality and pluralism* indicates that jurisdictional bounds lose much of their significance in the context of constitutional adjudication.

Originally, modern constitutional law was supposed to be, in Madison's famous phrase, a charter of power granted by liberty.[20] The point of constitutional legality used to be – and in certain areas continues to be – to determine whether the agents created by that charter also stay within the scope of their respective powers. Quite naturally, tests examining the means–ends relationship between a measure chosen and the objective pursued establish whether a particular power to legislate or to act has been used either properly or excessively. Hence, standards of rationality are part and parcel of constitutional law, in particular where courts adjudicate questions of the allocation of competence.[21]

The point of the requisite tests, however, is to scrutinise the link between the power in the abstract, on one hand, and its concrete exercise, on the

---

[20] See the quotation from Madison in B. Bailyn, *The Ideological Origins of the American Revolution* (Cambridge, MA: Harvard University Press, 1967), p. 55.

[21] For a *locus classicus*, see *McCulloch v. Maryland*, 17 US 316 (1819).

other. Assessing the rationality of an act is the way to determine whether an existing limit has been respected.

American constitutional law has long embraced this idea. Modern European tests of proportionality, by contrast, are not geared to such a task. In the field of fundamental rights, at any rate, the picture becomes reversed. A subject enjoys immunity from interference – and the organ of the state lacks the requisite power – if the measure turns out to interfere disproportionately with rights. The lack of the power *in abstracto* is the consequence of a negative finding concerning the rationality and reasonableness of action *in concreto*.

This represents a remarkable shift in the normativity of constitutional law. Again, in the field of fundamental rights, but even beyond that field, the constitution changes from being a charter of power to – borrowing the late David Currie's felicitous phrase – a repository of standards for assessing the rationality and reasonableness of government action.[22] The normativity of constitutional law is manifest in standards of rationality and not in limits established by legal rules. The text of the constitution merely indicates the instances in which it is imperative to exercise a more or less thorough test of practical rationality. In principle, however, the constitution loses its mooring in a written document. In this case, as well, it is no longer firmly tied to the history of a particular community.

The consequences of this shift are quite momentous. The prevalence of this altered understanding of the constitution explains, above all, the emerging juristocracy in constitutional law.[23] The constitution means what the judiciary says it means, and its members brim with confidence that they have much to say on questions of practical rationality.

What is more, since reasonableness and rationality of action are at stake and not compliance with a positive norm, constitutional authority begins to float freely in an amorphous jurisdictional space. Any tribunal is in principle capable of adjudicating any question that is brought before it. The allocation of jurisdiction becomes a question of second-order rationality as expressed, for example, in the principle of subsidiarity.[24] In principle, however, the normativity of constitutional legality is no longer tied to a specific legal instrument or a collective subject authorising its

---

[22] D. P. Currie, '*Lochner* abroad: substantive due process and equal protection in the Federal Republic of Germany', 11 *Supreme Court Review* (1989), 333–72.

[23] See R. Hirschl, *Towards Juristocracy: The Origins and Consequences of the New Constitutionalism* (Cambridge, MA: Harvard University Press, 2007).

[24] See M. Kumm, 'The cosmopolitan turn in constitutionalism: on the relationship between constitutionalism in and beyond the state' in Dunoff and Trachtman, note 5 above, p. 290.

adoption. All competing sites of constitutional authority are equal. They are equally universal.

The resulting pluralism of constitutional authority can only be stabilised on the basis of conditional deference. Jurisdiction A yields to how jurisdiction B protects fundamental rights so long as it sees B observing a certain standard of protection. B would act in the same manner towards A.

4. Constitutional authority

In light of the third transformation, it becomes necessary to reconsider the constitution's authority. In this context, it needs to be borne in mind that there is a nexus between the reasons decisive for a constitution's acceptability and how these reasons are to be given effect in singular cases.

The exploration of the constitution's authority applies this binocular view concerning the 'that' as well as the 'how' of its normative force.

4.1. The modern conception

According to the core idea of modern constitutionalism, the constitution is an instrument that both enables and constrains the exercise of public power.[25] The concept presupposes, thus, a certain idea of what that power is. Ordinarily, it is equated with the state, but it is not limited to it. Roughly speaking, public power is typically encountered in relations of subordination.

The constitution is law. This means not only that it establishes, to some extent, enforceable constraints but also that the very point of these is to effect respect that is due to the free choices of others. If legislation is void on the ground of an excess of legislative powers it is the will of the people that is enforced *vis-à-vis* the legislature. If an act of government is found to interfere with fundamental rights, the freedom of its subjects becomes reasserted.

The constitution is comprehensive. It provides the basis for any exercise of public power, even if only by means of broad delegations. The implication of comprehensiveness is the continuity of power. That is, once the effect of all legal acts is seen to be mediated by public power, all power, be it private or public, can be connected to constitutionally established

---

[25] See D. Grimm, *Die Zukunft der Verfassung* (Frankfurt: Suhrkamp, 1991).

spheres. Moreover, this continuum does not admit of any exceptions. Any claim to authority needs to be traceable to constitutional law. In other words, by virtue of being comprehensive, the constitution is also a monist ordering of authority. This explains why 'constitutional pluralism' is so much talked about as a phenomenon. It challenges profoundly the imagery of constitutional law.

The constitution serves three functions.[26] First, in some manner it has to guarantee fundamental rights, which are basic goods that are to be enjoyed by everyone on fair terms; second, the constitution is supposed to facilitate effective problem-solving and common action; and, finally, it has to give a structure to political self-determination.

It should go without saying that *originally*, that is, in the course of the English revolutions, the first function was supposed to be served by the third. The major emphasis that thus rested initially on the third function is consistent with a certain view of what lends authority to the constitution. According to the public philosophy of the bourgeois revolutions, the constitution originates from 'the people' or 'the nation'. Regardless of what the difference between these entities may come to, it indicates that the constitution is binding by virtue of having its origin in political self-determination. Indeed, it is through an act of self-constitution that collective self-determination is given presence and continuity by virtue of being given legal form. The authority of a constitution does not derive merely from the universal principles of freedom, equality and solidarity. It is rooted also in giving form to what would otherwise remain an amorphous, and potentially dangerous, mix of public opinion and spontaneous acclaim for resolute action. The form-giving quality of a constitution explains why its oft-derided 'mystical' origin is part of what gives it authority.[27]

As the origin and one of the major aims of the constitution, political self-determination accounts for the *particularistic* element of the constitutionalist cause. It was one of the defining features of constitutionalism up to the end of decolonisation in the twentieth century. This is not to say that the *universalistic* element, represented by the rights of man, becomes thereby submerged, for it is understood that any

---

[26] What follows is a variation on a theme found in B. Ackerman, 'The new separation of powers', 113 *Harvard Law Review* 3 (2000), 633–729.

[27] For a very serious exploration of the concept of the constituent power, see H. Lindahl, 'Constituent power and reflexive identity: towards an ontology of collective selfhood' in M. Loughlin and N. Walker (eds), *The Paradox of Constitutionalism: Constituent Power and Constitutional Form* (Oxford: Oxford University Press, 2007), pp 9–24.

people with mature reason will incorporate fundamental rights into their constitution.

4.2. The contrast with the pre-modern world

It is important that modern constitutions are understood to be *creations* of *one* collective subject. Law is the *form* by virtue of which this entity sustains itself over time. In contrast to their pre-modern counterparts, modern constitutions are not made up of various estates or social groups, each bringing its virtues and potential vices to the social ordering; it is in the pre-modern situation that the central task of the constitution is believed to be striking an adequate balance among groups so that their respective virtues can be preserved while the vices are supposed to cancel each other out.[28] The modern constitution, in other words, is *not* a mixed constitution.

This is reflected in the manner in which constitutional arrangements are imagined to be binding. Pre-modern constitutions were not deemed to be legal instruments. They were composed of precarious equilibria between and among the participating orders of society. The art of constitutional design consisted in creating institutions in which the relevant groups had to co-operate with potential contenders in a manner conducive to the common good. The constitution, in a sense, enforced itself through its constituted actors provided that the mechanisms of co-operation had been calibrated well enough.

While this idea has not completely disappeared from the horizon of modern constitutionalism, it is understood, nonetheless, that a constitution constrains conduct by virtue of being *law*. Moreover, the separation of powers is aligned to the branches of government in order to prevent abuses. It does not involve an adequate mix of groups and their relevant virtues. Once the constitution is taken to be law, respecting its binding force becomes a matter of constitutional interpretation and not of political prudence. Ordinarily, the contentious issue is whether it is parliaments or courts that are to divine the specifics of this special type of law.

4.3. Renewing the modern understanding

The emergence of the cosmopolitan constitution represents a momentous transformation of modern constitutionalism. For example, this

---

[28] For a well-known, beautiful outline of the idea, see Charles I, 'Response to the nineteen propositions' (1648), reprinted in Kenyon, note 7 above, p. 19.

transformation would be captured only inadequately if one were to say that the development of protection for international fundamental rights is a matter of international obligations that states may choose to incur or not to incur. Rather, submitting to peer review goes to the heart of the legitimacy of any political authority.

The cosmopolitan constitution can be understood, and also defended, as an attempt to rescue the universalistic ambition of modern constitutionalism from being suffocated by its particularistic mode of realisation. At least throughout the first one-and-a-half centuries of modern constitutionalism it was taken for granted that the locale for the realisation of the 'rights of man' was the nation state. Indeed, the 'right to have rights' was believed to require some form of belonging.[29] While this has not changed, what has indeed changed is the mode of remaining faithful to their universal dimension. While particularity is necessary in order to realise universal principles, the latter are systematically liable to be absorbed by it. In response to this threat, the cosmopolitan constitution reintroduces the universal ambition *vis-à-vis* the particular *via* the particular. Through the encounters with others, national particularity is challenged to confront its contingency.

The modern constitution owes its authority to collective authorship. But this authorship has so far conceived of the collective authors as belonging together in some way. It has ignored the possibility of common authorship among foreigners. The cosmopolitan constitution complements the picture by recognising the more universal relationship of 'foreignness' that obtains among humans.

Traditionally, the preferred mode of drawing out the meaning of constitutional norms, at any rate under constitutionalism 1.0, has been constitutional interpretation. The growing use of non-interpretative principles for assessing the rationality of action, such as proportionality,[30] or 'equality *qua* reasonableness',[31] indicates different sensibilities.

Such changes, however, can only be seen as continuous with modern constitutionalism when they can be accounted for from *within* its tradition. It has been pointed out above that political self-determination is the source of the constitutional authority. If the cosmopolitan constitution can be perceived as an outgrowth of modern constitutionalism then

---

[29] See H. Arendt, *The Origins of Totalitarianism* (New York: Schocken Books, 1991), p. 376.

[30] See D. Beatty, *The Ultimate Rule of Law* (Oxford: Oxford University Press, 2004), pp 171–6.

[31] For an introduction, see my 'Equality as reasonableness: constitutional normativity in demise' in A. Sajó (ed.), *The Dark Side of Fundamental Rights* (Utrecht: Eleven International, 2006), pp 191–215.

the three threads of development identified in section 3 of this chapter have to be accounted for on the basis of a conception of collective
self-determination, more precisely, as *appearances* of both political *and*
cosmopolitan self-determination.

5. Two forms of collective self-determination

The core explanatory task of distinguishing between defensible and indefensible forms of constitutionalism 3.0 has to be performed by drawing a
line between political and cosmopolitan self-determination. With regard
to the latter, two forms can be distinguished in turn. The second distinction is just as important as the first.

In its *mixed* form, cosmopolitan self-determination is compatible with
its political counterpart. In its *pure* form, it is not. Mixed cosmopolitan
self-determination explains why the cosmopolitan constitution is defensible. By contrast, pure cosmopolitan self-determination is the source of
defective renderings of constitutional ideas and the nemesis of constitutional legality.

5.1. The basic concept

Any self-determination involves, on the part of the determining self, an
active as well as a passive component (which is also active essentially for the
reason of being action). The active component consists of identification.
One is self-determining when one invests and encounters oneself in what
one chooses to do. If one did not, one would rather suffer from some
strange affliction. The passive component consists of allowing oneself to
be determined by that with which one identifies. Interestingly, this always
involves a partial *loss* of control.

For both activity and passivity, the self-reflexive element is essential.
Both identification and passive affection have to be authorised by oneself.
One must not have been tricked into identification, nor haphazardly
yield to whatever drive one might happen to possess. In order to rule
this out, identification and affection have to be governed by a principle
that lends expression to who or what one is. Intriguingly, activity and
passivity are involved here, too. The activity of authorisation is mediated
by passive awareness of, and receptivity towards, the identity that is at stake
here.

Self-determination is self-constitution. One becomes who one is
through authenticated acts of identification and 'self-affection'. This is

fairly obvious for cases of personal autonomy. One's acts can count as autonomous acts so long as one can see them as one's own and does not have to concede that they have happened to oneself when one was 'beside oneself'. When this condition is met one will make room for a desire to determine one's life. That is, one will try neither to repel nor to suppress it, and to accept it as one's own even if this desire may, from a certain angle, appear to be strange or even threatening. As long as one remains thereby explicable to those whom one regards as other rational beings one acts autonomously,[32] for a rational being is what one essentially is. Self-determination has a 'synthetic' quality. It has the power to make familiar the unfamiliar.

On the basis of these preliminary observations, collective self-determination can be understood as involving the interplay of an active and a passive element and their synthesis on the basis of a principle, the application of which is both active and passive.

5.2. Political self-determination

Political self-determination is situated in a space that is shared with others. The boundaries constituting this space are the condition for sharing a common concern for a place.

This place is occupied by real people. It is inevitable to engage with and to answer to them. Decisions cannot be based only upon aggregate data, models, projections and extrapolations. They are often preceded by effective encounters. Arriving at constructive solutions from such encounters requires judgement in the sense of an ability to assess the acceptability of certain solutions from the perspective of concrete others.[33] Getting along is an important aspect of political self-determination.

Owing to a shared responsibility for a common place the temporal horizon of political self-determination spans across generations. Not only is leaving ('exit') generally understood to be a means of last resort, the participants in political processes act as though their lives were going to take place in this place for an indefinite period of time. Its fate matters to them even beyond their own physical existence.

---

[32] As has been pointed out by J. D. Velleman, all normative questions are ultimately about how one explains to oneself one's own conduct. One must not do what would appear inexplicable in the manner in which one has come to conceive of oneself: J. D. Velleman, *How We Get Along* (Cambridge: Cambridge University Press, 2009), pp 15, 19–20.

[33] The above refers to I. Kant in the interpretation given by H. Arendt and E. Vollrath. See E. Vollrath, *Die Rekonstruktion der Politischen Urteilskraft* (Stuttgart: Klett, 1977).

The political world is experienced as the world where people are not unlikely to spend their whole lives. It is the place, therefore, where it is possible to negotiate and to agree upon the conditions under which people can develop, adopt and revise a plan of life.[34] The conditions under which this is possible are the core focus of distributive justice. Debates over just distributions are *essential* to political self-determination.

If the world upon which political self-determination has an impact is the world in which one can see whole and meaningful lives realised, then this world is also perceived as an overarching *form of life*. Individual life can take place only if lived in reasonable balance and interconnected with other lives. One may not be able to arrive at a concept of what that form of life is all about, but it is nonetheless presupposed in any consideration affecting its integrity and persistence over time.

Political self-determination involves a deep commitment to a bounded form of life. Since the political choices made by others with whom one shares this place are an integral part of it, one allows oneself to be determined by their choices. Greens grudgingly concede defeat to Christian democrats because they belong to their world. The principle mediating self-determination is *loyalty* to the community. Loyalty is a rational principle, for it is a condition for seeing one's life in the future, and not just now, located within a certain form of life that accounts for its significance and its success.[35]

5.3. Cosmopolitan self-determination: human rights

By definition, cosmopolitan self-determination is not tied to a given place. It does not involve encounters with particular people. No actual exchanges are taking place. Cosmopolitans do not share a concern about the future of one *particular* place.

Cosmopolitans inhabit one world, which is their *cosmopolis* (or cosmopolity). Yet, this *polis* exists only in the form of a variety of particular *poleis* (or polities). Hence, cosmopolitans can inhabit the cosmopolity by residing in *any* polity. Indeed, as long as there is one remaining, they do not care how many may go under. Yet, since by definition they do not belong to a particular community they inhabit these as foreigners or as *hospites* – guests, as Immanuel Kant would have put it.

---

[34] See J. Rawls, *Political Liberalism* (New York: Columbia University Press, 1993), pp 74–5.

[35] For a most remarkable phenomenology of loyalty, see G. Fletcher, *Loyalty: An Essay on the Morality of Relationships* (New York: Oxford University Press, 1993).

Foreigners are not tied to any particular polity through the bonds of loyalty. They are always ready to move on. Indeed, from their perspective any community has to be as good as any other provided, however, that the community fulfils conditions of inhabitability for humans. Evidently, it is *human rights* that formulate these conditions.

6. Mixed cosmopolitan self-determination

6.1. The concept

As foreigners, that is, as people who do not participate in a people's common self-determination, cosmopolitans can be at home anywhere in the world so long as the local political process respects human rights. This implies, however, that cosmopolitan self-determination can be fully reconciled with political self-determination and serve as a medium for its enactment. Political self-determination that abides by human rights standards is an apt vehicle for cosmopolitan self-determination. If the latter is linked to the former, one can speak of *mixed* cosmopolitan self-determination.

Abiding by human rights standards, however, in and of itself, is not sufficient to constitute self-determination. Allowing oneself to be determined by the political choices of others may well be an acceptance of heteronomy, which one may have even private reason to endure. Human rights alone merely circumscribe the conditions under which this type of heteronomy is reasonable.

In order to establish self-determination, it has to be shown how cosmopolitan subjects – or *we* in our capacity as cosmopolitan subjects – are able to identify with the will of a foreign polity and allow ourselves to be determined by it. Moreover, a principle needs to be found that explains why such behaviour is rational.

The idea providing the key is the old Burkean notion of virtual representation.[36] Indeed, repugnant as the use of the concept has been in the context of political self-determination, it is all the more apt to illuminate the relation between foreigners and a political process. One is virtually represented as a foreigner, that is, as someone who does not participate internally, wherever the process does not rule out that one's interest *can* be represented. Foreigners do not participate. But they participate

---

[36] For an excellent reconstruction, see M. Williams, 'Burkean "descriptions" and political representation: a reappraisal', 29 *Canadian Journal of Political Science* 1 (1996), 23–45.

through their absence, as it were, when their interests are present relative to the support that exists locally. Their interests, seen from a person-neutral perspective, appear on the horizon of the polity in question depending on local traditions and the relative strengths and composition of groups. These factors and others explain why some interests may be worse or better represented in one society than another. At any rate, foreigners are virtually represented as long as it is not impossible to articulate interests that they happen to have. They are adequately represented through the medium of a foreign body politic.

The concept of virtual representation also evokes the respect that foreigners have to pay to the political processes of other countries. Any other expectation, that is, to be more than merely virtually represented, would indeed be imperialistic. As a foreigner one needs to take into account, and respect, that various political communities are composed of different groups and reflect different traditions.

However, virtual representation fails, as John Ely explained, if people are discriminated against.[37] Hence, the conditions for cosmopolitan self-determination (identification with any foreign political process) obtain only if there is no discrimination on the ground of nationality. When this condition is met, it makes sense for foreigners to allow themselves to be determined by the result of foreign political self-determination, for they are then 'at home' in the relevant polities, albeit 'as foreigners'. They can identify with any polity.

As we shall see below, the principle mediating the rationality of this form of self-determination is the principle of cosmopolitan reciprocity.

6.2. Its relevance to constitutional adjudication

The analysis above may be read as suggesting that mixed cosmopolitan self-determination is a preserve of outsiders only, that is, a meagre substitute for political freedom available to those who do not participate. But such a reading would miss the universality of the cosmopolitan point of view. As rational beings – indeed, as bearers of human rights – we are all cosmopolitan subjects. Therefore, anyone who is a citizen is also 'visitor' (*hospites*)[38] to his or her own country.

---

[37] See J. Ely, *Democracy and Distrust: A Theory of Judicial Review* (Cambridge, MA: Harvard University Press, 1980), pp 153, 161–2, 165–6, 168.

[38] See I. Kant, 'Zum ewigen Frieden: Ein philosophischer Entwurf' in W. Weischedel (ed.), *Werke in Zwölf Bänden* (Frankfurt: Insel Verlag, 1968), vol. 11, p. 213.

It is submitted that this dual perspective is not alien to modern constitutionalism; on the contrary, it promises to preserve the universalistic component of such constitutionalism *vis-à-vis* its invariably particularistic mode of realisation. It underpins, essentially, the normative relevance of comparison and of peer review.

Comparisons in the context of constitutional adjudication involve horizontal confrontations of particularity that force countries to throw their own constitutional identity into sharper relief. For example, when a criminal justice system that permits life imprisonment without any prospect of parole is confronted with a jurisdiction under which creating a hopeless situation for prisoners is taken to offend human dignity,[39] this system is forced to face up to the fact that it embraces a comparatively harsh standard of retribution. Critical comparisons render explicit what would otherwise have been accepted as a matter of course. The point is not, however, that the relevant constitutional tradition is forced to defend its ways *vis-à-vis* others, which would indeed offend cosmopolitan reciprocity (see below), but rather that the tradition is challenged to come to terms *with itself*. It examines itself internally from the outside.

This presupposes, of course, a reading of the constitution in the fundamental rights sphere that Ronald Dworkin has called the 'moral reading'.[40] It treats fundamental rights as universal principles of political morality and, indeed, severs constitutional adjudication from any purported exegesis of a text. Originalism, hence, is inconsistent with a cosmopolitan perspective, for it ignores the dual nature of political and cosmopolitan self-determination.

This gives rise to the concern that the cosmopolitan constitution necessarily empowers courts at the expense of legislatures. In a sense, this appears to be its implication. Fundamental rights adjudication is vested in disembedded expertise. It does not invoke pedigree as ultimate criterion of validity, but focuses rather on results. As will be seen below, the focus on output is consistent with a transformation of belonging. Nonetheless, even as comparisons raise awareness of the contingent nature of settled understandings, courts retain the option to afford legislatures much leeway to affect the balance between fundamental rights and the public interest. Whether they do so or not depends on their national

---

[39] See the decision by the German Federal Constitutional Court in 45 BVerfGE 187, 21 June 1977, para. 187.

[40] See R. Dworkin, *Freedom's Law: The Moral Reading of the American Constitution* (Cambridge, MA: Harvard University Press, 1996).

constitutional tradition. Deference only has to come to an end *vis-à-vis* the peer review system.

6.3. *Its relevance to peer review*

The dual perspective also accounts for the legitimacy of regional fundamental rights regimes. They are the *authoritative* means by which political self-determination looks at itself from an external perspective. The minimal limits defined by a supranational tribunal (and the ECHR system can be said to be a supranational system in a weak sense)[41] define common standards of public decency below which no state may fall. Regional regimes retain a particularistic element, which is necessary to reconcile political self-determination with its other. Otherwise, the trust underpinning such regimes could not be sustained. Participating polities need to know that it is the authority of *peers* to which they submit themselves. Hence, the common morality of a regional regime will define threshold requirements for peerage, such as, in the case of Europe, the abolition of the death penalty.[42]

From the perspective of cosmopolitan self-determination, a polity's participation in a regional system of fundamental rights protection is not within the discretion of governments. That is, it is not up to the polity whether to enter into a relevant international agreement. It *has* to participate, for this is a precept of constitutional legitimacy.

6.4. *Its relevance to belonging*

It should go without saying that the dual perspective is also relevant to the transformation of our sense of belonging. Indeed, another shared experience coincides with the experience of submission to political authority. Political authority is co-authored by us and arises from our midst. By contrast, the cosmopolitan experience is that of being equally exposed to authorities that are ours insofar as we are alien to them. This second experience shifts the emphasis from the input legitimacy of democratic processes to output legitimacy in the eyes of those who view themselves as

---

[41] The explanation is that Art. 13 of the Convention requires Signatory States to provide effective domestic remedies against violations of convention rights. See M. Janis, R. Kay and A. Bradley, *European Human Rights Law: Text and Materials* (Oxford: Oxford University Press, 2008), pp 831–4.

[42] See I. Manners, 'Normative power Europe: a contradiction in terms?', 40 *Journal of Common Market Studies* 2 (2002), 235–58.

strangers among others.[43] This means, in particular, that the absence of discrimination on the ground of nationality plays a role that is equivalent to democratic legitimacy. This, in turn, indicates that denizenship, as a status, is just as respectable as citizenship.

In and of itself, however, the dual perspective cannot explain *which* interpretation ought to be chosen in order to make sense of the obligation to abstain from discrimination on the ground of nationality.

6.5. The principle of cosmopolitan reciprocity

The key to understanding the difference between mixed and pure cosmopolitan self-determination lies in the political element of the former.

Political self-determination presupposes seeing oneself as part of a form of life that one shares with others. Even if those others decide in a manner that one considers wrong their choice is still experienced as part of one's own existence, for to exist in this form of life means to live among people who have certain views. Indeed, the loyalty to a form of life can be expressed as loyalty to oneself as a component of that form. Respect for choices by others is part of what it means to see oneself as one of its parts. This is what anchors political self-determination. One is *not* a component of a common situation where unanimity is the rule governing common action. Unanimity is the decision-making rule for individuals considered in isolation.

Mixed cosmopolitan self-determination perceives human life as taking place within political communities. It is a matter of cosmopolitan reciprocity that one can claim respect for the choices of one's own polity if one respects the choices of others. The principle of cosmopolitan reciprocity recognises the universal existential relevance of belonging to a place.

6.6. The relevance of the will

Mixed cosmopolitan self-determination implies distanced identification with any respectable polity. It allows for determination by a foreign will and is based on the principle of cosmopolitan reciprocity.

Indeed, it is respect for *choices* that distinguishes mixed cosmopolitan self-determination, for it recognises the decisions made by the

---

[43] On the distinction between input and output legitimacy see F. Scharpf, *Governing in Europe: Effective and Democratic?* (Oxford: Oxford University Press, 1999), pp 7–21.

particular polities comprising the cosmopolity. One is collectively self-determining as a cosmopolitan subject if one sees oneself as inhabiting a world in which one is represented *as a foreigner* in the choices made by others.

Political self-determination also involves the same attitude towards others. Members of the defeated minority accept the choices of the majority since loyalty ties them to their community.

Respect for choices, I add in passing, is the major imprint of a legal relationship.

7. Pure cosmopolitan self-determination

The turning point for the emergence of pure cosmopolitan self-determination is a reinterpretation of political choices. Instead of seeing them as acts of volition they are regarded as practical manifestations of fallible knowledge. They are treated, then, not as acts by which an entity asserts its own *presence* in the social world, but as reflections of either provisional insights or beliefs over which it is reasonable to disagree. Acting is what we must do. Our acting is beyond reproach so long as it is based on sufficiently defensible knowledge. However, any course of action needs to be susceptible to correction on the basis of new insight. Thus understood, resolutions are nothing but unavoidable temporary resting points for inquiry.

7.1. From choices to tentative solutions

It is through a choice that a subject constitutes itself into the cause of an end and thus creates its appearance in the social world:[44] *hoc volo, sic iubeo*. But the determination of action can also be seen as an invariable selection of certain options under conditions of notoriously imperfect knowledge. When choices become perceived as reflecting provisional beliefs that enter into some organism's interchange with its environment, they are treated as though they were essentially nobody's choices. They become faceless, in particular, when they are seen as instances of rational maximisation (of whatever) for random sets of preferences. They are not expressions of *somebody's* will but of *anybody's* reasons.

---

[44] I am indebted, at this point, to C. Korsgaard, *Self-Constitution: Agency, Identify, and Integrity* (Oxford: Oxford University Press, 2009), pp 84–90.

Mixed   cosmopolitan   self-determination   reflects   our   self-understanding as both political and cosmopolitan subjects. People are believed to be loyal to their polities and to respect the loyalties of others as a matter of cosmopolitan reciprocity. *De facto* we conceive of ourselves as citizens and respect the same self-understanding in others.

When people no longer conceive of themselves as citizens but rather as the denizens of disembedded private projects, the respect for choices disappears for the simple reason that the political entities engaging in choosing no longer matter. Choices are then treated as though they were tentative conclusions arrived at along some path of intelligent problem-solving. The perspective on the social world becomes fundamentally altered thereby.

7.2. Jurisdictionally unanchored demand for measures

When political entities become submerged, the world necessarily appears to be composed of networks of horizontal transactions, the shape of which can be more effectively influenced by some at the expense of others. The world is composed of markets and voluntary associations. Both transcend, by definition, national bounds.

Individuals inhabiting the 'flat' world of horizontal interactions recognise, of course, that living among others creates a demand for facilitating measures. What enters into their field of perception, in particular, are various, aggregate, adverse consequences of social co-operation. Consequences of this kind are called 'risks'. Individuals realise that being in society with others requires various forms of *risk-management*, which can be best provided by bodies that are privy to relevant expertise. In addition, there is a high demand for *crisis intervention* since capitalist economies are prone to crisis. Competence in risk management and crisis intervention is the twin source of the suprapolitical authority that is in high demand under cosmopolitan conditions. The root of normativity is distress. The felt need to have order sustained and societal accidents averted has no time for jurisdictional bounds. Any effective regulation or intervention is likely to be welcomed. Action takes precedence over norms governing conduct. Since norms, in a sense, establish jurisdiction over whatever is alleged to be their application, the distinction between norms and their applications is in a state of collapse. Without jurisdictional bounds, authority is immediately active. Flexible rationality supersedes normativity.

7.3. Self-determination as herding

Pure cosmopolitan subjects are interested in having the pursuit of their private projects channelled by rational precautions. They can be *collectively* self-determining inasmuch as they yield to epistemic and practical authority when they sense that others do so as well. They *identify* with similarly smart individuals, even if the underlying reasons may simply be that it is better to have some co-ordinated conduct rather than none. They allow themselves to be determined by expertise, regulations and effective interventions, for they sense that this is a smart thing to do. The principle mediating their self-determination is *rational deference*.

The bodies relevant to this form of self-determination are of an administrative kind.[45] Indeed, it is one of the more radical and seemingly far-fetched claims submitted here that administrative authority is best reconstructed in terms of pure cosmopolitan self-determination. Old-fashioned doctrines of delegation, which have been applied in the national as well as in the international realm, were attempts to rein in jurisdictionally unbounded and expertise-driven claims to authority submitted by administrative processes. Administrative problem-solving has always had a life and a dynamics of its own. Its authority lies outside the political realm. All that has been added by the shift of focus to sites of transnational authority was to make their overweening influence more visible.

When the transnational relevance of private standard-setting bodies, of informal modes of policy co-ordination or of multilevel interaction among international and national administrators, can no longer be ignored by rationalising their existence in terms of delegation, one needs to face up to their independent source of authority. Jurisdictional anchors matter only at a remove, if they matter at all. In a sense, the demands for risk management and crisis intervention are jurisdictionally neutral. They are cognate to the normativity of distress underpinning global crisis-management. Pedigree does not matter. The promised effectiveness of a response to a perceived exigency reveals whether measures ought to be followed or not. Management and intervention partake of the features that Carl Schmitt attributed to sovereignty, even though in merely partial and non-comprehensive form.

---

[45] See N. Krisch, *Beyond Constitutionalism: The Pluralist Structure of Postnational Law* (Oxford: Oxford University Press, 2010).

8. The task ahead

The discussion of both forms of cosmopolitan self-determination gives rise to at least three normative questions, which cannot be explored here.

The first question concerns the adequate *interpretation* of the non-discrimination principle.[46]

The second question asks how the *limits* to the application of this principle ought to be drawn.

The third question concerns the *legitimacy* of pure cosmopolitan self-determination.

---

[46] Answering the first question presupposes an analysis of the transnational effects argument. For a first foray, see my 'The argument from transnational effects', 16 *European Law Journal* (2010), 315–44, 375–95.

5

On liberalism and legal pluralism

RALF MICHAELS

1. Introduction

Is legal pluralism compatible with liberalism? Does liberalism even require the endorsement of legal pluralism? For a long time, for many the answer to both questions seemed, clearly, no. John Griffiths directed his influential defense of legal pluralism explicitly against 'the ideological heritage of the bourgeois revolution and liberal hegemony of the last few centuries.'[1] That ideological heritage, he argued, led to the rise of the state as the umbrella of all society, and to the normative paradigm of the rule of law, understood as the centralized guarantee of societal order and legitimacy.[2] Modern legal pluralism, the emphasis on legal orders other than state law, was formulated in the 1980s as a challenge to these ideas, on both an empirical and a normative level. And, quite consequentially, defendants of liberalism and the rule of law have long viewed legal pluralism with suspicion.

Still today, the antithesis of liberalism and legal pluralism persists in the work of many.[3] John Gray, for example, argues for legal pluralism as an explicit alternative to the 'liberal ideal of the neutral state' that he

Thanks to helpful feedback from audiences in Helsinki and at Tillar House in Washington, DC. Special thanks to Victor Muñiz-Fraticelli, who helped tremendously in improving the argument; he is of course blameless for its remaining insufficiencies.

[1] J. Griffiths, 'What is legal pluralism?' (1986) 24 *Journal of Legal Pluralism* 1–56, at 2–3; Griffiths, 'Preface' in B. Dupret, M. Berger and L. al-Zwaini (eds), *Legal Pluralism in the Arab World* (1999), pp vi–x; see also J. Gray, 'From post-liberalism to pluralism' in I. Hardin and R. Shapiro (eds), *38 NOMOS: Political Order* (New York: New York University Press, 1996), pp 345–62; B. de Sousa Santos, *Towards a New Common Sense: Law, Science and Politics in the Paradigmatic Transition*, 2nd edn (Cambridge: Cambridge University Press, 2003), pp 89–90.

[2] See, e.g., H. W. Arthurs, *'Without the Law': Administrative Justice and Legal Pluralism in Nineteenth-Century England* (Toronto: University of Toronto Press, 1985), and the review by R. W. Gordon, 'Without the Law II', 24 *Osgoode Hall Law Journal* (1986), 421–36.

[3] See, e.g., G. Anderson, *Constitutional Rights after Globalization* (Oxford: Hart, 2005), pp 39ff.

considers indefensible.[4] Amongst other authors, however, it appears that this heritage of legal pluralism as opposed to liberalism has been overcome – or it has been forgotten. Several of today's new legal pluralists are, for whatever reason, liberals at the same time. (Or, perhaps more appropriately, contemporary liberals have become legal pluralists.) Thus, Will Kymlicka suggests that proper accommodation of minorities requires accepting these minorities' own normative orders as law – though with restrictions made especially for human rights.[5] Mattias Kumm presents a theory of 'liberal legal pluralism' as the proper model for the relation between EU law and Member State law.[6] Alec Stone Sweet suggests a constitutionalization of legal pluralism, on recognizably liberal terms.[7] Jan Smits, in what he calls (somewhat misleadingly) a 'radical view of legal pluralism', conjures a plurality of legal systems that greatly enhance a liberal ideal, namely freedom of choice for rational agents.[8] Paul Schiff Berman even goes so far as to suggest that his so-called cosmopolitan pluralist jurisprudence must necessarily be 'consonant with liberal principles' as 'there is no way to extricate oneself from this concern if one wants to have any type of functioning legal system for negotiating normative difference.'[9] The recent decision by a lower German court that

[4] J. Gray, *Enlightenment's Wake. Politics and Culture at the Close of the Modern Age* (London: Routledge, 2007), pp 203–5 (but see also p. 207ff). For critique, see e.g. G. Morgan, 'Gray's elegy for progress' in J. Horton and G. Newey (eds), *The Political Theory of John Gray* (London: Routledge, 2006), pp 115–30 at 124–5.

[5] E.g. W. Kymlicka, *Multicultural Odysseys: Navigating the New International Politics of Diversity* (Oxford: Oxford University Press, 2007), pp 152–3.

[6] M. Kumm, 'Who is the final arbiter of constitutionality in Europe?' available at http://www.jeanmonnetprogram.org/archive/papers/98/9810/V.html. In the published version in 36 *Common Market Law Review* (1999) 351, at 374, section IV is retitled 'European constitutionalism'. But see the discussion of liberal pluralism in the same article at 375.

[7] A. Stone Sweet, 'A cosmopolitan legal order: constitutional pluralism and rights adjudication in Europe', 1 *Global Constitutionalism* (2012), 53–90.

[8] J. Smits, 'Plurality of sources in European private law, or: How to live with legal diversity?' in R. Brownsword et al. (eds), *The Foundations of European Private Law* (Oxford: Hart Publishing, 2011) 323; Smits, 'A radical view of legal pluralism' in L. Niglia (ed.), *Pluralism and European Private Law* (Oxford: Hart, 2013), pp 161–71; for criticism, see R. Michaels, 'Why we have no theory of European private law pluralism', in *ibid.*, pp 139–71, at 149–53; B. Lurger, 'A radical view of pluralism? Comments on Jan Smits', in *ibid.*, at 173.

[9] P. S. Berman, *Global Legal Pluralism: A Jurisprudence of Law Beyond Borders* (Cambridge: Cambridge University Press 2012), p. 146. For a recent, careful critique of Berman's approach that accords with much of what I write more generally here, see A. Galán and D. Patterson, 'The limits of normative legal pluralism: Review of Paul Schiff Berman, *Global Legal Pluralism*, 11 *International Journal of Constitutional Law* (2013) 783–800, especially at

circumcision, as required by Islam and Judaism, is criminal,[10] has been called 'a blow against liberal legal pluralism.'[11] If legal pluralism was once the opponent of legal liberalism, now it looks as though it has become its apotheosis.

Is this newly found alliance between liberalism and legal pluralism a regression or an advance? In what follows, I want to suggest that it might be both at the same time. My results will be tentative, as they must be. But they suggest that the relation between liberalism and legal pluralism is more complex than one of compatibility, incompatibility, or compromise. Much depends on what we understand by liberalism, and what we understand by legal pluralism. Clarifying these terms goes a long way towards clarifying the relation between them.

In short, my findings are these: First, liberalism does indeed require some kind of pluralism, but it does not require legal pluralism. We must be careful not to equate *societal* pluralism on one hand (which may be ordered by a unitary law) with *legal* pluralism on the other.

Second, liberalism in a traditional sense – that is, liberalism understood as the order of the liberal state – is compatible with non-state legal orders only as long as state law remains normatively at a higher level than non-state orders. One speaks here, typically, of weak legal pluralism. States will typically recognize only non-state orders that are on one hand strong enough to successfully demand their recognition as law, and on the other not so strong as to threaten the state's legal monopoly.

Third, strong legal pluralism may be compatible with liberalism, too, but that liberalism would have to be liberalism beyond the state, a neo-liberalism. Further, although neo-liberalism is compatible with, indeed

---

p. 793ff. In response, Berman has considered such criticism or analysis irrelevant: P. S. Berman, 'How legal pluralism is and is not distinct from liberalism: A response to Alexis Galán and Dennis Patterson', 11 *International Journal of Constitutional Law* (2013) 801–8, at 803 ('for me very little turns on whether my vision of legal pluralism is or is not consonant with one or more of the many variant strands of liberalism articulated by political theorists').

[10] Judgment of 8 May 2012, No 151 Ns 169/11, [2012] *Neue Juristische Wochenschrift* 2128; [2012] *Juristenzeitung* 805. NStZ. An English translation can be found at www.dur.ac.uk/resources/ilm/CircumcisionJudgmentLGCologne7May20121.pdf. A comment in English by a German expert is B. Fateh-Moghadam, 'Criminalizing male circumcision? Case note: Landgericht Cologne, Judgment of 7 May 2012 – No. 151 Ns 169/11', 13 *German Law Journal* (2012), 1131–45.

[11] R. Yael Paz, 'The Cologne circumcision judgment: A blow against liberal legal pluralism', available at http://verfassungsblog.de/cologne-circumcision-judgment-blow-liberal-legal-pluralism/.

conducive of, strong non-state laws, it poses a threat to weaker non-state laws.

2. Pluralism in the *Refah Partisi* decision

2.1. *The* Refah Partisi *decision*

Instead of arguing these points in the abstract, I want to demonstrate these three findings on the basis of a concrete example: *Refah Partisi* v. *Turkey*, the decision by the European Court of Human Rights (ECtHR) on the ban of the Turkish Welfare Party.[12] Leaders of the party had proposed, amongst other things, the introduction of a system of legal pluralism into Turkish law,[13] in particular the applicability of Shari'ah to Turkish Muslims:

> We want despotism to be abolished. There must be several legal systems. The citizen must be able to choose for himself which legal system is most appropriate for him, within a framework of general principles... – ... Why then, should I be obliged to live according to another's rules? ... – ... The right to choose one's own legal system is an integral part of the freedom of religion.[14]

This proposal was one of the reasons for which the Turkish constitutional court banned the party in 1998. The ban was upheld by the ECtHR, first in a chamber decision and then in the full Court. The Court neatly distinguished individual *conscience* (which is protected) from privately made *law* (which is not):[15]

> [The Court] reiterates that freedom of religion, including the freedom to manifest one's religion by worship and observance, is primarily a matter of individual conscience, and stresses that the sphere of individual conscience is quite different from the field of private law, which concerns the organisation and functioning of society as a whole.

It then went on to conclude that Turkey was free, perhaps even obliged, to prevent the emergence of such privately made law – especially where

---

[12] *Refah Partisi* v. *Turkey*, (2003) 37 EHRR 1.

[13] The ideological basis for such legal pluralism was laid by Ali Bulaç, who in turn invoked the Medina agreement, in which Muhammad granted Jews the right to live by their own laws. See A. Bulaç, 'The Medina Document' in C. Kurzman (ed.), *Liberal Islam – A Sourcebook* (New York: Oxford University Press, 1998), 169–78. For a critique of Bulaç, see T. Akyol, *Medine'den Lozan'a [From Medina to Lausanne]* (Istanbul: AD Yaincilik A.S., 1996) and the book review by S. Özel, 109 *Foreign Policy* (1997–8), 164–6.

[14] *Refah Partisi*, note 12 above, at 28.   [15] *Ibid.*, at 128.

such law would go against the public order and the value of democracy, and especially where it would discriminate against women.[16]

> It has not been disputed before the Court that in Turkey everyone can observe in his private life the requirements of his religion. On the other hand, Turkey, like any other Contracting Party, may legitimately prevent the application within its jurisdiction of private-law rules of religious inspiration prejudicial to public order and the values of democracy for Convention purposes (such as rules permitting discrimination based on the gender of the parties concerned, as in polygamy and privileges for the male sex in matters of divorce and succession).

Reduced to contract, privately made law is obviously subject to mandatory state law:[17]

> The freedom to enter into contracts cannot encroach upon the State's role as the neutral and impartial organiser of the exercise of religions, faiths and beliefs.

In opposing legal pluralism, the Court, quoting at length from its own earlier Chamber decision, brings classical tropes of liberalism: individualism, individual rights, state neutrality (in particular the separation of church and state), and non-discrimination:[18]

> ... the Court considers that Refah's proposal that there should be a plurality of legal systems would introduce into all legal relationships a distinction between individuals grounded on religion, would categorise everyone according to his religious beliefs and would allow him rights and freedoms not as an individual but according to his allegiance to a religious movement.
>
> The Court takes the view that such a societal model cannot be considered compatible with the Convention system for two reasons.
>
> Firstly, it would do away with the State's role as the guarantor of individual rights and freedoms and the impartial organiser of the practice of the various beliefs and religions in a democratic society, since it would oblige individuals to obey, not rules laid down by the State in the exercise of its above-mentioned functions, but static rules of law imposed by the religion concerned. But the State has a positive obligation to ensure that everyone within its jurisdiction enjoys in full, and without being able to waive them, the rights and freedoms guaranteed by the Convention.
>
> Secondly, such a system would undeniably infringe the principle of non-discrimination between individuals as regards their enjoyment of public

---

[16] *Ibid.*   [17] *Ibid.*   [18] *Ibid.*, at 119.

freedoms, which is one of the fundamental principles of democracy. A difference in treatment between individuals in all fields of public and private law according to their religion or beliefs manifestly cannot be justified under the Convention, and more particularly Article 14 thereof, which prohibits discrimination. Such a difference in treatment cannot maintain a fair balance between, on the one hand, the claims of certain religious groups who wish to be governed by their own rules and on the other the interest of society as a whole, which must be based on peace and on tolerance between the various religions and beliefs.

The result is in many ways contradictory. In the end, the Court upholds, in the name of democracy, the banning of a party that has been elected by democratic means.[19] In the name of liberal tolerance, it finds intolerable the existence of a party that holds certain values that it does not approve of. In the name of protecting suppressed groups (women) it upholds the repression of other groups (political Muslims). In order to protect the agency and freedom of women, it effectively strips these women, many of whom had voted for the welfare party, of agency.[20] And in the name of self-determination and freedom of contract, it rejects the self-determination exercised by choosing non-state law to govern oneself.

And the decision has other problems, too. In particular, the depiction of Shari'ah as stable and invariable is inaccurate.[21] Its view that Shari'ah is necessarily incompatible with democracy is therefore at least doubtful, especially when we consider other parties that have passed muster. The argument against discrimination is put into question by the fact that there was an unusually high number of women among Refah Partisi's supporters.[22]

---

[19] I leave open the question how well Turkish democracy functions; for doubts in the context of Refah Partisi, see M. Kamrava, 'Pseudo-democratic politics and populist possibilities: The rise and demise of Turkey's Refah Party', 25 *British Journal of Middle Eastern Studies* (1998), 275–301.

[20] For criticism of the lack of agency in the critique of Islam see, for example, S. Mahmood, 'Feminist theory, embodiment, and the docile agent: Some reflections on the Egyptian Islamic revival', 16 *Cultural Anthropology* (2001), 202–36.

[21] *Refah Partisi*, note 12 above, at 123. For a critique of such assumptions of invariability in the decision, see e.g. A. Büchler, *Islamic Law in Europe? Legal Pluralism and its Limits in European Family Laws* (Farnham: Ashgate, 2011), p. 92; more generally L. Gannagé, 'Droit immobile ou droit en mouvement? Quelques remarques à propos du droit musulman' in *Études à la memoire du Professeur Bruno Oppetit* (Paris: LexisNexis Litec, 2008), pp 203–46.

[22] Y. Arat, *Rethinking Islam and Liberal Democracy: Islamist Women In Turkish Politics* (Albany: State University of New York Press, 2005).

2.2. Societal and legal pluralism

But is the Court really anti-pluralist, or anti-liberal, as critics have suggested? Notably, the Court, like its sister institution, the European Court of Justice, has in the past emphasized the importance of pluralism.[23] As early as 1976, the ECtHR emphasized the need to protect 'pluralism, tolerance and broadmindedness without which there is no "democratic society"' through the protection of free speech.[24] For the Court, this encompasses pluralism of the media, pluralism of political parties and other associations, pluralism of thoughts and of religions, pluralism of education, etc. Indeed, the Court of Justice has emphasized such pluralism, which we may call societal pluralism, as a necessary element of a democratic society.[25]

Moreover, the Court has not confined protection to individuals, especially in the area of religious freedoms. Instead, the self-determination of religious groups (the ground on which Refah Partisi proponents based their claim for legal pluralism) has long been a cornerstone of the Court's case law; arguably, for some time it was even more prominent than individual protection.[26] Religious freedom is not just an individual right, it is also a right of communities (and of institutionalized churches).[27] Thus, churches have been allowed to determine their own leaders, independently of the state government.[28] Churches have been allowed to dismiss their

---

[23] For the ECtHR, see A. Nieuwenhuis, 'The concept of pluralism in the case-law of the European Court of Human Rights', 3 *European Constitutional Law Review* (2007), 367–84. More doubtful, but with a different perspective, is M. Everson, 'Social pluralism and the European Court of Justice: A court between a rock and a hard place', 8 *Journal of Legislative Studies* 4 (2002), 98–116.

[24] *Handyside* v. *UK*, 7 December 1976, 1 EHRR 737, para. 49.

[25] Case C–288/89 *Collectieve Antennevoorziening Gouda* [1991] ECR I–4007, para. 23; Case C–148/91 *Veronica Omroep Organisatie* [1993] ECR I–487, para. 10; Case C–23/93 *TV10* [1994] ECR I–4795, para. 19; Case C–250/06 *United Pan-Europe Communications Belgium and Others* [2007] ECR I–11135, para. 41; and Case C–336/07 *Kabel Deutschland Vertrieb und Service GmbH & Co. KG* v. *Niedersächsische Landesmedienanstalt für privaten Rundfunk* [2008] ECR I–10889.

[26] B Meyler, 'Religious institutions and religious minorities in international law', *St John's Journal of Legal Commentary* (2007), 535; C. Evans, 'Individual and group religious freedom in the European Court of Human Rights: Cracks in the intellectual architecture', 26 *Journal of Law and Religion* (2010–11), 321–44.

[27] But see R. Schragger and M. Schwarzman, 'Against religious institutionalism', 99 *Virginia Law Review* (2013) 917–86, and the response by P. Horwitz, 'Defending (religious) institutions', 99 *Virginia Law Review* (2013) 1049–64.

[28] *Hasan and Chaush* v. *Bulgaria* (App. No. 30985/96) (2002) 34 EHRR 55.

employees for conduct in violation of religious norms, like separation from one's spouse or extramarital affairs.[29]

Notably, such a focus on groups is compatible with most versions of liberalism. Recognition of religions as groups would be incompatible with liberalism only if liberalism were understood as interested exclusively in the individual, and thus hostile to any group. But such a concept of liberalism, if it was ever defensible, no longer represents the exclusive understanding of liberalism today. In one concept of liberalism, influenced by Gierke and Maitland, groups, institutions, can themselves be bearers of rights.[30] But even liberals who would not go so far as to treat groups and communities just as though they were individuals nevertheless account for them. For example, in the kind of liberalism promoted by Will Kymlicka, recognition is granted not just to individuals, but also to groups.[31] This seems plausible (though not unproblematic) even from an individualist position: if groups are not recognized, this curtails at the same time the individual freedom to participate in such groups. In this sense, Kymlicka's plea for the recognition of groups is a recognition of the rights of their members, not of the groups as such.

Still, the important question remains. Does the recognition granted to groups that is at least compatible with, and possibly required by, liberalism, encompass the recognition of these groups' ability to make law, or to choose another law to govern them than that of a state? In other words, does societal pluralism require legal pluralism? The answer is not obvious. Note that the concept of pluralism that the Court employs is not *legal* pluralism but *societal* pluralism.[32] Societal pluralism, at least in the sense in which the Court and its commentators use the term, is the idea that

---

[29] *Schüth* v. *Germany* (App. No. 1620/03) (2011) 52 EHRR 32; *Obst* v. *Germany* (App. No. 425/03) 23 September 2010, nyr.

[30] H. Laski, 'On the personality of associations' in *The Foundations of Sovereignty and Other Essays* (New York: Harcourt, Brace and Company, 1921).

[31] E.g. W. Kymlicka, *Liberalism, Community and Culture* (Oxford: Clarendon Press, 1989); Kymlicka, *Multicultural Citizenship* (Oxford: Oxford University Press, 1996); cf. C. Taylor, *Multiculturalism and 'The Politics of Recognition': An Essay by Charles Taylor* (Princeton, NJ: Princeton University Press, 1992). This, of course, is a contentious issue. For a powerful opposition, see G. Kateb, 'Notes on pluralism', (1994) 61 *Social Research*, 511–34, reprinted in Kateb, *Patriotism and Other Mistakes* (New Haven, CT: Yale University Press, 2006), pp 21–40.

[32] The Court often speaks of political instead of societal pluralism, but that is a misleading term. A different understanding of political pluralism would link it to the tradition especially of the British pluralists. See A. I. Eisenberg, *Reconstructing Political Pluralism* (Albany: SUNY Press 1995); J. T. Levy, 'From liberal constitutionalism to pluralism' in

the liberal and democratic state must tolerate and recognize diversity – of viewpoints, of groups, of media, etc. Such diversity is not only what liberalism supports. It is what liberalism is grounded upon. This is not the same as *legal* pluralism – the idea that there are plural legal orders, not all of them state law. The question for legal pluralism is not whether groups are granted some type of autonomy, but whether that autonomy is supposed to include lawmaking power.

3. State liberalism and the doubly weak legal pluralism

Our question is not, then, whether liberalism must be pluralist. The answer is yes, it must, at least in the sense described above. The question is whether this *societal* pluralism that is intrinsic to liberalism in turn necessitates *legal* pluralism.

Some people have suggested this. For them, recognition of political, cultural, and religious pluralism – a hallmark of political liberalism – necessitates legal pluralism.[33] Intellectuals belonging to Refah Partisi had argued similarly.[34] The Court, as we have seen, takes the exact opposite view. It suggests, at least implicitly, that liberalism can be guaranteed only through the *denial* of legal status to normative orders other than itself. According to this argument, the liberal state is able to accommodate plurality of groups, views, cultures, precisely because it refuses legal pluralism. It requires its superior position for its own way of accommodation. Consider again this passage from the decision:[35]

> The Court takes the view that such a societal model . . . would do away with the State's role as the guarantor of individual rights and freedoms and the impartial organiser of the practice of the various beliefs and religions in a democratic society, since it would oblige individuals to obey, not rules laid down by the State in the exercise of its above-mentioned functions, but static rules of law imposed by the religion concerned. But the State has a positive obligation to ensure that everyone within its jurisdiction enjoys

M. Bevir (ed.) *Modern Pluralism: Anglo-American Debates since 1880* (Cambridge: Cambridge University Press, 2012), p. 21. See also Bengoetxea in Chapter 6 of this volume.

[33] J. Gadirov, 'Freedom of religion and legal pluralism' in T. Loenen and J. E. Goldschmidt (eds) *Religious Pluralism and Human Rights in Europe: Where to Draw the Line?* (Antwerp: Intersentia, 2007), pp 81–95. See also F. Tulkens, 'The European Convention on Human Rights and church–state relations. Pluralism vs. pluralism', 30 *Cardozo Law Review* (2008–9), 2575–91.

[34] B. Zengin, *Özgürleserek Birlikte Yasamak* (Ankara: Birleşik Yayıncılık, 1995), pp 87–93.

[35] *Refah Partisi*, note 12 above, at 119.

in full, and without being able to waive them, the rights and freedoms guaranteed by the Convention.

What makes the liberal state liberal, in this conception, is precisely its ability to allow for plurality *without* recognizing separate legal orders.

3.1. Accommodation of non-state law in the liberal state

Actually, the case is more complicated than this in more than one way. The first is this: The liberal state is open to non-state normative orders, but it usually denies them the status of law and recognizes them as something other than law. It is worth remembering that legal pluralism is not the only way in which the normative commitments of minority groups could be accommodated in a liberal way. The state has various other ways of accommodating non-state rules without recognizing them as law, as I demonstrate elsewhere.[36] The state does not ignore non-state law, but it treats it in a special way: It 'restates' these norms by translating or even transposing them into the semantics of its own system.

One such mode is *incorporation*: the copying of non-state norms into state-based norms, for example in the form of a commercial code. A famous (though disputed) example for this is the law merchant, which was allegedly incorporated into the common law. A second mode is *deference*: the transformation of non-state laws into facts, for example by treating the law merchant as custom. A third mode is *delegation*: the transformation of non-state law into subordinated law, for example by allowing commerce, in the form of contract autonomy, a space for the development of autonomous norms – norms that achieve their validity, from the state's perspective, only because and insofar as the state recognizes them as such.

Islamic law has, in fact, played all three roles *vis-à-vis* the state. It has, obviously, been incorporated into the law of Islamic states[37] – which has

---

[36] R. Michaels, 'The re-state-ment of non-state law: The state, choice of law, and the challenge from global legal pluralism', 51 *Wayne Law Review* (2005) 1209, at 1227–35. For a more extended list, see W. Twining, 'Normative and legal pluralism: A global perspective', 20 *Duke Journal of Comparative & International Law* (2009–10) 473–518, at 503 (recognition, rejection, incorporation, integration, subordination, assimilation, ignorance). Yet a different list on the relation between state and non-state judicial or quasi-judicial institutions is given by M. Forsyth, 'A typology of relationships between state and non-state justice systems', 56 *Journal of Legal Pluralism* (2007), 67–112.

[37] J. M. Otto, *Sharia Incorporated: A Comparative Overview of the Legal Systems of Twelve Muslim Countries in Past and Present* (Amsterdam: Amsterdam University Press, 2011).

posed a challenge not just to state law but also to the nature of Islamic law.[38] Deference to Islamic law exists, as well – not just in Islamic countries, but also in the West. Take only the references to *murabaha* and *musharaka*, both Islamic financing devices, in the UK Finance Acts 2005 and 2006.[39] In view of the rise of Islamic banking, and competition for investors who want to invest in accordance with Islamic law, several countries, including France and the UK, adapted their tax laws to take these developments into account. Delegation, finally, is perhaps the trickiest of the three issues, because it is the most contested. The discussions over faith-based arbitration in Ontario and the UK concerned suggestions of such delegations.[40]

There is, then, a certain (though limited) readiness of states to give some recognition to Islamic law – as long as this recognition does not grant the status of law. I demonstrate elsewhere why, in principle, it seems less attractive for a state to recognize a non-state on an equal footing than to recognize another state: only the latter maintains and indeed enhances the states' monopoly on lawmaking.[41] However, sometimes the pressure for recognition from non-state groups may make such recognition necessary. This suggests a dual hypothesis. Presumably, a state will recognize non-state law as law only if the group supporting that law is neither too weak, nor too strong. If the group is too weak, it cannot exert the necessary pressure on the state to be granted the quite substantial privilege of partial legal autonomy. If the group is too strong, on the other hand, the liberal state will feel threatened by it and thus deny legal autonomy as well. At

---

[38] See S. A. Jackson, *Islamic Law and the State: The Constitutional Jurisprudence of Shihāb al-Dīn al-Qarāfī* (Leiden: Brill, 1997).

[39] UK Finance Act 2005 s. 47; UK Finance Act 2006 s. 168. See e.g. A. K. K. Aldohni, *The Legal and Regulatory Aspects of Islamic Banking: A Comparative Look at the United Kingdom and Malaysia* (London: Routledge, 2012).

[40] Two recent collections provide helpful overviews of the respective discussions: A. C. Korteweg and J. A. Selby (eds), *Debating Sharia: Islam, Gender Politics, and Family Law Arbitration* (Toronto: University of Toronto Press, 2012); R. Griffith-Jones (ed.), *Islam and English Law: Rights, Responsibilities and the Place of Shari'a* (Cambridge: Cambridge University Press, 2013). For an insightful analysis of the deference to Islamic arbitration as a sign not of multiculturalism but of neoliberalism, see A. Macklem, 'Multiculturalism meets privatisation: the case of faith-based arbitration', 9 *International Journal of Law in Context* (2013), 343–65.

[41] Michaels, above note 8, at 1243–4. A related argument can be found in A. Shachar and R. Hirschl, 'The new wall of separation: Permitting diversity, restricting competition', 30 *Cardozo Law Review* (2009), 2535–60 (with examples from Canada and South Africa).

most, the liberal state will recognize a non-state legal order insofar as that order does not challenge its (the state's) predominance.[42]

3.2. The weak pluralism consistent with liberalism

The first precondition set by the liberal state is this: The non-state law to be recognized must be hierarchically inferior to the state's own law. If non-state law is inferior to all state law, we have a situation of legal pluralism that exists in all legal orders that give a subsidiary role to custom and the like. But non-state law remains inferior even when it is on an equal footing with state law but subject to the constitution. This is so because the constitution remains tied to the state.

A summary look around the world suggests that different states view this question differently.[43] States like India and Israel, famously, endorse such weak legal pluralism – they recognize religious law as law, but maintain certain checks on the application of such religious laws. Other states, like Canada and the UK, after long debates, have decided not to grant the status of law to religious law (in particular Islamic law).[44] Many factors may contribute to the variance – colonial history (including the British heritage of indirect rule), historical specificities, contingent political decisions made in the past, perhaps also the heightened fear in the West of Islam (as opposed to other religions). However, we can observe some regularities. The first of these seems to be this: States, typically, prefer granting group freedom through mere political pluralism, instead of legal pluralism, because this makes it easier for them to control the group. In order to be able to claim the status of law, the religious group must be so strong that its claims *vis-à-vis* the state have weight. A marginal, minor, religious group will rarely achieve law status.

This kind of accommodation of non-state law as inferior is what legal pluralists call 'weak legal pluralism.' Weak pluralism is opposed to strong

---

[42] This is the implicit position e.g. in A. Shachar, *Multicultural Jurisdictions. Cultural Differences and Women's Rights* (Cambridge: Cambridge University Press, 2001) and in S. Benhabib, *The Claims of Culture. Equality and Diversity in the Global Era* (Princeton, NJ: Princeton University Press, 2002). See also S. Benhabib, 'Beyond interventionism and indifference. Culture, deliberation and pluralism', 31 *Philosophy & Social Criticism* November (2005) 753–71, at 758–63.

[43] See, in general, W. Menski, *Comparative Law in a Global Context: The Legal Systems of Asia and Africa* (Cambridge: Cambridge University Press 2006).

[44] Above note 40.

legal pluralism, which denotes a situation in which non-state law is not subordinated to state law.[45] This means not only that non-state law is inferior to the state in some unspecific way. It also means, more importantly, that the validity of non-state law, its character as 'law', follows not from some intrinsic nature but instead from its recognition by the state. And this means that this validity is also limited: Non-state law is valid only insofar as it is recognized as such by the state. Islamic law, according to this conception, can perhaps be recognized as law, but only insofar as its norms do not violate the rules of state law – in particular those on the treatment of women. In an important way, thus, non-state orders are not treated as law at all. Instead, they are more akin to contracts, or perhaps corporate charters.

This not only limits the content of non-state law, it also impacts its nature. What 'weak' legal pluralists ask for is recognition of non-state law: The state creates and administers legal pluralism through the recognition of non-state law. This recognition is often less innocent, or benevolent, than one may think.[46] In the colonial context it has been shown that often local, 'customary' law was not taken as found, but rather was created through the very act of recognition. This act of recognition-creation changed the nature of prior custom into law and thereby regularly changed it. This is a violent act in more than one regard: First, because information about the assumed non-state law requires informants, the act of recognition empowered certain informants whom the colonizers chose, and disempowered other members of the group, often those with whom the informants had been in contest before. Since culture is always internally contested, an outside observer cannot recognize the content of a culture without interfering in these internal negotiations. Second, recognition is a form of domestication of the other – a way of managing legal culture by subordinating it to the state's own system and logic. The well-meant attempts to codify African customary law are a good example of a setting in which the recognition and management of customary law amounted to its invention.

Duncan Ivison has indeed argued that such weak legal pluralism (which he tellingly calls liberal legal pluralism) is a continuation of colonialism:

---

[45] See Griffiths, 'What is legal pluralism?', above note 1, at 5–8.

[46] See also R. Bolens, R. Bustamante and H. de Vos, 'Legal pluralism and the politics of inclusion: Recognition and contestation of local water rights in the Andes' in B. van Koppen, M. Giordano, and J. Butterworth (eds), *Community-based Water Law and Water Resource Management. Reform in Developing Countries* (Oxfordshire: CABI, 2007), pp 96–113, especially pp 99–101.

Liberal legal pluralism, on this reading, is basically a means of re-subordinating marginal groups within a legal system that leaves their substantive disadvantage intact. Liberal pluralism might be subtle and less heavy-handed than earlier forms of colonialism, but liberal multicultural government (understood in the broadest sense of the term) is basically continuous with it.[47]

This problem can be observed in the *Refah Partisi* case. The recognition of 'Islam' as a legal system is very unspecific. It would work little harm if Islamic law were a clearly identifiable entity (like French law) but in fact it is not. It does not seem irrational to assume that the Welfare Party had a particular conception of Islamic law in mind, and it seems quite possible that this conception might not be to the liking of many Turkish Muslims whose understanding of Islam is different. If so, then these Muslims might be better off with a system in which 'Islamic law' is *not* recognized as a separate legal system, because their own freedom of religion may actually be greater *vis-à-vis* the state than *vis-à-vis* some possibly intolerant definition by the Welfare Party.

3.3. Minority and majority pluralism

This suggests why Griffiths could say that weak legal pluralism – non-state orders that are subject to recognition by the state – is not really legal pluralism at all. It does not suggest, however, why such legal pluralism should be a problem for the state, if it only enhances the power of the state. Why could the ECtHR not have allowed such a weak legal pluralism? Judge Kovler's concurring opinion rightly deplored that the Court did not analyze legal pluralism more fully.[48] Indeed, critics have suggested that legal pluralism would be compatible with, perhaps even beneficial to, democracy in Turkey.[49] In their view, the liberal legal state may even be required to grant a limited degree of legal pluralism, because a right to a religious legal order emerges from the right to religious freedom. Earlier, I have suggested that such an argument confuses legal with societal

---

[47] D. Ivison, 'Introduction: Multiculturalism as a public ideal' in Ivison (ed.), *The Ashgate Research Companion to Multiculturalism* (Farnham: Ashgate, 2010), pp 1 and 4.

[48] See *Refah Partisi*, note 12 above.

[49] E.g. K. Meerschaut and S. Gutwirth, 'Legal pluralism and Islam in the scales of the European Court of Human Rights: The limits of categorical balancing' in E. Brems (ed.), *Conflicts between fundamental rights* (Antwerp: Intersentia, 2008), pp 431–65; see also E. Hughes, *Turkey's Accession to the European Union: The Politics of Exclusion?* (London: Routledge 2010), p. 170.

pluralism. The Court makes a plausible point when it suggests that the freedom of religion encompasses freedom to act, not freedom to live by one's own laws. Quite arguably, then, freedom of religion does not *require* the recognition of non-state law as law. But this does not answer the question why the state is so afraid of a weak legal pluralism. Would it not strengthen, rather than weaken, the liberal state to recognize religious law as law?

The answer, I suggest, lies in a second regularity concerning the relation between the liberal state and the non-state group. In the previous section I suggested that such groups will only see their norms be recognized as law if the group is strong enough. Here, I want to suggest that the group will find such recognition denied if it is *too* strong. The religious group must not be so strong that its claim for an autonomous legal order could in fact threaten the actual superiority of the state.

This has to do with the requirements of weak legal pluralism. It is not enough for the state to assume *normative* superiority over non-state law. It also requires *effective* superiority over non-state law. If the state lacks the power to subordinate the non-state group, it will view that group as a challenger, and will not be willing to strengthen it by giving it legal autonomy. Here is the connection between (limits to) legal pluralism and militant democracy.[50] The idea of militant democracy suggests that democratic states will limit democracy if such limits are deemed necessary for democracy at large to prevail. The fear of legal pluralism in *Refah Partisi* arises from the fear that Refah Partisi did not merely want to subordinate Islamic law to the state, it also wanted to change the nature of the state itself. (A similar fear appears to underlie the strong opposition to Islamic law in Western countries, like the USA and France.)

Whether such a fear is justified or not is beyond this chapter (though, arguably, it should not have been beyond the Court's reasoning). Here, the Court's rejection of a legal pluralism may have been inspired by the expectation that such recognition would not in fact amount to subordination, that what Refah Partisi wanted was, rather, establishment of Islamic law as state law – whether openly (which would likely be unconstitutional) or clandestinely.

---

[50] P. Macklem, 'Militant democracy, legal pluralism, and the paradox of self-determination', 4 *International Journal of Constitutional Law* (2006), 488–516; J. Gadirov, 'The principles of legal pluralism and militant democracy' in W. Cole Durham, Jr et al. (eds), *Islam, Europe and Emerging Legal Issues* (Farnham: Ashgate, 2012), pp 273–90.

4. Neo-liberalism and strong legal pluralism

This is not the end of the analysis, however. It is still possible that strong legal pluralism is compatible with legal pluralism, too. Maybe, the true foe of strong legal pluralism is not liberalism in a general sense, but liberalism in a particular form that can be called state liberalism.[51] The court of a state, like the Turkish Constitutional Court, will necessarily take the perspective of the state, and thus of state liberalism. The ECtHR, in endorsing this position, replicates the idea of liberalism as mediated and guaranteed by the state.

4.1. The precarious role of the state

Of course, state liberalism is not the only perspective of liberalism. We can also think of a liberalism that is not tied to the state but transcends it. Such liberalism – I will refer to it here as neo-liberalism, without wanting to engage in a more specific definition – could indeed, prima facie, be compatible with strong legal pluralism. Just as strong legal pluralism emphasizes that the state is not automatically hierarchically superior to non-state law, so neo-liberalism emphasizes that the state is only one of many legitimate orders, and not automatically normatively (or empirically) superior to private institutions or groups, like corporations, or markets. Under neo-liberalism, the state is not the guarantor of the freedom of the market; instead, the state itself is subject to the forces of the market, and finds its justification against them. I am, for the sake of simplicity, using ideal types here. But the difference between state liberalism and neo-liberalism, in this sense, could be summarized thus: Whereas in state liberalism the idea is that maximum freedom is guaranteed through the framework that the state provides, in neo-liberalism the idea is that maximum freedom is guaranteed through subjecting the state itself to the forces of the market.

Neo-liberalism, in this view, has its origins in classical liberalism, but it finds its particular characteristics in a certain understanding of globalization. Viewed in this way, states have been, if not weakened, then at least fundamentally transformed under the impact of globalization. This transformation concerns both their actual role and their normative

---

[51] State liberalism in this sense is connected with what Samuel Freeman calls 'high... liberalism': Freeman, 'Illiberal libertarians: Why libertarianism is not a liberal view', *Philosophy and Public Affairs* (2001) 105–51, at 106.

justification.[52] Concerning their actual role, states can no longer claim (if they ever could) to have the power to regulate everything. Their territorial character makes them weak in the face of general deterritorializing tendencies, be they in the area of communication (the Internet), people (migration), or markets (multinational corporations, global markets). In addition, states do not stand side by side in relative isolation; instead, they compete with each other over investment. Concerning their normative justification, states are still expected to guarantee maximum freedom, just as in state liberalism. What is new is that such freedom is no longer owed merely to the state's own citizens, but to all people and actors. And it is no longer, primarily, a political freedom, but instead an economic freedom.

4.2. The precarious role of non-state law

Now, neo-liberalism and legal pluralism do share an obvious affinity. This affinity can be found in arguments for a new *lex mercatoria* – a law made not by states but by markets, deriving its legitimacy not from deference by the state but instead from the consent of all its participants.[53] Such a *lex mercatoria*, it is often argued, is superior to state law, at least insofar as merchants (or their modern equivalent, multinational corporations) are concerned. Merchants, it is said, should be entitled to opt out of state regulation altogether, and instead find their dealings regulated entirely by their own legal rules, created through the process of the market. Proponents of *lex mercatoria* frequently invoke legal pluralism, although their economic law has relatively little to do with old community-based sets of norms as found in the colonial context. (If the community of merchants were an actual community in this sense, it would certainly run foul of anti-trust laws.)[54] What *lex mercatoria* shares with those other non-state laws is that it is a non-state normative order – and,

---

[52] For the distinction between empirical, theoretical, and ideological dimensions of globalization, see R. Michaels, 'Globalisation and law: Law beyond the state', in R. Banakar and M. Travers (eds), *Law and Social Theory*, 2nd edn (Oxford: Hart, 2013), pp 287–304 at 289, 290–95.

[53] For a critical analysis, see A. C. Cutler, *Private Power and Global Authority: Transnational Merchant Law in the Global Political Economy* (Cambridge: Cambridge University Press, 2003).

[54] As can ethnic communities when they engage in economic conduct. See B. D. Richman, 'The antitrust of reputation mechanisms: Institutional economics and concerted refusals to deal', 95 *Virginia Law Review* (2009), 325–87.

relatedly, that it merges law and society in ways unfamiliar from state legal positivism.[55]

But ethnic or religious communities can profit from neo-liberalism, too.[56] The Turkish Welfare Party presented a fascinating mix of resistance to globalization (and the decline of the welfare state) with, at the same time, the emergence of another kind of globalization movement, namely that of political Islam.[57] Contemporary Islam, too, is a globalization movement. The perceived threat from legal pluralism in the *Refah Partisi* judgment may not just have been that Islamists might take over the state. Instead, the fear may have been that a certain view of Islam might question governance by the state altogether.[58] Arguably, much of the current conflict between state laws (in Europe as in the Arab world) and so-called radical Islam is less about different substantive values and more about the primacy of the territorial state over the community-based (and transnational) religious group. There has always been a strand in Islam that aimed not at appropriating the state so much as overcoming it altogether, in the name of a transnational Islamic community, the *umma*.[59]

Both *lex mercatoria* and Islamic law present radical threats to the state. This makes their somewhat inconsistent treatment by state courts surprising. The threat is clearly recognized and quite likely exaggerated in *Refah Partisi*. It is taken far less seriously in the deference that is given *de facto* to non-state economic law, in particular international arbitration.

But does such a threat to the state's dominance already favor legal pluralism? Note that many view neo-liberalism not as a boon for but as a threat to legal pluralism. The non-state legal orders that such critics view as endangered are not, typically, economic orders like *lex mercatoria*, nor strong religious laws like Islamic law. Instead, the critics see a threat for smaller, local and community-based legal orders. The fear is, here,

---

[55] See P. Zumbansen, 'Transnational legal pluralism', 1 *Transnational Legal Theory* (2010), 141–89; Macklem, note 40 above.

[56] See O. Roy, *Globalized Islam: The Search for a New Ummah* (New York: Columbia University Press, 2006).

[57] See H. Gülalp, 'Globalization and political Islam: The social bases of Turkey's Welfare Party', 33 *International Journal of Middle East Studies* (2001), 433–48.

[58] On the complex relation between state and Islam, see W. B. Hallaq, *The Impossible State: Islam, Politics, and Modernity's Moral Predicament* (New York: Columbia University Press, 2012).

[59] P. Mandaville, *Transnational Muslim Politics: Reimagining the Umma* (London: Routledge, 2003).

that the dominance of the market will atomize local communities and reduce their members into market participants. Small communities in particular, it is feared, cannot withstand the powers of globalization. Law and development are viewed as insufficiently attentive to non-state law, focusing too exclusively on the state as the agent of change.[60] Beyond the market (defined through contract) and the state (defined through state law), no other legal systems seem available. And similar concerns exist *vis-à-vis* Islamic law. Historically, Islamic law was open to a legal pluralism that recognized other legal orders, but this attitude may have weakened its economic success.[61] Nowadays, Islamic legal scholars are not always so tolerant of other laws. Refah Partisi may have presented Islamic law as a choice for believing Muslims, but the choice of laws other than Islamic law does not always find the same favor with Islamic legal scholars.

4.3. The centrality of power

In the end, then, neo-liberalism is not necessarily more favorable towards a true legal pluralism than is state liberalism. Indeed, on closer inspection the problems of state liberalism and neo-liberalism tend to resemble each other. The problem with state liberalism was that the state retained its dominance, thereby reducing non-state laws to secondary legal orders. The problem with neo-liberalism might be that strong non-state orders retain their dominance, thereby reducing weak non-state laws to secondary legal orders. Once the state is reduced in importance, it can no longer threaten non-state laws, but also it can no longer protect them. Neo-liberalism favors non-state law, but only non-state law of the kind that is strong enough to hold its own under the pressures of globalization.

In the legal pluralism literature, this radicalism of neo-liberalism is not always, it seems, fully acknowledged. Mattias Kumm, for example, gestures towards neo-liberalism when he suggests 'that the liberal ideal of the Rule of Law is analytically divorced from the conception of the sovereign nation state, with whom *[sic]* it was wedded as a matter of

---

[60] See P. Orebech, F. Bosselman, J. Bjarup, D. Callies, M. Chanock, and H. Petersen, *The Role of Customary Law in Sustainable Development* (Cambridge: Cambridge University Press, 2006); B. Z. Tamanaha, C. Sage, and M. Woolcock (eds), *Legal Pluralism and Development: Scholars and Practitioners in Dialogue* (Cambridge: Cambridge University Press, 2012).

[61] Thus at least the argument in T. Kuran, *The Long Divergence: How Islamic Law Held Back the Middle East* (Princeton, NJ: Princeton University Press 2010), p. 228ff.

historical contingency only'.[62] But in the end he places his liberalism somewhere between the state and the EU as a quasi-state, not truly outside the state. Similarly, Berman may explicitly reject a monopolistic position of the state. But even if he leaves the state behind, he does not really leave the state paradigm behind. In the end, all his strategies for 'managing legal pluralism' are not just addressed explicitly to the state; his managerialism also presupposes some superior position from which such management is possible.[63]

The challenge of neo-liberalism (and, incidentally, also of strong legal pluralism) is that such management is not possible, at least not from a central position or even in a strictly coordinated way. This is a hope for radical anarchists in the tradition of Austrian economics. It may also be a hope for radical Islamists. But neither the totalitarianism of the market nor the totalitarianism of one religion would be truly pluralist. Whether legal pluralists, be they of the liberal kind or not, are really willing to embrace such a brave new world is an open question as well. Until and unless they are, I think, the compatibility of legal pluralism with liberalism cannot be demonstrated.

5. Conclusion

In one way, the result is trivially simple. It turns out that there are two concepts of liberalism: state liberalism and what I call here neo-liberalism. Likewise, there are two concepts of legal pluralism: weak and strong legal pluralism. State liberalism is compatible only with weak legal pluralism, because both of them rest on a central position for the state. Similarly, neo-liberalism and strong legal pluralism are compatible, at least in one way: both of them overcome the normative superiority of the state. If, in talking about legal pluralism and liberalism, we want to become clearer in the use of our concepts, we need to take these respective compatibilities into account.

But the trivially simple result carries with it important insights. Griffith's criticism of weak legal pluralism as subordinated to the state was based on a critique of the state, but certainly not of the kind that we find in neo-liberalism. The state is undoubtedly an imperfect guarantor of legal pluralism, and the *Refah Partisi* decision makes this amply clear. But neo-liberalism does not necessarily present greater hope for

---

[62] Kumm, above note 6, at 374.
[63] Berman, above note 9. See also Galán and Patterson, note 9 above, at 798.

true legal pluralism. As a theory of relentless competition, it does not guarantee what legal pluralists hope for: relative autonomy of different legal systems. Instead, it puts such systems under constant pressure to justify themselves against the forces of competition. And it implies the possibility – indeed, the likelihood – that dominant legal systems will come to dominate weaker ones. In state liberalism, the dominant legal system is that of the state. In neo-liberalism, the dominant legal system is, eventually, some global economic law.

In the end, then, it seems that Griffiths was right: liberalism and legal pluralism remain incompatible. Both state liberalism and neo-liberalism have insufficient means to protect the autonomy of weak, non-state legal orders. This may or may not be more attractive for the world, and I take no position on this here. But it is not certain that this is more attractive for legal pluralism. Liberal legal pluralism remains an incoherent concept.

PART II

European Law

6

Rethinking EU law in the light of pluralism and practical reason

JOXERRAMON BENGOETXEA

1. Overture – rethinking 'official law' and 'pluralism' in the EU

This chapter discusses two sets of interrelated contrasts that give interesting insights when analysed comparatively in an endeavour to rethink law and legal thinking, especially in the European Union context: legal plurality vs. legal pluralism on one hand and cultural plurality vs. multiculturalism on the other. The analytical argument is that legal and cultural *plurality* are ideas or concepts linked to sociological, cognitive, theoretical or descriptive interest whereas legal and constitutional *pluralism* or *multiculturalism* are better understood as normative concepts, even though their usage is sometimes meant theoretically and descriptively.

1.1. Plurality and pluralism

The term 'pluralism' has two distinct dimensions that can be confused: one is descriptive or interpretative and it identifies diversity or plurality in law and in society; the other is normative and it provides a solution, a programme or a proposal to deal with such diversity and plurality: either to see it as a challenge (or as a dissonance)[1] and then try to solve it, or

Research for this paper has been carried out in the framework of a research project on the Lisbon Treaty and fundamental rights protection (MiCin, der2010–19715), funded by the Spanish Ministry for Sciences and Innovation. The author is also a member of the Consolidated Research Group on fundamental rights in the EU (GIC07/86-IT-448-07) financed by the Basque Autonomous Government.

[1] A. Somek, 'The emancipation of legal dissonance' in H. Koch, K. Hagel-Sørensen, U. Haltern and J. H. H. Weiler (eds), *Europe: The New Legal Realism. Essays in Honour of Hjalte Rasmussen* (Copenhagen: Djøf, 2010), pp 679–713 at 712–3:

> Legal science needs to address not only the tricky question of what it takes to adjudicate responsibly, but also to confront the question of what we actually mean by 'law' in the European Union. Do we think that the law is a means of social control? If we do we

to consider diversity and conflict as normal states of affairs and then aim to preserve it, even to celebrate it.[2] Both positions ultimately rely on a different concept of law.[3] Kaarlo Tuori has put it clearly: 'Plurality is not the same as pluralism. . . . Emphasis on overlapping, interpenetration and dialogue is common to interventions espousing constitutional pluralism. The term "plurality", in turn, is neutral with regard to the nature of the relationship between the units making up the plurality. Thus, "plurality" should not be confounded with the idea of self-containment and strict boundary-maintenance of the many constitutions either.'[4]

The pluralist challenge leads to a revision of some fundamental concepts traditionally linked to the identification of state and law, which is one of the classical *topoi* that need rethinking in the theory of law and in constitutional law doctrines. The pluralist challenge shakes three important constitutional implications of the state-centred theory of law:[5]

1. basic features of the legal system like *legal unity* (and the ensuing authority and legitimacy of the constitution, ensuring the place of such unity at the top of the validity chain) are challenged by a plurality of legal orders, of legal systems,[6] and of normative claims based on culture that resist such hierarchical relations;

> may have reason to distinguish law from other forms of control. Alternatively, the law might be conceived of as one method of social problem solving among others, which is continuous with other forms of human co-ordination.

[2] See M. P. Maduro, 'Three claims of constitutional pluralism' in M. Avbelj and J. Komárek (eds), *Constitutional Pluralism in the European Union and Beyond* (Oxford: Hart Publishing, 2012), pp 67–84 at 77: 'As long as the possible conflicts of authority do not lead to disintegration of the European legal order, the pluralist character of European constitutionalism should be met as a welcome discovery and not as a problem in need of a solution.'
[3] R. Alexy, 'Hauptelemente einer Theorie der Doppelnatur des Rechts', *Archiv für Rechts- und Sozialphilosophie* 95 (2009), 151–66.
[4] K. Tuori, 'The many constitutions of Europe' in K. Tuori and S. Sankari (eds), *The Many Constitutions of Europe* (Farnham: Ashgate, 2010), pp 3–30 at 3.
[5] For a critique of state-centred theories of law see N. MacCormick, *Questioning Sovereignty: Law, State, and Nation in the European Commonwealth* (Oxford: Oxford University Press, 1999), Ch. 1.
[6] The distinction between legal order and legal system is not unanimously maintained and has different versions. In its meta-logical version, the system is a reconstructed legal order, which is itself a reconstruction from the valid norms in a given law; legal system would be a higher systematisation, a regulative ideal: see J. Bengoetxea, 'Legal system as regulative ideal', *Archiv für Rechts- und Sozialphilosophie* 53 (1991), 65–80. In another version the legal system includes the legal order but adds the sociological dimension of legal agents or operators. Legal pluralism *stricto sensu* would imply a plurality of legal systems, not just of sources of law, within one society, territory or jurisdictional entity.

2. *ideological coherence*, characterised by the values of the body politic as stated in and interpreted from the constitution, is also threatened by cultural, political and legal plurality of normativities;
3. *national identity* and citizenship, the institution providing the structural link between persons and the body politic through status and political function, is threatened by a new plurality of forms of allegiance and legitimacy (versions of citizenship and identity removed from statehood and nationality).

As a result, the traditional binary logic based on the *summa divisio* – the laws of identity, non-contradiction and the excluded middle[7] – that follow the binary code according to which, for instance, a person cannot be a citizen of two distinct systems and a norm cannot be valid and invalid at the same time – and which informs the whole constitutional project: separation of powers, division of competences, fundamental rights, legality, hierarchy and the rule of law – is also shaken by pluralist phenomena.[8]

Not only have legal pluralistic developments in public *inter*national law – *ius cogens*, human rights and universal jurisdiction, international soft law, alternative dispute resolution systems such as international arbitration, new actors – challenged the still dominant trend to conceptually link state and law,[9] but also, and perhaps more importantly, challenges have been issued by *supra*national phenomena such as European law – i.e. both EU law and the law of the ECHR (the Convention) – or by *trans*national law – *lex mercatoria, lex digitalis, lex sportiva*[10] – or soft law and new governance or multilevel governance,[11] even by constitutional principles that inspire the structure of power and the distribution of

---

[7] See P. Glenn, 'Sustainable diversity in law', *Hague Journal on the Rule of Law* 3 (2011), 39–56; see also Glenn in Chapter 2 of this volume.
[8] This statement is not meant as an objection to system theories (Luhmann, Teubner). In pluralist situations the validity of a norm belonging to a system can be explained in terms of how closed or open the system is. However, closed systems of law simultaneously operative in a society do seem to strengthen a radical legal pluralism.
[9] J. Bengoetxea, 'L'État, c'est fini?', *Rechtstheorie* 15 (1993), 93–108.
[10] See Tuori in Chapter 1 of this volume.
[11] Again, new governance refers to a multiplicity of actors besides public actors or institutions involved in norm- and policy-making and application; and to the interactions – networks, cooperation, coordination, delegation, participation, consultation etc. – between these actors. Multilevel governance refers to the multiple, institutional, norm and policy decision-making spheres, from the local to the international where this multiplicity of actors and procedures interact. The literature on EU governance is immense since the seminal work by C. Joerges and R. Dehousse (eds), *Good Governance in Europe's Integrated Market* (Oxford: Oxford University Press, 2002).

competences in territorially complex states but that can equally be applied to suprastate organisations, such as federalism, asymmetric federalism, variable geometry, multiple speed integration and subsidiarity.

1.2. A pluralist theory of law

The distinction between the descriptive, cognitive and interpretative dimensions – analysing plurality or diversity – and the normative dimensions – advocating, tolerating or rejecting pluralism in the legal sphere – is relevant for rethinking the 'legal'. A background theory of law is required in order first to identify phenomena as legal or law-related and to be able to conceive of soft law, customary law and 'other' normative forms alongside official law; second, to postulate that such phenomena belong to different legal 'orders'; and third, to assert that such 'legal' orders coexist and operate simultaneously, albeit not with the same intensity and effectiveness, in the same society – in the same jurisdiction, thus leading to different normative contentions concerning rights, obligations and legal positions of actors. This pluralist theory of law can be state-centred and oriented towards official sources and jurisdictions, even interstate centred; in other words, more focused on the surface level of law; or it can be hermeneutic and interpretative and focus more on the deeper layers such as legal culture, or the deeper, sedimentary level.[12]

A pluralist, surface-based concept of law will elaborate on the plurality and diversity of sources of law – custom, principles, legislation, regulation, treaties and soft law. Custom and general principles of law are sources of law incorporating plurality and diversity in the system by opening it to social norms; but could they be operating as sources of other normative orders – religion, morality – in the same, pluralistic, society? A pluralist, hermeneutic concept of law will see law as embedded in the domain of practical reason and will look for the plurality of normative orders and aspirations to justice that each order represents in a multicultural, pluralist and complex society. A plurality of legal cultures can also obtain within this type of society, and some of these legal cultures can share important elements while diverging in other respects. MacCormick's view of law

---

[12] This geological and historical metaphor distinguishing between the different 'layers' of law is a major contribution by Tuori: see his *Critical Legal Positivism* (Farnham: Ashgate, 2002), and *Ratio and Voluntas* (Farnham: Ashgate, 2011). Legal culture interestingly appears as a bridge or commuter between the deeper, sedimentary layers and official sources.

as *institutional normative order* is one of the most interesting theories to capture both dimensions,[13] surface law, sub-surface practical reason and all the diversity and plurality of legal phenomena going beyond the state (transnational), below the state (subnational or infrastate), between states (international) and above the state (supranational) as well as state or national law.

1.3. Varieties of plurality in the law

Varieties of plurality in the law need to be identified, as they relate to territorial, historical, cultural, ethnic-indigenous, religious or status-related causes having social, political and economic explanations. One expression of such pluralities in state law, in suprastate law and in transnational law requires special attention: 'constitutional pluralism'. It starts from the recognition of constitutional *plurality*, a diversity of constitutions or constitutional expressions with different claims to validity, authority and legitimacy within the same polity, and then it uses the term 'pluralism' to suggest accommodation strategies between these claims, somehow indicating a normative preference for retaining the complexity and diversity with polycentric models, for not solving the possible tension arising from normative constitutional plurality with sometimes competing claims to authority. *Constitutional pluralism* is but one version of legal pluralism,[14] one concerned with sovereignty, authority and power. It reveals a preoccupation with supremacy or sovereignty in some legal cultures and with the issue of courts' authority (who has the last word?), but also with new ways of thinking about European Union law in its relationship with the (authority-claims of the) law of the Member States. The view from the EU runs along these lines: each system sees itself as endowed with authority; in the case of the EU this is an attributed sovereignty, in the case of the Member States, the original sovereignty or authority is either relinquished to the EU or residual and subsidiary for the areas not transferred to the EU, but the general principles of EU law still have to be

---

[13] This theory is most elaborated in N. MacCormick, *Institutions of Law: An Essay in Legal Theory. Law, State, and Practical Reason* (Oxford: Oxford University Press, 2007); see also MacCormick and O. Weinberger, *Institutional Theory of Law: New Approaches to Legal Positivism* (Dordrecht: D. Reidel Publishing Company, 1986).

[14] The term was coined by MacCormick, note 5 above, Ch. 7, who started from the Member State perspective to observe the existence of not one but two legal orders, Member State law and EU law, each claiming final authority and each claiming to account for the other's derived authority.

observed at all times.[15] The view from the Member States is different: the EU only has conferred powers and cannot overstep those powers, subject to constitutional courts' control.

Constitutional pluralism predominantly focuses on hard concepts of power and on authority clashes, on claims to sovereignty and the supremacy of EU law and resistance to such claims by Member States' top judiciaries along the binary logic mentioned above, according to which authority is absolute and non-negotiable. To be a credible interpretative and normative project constitutional pluralism has to be multilevel and focus on *softer* concepts of multiple authorities and multi-value logics, on coordination and multilevel governance structures, on cooperative administrative law – the single administration and the principle of loyalty – on polycentric models using concepts like subsidiarity, the rule of reason, proportionality, institutional and procedural autonomy, and primacy (as distinguishable from supremacy, as in the jurisprudence of the European Court of Justice).[16] These are appropriate tools with which to build cognitive and normative accommodation for the complexity resulting from the plurality, diversity and polycentricity of legal (constitutional) orders, each with its own, reconcilable, claim to autonomy, validity and legitimacy.

Constitutional pluralism has heretofore shown little interest in those other important sources of plurality, distinct from the constitutional forms, namely cultural, social, economic and political normative systems. Perhaps this can be seen as a suggestion for future research rather than a criticism of its focus. After all, the type of pluralism it is interested in is qualified by 'constitutional' aspects and 'highcourt-itis', but it should open up to the other, the multiple constitutions: the economic, the social, the juridical,[17] the political, the religious, the governance, the transnational and the security 'constitutions'.[18] Amongst these, multicultural societies

---

[15] C. Joerges suggests the term 'deliberative supranationalism' in 'Rethinking European law's supremacy', No. 2005/12, Law Working Papers, European University Institute, at 15.

[16] As the Spanish Constitutional Court correctly theorised in its 2004 declaration on the Constitutional Treaty DTC 1/2004, of 13 December 2004. There has been much debate on the suitability of this distinction – see below.

[17] Soft law, too, poses a challenge in this set of concepts since it has more to do with the recognition of official operative sources of law, where it does not fit; and yet it can be observed to operate like other 'official' legal phenomena, which reopens the debate on plurality at the level of sources of law also related to the discourse on new governance in the EU.

[18] I have added transnational and governance constitutions to the list proposed by Tuori in Chapter 1 of this volume; one could perhaps think of other expressions of 'constitution', such as the secular or religious constitution.

pose interesting challenges to constitutional pluralism. Cultural plurality or cultural diversity and *multiculturalism* in the wider discussion concerning practical philosophy, including law (multicultural jurisprudence), originate in contemporary societies from different sources of such cultural plurality, like religious diversity, ethnic and linguistic diversity related to migration, social class, subcultures and the urbanization process, and the territorial plurality of native, indigenous, substate, national cultures.

From both communitarian and liberal standpoints, some of the issues raised by cultural plurality extend from full acceptance to outright rejection of different normative – cultural, religious – practices and the norms behind them; from a sort of segregated coexistence of forms of life to the imposition of hegemonic cultural standards or languages. Somewhere in between such stereotype positions we could find cosmopolitan and dissent-oriented interpretations of human rights. The major legal strategies for dealing with cultural normative plurality reveal a great deal about the potentially manipulative use of concepts related to fundamental rights discourses, such as some theories based on *égalité*. Legislative strategies are often the first reactions, as in France,[19] Belgium,[20] and Switzerland,[21] but reasonable accommodation strategies, equity or fairness, and cultural sensitivity all need rethinking in this light. Through litigation or mediation, through legal discourse and argumentation, closely embedded in practical reason (Alexy's *Sonderfall* or special case in discourse theory),[22] through the weighing and balancing of rights and analyses of necessity and proportionality, new forms of accommodation are developing for concrete negotiated solutions based on the fundamental values of the law with which the legislator is unable or unwilling to cope: unable, for reasons technical or related to separation of powers or federal structure; unwilling, for reasons political and strategic (structure of voting patterns, powerful lobbies, pragmatic calculations, the inadequacy of political ideology based on grand principle). This limitation of the legislature opens up new avenues and new 'policy' challenges for the judiciary.

---

[19] French law prohibiting use of the *burqa*, the *niqab* or the full veil in public; loi du 11 octobre 2010, entered into force on 11 April 2011.

[20] By local police regulations, several Belgian communes have banned the wearing of the full veil in public but no law has yet been passed since legislative initiatives for a law on the *burqa* by the Mouvement Réformateur were rejected by the Chambre des Représentants.

[21] In a referendum, November 2009, 57.5 per cent of participating Swiss voters, and twenty-two of the twenty-six Swiss cantons, accepted a constitutional amendment banning construction of new minarets. Cantons in the French-speaking part of Switzerland, mostly, opposed the initiative.

[22] See R. Alexy, *A Theory of Legal Argumentation* (Oxford: Oxford University Press, 1989).

1.4. Dealing with plurality in law

Courts and judges are often thought to reintroduce unity by determining which law amongst possibly applicable alternatives shall be valid. An important issue arises, then, when plurality is brought back to the Alternative Dispute Resolution (ADR) field and courts no longer control litigation – e.g. shari'ah courts in the United Kingdom. In the EU, this phenomenon can be seen in operation even as regards litigation in official courts, as strategies for avoiding or opting out of some national, hierarchically lower or higher courts can be seen as related to a plurality of dispute resolution mechanisms. This can lead to interesting dynamics affecting the role of the CJEU and the ECtHR in reintroducing unity and uniformity, e.g. as regards arbitration.

We should not ignore the risk of getting lost in the complex map of legal and cultural pluralities, fragmentation and contested legitimacies, a risk largely enhanced by polycentricity, decentralised sovereignty, and transnational legal phenomena involving hegemonic actors not always linked to states and public authorities. What intellectual tools do we have within our reach to guide us through these complex maps and paradoxes? Do we, can we, share criteria to understand these phenomena and the challenges they pose to our traditional ways of thinking about the law and about legal theories? Can we develop new ways of thinking about these two sets: the law or the legal dimension and legal thinking or theory? These are some of the questions related to the concept of law and the issue of plurality within legal and constitutional pluralism and a possible answer would be to adopt a form of perspectivism or methodological pluralism.[23] And next come the normative questions concerning practical reason: can we share overarching normative criteria to cope with the plurality of normative standards originating in the diversity of laws, constitutions and cultural plurality of all sorts? Do we go for a radical pluralism that gives up on the normative attempt to reintroduce some communication between systems? Do we seek some version of interlegality, emphasising common values, international *ius cogens* or some natural law?

In my opinion, a rational discourse theory backed by procedural guarantees – securing safeguards, protection and participation – and by fundamental rights, or at least a forum where such rights can be debated, can provide a tentative solution. The most important point here is the

---

[23] The term has been coined in another context by M. Keating and D. Porta, 'In defence of pluralism in the social sciences', *European Political Science* 9 (2010), 111–20.

process of dialogue itself, not the substantive, reflective equilibrium that results in each of these discursive processes. If we emphasise the substantive, shared standards seeking legitimacy we will probably abandon (radical) pluralism and reintroduce some form of overarching unity (or relative pluralism), a normative system where those substantive criteria are recognised as valid, and perhaps end up defending Kelsen's monist view of international law. If we only seek a procedural solution, we will not be able to offer any normative synthesis, nor any norm other than those governing discourse.[24]

2. Developments – pluralisms and practical reason

The classic definitions of legal pluralism, e.g. as developed by historians, sociologists and anthropologists of law, point to the existence of more than one law addressing the same problem-situation in one and the same society, each providing a different solution. Leaving aside the difficulties in identifying 'society', itself ultimately depending on legal definitions,[25] this is essentially a descriptive-interpretative statement about plurality. There was no normative follow-up to this description-interpretation, for instance a claim that such plurality was worth preserving, even developing, or should rather be 'resolved' into a single system. Indeed, considering coexisting normative orders as 'legal' was already a pluralistic stance, since dominant theories of law tended to identify law with state, and non-state normative phenomena would be considered not proper 'law' but at most quasi-legal.

2.1. A background concept of law as practical reason

The classic view of legal pluralism would thus fall within the 'plurality' category, but that the term pluralism should have been chosen instead of plurality might already indicate that a normative standpoint was already

---

[24] References are omitted here, but the Habermasian inspiration of this proposal is hard to deny.

[25] For an interesting comment on the term 'das Volk', or 'nation', and its relation to constitutional discourse, see D. Edward, 'Was denn ist ein Volk?', in *50th Anniversary of the Europa Institut of the Universität des Saarlandes*, Saarbrücken, 2011, 5–10. 'Society', 'people', 'nation', 'culture', '*Volk*', '*demos*' are hermeneutic concepts where pre-understandings are methodologically useful before their multitude and complexity is analysed.

being adopted in favour of the maintenance of plurality, a position probably held by many legal anthropologists, who tended to affirm the *a priori* value of diversity.

This discussion shows that a background, working concept of law is necessary in order to identify the plurality of the legal. Twining has put the issue in clear terms:

> Confining ourselves to legal texts and external observers simplifies the analysis. However, in the present context it is sensible to have a reasonably broad conception of 'law' because some of the standard contrasts are made between explicit statements of legal rules and something else: 'the law in action', 'real rules', 'unofficial law', hidden normative and legal orders, interposed norms and institutions, underlying principles, ideologies and so on. In diffusion a common contrast is often made between 'official' imported law and pre-existing 'unofficial law' – typically customary or religious normative orders that exist below the surface and the interaction with which is often overlooked. So without entering into debates about definitions or conception of 'law', I shall here treat these contrasted phenomena as falling within the ambit of the 'legal'.[26]

The problem is that replacing 'law' with the (domain of the) 'legal' does not really solve our conceptual struggles. We have no option but to try to provide a working concept of law, which we can do by following MacCormick's definition of law as 'institutional normative order'.[27] This understanding is broad enough to comprehend state and non-state legal forms like those below, beyond, beside, above, between states. On top of this definition we add to the law the claim of (at least procedural) validity, following Alexy,[28] with the effect that a debate over the conditions for validity and legitimacy opens up. Whether the law actually achieves such validity and legitimacy is something that cannot be (ultimately) settled from the standpoint of the law itself, since the claim of validity is made to a broader, higher or larger sphere of normative and practical reason, i.e. discourse ethics, justice as fairness or political morality. All orders of practical reason containing norms actually make such a claim to validity and, as a result, where systems of norms differ in the normative solutions they propose for concrete problem-situations in the same space and time coordinates within society, a pluralist situation obtains. Amongst these,

---

[26] W. Twining, 'Surface law' in H. Petersen, A. L. Kjær, H. Krunke and M. R. Madsen (eds), *Paradoxes of European Legal Integration* (Farnham: Ashgate, 2008), pp 157–84 at 178–9. Watson's transplants can work at surface level.

[27] MacCormick, *Institutions of Law*, note 13 above.

[28] Alexy, *Legal Argumentation*, note 22 above.

normative differences flowing from cultural plurality (the descriptive side of multiculturalism) figure prominently.

2.2. Cultural plurality and reasonable accommodation

Cultural plurality as a sociological fact adopts different expressions in politics, in the economy, in social relations, in the symbolic universe, in the cultural products and references created, produced and consumed in our societies, and also in law. Cultural plurality therefore implies diversity (also) of normative standpoints rooted in cultural forms and patterns. Cultural plurality or pluri-culturality or multiculturality can also, although need not, be related to a sociological or a political theory with normative claims: multiculturalism or some of its spin-offs like the more hybrid interculturalism or the more bureaucratic, and apparently neutral, management of cultural diversity. This fact is not exclusive to the European Union but is shared with other modern societies, some of them further ahead than others in thinking about these issues.[29]

The normative question following from 'cultural plurality' is whether a society goes for an outright relativist approach in which anything goes (pluralism and full inclusion but standards shared nowhere except the market), for a tolerant, 'relative inclusion' approach (minimum shared normative standards)[30] or for a monist reduction to a preferred, hege-monic, culture and 'way of life' that it makes prevail, imposing limits on multiculturalism following from 'ways of life' and cultural preference rather than from human rights.

Reasonable accommodation is based on calculated institutional toler-ance, freedom and personal autonomy in choosing one's model of the good life, and access to scarce resources and other structural social and educational institutions configuring a person's life-chances (and their correlative, group preferences). Are there any limits to such autonomous choice? Can it lead to denying other persons' autonomy and access to mini-mal conditions? Are the postulates of the dignity of human beings, equality

---

[29] Compare the debates in Canada and Quebec with those in France, Switzerland or Germany. A Council of Europe expert group on multicultural Europe, headed by Joschka Fischer, addressed issues such as intolerance and discrimination in the context of multiculturalism and religious pluralism. It called on Europe to embrace diversity, while acknowledging equality before the law, respect for human rights and the need to share certain rights and obligations in our societies.

[30] Strategies of 'reasonable accommodation' and equity are the most interesting inclusive solutions.

and autonomy of persons paramount? And does reasonable accommodation set any limits on tolerance? Does anything go? If we can agree
beforehand on anything more concrete than general principles – equality,
freedom, dignity – then we can build a strategy seeking commensurable
values and norms.[31] Again, the proposal is that we can agree on a deliberative, inclusive and participatory process that can lead to deciding and
negotiating each situation on its merits. When it comes to the making of
legal norms or to the design and implementation of policies, we would
stress the need for the state to be neutral as regards conceptions of the
Common Good (Rawls), for law- and policymakers to be sensible and
sensitive to plurality but faithful to the values of personal autonomy and
toleration, for legal procedures and information and communication systems, at domestic but also at the supra-, inter- and transnational levels,
to be inclusive of existing cultural plurality and participatory, through
dialogue and participatory discourse, and for all actors involved in governance to seek a reflective equilibrium between the majority principle and
the protection of minorities.

Reasonable accommodation requires a rights-balancing and proportionality test. In the EU, these forms of cultural diversity receive visibility as
a problem to be analysed from the point of view of racial discrimination,[32]
human rights abuses, politics,[33] and a challenge to 'forms of life' rather
than as challenges to the law only;[34] and sometimes the official legal
responses adopted to manage such plurality can themselves challenge the
law of a higher order.[35]

While this type of plurality can be seen as a source of social development, the strategies normally adopted to deal with cultural plurality or
multiculture inevitably pose a challenge to European standards of fundamental rights and freedoms and strike at the heart of European legal

[31] The international law of the Charter of the UN refers to the principles of law recognised
by civilised nations; but one can enquire what exactly lay behind this enlightened ideal at
the time or what it might mean currently.
[32] E.g. the expulsion of the Roma from France or Italy, or anti-Maghreb expressions in parts
of Spain.
[33] E.g. right-wing, populist or xenophobic discourse in extreme or mainstream political
parties and groups.
[34] In some cases these practices directly challenge the law, in others they simply challenge
the form of life or culture of a majority in a given society. Thus the wearing of the *burqa*
in public is an offence in some countries or boroughs, but not in most.
[35] Thus in the fight against illegal immigration, abuses of EU law or of the ECHR can be
committed. Suspension of the Schengen Agreement (France), and the establishment of
'detention' centres, are examples of this point.

identity and citizenship.[36] From the modern standpoint of human rights, this fact of plurality and diversity is often regarded as an asset.[37] But this does not mean that in any given society or community where a dominant, majoritarian and hegemonic, normative framework exists (liberal, communitarian or other) and impregnates official law, different, identifiable, cultural practices and their normative claims, commensurable or not, will or even should be catered for, supported or accommodated. This stronger multicultural claim is related to ethical relativism, which ultimately clashes with the discourse on the core of fundamental rights. Accommodation and relativism can sometimes clash. This is because the first assumes that a majority is making room and allowing a minority to be accommodated within a larger frame. In relativism, there is no reference into which plural values and cultures would settle. Radical pluralism has sometimes been identified with this extreme relativism of incommensurability.

2.3. Constitutional pluralism

Plurality of and/or within laws in the same jurisdiction, so-called legal pluralism and versions of this can be a consequence of the sociological fact of cultural plurality or of the diversity, within the same territory, of mutually competing or else shared official, institutional, normative systems. This plurality of legal systems can also be related to constitutional plurality and integrated into a theory of constitutional pluralism,[38] as opposed to classic constitutionalism. This plurality of laws in the same territory can, again, be seen as a sociological or socio-legal fact – legal plurality or diversity – or as a theory of law and state – legal pluralism

---

[36] Especially at civic citizenship, as distinguishable from market citizenship. On legal reasoning followed by the Court of Justice in the interpretation of Arts 20 and 21 TFEU, see S. Sankari, *European Court of Justice Legal Reasoning in Context* (Groningen: Europa Law Publishing, 2014, forthcoming), an excellent doctoral thesis I had the honour to examine as opponent (June 2011, University of Helsinki).

[37] See, for example, Art. 2 TEU.

[38] On constitutional pluralism see MacCormick, *Institutions of Law*, note 13 above, and *Questioning Sovereignty*, note 5 above. This concept was taken up by Neil Walker in 'The idea of constitutional pluralism', No. 2002/01, Law Working Papers, European University Institute, and has since become the subject of heated debate in European legal scholarship. For a very good approach from legal theory see M. Borowski, 'Legal pluralism in the European Union' in A. J. Menendez and J. E. Fossum (eds), *Law and Democracy in Neil MacCormick's Legal and Political Theory: The Post-Sovereign Constellation* (Dordrecht: Springer, 2011), Ch. 10.

vs. monism.[39] Much will turn around the contemporary notion of the nation state as the dominant but no longer exclusive normative framework in the European context. According to the Parliamentary Assembly of the Council of Europe, 'the general trend of the nation-state's evolution is towards its transformation depending on the case, from a purely ethnic or ethnocentric state into a civic state and from a purely civic state into a multicultural state where specific rights are recognized with regard not only to physical persons but also to cultural or national communities'.[40]

Amongst the varieties of pluralism, classic legal pluralism was largely based on personal – ethnic, religious – status. Some examples can be seen in the laws in the Middle Ages in Europe including feudal law, canon law, free cities laws, the interaction of indigenous and colonial law, Ottoman empire pluralism or currently, *adat* and official law in Indonesia. New forms of pluralism relate the plurality of 'consociational' forms of modern society to all sorts of organisations, incorporations, corporations, trusts and institutions producing norms that are legally recognised as valid and parallel to official state law such as the law of churches or religions, of sports and other associations, of collective agreements, of universities, of large companies, or voluntary codes of conduct in industry. Some of these forms are soft private norms, others quasi-official or public norms. Some of these forms rely largely on state institutions for recognising and enforcing the law. The most interesting development in this sphere is that most of these phenomena are not confined to 'national' or state society but are largely transnational because of the effects of intensified globalisation. Governance theories largely deal with these forms of 'coordinated' plurality. Another important version of legal pluralism is related to national and international litigation and the ADR markets. Enter the transnational dimension and the complexity of legal pluralism is greatly increased.

As a result of these developments of legal pluralism, a matrix could be constructed combining

---

[39] From a systems-theoretical point of view, plurality involves a recognition of cognitive complexity, and whereas monism attempts a normative reduction of that complexity by imposing the binary code of one legal system (valid/invalid), pluralism attempts no such reduction but reconciles cognitive and normative complexity in a legally polycentric context (not invalid/possibly valid/possibly invalid).

[40] Recommendation 1735 (2006) on 'The Concept of "Nation"', Assembly debate on 26 January 2006 (7th Sitting), see Doc. 10762, Report of the Committee on Legal Affairs and Human Rights, Rapporteur: Mr Frunda.

1. state and non-state – transnational – axis,
2. public/private axis related to spheres of law – personal status and citizenship, official institutions vs. market, religious and civil society – and
3. an axis of substantive norms vs. dispute resolution mechanisms.[41]

Constitutional pluralism, only one small cell in this matrix, probably originates with the confrontation between claims for institutional legitimacy made by the highest courts of some Member States and the European Court of Justice, each of them concerned to safeguard the validity chain of its own system, its constitutional charter. As Müller-Graff explains,[42] the German Federal Constitutional Court (BVerfGe) has not given up the principle that it can declare a European act to be *inapplicable* even if the European Court of Justice has found it to be *compatible* with the fundamental rights of the Union; the BVerfGe does not recognise the CJEU 'as having the last word' in questions of European law that concern the Federal Republic with regard to fundamental rights.[43] On the basis of the 'eternity clause' contained in Article 79, 3 of the German Constitution (GG) the principles of Article 1 of the Basic Law – respect for human dignity, recognition of human rights and the binding force of the ensuing basic rights on public authorities – cannot be amended. The issue of clashes of authority and sovereignty between custodian constitutional courts is clearly raised to the fore for discussion: imposing limits on the transfer of powers and on the authority to rule on legal validity.

---

[41] As Joerges ('Rethinking', note 15 above, at 13) has put it, from a more private law outlook:

> In terms of conflict resolution, ... the law should encourage the concerned actors themselves to take up the search for problem solving and interest-mediation. It should ensure that their activities respect principles of fairness, enhance their deliberative quality, and then eventually acknowledge such societal norm-generation. It is in this way that law can respond to collisions and contestations, and it can thus be characterized as conflict of laws.

This is Joerges's interesting proposal for dealing with clashes of supremacy, a comity and conflict-of-laws approach.

[42] P. Müller-Graff, 'The European openness of the German Constitution in the light of the jurisprudence of the Federal Constitutional Court' in Koch, Hagel-Sørensen, Haltern and Weiler, note 1 above, at 509.

[43] *Solange I*, BVerfGE 37, 271, 2 CMLR (1974) and *II*, BVerfGE 73, 339 (1986), 3 CMLR (1987), the Maastricht *Urteil* of 1993 (*Brunner* v. *European Union Treaty* [1994] 1 CMLR 57) and the *Lisbon* judgment, BVerfGE (2 BvE 2/08, 30 June 2009).

2.4. Sources of constitutional pluralism

Clashes of authority are only one of the sources of constitutional pluralism.[44] According to Maduro,[45] there are internal and external sources of constitutional pluralism in the European Union legal order, all having an impact on the role of courts. External pluralism derives from:

1. increased communication between and interdependence of the EU legal order with international and foreign legal orders,
2. legal integration relationships in which the EU participates in another legal order,
3. interpretative competition in which the EU is not formally part of another legal order but shares norms and, possibly, jurisdiction with that legal order and
4. legal externalities where the decision taken in one jurisdiction has a social or economic impact in another and where the Court of Justice takes into consideration the jurisprudence of other courts on specific issues.

All these phenomena contribute to complexity and interlegalities, rather than constitutional pluralism, but (2) is possibly the closest to constitutional pluralism since the EU might take a position, e.g. towards the European Convention on Human Rights (ECHR), similar to that taken by Member States towards the EU.

Maduro sees internal pluralism as following from:

1. a plurality of constitutional sources (both European and national) feeding the EU constitutional framework and its general principles of law,

---

[44] The earlier analysis of constitutional pluralism is represented by M. P. Maduro, 'Contrapunctual law: Europe's constitutional pluralism in action' in N. Walker (ed.) *Sovereignty in Transition* (Oxford: Hart Publishing 2003), pp 501–37. See also M. Kumm, 'Who is the final arbiter of constitutionality in Europe? Three conceptions of the relationship between the German Federal Constitutional Court and the European Court of Justice', *Common Market Law Review* 36(1999), 351–86; J. Komárek, 'European constitutionalism and the European Arrest Warrant: contrapunctual principles in disharmony', Jean Monnet Working Paper 2005, No. 10/05; and N. Walker, 'The idea of constitutional pluralism', *Modern Law Review* 65 (2002), 317–59.

[45] M. P. Maduro, 'Interpreting European law: judicial adjudication in a context of constitutional pluralism', 1 *European Journal of Legal Studies* 2 (2007), *passim*. See also the amended version 'Interpreting European law – on why and how law and policy meet at the European Court of Justice' in Koch, Hagel-Sørensen, Haltern and Weiler, note 1 above, p. 458.

2. acceptance of the supremacy of EU rules over national constitutional rules posing challenges and creating a situation in which the normative authority of EU law is negotiated,
3. new forms of power challenging the traditional private/public distinction and other legal categories upon which EU rules have been framed, often overlooking this public/private distinction, and
4. conflicting political claims of political authority leading to a political or ideological pluralism.

Constitutional pluralism is normally identified with (2).

Classic non-pluralist approaches – monism or singularism – see plurality as a problem that needs solving, especially if it means making claims to alternative sources of authority and validity. Constitutional pluralist positions are not perturbed by such clashes and do not intend to develop a comprehensive normative solution to solve them; seeing a clash as somewhat incommensurable, but not fatal when understood as disputes over ultimate claims to supremacy. The normative question for Maduro is how should the Court of Justice address some of the challenges brought by increased political and legal pluralism? If it placed great emphasis on supremacy it would probably feed the clashes between claims to authority and sovereignty made by each constitutional system, the Member State system and the EU system, and claims of unity and hierarchy made in relation to the legal system (Kelsen's pyramid). But if the Court underscored supremacy and instead focused the debate around the milder concept of primacy,[46] as it has tended to do in its jurisprudence, perhaps the binary logic of the clash could be defused and the question would be one of setting aside or leaving unapplied an incompatible norm of domestic law rather than quashing or annulling that norm as outranked by the EU norm.

---

[46] 'Primacy' is not often referred to in debates on constitutional pluralism, and yet it was the term used by the Court: *primauté*. It would be interesting to enquire into why it was transformed into a matter of supremacy and who was behind this transformation. What seems clear is that, in spite of the CJEU's care in avoiding the term supremacy and the juridical consequence of invalidity that would follow from the declaration that a norm of domestic law was incompatible with CJEU primacy, many constitutional courts in the Member States have misunderstood primacy as meaning supremacy; and scholars have not always corrected this misunderstanding, with some notable exceptions (see M. Avbelj, 'Supremacy or primacy of EU law – (why) does it matter?', 17 *European Law Journal* 6 (2011), 744–63). Even the translation services at the Court of Justice, and therefore the Court itself as an institution, probably deserve part of the blame for turning *primauté* into supremacy.

In my own legal/constitutional culture an interesting tool was developed to cope with such clashes, the 'foral pass' (*pase foral* or *sobrecarta* in Navarrese law), i.e. a 'power of disallowance' or 'confederal veto'. The *fueros* were historic covenants between the Southern Basque territories, and the kingdom of Castille, and after forced accession in 1515, also between the kingdom of Navarre and the Spanish Crown. Certain legal and political liberties, privileges and immunities were recognised. One interesting constitutional convention, the *pase foral*, developed during the five centuries of the life of the *fueros*, consisted in rejecting the application of a law of the Crown that was considered to be contrary to the *fueros*. This foral pass used the formula '*sea acatado pero no cumplido*', meaning 'let the law be received but not executed'. Interestingly, the principle had 'direct effect' since it could be invoked before the provincial council as an immunity or defeating norm. This objection was raised to the Cortes (Crown parliament which had to resolve grievances before new laws could be passed).[47] The doctrine of primacy would do something similar to help EU law bypass domestic law, which would not be applied or executed but remain valid law in strictly domestic contexts of application. A certain logic of subsidiarity inspired the foral pass whereas a logic of preemption applies to EU law primacy, but the result is to negotiate dissonance or conflict, the existence of an antinomy and of asymmetry.

2.5. Primacy and supremacy as responses to constitutional pluralism

So primacy is an interesting concept to develop in order to favour constitutional pluralist approaches, as the Court of Justice has done. It might not solve all the clashes between highest courts (the CJEU and the 'constitutional courts' of the Member States) but it might defuse much of the tension. Clashes between legal/constitutional systems are mostly related to three issues:

1. *Kompetenz-Kompetenz*, or the final authority to decide on the distribution of competences between the Member States and the Union;
2. authoritatively deciding the scope, core meaning and consequences of fundamental rights in a multilevel system where these are contained in different constitutional charters; and

---

[47] The foral pass was abolished in 1830 during the first Carlist war. See R. Gomez Rivero, 'Análisis comparado del pase foral en el País Vasco a partir de siglo XVIII', 39 *Boletin de la Real Sociedad Bascongada de Amigos del País* (1983), 533–82.

3. deciding the validity of norms of the legal (constitutional) system and therefore striking out/defeating incompatible norms (antinomies) even where they have a constitutional pedigree.

The distinction between primacy and supremacy relates to this third set of conflicts or tensions. This interesting distinction was actually made, in cryptic language, by the Spanish Constitutional Court in its declaration on the compatibility with the Spanish Constitution of the Treaty establishing a Constitution for Europe.[48]

According to the Tribunal Constitucional, primacy and supremacy are categories that operate at different levels: whereas primacy has to do with the scope of application of valid norms, supremacy has to do with norm-making procedures, expresses the higher hierarchical rank of a norm and acts as a source of validity for those norms of a lower rank, so that the lower norms will be invalid if they contradict a higher norm within the same system. Primacy does not question the validity of the contrary norm but simply sets this norm aside for the purposes of application.

In my opinion the Spanish Constitutional Court has taken one step in the right direction but does not go far enough and does not correctly interpret the claims made by EU law. The distinction between primacy and supremacy holds, and is correctly understood as one between the scope of application of norms that might continue to be valid, even when displaced or disapplied, and the concept of norms acting as sources of validity in Kelsenian fashion and therefore being liable to nullity or nullification. However the Spanish Court seems to forget that EU law also makes claims to hierarchical superiority in areas of its competence, and that if an infringement action, brought by the Commission or by a Member State against a legal norm of a Member State (even one having constitutional rank), declares that norm to be incompatible with the EU Treaties, this norm will need to be not simply displaced or defeated but annulled, deprived of its validity, removed from the legal order. Not just primacy but also supremacy applies over systems, but the Declaration

---

[48] Declaration 1/2004 of 13 December, point 4: 'the claim to the primacy of Union Law made by Article I–6 of the Treaty does not contradict the supremacy of the Constitution'. This interpretation simply avoids the tension between the final claims to authority made by the EU and by the Member State legal systems. The declaration on primacy attached to the Constitutional Treaty carefully referred to the understanding of primacy according to the case law of the Court, a point also underlined in the House of Lords Select Committee report on the Constitutional Treaty.

gives the impression that supremacy only exists internally, within the legal system. I believe commentators have criticised not only the way in which the Tribunal Constitucional has drawn the distinction between primacy and supremacy but also the distinction itself.[49] This is where I disagree: the distinction is to the point, but the Constitutional Court's theory is flawed because supremacy also befits EU law.

Supremacy involves a hierarchical relationship between legal systems leading to the *lex superior* nature of the norm belonging to the higher system and therefore striking out as invalid the incompatible *inferior* norm belonging to the subordinate system. In order to strike down an incompatible norm and declare it invalid a special court action and procedure has to be followed, a direct action brought to quash an incompatible norm. This can be a norm belonging to secondary EU law, under a preliminary procedure on its validity, centralised in the Court after *Foto-Frost*,[50] or more likely an action to annul the invalid norm. It can also be an infringement proceeding against the norm of a Member State that is declared by the Court to be incompatible with EU law. On the other hand, primacy would be a mere question of the (scope of) applicability of norms. The fact that a norm 'has primacy' over another simply means that in the application of those norms to the case at hand, the other norm yields and is left unapplied or defeated but still valid within its legal system and operative in internal law if no clash with an EU norm is found. Defeasibility is an interesting feature of the application and formulation of norms.[51] The special action and procedure for this non-application or defeasibility is the preliminary reference, which allows the Court to adopt a minimalist approach.[52] The effect of a declaration of primacy differs in important ways from those following from hierarchy.

---

[49] Víctor Ferreres Comella is an interesting exception, since he admits that the distinction might make sense, but cannot be carried very far; see 'La Constitución Española ante la cláusula de primacía del derecho de la UE' in A. López Castillo, A. Saiz Arnaiz and V. Ferreres Comella (eds), *Constitución Española y Constitución Europea* (Madrid: Centro de Estudias Políticos y Constitucionales, 2005), pp 89–99. See also M. Kumm and V. Ferreres Comella, 'The primacy clause of the Constitutional Treaty and the future of constitutional conflict in the European Union', Jean Monnet Working Paper 2004, No. 5/04.

[50] Case 314/85 *Foto-Frost* [1987] ECR 4119.

[51] See N. MacCormick, *Rhetoric and the Rule of Law* (Oxford: Oxford University Press, 2005), at 252–3.

[52] See D. Sarmiento, 'Half case at a time: dealing with judicial minimalism at the European Court of Justice' in M. Claes, M. de Visser, P. Popelier and C. van de Heyning (eds), *Constitutional Conversations in Europe* (Cambridge: Intersentia, 2012), pp 13–40, at 16–17.

That is why the distinction between primacy and supremacy and the minimalist, gradual approach by the Court is a relevant and useful tool for diffusing the tensions of constitutional pluralism, of mutually incompatible claims to final authority.

2.6. Further tools for defusing pluralist tensions

Other tools for defusing the tension at the three levels identified would be the general principle of EU law known as institutional and procedural autonomy, the technique of harmonisation by common standards, the very nature of the directive as a legal instrument, a source or a regulatory tool related to the plurality of systems, development of the general principle of law known as effectiveness – in EU law this has delivered important consequences such as the doctrines of indirect effect, Member State liability for breaches and incidental direct effect[53] – also subsidiarity and proportionality as general principles of EU law.

As regards the question who has the ultimate decision regarding competences (*Kompetenz-Kompetenz*), it seems that a culture of subsidiarity developed by the agents involved might help defuse tensions or moderate resulting pluralistic situations. In any case, if competences are pooled in the Union by the Member States and if EU competence is to be uniformly exercised throughout the Union, leaving with each of the Member States' constitutional courts the ultimate decision on the extent to which competences will be conferred would amount to having potentially different approaches to the scope and intensity of competences within the Union. On the other hand, an abusive interpretation by the CJEU of the extent and intensity of conferred powers might preempt Member State competences. In the end a reflective equilibrium will be found between the ultimate umpires involved in the *Kompetenz-Kompetenz* debate, so that a certain kind of pluralism is reintroduced.

Subsidiarity also goes beyond the binary logic of distribution of competences belonging to the Member States exclusively or to the Union exclusively. Subsidiarity applies in relation to shared powers and will take several factors into account – proximity to citizens, the effectiveness and efficiency of the measure, economies of scale – in order to decide on the actual level at which and the intensity with which norms ought

---

[53] See the author's 'Is direct effect a general principle of EU law?' in U. Bernitz, J. Nergelius and C. Cardner (eds), *General Principles of EC Law in a Process of Development* (Alphen aan den Rijn: Kluwer Law International, 2008), pp 3–23.

to be adopted (proportionality and subsidiarity being functionally and conceptually linked).

Clashes regarding fundamental rights are related to the fact that fundamental rights are nowadays recognised, guaranteed, controlled and protected at different levels – substate, state, suprastate, international – and the definition of their scope and their intensity at one level, e.g. under supranational EU law, will have an impact on the definition at another level, e.g. domestic law. In a moderate, external, pluralistic scenario,[54] this complex interaction will be altered further when the EU adheres to the ECHR but also through increased communication between and interdependence of the European Union legal order with international and foreign legal orders, the EU participating in another legal order like the UN.[55] A certain interpretative plurality in which the Union shares norms and, possibly, jurisdiction with another legal order, like the ECHR, and legal externalities that see the decision taken in one jurisdiction have a social or economic impact in another and the Court of Justice taking into consideration the jurisprudence of other courts on specific issues, might also alter this interaction.[56]

These complex interactions might create new tensions in such an external (moderate) pluralist scenario. But the sources of tension contain at the same time the seeds of understanding and communication between systems and potential for reasonably accommodating other normative solutions. Tools for defusing these tensions and making plurality seem amenable, manageable and accommodating include hybridity, interlegality, the developing legal culture of human rights, general principles of practical reason and porosity of legal cultures.

3. Finale – role of jurists in balancing pluralisms and a cosmopolitan order

As Sally Engle Merry has observed,[57] there is a contrast or a gap between the attitude of human rights lawyers and activists who are part of an

---

[54] Maduro, 'Interpreting European law', note 45 above.

[55] The tensions reflected in cases such as *Kadi* or *Bosphorus* are illustrative of this interaction. See Joined Cases C–402/05 P and C–415/05 P *Kadi* [2008] ECR I–6351 and *Bosphorus* v. *Ireland* (App. No. 45036/98) ECtHR 2005–VI. See also Besson in Chapter 7 of this volume.

[56] As when the ECJ took into account the case law of the US Supreme Court concerning sex discrimination, especially in *Kalanke* (Case C–450/93 *Kalanke* v. *Freie Hansestadt Bremen* [1995] ECR I–3051).

[57] *Human Rights and Gender Violence: Translating International Law into Local Justice*, Chicago Series in Law and Society (Chicago: Chicago University Press, 2006), at 164.

academic, international elite committed to the universality of human rights, and lawyers and other professionals working at the level of ordinary, daily practice, who must cope with the fragmentation and plural condition of law among other rule systems, seeking justice in concrete instances, seeking equitable, fair solutions in actual cases. It is an open question whether more interaction will take place between the two types of jurist or whether fragmentation will continue, but in any event all jurists can develop some shared values and tools for dealing with plurality and foster accommodation strategies. Courts therefore play an important role in reintroducing order and unity to diversity, and the CJEU is no exception.

In my opinion, the interesting question for contemporary European socio-legal studies of legal pluralism goes beyond enquiring into the attitudes of legal actors in the face of different, competing, legal orders in constitutional pluralism to examining attitudes towards these concrete manifestations or expressions or pluralistic phenomena – constitutional but also related to multiculturalism in a context in which official state law still dominates, but no longer monopolises, the elaboration and application of law and internal legal cultures. Such specific expressions of pluralistic phenomena are linked to cultural plurality or diversity and in the law deliver results such as accommodation formulae. But if the legislator or the policymaker, representing the majority in a parliamentary system, fails or decides not to accommodate through general norms, then the interpreter, the jurist, the judge will have a second chance to apply (reasonable) accommodation, cultural defences as developed in cultural jurisprudence or sensitivity or empathy, or equity. In either case, the accommodation is performed in or on official law. Here, equity,[58] empathy,[59] sensitivity or reasonable accommodation,[60] all require going beyond the formalism of state official-law monism and being aware of

---

[58] We cannot here examine this concept, which was introduced by the Roman *praetors* and authors as '*summum ius, summa iniuria*' (Cicero, *De Officiis*, I, 33). It was later developed by medieval scholastics, canonists and glossators inspired by the rediscovery of Aristotle, and to some extent by English lawyers to distinguish it from the common law, but not as this later developed in the Chancery courts. See Thomas of Aquinas's *Summa Theologiae*, 2a, 2ae, 60.5. See generally J. M. Kelly, *A Short History of Western Legal Theory* (Oxford: Clarendon Press, 1992), Ch. 2.

[59] See G. Stone, 'Our fill-in-the-blank Constitution' in *The New York Times*, 14 April 2010: 'empathy helps judges understand the aspirations of the framers, who were themselves determined to protect the rights of political, religious, racial and other minorities. Second, it helps judges understand the effects of the law on the real world.'

[60] See Bouchard-Taylor Commission (www.accommodements-quebec.ca/) and the first case *Ontario Commission of Human Rights and Theresa O'Malley (Vincent)* v. *Simpsons-Sears Ltd* [1985] 2 SCR 536, although similar developments had taken place in the USA in the field of labour relations.

legal pluralist phenomena that might have a bearing on equal treatment and the prohibition of discrimination.

A particular attitude is expected from jurists, law-interpreters and officials. Democratic states must ensure that all persons take part in the life of the community (equal and active citizenship), while taking due account (recognition) of their diversity and difference. Religious, linguistic, cultural and social differences might require different treatment.[61] If the legislator were to face the particular situation the judge is facing, the law would have been drawn up in a special way to take account of the particulars. The judge would then become a sensitive, interstitial legislator and would modulate the rigid interpretation of the law.

This special, accommodating attitude facilitates both adoption of a monist standpoint by the legal system and the cherished unity of the rule of recognition and sources, while achieving equity in individual cases.[62] This seems to be the message sent by the Strasbourg Court (ECtHR): no need for the legislator to accept legal pluralism,[63] but calls for special awareness to the attitudes of actors in the legal field. This will require special practical argumentation, reasoning and legal techniques but furthermore it requires a special attitude on the part of judges. Courts must assume this idea of plurality and social change in their reasoning, seeking a balance between the values of autonomy, dignity, equality and security and this will require the judge to cultivate the virtue of openness and readiness to listen.[64]

When facing plurality, the major lawmakers – constitution framers, amendment drafters or constitution interpreters, legislators, but also lawyers and judges generally – develop different strategies: democratic legislators, at the level of sources of law, tend to accept cultural plurality and diversity within the confines of democratic constitutions, human rights bills and international human rights instruments. This cultural

---

[61] See P. Bosset and M. Foblets, 'Accommodating diversity in Quebec and Europe: different legal concepts, similar results?' in *Institutional Accommodation and the Citizen: Legal and Political Interaction in a Pluralist Society* (Strasbourg: Council of Europe Publishing, 2009), pp 37–65.

[62] *Ibid.*, p. 41: '. . . the issues raised by legal pluralism are quite distinct from those connected with the duty to accommodate, which in principle simply requires institutions' rules and practices to be adjusted in individual cases to redress established forms of discrimination.'

[63] Indeed, the ECtHR is not keen on legal pluralism at all; see *Refah Partisi* (App. Nos 41340/98, 41342/98 and 41343/98), Judgment of 13 February 2003. See also Michaels in Chapter 5 of this volume.

[64] See M. Rivet, 'Introduction' in M. Jézéquel (ed.), *La Justice à l'Épreuve de la Diversité Culturelle* (Cowansville, Quebec: Yvon Blais, 2007), p. 15.

plurality can even become a major feature of modern constitution-states. However this acceptance of *cultural* plurality does not amount to recognition of *legal* plurality, of the normative claims made by individuals invoking their own different cultures, at the more fundamental level of the rule of recognition of the sources of law. Such plurality and diversity of laws, which is denied at the level of sources, might nevertheless be recognised in the interpretation and application of the law, through the mediation of cultural plurality. This happens when judges and legislators, inspired by notions of cultural openness, recognise some relevance and effect of cultural plurality, this recognition being facilitated by theories of human rights-conforming interpretation. Some similar attitude might be detected in the careful approaches of the CJEU (primacy, institutional and procedural autonomy, conforming interpretation) and of the ECtHR (margin of appreciation) towards constitutional pluralism. Tools, techniques and doctrines are thus developed in the context of legal discourse – the application of law, legal argument and judicial reasoning – to defuse the tension that can arise from a plurality of potentially conflicting norms and to achieve results that reconcile cultural diversity and non-discrimination, or alternative claims to constitutional authority, with denial of (radical) legal pluralism at a more foundational, conceptual level.

7

European human rights pluralism

Notion and justification

SAMANTHA BESSON

The present volume sets itself the daunting, and somewhat presumptuous task of 'rethinking legal thinking'. This undertaking strikes us as particularly difficult when transposed to the blooming field of international and European legal theory: after all, we are still having a hard time thinking about international and European law, so how can we be expected to be rethinking our legal thinking yet? At the same time, however, we also know that, when thinking about new forms of law developing outside the boundaries of the state, it is essential not to apply too hastily traditional conceptions and approaches in legal theory. Not only might those conceptions not fit the practice of European and international law but, given the integrated nature of the European legal order and of parts of the international legal order, they might no longer fit that of domestic law either. Building this new boat on an open sea, to borrow an expression from Neurath and Habermas, may be a necessary project as a result, however difficult it may be.[1]

This chapter was written while a Fellow of the Wissenschaftskolleg zu Berlin (Germany) in 2011–12. It is a revised version of a paper I presented at the Rethinking Legal Thinking Conference, Centre of Excellence Foundations of the European Polity, University of Helsinki, 26–7 August 2010. Many thanks to Kaarlo Tuori for the invitation and to Julen Extabe for his comments. Last but not least, I would like to thank my research assistant Eleonor Kleber for her help with the editing of the chapter.

[1] See e.g. M. Giudice and K. Culver, 'Not a system but an order: explaining the legality of the European Union' in J. Dickson and P. Eleftheriadis (eds), *Philosophical Foundations of European Union Law* (Oxford: Oxford University Press, 2012), pp 54–76; W. Waluchow, 'Legality's frontier: a review of Keith Culver and Michael Giudice, *Legality's Borders: An Essay in General Jurisprudence*', 1 *Transnational Legal Theory* 4 (2010), 575–85; S. Besson and J. Tasioulas, 'Introduction' in Besson and Tasioulas (eds), *The Philosophy of International Law* (Oxford: Oxford University Press, 2010), pp 1–27; K. Culver and M. Giudice, *Legality's Borders* (Oxford: Oxford University Press, 2010); W. Twining, *General*

In this chapter, I would like to take the title of the volume to imply primarily a change of perspective in legal theory; a change of perspective that is important if one wants to embrace the most difficult issues in international and European legal theory, issues that seem to be resisting existing paradigms in traditional legal theory. My topic pertains to the now famous (or infamous) idea of legal pluralism in European and international legal theory, i.e. the idea that not all legal norms applicable in a given legal order ought to be regarded as validated by reference to the same criteria and hence as situated within a hierarchy, and that, accordingly, some normative conflicts may get no legal answer as a result.[2]

Importantly, however, I will try to look at the question of legal pluralism from a different perspective: that of human rights law in the context of human rights legal theory. This new focus is particularly topical as it is in the human rights context that most authors endorsing one form or the other of legal pluralism see evidence to support their view. They either understand human rights pluralism as a case of legal pluralism,[3] and

---

Jurisprudence: Understanding Law from a Global Perspective (Cambridge: Cambridge University Press, 2009); S. Besson, 'How international is the European legal order?', *No Foundations* 5 (2008), available at www.helsinki.fi/nofo/; S. Besson, 'The concept of constitutionalism in Europe: interpretation *in lieu of* translation', *No Foundations* 4 (2007), available at www.helsinki.fi/nofo/; N. Walker, 'Legal theory and the European Union', 25 *Oxford Journal of Legal Studies* 4 (2005), 581–601 at 592.

[2] See e.g. G. Davies, 'Constitutional disagreement in Europe and the search for pluralism' in M. Avbelj and J, Komarek (eds), *Constitutional Pluralism in the European Union and Beyond* (Oxford: Hart Publishing, 2012), pp 269–83; M. Maduro, 'Three claims of constitutional pluralism' in *ibid.*, pp 67–84; S. Besson, 'The truth about legal pluralism: a review of Nico Krisch, *Beyond Constitutionalism*', 8 *European Constitutional Law Review* 2 (2012), 354–61; N. Krisch, *Beyond Constitutionalism: The Pluralist Structure of Postnational Law* (Oxford: Oxford University Press, 2011); S. Besson, 'European legal pluralism after *Kadi*', 5 *European Constitutional Law Review* 2 (2009), 237–64; N. Krisch, *The Case for Pluralism in Postnational Law* (London: LSE Legal Studies Working Papers, 2009); J. Baquero Cruz, 'The legacy of the Maastricht-*Urteil* and the pluralist movement', 14 *European Law Journal* 4 (2008), 389–422 at 397–403; Besson, 'How international', note 1 above; M. Maduro, 'Interpreting European law: judicial adjudication in a context of constitutional pluralism', *European Journal of Legal Studies* 1 (2007); N. Barber, 'Legal pluralism and the European Union', 12 *European Law Journal* 3 (2006), 306–29; M. Kumm, 'The jurisprudence of constitutional conflict: constitutional supremacy in Europe before and after the Constitutional Treaty', 11 *European Law Journal* 3 (2005), 262–307; M. Maduro, 'Contrapunctual law: Europe's constitutional pluralism in action', in N. Walker (ed.), *Sovereignty in Transition* (Oxford: Oxford, Hart Publishing, 2003), pp 501–37; N. Walker, 'The idea of constitutional pluralism', 65 *Modern Law Review* 3 (2002), 317–59; N. MacCormick, 'The Maastricht-*Urteil*: sovereignty now', 1 *European Law Journal* 3 (1995), 259–66 at 259.

[3] See e.g. N. Krisch, 'The open architecture of European human rights law', 71 *Modern Law Review* 2 (2008), 183–216; Maduro, 'Three claims', note 2 above.

sometimes even as the only case they can think of,[4] or envisage human rights as a solution to the more widespread phenomenon of legal pluralism, for instance in judicial settlements of normative conflicts.[5] Against this new trend in European and international legal scholarship,[6] however, I will argue that human rights plurality certainly exists through the coexistence of multilevel human rights norms and judicial interpretations of those norms stemming from different international or European and domestic legal orders and institutions, but that we should be more cautious before referring too quickly to that plurality as human rights pluralism of the kind the use of the term 'legal pluralism' is meant to indicate. Contrary to what many authors claim when conflating the two terms,[7] the plurality of human rights does not necessarily imply their pluralism,[8] and the necessary normative arguments for the latter have not actually been provided in the literature, which tends to be empirical and largely descriptive.[9] Furthermore, human rights norms are legitimating norms, and as a result their pluralism is bound to be very different from that of other legal norms. If there is a form of human rights pluralism at work in Europe, I will argue that it is one of a very different kind: one that is about mutual legitimation, and that is situated at the core of the complex process of democratic legitimation of European legal orders.

---

[4] If one looks at the examples in Maduro, 'Three claims', note 2 above, or M. Kumm, 'The cosmopolitan turn in constitutionalism: on the relationship between constitutionalism in and beyond the state' in J. L. Dunoff and J. P. Trachtman (eds), *Ruling the World? International Law, Global Governance, Constitutionalism* (Cambridge: Cambridge University Press, 2009), pp 258–326, human rights feature almost exclusively in their examples of legal pluralism. For Krisch, 'Open architecture', note 3 above at 186 and 215, and *Beyond Constitutionalism*, note 2 above, by contrast, human rights pluralism is one kind of legal pluralism among many others. The same may be said paradoxically about the non-pluralist account of G. Letsas, 'Harmonic law – the case against pluralism and dialogue' in Dickson and Eleftheriadis, note 1 above, pp 77–108, who focuses on human rights in his argument against legal pluralism (although he does argue later on that human rights are different from other issues arising within ordinary EU law).

[5] See e.g. L. Azoulai, 'Conclusions' in E. Dubout and S. Touzé (eds), *Les droits fondamentaux: charnières entres ordres et systèmes juridiques* (Paris: Pedone, 2010), pp 327–33.

[6] See e.g. Krisch, 'Open architecture', note 3 above; the essays in Dubout and Touzé, note 5 above.

[7] See e.g. Maduro, 'Three claims', note 2 above; Krisch, 'Open architecture', note 3 above; Krisch, *Beyond Constitutionalism*, note 2 above.

[8] See e.g. Letsas, note 4 above.

[9] Krisch, 'Open architecture', note 3 above at 198 fn. 92, 209ff., for instance, only provides empirical evidence of heterarchy and discusses strategic explanations for domestic and European courts' attitudes.

Context matters if we are to understand this topic, and a few words are therefore in order about the circumstances in which the issues of European legal pluralism and human rights have come together. Lately, circumstances of legal pluralism in the European Union (EU) have led to an increased focus on values,[10] on one hand, and on courts,[11] on the other. Values have been identified, by legal scholars and practitioners equally, as constitutive of the common standards that democratic political and institutional structures and legal rules no longer provide in a context of competing legal orders, regimes and sources – or at least, provide only at the price of very high complexity. Unsurprisingly in those conditions, courts have become the privileged forum for decision making and have used values as guidance in complex normative conflicts. This conjunction of values and judicial power actually explains why human rights have become so central to the articulation of European legal orders and regimes in recent years. Increasingly, indeed, human rights are used as common standards for adjudicating normative conflicts in Europe, and hence as a solution to the normative consequences of legal pluralism.[12] The idea is indeed that all legitimate orders protect human rights and that their respective human rights norms provide common ground for judicial settlements in cases of normative conflict.

Increasing references to human rights as the solution or part of the solution to legal pluralism in Europe do not come without difficulties, however. First, the multilevel and multisourced guarantees of human rights have been said to give rise to a legal pluralism of their own. This is the idea of human rights pluralism defended by many authors in the absence of a clear hierarchy between those guarantees.[13] Second, even if one disagrees with the possibility or idea of human rights pluralism, the plurality of courts and bodies interpreting human rights law in Europe has triggered jurisdictional conflicts over the correct interpretations of those rights. This kind of interpretative or judicial pluralism, and conflict over human rights interpretations, are an even more serious concern. Finally, a more careful and informed approach to the nature and legitimacy of the

---

[10] See A. Rosas, 'The European Court of Justice in context: forms and patterns of judicial dialogue', 1 *European Journal of Legal Studies* 2 (2007).

[11] See *ibid.*, Maduro, 'Interpreting European law', note 2 above.

[12] See e.g. M. Maduro, 'La fonction juridictionnelle dans le contexte du pluralisme constitutionnel: l'approche du droit communautaire' in Dubout and Touzé, note 5 above; V. Champeil-Desplats, 'Les droits fondamentaux et l'identité des ordres juridiques: l'approche publiciste', in *ibid.*, pp 149–64; and Azoulai, note 5 above.

[13] See e.g. Krisch, 'Open architecture', note 3 above; Maduro, 'Three claims', note 2 above.

various human rights guarantees applying in Europe shows how the reference to human rights pluralism merely obfuscates the real stakes of legal pluralism. It reveals a misunderstanding of both what European human rights are and what they are used for in European adjudication. Clarifying why this is the case in this chapter is not only part of our collective endeavour to devise a new European legal theory, but should also contribute to the nascent international law theory and international human rights theory in particular, as we may be able to learn from experiences gained within the European Union.[14]

My argument about European human rights pluralism will be four-pronged. The first step will clarify what European legal pluralism really amounts to as it means different things to different people – and sometimes even to the same people. In section 2 of this chapter, I will turn to European human rights pluralism, and to its different understandings and roles in practice. The final section of the chapter will re-examine the question of European legal pluralism from a more political and, in particular, a more democratic approach.

1. European legal pluralism

Over the last twenty years or so, the concept of legal pluralism has developed and consolidated in Europe. It emerged from the current circumstances of increasing density in European law,[15] and stems from the limitations of the monist/dualist divide when faced with the immediate validity of and/or lack of hierarchy among norms stemming from different legal orders, regimes and sources within the European Union.[16]

---

[14] See S. Besson, 'Human rights and democracy in a global context: decoupling and recoupling', 4 *Ethics and Global Politics* 1 (2011), 19–50.

[15] I am consciously avoiding the term 'constitutional pluralism', as I am assuming that the autonomy of a legal order implies a rule of recognition and hence some kind of constitution in a material sense. As a result, legal pluralism in the sense it is understood in this chapter can only be constitutional pluralism (and see Letsas, note 4 above, indirectly). See also Opinion of Advocate General Maduro, Joined cases C–402/05 P and C–415/05 P *Yassin Abdullah Kadi and Al Barakaat International Foundation* v. *Council of the European Union and Commission of the European Communities* [2008] ECR I–6351, para. 21, by reference to Case 294/83, *Les Verts* v. *Parliament* [1986] ECR 1339, para. 23.

[16] On those limitations, see the introduction in A. Nollkaemper and J. Nijman (eds), *New Perspectives on the Divide between International Law and National Law* (Oxford: Oxford University Press, 2007). See e.g. the references in footnote 2. See also, more generally, Besson, 'European legal pluralism', note 2 above.

Needless to say, legal pluralism remains an ambiguous or 'fuzzy' concept.[17] Two dimensions of meaning at least need to be distinguished. In a first meaning, pluralism can be used to refer either to the normative consequences of the existence of a plurality or multiplicity of legal norms, sources or regimes applicable within the same legal order (internal legal pluralism). This is what is usually meant by reference to pluralism within international law.[18] In a second meaning, and this is its most common meaning and the one that is used in this chapter, it refers to a multiplicity of legal orders the norms contained in which can apply within a given legal order, usually the domestic one, albeit stemming from different legal orders (external legal pluralism). Of course, both types of legal pluralism can overlap and usually external legal pluralism is also characterised by some form of internal legal pluralism.[19]

In practice, and this is what distinguishes a situation of legal pluralism from the legal situation that used to prevail, those plural legal norms coincide in the same social sphere and overlap on the same issues, people and territory, thus sharing the same material, personal and territorial scope.[20] As a result, legal pluralism is usually experienced within a domestic legal order where norms stemming from the European and international legal orders meet and interact upon direct application to their subjects. In this respect, it is important to distinguish between legal pluralism in an

---

[17] 'Fuzzy': Letsas, note 4 above. I am not looking here at moral pluralism or social and cultural pluralism, but only at legal pluralism. Of course, legal pluralism can be a consequence of moral, social or cultural pluralism, but is not necessarily so. Moreover, I am not looking at non-official forms of law and social norms and hence am not considering those forms of pluralism of social norms: see e.g. S. Moore Falk, *Law as Process: An Anthropological Approach* (London: Routledge, 1978); B. de Sousa Santos, *Toward a New Common Sense: Law, Science and Politics in the Paradigmatic Transition* (London: Routledge, 1995). See also K. Günther, 'Rechtspluralismus und universaler Code der Legalität: Globalisierung als rechtstheoretisches Problem' in L. Wingert and K. Günther (eds), *Die Öffentlichkeit der Vernunft und die Vernunft der Öffentlichkeit* (Frankfurt: Suhrkamp, 2001), pp 539–67; J. Griffiths, 'What is legal pluralism?', 24 *Journal of Legal Pluralism* (1986), 2–55; W. Twining, *Globalisation and Legal Theory* (London: Butterworths, 2000).

[18] See e.g. International Law Commission, 'Fragmentation of international law: difficulties arising from the diversification and expansion of international law', Final Report, 13 April 2006, UN Doc. A/CN.4/L.682. See also S. Besson, 'Whose constitution(s)? international law, constitutionalism and democracy' in Dunoff and Trachtman, note 4 above, pp 381–407; S. Besson, 'Theorizing the sources of international law' in Besson and Tasioulas, note 1 above, pp 163–85.

[19] This is also why external legal pluralism is the more complete of the two and entails both the validity-related and authority-related dimensions discussed below.

[20] See e.g. Griffiths, note 17 above at 8; Twining, *Globalisation and Legal Theory*, note 17 above, p. 8.

integrated legal order such as that made up of the EU and domestic legal orders, on one hand, and legal pluralism in other legal orders, on the other. An example of the latter is the legal pluralism that prevails in any domestic order to which different international law regimes apply at the same time, such as the European Convention on Human Rights (ECHR) and UN law in the domestic legal order. Importantly, however, a more advanced form of legal pluralism is very characteristic of the former integrated legal orders. An integrated legal order is indeed an autonomous legal order made up of many autonomous legal orders that do not lose their autonomy as a result.[21] The identification of the particular legal order within which legal pluralism is experienced is important not only in determining the norm-applying actors in charge of validating legal norms stemming from different legal orders and hence of settling their potentially conflicting claims to (exclusionary) legitimate authority. It also matters if one is to avoid the slippery transitions, that are common in the legal pluralism literature, from a discussion of plural legal 'norms' to considerations of a 'pluralist legal order'.[22]

Two further meanings of the concept of external legal pluralism may be identified: first of all, pluralism *qua* validity and pluralism *qua* rank, and, second, within either of them, pluralism of norms/sources/regimes and pluralism of orders (or more exactly of norms stemming from different orders) applying to the same subjects.

When pluralism is used to refer to a plurality of legal orders overlapping within the same social sphere, this is usually meant to distinguish pluralism from monism.[23] As such, it constitutes an elaborate and interlocking version of dualism. Legal validity does not, however, depend on transposition or reception in different legal orders contrary to what is the case in a dualist legal order. What matters is that the validity of those different

---

[21] On the notion of integrated legal order, see Besson, 'How international', note 1 above and 'European legal pluralism', note 2 above. On the place of international law within the EU's integrated legal order, see *ibid.*, and both the judgment and the Opinion of Advocate General Kokott in Case C–366/10 *Air Transport Association of America*, nyr.

[22] See e.g. Krisch, 'Open architecture', note 3 above at 185–6 on human rights pluralism *qua* pluralistic legal 'order'; he moves swiftly from 'human rights law' (domestic and international) to the opposition between 'different', 'integrated' and 'pluralistic' 'legal orders'. I do not plan, however, to explain how to distinguish between legal pluralism within a particular legal order, usually the domestic one, and a pluralistic legal order, but merely to draw attention to the importance of the distinction.

[23] Note that monism is a theory of legal validity within a given legal order, and not of legal autonomy. As a result legal monism is entirely compatible with the coexistence of separate, autonomous, legal orders, provided they do not overlap entirely.

norms can be established together and at the same time in their respective legal orders, and this is best captured by the concept of plurivalidity.[24] Pluralism in this first meaning of the concept pertains therefore to the *validity* of legal norms. It assumes that legal norms' validity can have many autonomous sources within the same territory or political community and within the same legal order. More specifically, this may be explained, in legal positivist terms, by reference to the plurality of rules of recognition coexisting within the same legal order and identifying the criteria for validity of the legal norms to be applied in each case by the norm-applying institutions.[25]

The term 'legal pluralism' can also be used, however, having the meaning equivalence of legal norms or of legal sources, either within a legal order or between different legal orders. In that sense, pluralism is opposed to hierarchy. It provides a different answer to the question of first *primacy* and then *rank* among legal norms from the same legal order or from different legal orders that overlap in a given legal order. Of course, the plurality of valid and equally strong legal norms need not necessarily lead to normative conflict, but it might do so and this is how it usually attracts attention. In a case of normative conflict, pluralism is usually contrasted with the existence of a formal hierarchy of sources or of norms, and equated with heterarchy as a result; the legal order at stake entails no rules of conflict and the settlement of potential normative conflicts has to be left to judicial politics. More specifically, the equivalence in rank of legal norms within a pluralist legal order may be explained, in legal positivist terms, by reference to the coexistence of various rules of recognition with distinct validity criteria, on one hand, and to the absence of ranking rules in all legal orders, on the other.[26]

Those distinctions are important. First, not all those forms of legal pluralism present the same difficulty for legal theory. It is one thing for the law-applying institutions in a legal order to recognise the legal norms of another legal order as valid and hence as authoritative norms in their legal order, and another to discuss which ones should take priority in cases of conflict. Nor, secondly, need the remedies be the same in all cases. Thus, the principle of normative coherence can be regarded as a remedy for the absence of hierarchy or rules of conflict between norms in the same

---

[24] See Besson, 'How international', note 1 above, p. 14; Günther, note 17 above.
[25] See J. Raz, *The Concept of a Legal System* (Oxford: Clarendon Press, 1980), p. 35ff.; Barber, note 2 above.
[26] See Raz, *ibid.*, p. 35ff.; Barber, *ibid.*, at 322.

legal order. It is not so relevant, however, when the question pertains to the validity of one legal order's norms in another legal order. Of course, in general, often pluralism *qua* validity only really matters when questions of conflict between norms and hence issues of rank arise; normative conflicts are really of interest only if the legal norms at stake are concurrently valid legal norms. And this is what makes the distinction so difficult to draw in practice.

From a meta-theoretical perspective, legal pluralism is often used as a descriptive concept and hence presumably in order to qualify an empirical fact.[27] It is important, however, to distinguish the mere plurality of legal norms from legal pluralism.[28] Legal pluralism implies some kind of normative statement about how the legal validity and legal authority of that plurality of norms ought to be organised. Those cannot merely be described. True, practices around them or even the legal actors' cost–benefit calculus and attitudes may be,[29] but not the legal norms' validity and authority themselves. Regrettably, no normative argument for legal pluralism is to be found in that scholarship, except for a few contributions that are usually sceptical about its existence.[30]

Of course, this normative onus on theories of legal pluralism raises the broader issue of whether legal theory can ever be purely descriptive. My answer is that it cannot. Legal positivism, which is the kind of legal theory endorsed here, is itself normative *qua* legal theory. And legal pluralism, as part of legal positivism,[31] needs to be argued for normatively. It is important, therefore, to provide a normative defence of legal pluralism within the realm of legal positivism. The argument is that legal pluralism may be justified by reference to democratic legitimacy and, more specifically, to the multilevel democratic legitimation of different legal sources,

---

[27] See e.g. Krisch, 'Open architecture', note 3 above, and *Beyond Constitutionalism*, note 2 above.

[28] The same distinction may be drawn between 'ethical plurality' and 'ethical pluralism'.

[29] This is what Krisch, 'Open architecture', note 3 above at 209ff. does, for instance, by reference to political science literature in the field of international adjudication.

[30] See e.g. Besson, 'European legal pluralism', note 2 above; A. Somek, 'The concept of "law" in global administrative law: a reply to Benedict Kingsbury', 20 *European Journal of International Law* 4 (2009), 985–95; Letsas, note 4 above. See, however, most recently Maduro, 'Three claims', note 2 above; Davies, note 2 above.

[31] I agree with Letsas, note 4 above, and A. Zysset, 'Epistemological analysis of the "disorder" of European legal pluralism' in S. Besson and N. Levrat (eds), *Dés-ordres Juridiques Européens – European Legal Dis-Orders* (Zurich: Schulthess, 2012), on the legal positivist underpinnings of the notion of legal pluralism. However, I disagree with them about the fatality of the empirical nature of the legal positivist argument for legal pluralism.

regimes and orders by reference to the same democratic people.[32] This normative, democracy-based argument for legal pluralism also explains the judicial recourse to further principles in the resolution of normative conflicts, such as subsidiarity, for instance. As I will argue in the human rights context, judicial dialogue on its own cannot explain what judges are doing when settling those cases. Nor may it account on its own for the kind of normative cooperation and mutual reasoning they embrace.

Last but not least, it is important to distinguish the legal pluralism discussed in this section from *judicial* pluralism, i.e. the plurality of and lack of hierarchy between courts belonging to different legal orders albeit interpreting and applying the same legal norms in each of those legal orders. The two forms of pluralism are distinct, albeit often joint in practice. It is important to keep them apart, however. There may be many courts with jurisdiction over the application and interpretation of the same legal norms in the same political community, as exemplified by the adjudication over the ECHR in the EU by the Court of Justice of the European Union (CJEU), the European Court of Human Rights (ECtHR) and domestic courts. Conversely, the same court may be called on to apply a plurality of legal norms stemming from different legal orders as exemplified by domestic courts applying EU law. Of course, in most cases, judicial pluralism enhances legal pluralism by multiplying the interpretations of the same norms that stem from different legal orders within the same legal order. Moreover, judicial pluralism is largely a consequence of legal pluralism, given that normative conflicts need to be settled somehow and usually through judicial intervention. And in cases where those settlements are in the hands of many courts, legal pluralism is more or less regulated by judicial pluralism. In this chapter, however, I shall focus on legal pluralism as distinct from judicial pluralism so as to untie, as much as possible, the role of human rights in the articulation of legal orders from what courts hold of that role and from the function they play in that context.[33]

---

[32] See Besson, 'European legal pluralism', note 2 above, drawing a distinction in this respect between EU law and international law.

[33] Most discussions of human rights pluralism in Europe usually treat both issues together. See e.g. L. Scheeck, 'The relationship between the European Courts and integration through human rights', 65 *Zeitschrift für Ausländisches Öffentliches Recht und Völkerrecht* (2005), 837–85; S. Douglas-Scott, 'A Tale of Two Courts: Luxembourg, Strasbourg and the growing European human rights *acquis*', *Common Market Law Review* 43 (2006), 629–66; Rosas, note 10 above; G. Harpaz, 'The ECJ and its relations with the ECtHR', *Common Market Law Review* 46 (2009), 105–42; J. Callewaert, 'The European Convention on Human

Interestingly, one of the most severe challenges to legal pluralism stems precisely from its proponents' emphasis on judges and judicial politics in cases of normative conflicts. Letsas argues, for instance, that this emphasis implies that the non-legal and political role of judges becomes so important that it is untenable for legal positivists, who can only accommodate judicial discretion within certain limited boundaries.[34] This argument fails to convince, however. It is not only indeterminate in terms of threshold but, given that legal pluralism does not necessarily lead to normative conflicts, it lacks teeth. Legal pluralism is no less tenable for courts because it is no longer only internal but also external, to refer to the distinction I made before. Of course, Letsas is right to argue against judicial dialogue as the solution to legal pluralism, however. As I will argue, handling legal pluralism requires much more than dialogue. As a result, not all legal pluralist theories need to endorse judicial dialogue, and the objections to judicial dialogue need not be regarded as objections to legal pluralism.

2. European human rights pluralism

When transposed into the European human rights context, the issue of legal pluralism raises two distinct sets of questions: the issue of human rights pluralism itself and that of the role of human rights in the context of legal pluralism. Both need to be addressed in turn, as they raise separate difficulties and have too often been conflated, with the result that both are either endorsed or rejected at the same time, and usually for the wrong reasons.

2.1. Human rights pluralism in Europe

Interestingly, European human rights law is often invoked as a primary example of legal pluralism in Europe.[35] The human rights applicable to any given situation within a European state stem from many different legal

---

Rights and European Union law: a long way to harmony', *European Human Rights Law Review* 6 (2009), 768–83; Krisch, *Beyond Constitutionalism*, note 2 above. See on the legitimacy of supranational human rights review in Europe, e.g. S. Besson, 'European human rights, supranational judicial review and democracy – thinking outside the judicial box' in P. Popelier, C. van Nuffel and P. van den Heyning (eds), *Human Rights Protection in the European Legal Order: The Interaction between the European and the National Courts* (Cambridge: Intersentia, 2011), pp 97–145.

[34] Letsas, note 4 above.

[35] See e.g. Krisch, 'Open architecture', note 3 above; Maduro, 'Three claims', note 2 above.

orders, or at least from different sources and regimes within the same legal order: e.g. domestic human rights, EU fundamental rights and ECHR rights. Because those various sources of human rights interact in ways that allegedly can no longer be explained solely by reference to monism or dualism,[36] and, more precisely, because ECHR rights in particular are mostly immediately valid as domestic human rights within the domestic legal order, pluralism is usually regarded as the best explanation of their relationship, on one hand.[37] On the other, the relationship between domestic human rights, ECHR rights and EU fundamental rights, when interpreted by their respective adjudication bodies, is said to be unclear and conflicting claims to authority are said to be made in many cases. As a result, that relationship is usually approached as a pluralist one in the absence of a clear hierarchy between those rights.[38]

In line with the argument I made earlier about European legal pluralism, the key question, however, is whether, besides the empirical evidence given for those two dimensions of European human rights plurality, one may bring forward normative arguments for the existence of European human rights pluralism proper. As I argued earlier, indeed, legal validity and legal authority cannot merely be described as empirical facts, and the normative underpinnings of those descriptive statements need to be argued for. The plurality of human rights norms internationally and domestically, and of interpretations of human rights by international and domestic judicial bodies, need not yet imply a form of human rights pluralism.

I will make two sets of points here: one pertaining to the pluralism of human rights themselves and the other to the pluralism of human rights' interpretations. Within each, I will focus both on the plural validity and the plural authority of human rights norms. Of course, as I have explained and will explain again in relation to human rights, the distinction between human rights norms and their judicial interpretations and applications is artificial. All the same, it is important to draw that distinction between human rights norms and their judicial interpretations in order to stress the difference between plural validity and plural rank, and, more significantly, in order to dispel the idea, which I will address later in the chapter, that their abstract normative equivalence might be invoked to settle other normative conflicts without requiring a judicial interpretation of the

---

[36] See e.g. H. Keller and A. Stone Sweet (eds), *A Europe of Rights: The Impact of the ECHR on National Legal Systems* (Oxford: Oxford University Press, 2008).
[37] See e.g. Krisch, 'Open architecture', note 3 above at 184–5.   [38] *Ibid.*

human rights themselves and without having to consider the potential conflicts between distinct international or European and domestic judicial interpretations.

2.2. Pluralism of human rights law in Europe

By reference to what I said about legal pluralism in the previous section, the argument that would need to be made in favour of human rights pluralism would be, first, that European human rights norms are immediately valid on the domestic level regardless of whether the domestic legal order is monist or dualist and, second, that there are no hierarchies when European norms conflict with domestic human rights norms.

While both points appear to be arguable at first sight, they underestimate a crucial feature of international or European and domestic human rights norms: their mutuality, both in terms of validity and in terms of legitimate authority. Thus, while human rights law may indeed be regarded as pluralist, this, on its own, does not capture the core of the relationship at work between international or European human rights law and domestic human rights law. Since I have already developed an argument for the mutual validation and legitimation of domestic and international or regional human rights law elsewhere,[39] I will focus here on how that mutual validation and legitimation may be understood as a special instantiation of legal pluralism. Note that, as I explained earlier in relation to legal pluralism in general, the distinction between validity and legitimacy is merely conceptual given how closely related they are in practice, and the mutual validity of international or European human rights and domestic human rights has to be explained by reference to their mutual legitimation.

First of all, then, let us look at the plurivalidity of human rights law. A pluralist argument would read along the lines that international or European and domestic human rights legal norms draw their joint validity from separate rules of recognition within the domestic legal order. Actually, however, it would be more accurate to argue that their plurivalidity amounts to intervalidity or mutual validity to the extent that their validity is mutually determined.

---

[39] See S. Besson, 'Human rights and constitutional law' in R. Cruft, S. M. Liao and N. Renzo (eds), *Philosophical Foundations of Human Rights* (Oxford: Oxford University Press, 2014), forthcoming.

To start with, it is important to stress the existence of a so-called 'dual positivisation' of human rights in international or European law and domestic law.[40] Authors still disagree about the grounds for that dual positivisation and juxtaposition of human rights regimes in the domestic legal order. Those are neither chronological, substantive nor remedial. International and domestic human rights norms as we know them today date back roughly to the same post-1945 era, a time at which or after which the international bill of rights was drafted on the basis of existing domestic bills of rights and at which or after which most existing domestic constitutions were either completely revised or drafted anew on the basis of the international bill of rights.[41] Nowadays, in actual fact, constitutional rights either antedate the adoption of international human rights law or ought to be adopted on the ground of the latter – either in preparation for ratification or as a consequence thereof [42] – thus confirming the synchronic nature of their functions and the requirement that they coexist; one no longer goes without the other.[43] Interestingly, however, the content and the structure of the human rights protected are, by and large, the same.[44] Neither, finally, does the key to the relationship between domestic and international human rights lie in their enforcement, as both human rights regimes are owned by domestic institutions, implemented by domestic institutions and monitored in the same way.[45]

What is clear, however, is that the two regimes are not merely juxtaposed – with international human rights law *qua* gap-filling rights[46] – and hence should not be regarded as redundant regimes at best. The difference between the two legal regimes of human rights and the underlying ground for their dual positivisation and validation in the domestic legal order, as a result, pertains to their distinct albeit complementary functions.[47] International human rights law secures the external and minimal protection of the right to have domestic human rights in the political community of

---

[40] See G. Neuman, 'Human rights and constitutional rights', 55 *Stanford Law Review* 5 (2003), 1863–1900 at 1864.
[41] S. Gardbaum, 'Human rights as international constitutional rights', 19 *European Journal of International Law* 4 (2008), 749–68 at 750.
[42] See e.g. Art. 1 ECHR; Arts. 2 and 4 Convention on the Rights of the Child.
[43] See also Gardbaum, note 41 above at 764ff.   [44] *Ibid.*, at 750–51.
[45] See also R. Dworkin, *Justice for Hedgehogs* (Cambridge, MA: Belknap, 2011), pp 333–4. See also K. Hessler, 'Resolving interpretive conflicts in international human rights law', 13 *Journal of Political Philosophy* 1 (2005), 29–52 at 37.
[46] See Gardbaum, note 41 above at 764.   [47] See also Dworkin, note 45 above, pp 334–5.

which one is a member. That externalised human rights regime works on three levels domestically and has three functions accordingly:

1. a *substantive* one: it requires the protection of the minimal and abstract content of those rights against domestic levelling-down, and works therefore as a form of back-up;[48]
2. a *personal* one: it requires the inclusion of all those subjected to domestic jurisdiction,[49] territorially and extraterritorially and whether they are nationals or not, in the scope of those rights;[50] and
3. a *procedural* one: it requires the introduction of both internal and external institutional mechanisms to monitor and enforce those rights.[51]

Both levels of protection are usually regarded as complementary and as serving different functions, therefore, rather than as providing competing guarantees. This complementary relationship between international and domestic guarantees explains why the reception of international human rights into domestic law is favoured or even required by international human rights instruments. Domestic human rights law does more than merely implement international human rights, therefore: it contextualises and specifies them. This explains why international human rights are usually drafted in minimal and abstract terms, thus calling for domestic reception and specification.[52] They rely on national guarantees to formulate a minimal threshold that they reflect and entrench internationally. That entrenchment is dynamic and the minimal content of international human rights may evolve with time.[53] More importantly, they are usually abstract and meant to be fleshed out at the domestic level, not only in terms of the specific duties attached to a given right but also in terms of the right itself.

---

[48] See A. Buchanan, 'Reciprocal legitimation: reframing the problem of international legitimacy', 10 *Politics, Philosophy and Economics* 1 (2011), 5–19 at 11; Gardbaum, note 41 above at 764.
[49] See S. Besson, 'The extraterritoriality of the European Convention on Human Rights: why human rights require jurisdiction and what jurisdiction amounts to', 25 *Leiden Journal of International Law* 4 (2012), 857–84.
[50] See Buchanan, note 48 above at 12–13; Gardbaum, note 41 above at 765–7.
[51] I do not agree with the other functions of international human rights law suggested by Gardbaum, note 41 above at 766–8 and Buchanan, note 48 above at 11–14.
[52] See Besson, 'Decoupling and recoupling', note 14 above; Dworkin, note 45 above, pp 337–8.
[53] See S. Besson, 'The *erga omnes* effect of ECtHR's judgments – what's in a name?', in Besson (ed.), *The European Court of Human Rights after Protocol 14 – First Assessment and Perspectives* (Zurich: Schulthess, 2011), pp 125–75, on the interpretative authority of the ECtHR's judgments.

As a matter of fact, it is through the relationship of mutual reinforce-ment between domestic human rights and international human rights, and the productive tension between external guarantees and internal ones, that human rights law has consolidated at both domestic and international levels.[54] International human rights law places duties on domestic author-ities to include them within domestic human rights law and to implement them in a democratic fashion, and the latter feed into international human rights guarantees in return. This constant interaction between interna-tional and domestic human rights is reminiscent of Arendt's universal right to have particular rights and the to-ing and fro-ing between the universal and the particular. International human rights are specified as domestic human rights, but domestic human rights progressively consol-idate into international human rights in return.

This virtuous circle can actually be exemplified by reference to the sources of international human rights law. International human rights law is indeed deemed to belong to general international law and finds its sources both in general principles of international law, and arguably also in customary international law. Both sets of sources derive inter-national norms from domestic ones and this jurisgenerative process is actually epitomised by the sources of international human rights law.[55] Historically, much of the content of international human rights treaties was actually drawn from domestic bills of rights, and many of the latter were then revised after 1945 to come into line with the former.[56] The mutual relationship between international and domestic human rights can also be confirmed by recent human rights practice, whether it is of a customary, conventional or even judicial nature. Domestic human rights contribute to the development of the corresponding international human rights' judicial or quasi-judicial interpretations. This is clearly the case in the case law of the European Court of Human Rights where common

---

[54] See Besson, 'Decoupling and recoupling', note 14 above; J. Habermas, 'The concept of human dignity and the realistic utopia of human rights', 41 *Metaphilosophy* 4 (2010), 465–80 at 478; S. Benhabib, 'Claiming rights across borders: international human rights and democratic sovereignty', 103 *American Political Science Review* 4 (2009), 691–704; S. Benhabib, *Dignity in Adversity: Human Rights in Troubled Times* (Cambridge: Polity Press, 2011), pp 16 and 126; J. Habermas, *Zur Verfassung Europas: Ein Essay* (Berlin: Suhrkamp, 2011), pp 31–2, 36–8.

[55] See S. Besson, 'General principles in international law – whose principles?' in S. Besson and P. Pichonnaz (eds), *Les principes en droit européen – Principles in European Law* (Zurich: Schulthess, 2011), pp 21–68.

[56] See J. Morsink, *Inherent Human Rights: Philosophical Roots of the Universal Declaration* (Philadelphia: University of Pennsylvania Press, 2009), p. 149.

ground is a constant concern and is sought after when interpreting the ECHR.[57]

That mutual relationship between international and domestic human rights law may also be observed from the way in which international human rights norms are validated in the domestic legal order.[58] Unlike other international law norms, international human rights law claims, and is usually granted, immediate validity and direct effect in domestic legal orders.[59] This occurs in many cases through the joint and largely indistinct application of international and constitutional human rights by domestic authorities, and in particular domestic courts. There is, in other words, no difference between international human rights and domestic constitutional rights in terms of validity within the domestic legal order. Nor are they differentiated in most cases, as they are usually subsumed within a composite set of human rights norms. Once validated through this kind of indiscriminate application, what matters is the human right, and no longer its legal source.

Second, we must examine the heterarchy of human rights law. The second feature of legal pluralism may also be verified in the human rights context, which does not assign to international or European human rights law priority over domestic human rights law and vice versa. As a matter of fact, not only does neither take priority over the other, as in other cases of legal pluralism, but they should be seen, moreover, as standing in a relationship of mutual legitimation that is usually lacking in those other cases.

Importantly, indeed, the legal enforcement of international human rights is a two-way street that is not limited to a top-down reception of international law in domestic law, but also spreads from the bottom upwards and comes closer to a virtuous circle of legitimation. The recognition and existence of those rights *qua* international human rights that constrain domestic politics ought indeed to be based on democratic practices recognised on a domestic level. Their content reflects the outcome of democratic interpretations of human rights. And only those polities that both respect international human rights and are democratic are deemed

---

[57] See Besson, '*Erga omnes* effect', note 53 above.

[58] See Neuman, note 40 above at 1890–95.

[59] This is particularly striking in legal orders within which international law is not necessarily granted immediate validity and direct effect. See e.g. S. Besson, 'The reception of the ECHR in the United Kingdom and Ireland' in Keller and Stone Sweet, note 36 above, pp 31–106; and H. Keller and A. Stone Sweet, 'Introduction: the reception of the ECHR in national legal orders' in *ibid.*, pp 3–30.

legitimate in specifying the content of those rights further, and hence in contributing to the further recognition and existence of those rights *qua* international human rights that will constrain them in return.[60] This dynamic phenomenon is what Buchanan refers to as the mutual legitimation of domestic and international law.[61]

Of course, the mutual legitimation of international or European human rights law and domestic human rights law does not mean that normative conflicts cannot arise. This is the so-called 'divergence question', and it is usually described as a conflict of incompatible claims to legitimate authority stemming from domestic and international human rights law.[62]

Interestingly, the question is often misunderstood. One of the main difficulties with this understanding of the question and of the discourse pertaining to human rights pluralism in Europe is actually the tendency to conflate the plurality of judicial interpretations of the same human rights norms among European and domestic institutions, a serious issue in itself, with the plurality of human rights norms just discussed. Not only does the latter not imply the former, but their respective pluralisms need to be carefully distinguished from one another, as I explained earlier in relationship to the general distinction between legal and judicial pluralism.

Human rights themselves cannot enter into conflict as they share the same abstract content (i.e. protection of the same interests against the same standard threats) independently of their international or domestic sources. Instead, it is the interpretations of human rights and the specifications of the corresponding duties in concrete local circumstances by international and domestic institutions that may conflict with each other. And this is the case *a fortiori*, whether the human rights interpreted and specified by those institutions are the same international human rights, on one hand, or distinct international and domestic human rights, on the other. In other words, where two human rights norms stem from different legal sources, therefore, what may differ between them are not the abstract rights but the concrete duties and this can only be the case once the norms have been applied to the same set of circumstances by different authorities. Furthermore, as discussed above, in the reception

---

[60] See Hessler, note 45 above at 48ff.

[61] See A. Buchanan, *Justice, Legitimacy, and Self-Determination: Moral Foundations for International Law* (New York: Oxford University Press, 2004), pp 187–9; Buchanan, 'Reciprocal legitimation', note 48 above.

[62] Neuman, note 40 above at 1873–4 and 1874ff. for the various divergences.

process international human rights are usually subsumed within domestic human rights norms, and in particular within constitutional rights, and this turns them into valid domestic law; it not only grants them the legitimacy of domestic law, but also takes care, usually, of any potential conflict of authority as a result.

All this explains why the idea of human rights pluralism *qua* human rights heterarchy is misleading:[63] there may be a plurality of human rights institutions interpreting the same international human rights norms differently, but this does not entail a conflict between the international or domestic legal norms protecting those rights.[64] Of course, human rights may come into conflict when their corresponding duties conflict,[65] but again this is an independent question that has nothing to do with either the international or domestic sources of the rights themselves, on one hand, or the international or domestic nature of the interpreting institutions, on the other.[66] Finally, international human rights may conflict with norms of domestic constitutional law other than human rights, when the abstract content of the latter is clear, but this is another matter.

Once reformulated, the question is then how one should handle conflicts of interpretation or specification between international and domestic human rights institutions.[67] This means identifying which institution is legitimate or justified in its claim to final authority over the issue.[68] International human rights institutions may be tribunals, like the European or Inter-American Court of Human Rights, or independent treaty bodies, like the UN human rights treaty bodies. Domestic human rights institutions cover any domestic institutions implementing human rights, but mostly judicial bodies whether they specialise in human rights or have general jurisdiction. And this issue actually constitutes the object of the next section.

---

[63] See e.g. Krisch, *Beyond Constitutionalism*, note 2 above.

[64] See Besson, 'Human rights and constitutional law', note 39 above.

[65] See e.g. J. Waldron, 'Rights in conflict' in *Liberal Rights: Collected Papers 1981–1991* (Cambridge: Cambridge University Press, 1993), pp 203–24; S. Besson, 'Conflicts of constitutional rights: nature, typology and resolution' in Besson, *The Morality of Conflict: Reasonable Disagreement and the Law* (Oxford: Hart Publishing, 2005), pp 419–56; L. Zucca, *Constitutional Dilemmas: Conflicts of Fundamental Legal Rights in Europe and the USA* (New York: Oxford University Press, 2007).

[66] Contra: see e.g. A. Torres Perez, *Conflicts of Rights in the European Union: A Theory of Supranational Adjudication* (Oxford: Oxford University Press, 2009).

[67] See e.g. Hessler, note 45 above at 32–3.

[68] See S. Besson, 'The legitimate authority of international human rights' in A. Føllesdal et al. (eds), *The Legitimacy of International Human Rights Regimes* (Cambridge: Cambridge University Press, 2013).

2.3. Pluralism of human rights interpretations in Europe

The next question then is whether the plurality of human rights interpretations that stem from different competent judicial bodies in Europe may be equated with a form of legal pluralism. This is not so much a question of validity, but rather one of rank or hierarchy in response to potential conflicts between those plural interpretations. Allegedly, indeed, the relationship between European interpretations of human rights by their respective adjudication bodies is unclear, and conflicting claims to authority are made in many cases. In the absence of a clear hierarchy between them, that relationship is usually approached as a pluralist one.[69]

Here again, my argument will be that, while it is true that there is no hierarchy of human rights interpretations in Europe, their relationship is more complex than mere heterarchy: it is one of mutuality. Their different roles or functions preclude the possibility of a real conflict as a result.

To start with, there are various arguments one might articulate for the priority of domestic human rights institutions in the interpretation and specification of human rights.[70] I will restrict myself to two here: one is democratic and the other practical. First of all, domestic human rights institutions are the institutions of the democratic polity to which belong the members whose rights are affected and to which those members' duties need to be allocated. The egalitarian dimension of human rights ties them closely to political and more specifically to democratic procedures in the specification and allocation of duties. Only domestic institutions present those democratic and egalitarian qualities in relation to the human rights that bind them and which they ought to protect. Second, domestic institutions have the institutional capacity to allocate the burden of duties fairly in view of the resources available and in knowledge of the concrete threats to the protected interests. The concrete dimension of human rights duties makes their identification and distribution a necessarily local matter and the same applies to the resolution of conflicts of human rights duties or to the justification of required restrictions to human rights duties. Domestic institutions are clearly better situated to ensure

---

[69] See e.g. Krisch, 'Open architecture', note 3 above at 184–5.

[70] See Hessler, note 45 above at 42ff. On the legitimacy of international judicial review of human rights, see also Besson, 'Supranational judicial review', note 33 above; A. Føllesdal, 'International judicial human rights review – effective, legitimate or both?' in J. Sihvola, P. Korkman and V. Mäkinen (eds), *Universalism in International Law and Political Philosophy* (Helsinki: Helsinki Collegium for Advanced Studies, 2008); A. von Staden, 'The democratic legitimacy of judicial review beyond the state: normative subsidiarity and judicial standards of review', 10 *International Journal of Constitutional Law* 4 (2012), 1023–49.

that allocation and hence the interpretation of human rights duties in context.

Importantly, however, despite being situated outside the democratic polity to which belong those members whose human rights and duties are concerned, the parallel existence of international human rights institutions with a claim to final and legitimate authority does not mean that this should be understood as a juxtaposed and competing monitoring regime, situated in a heterarchical relationship to domestic ones. As a result, assigning priority to either domestic or international human rights interpretations should not be understood as implying a hierarchy or a higher legitimate authority in any way. The claims to legitimate authority of international and domestic human rights institutions are not in competition and potential conflict with one another.[71] Their mutuality dates back to the post-1945 human rights regime and needs to be fully grasped at last. This implies understanding that their claims to legitimate authority are not distinctly justified on different bases and in an exclusive fashion, but on the contrary share a mutually reinforcing, democratic justification.[72] Thus, it is the international human rights institutions' potential contribution to democratic processes or compensation for any domestic lack thereof that helps justify their legitimate authority in the cases in which they impose particular human rights interpretations on domestic authorities.[73] Just as international human rights contribute to protecting the rights to democratic membership and to have human rights in a democratic polity, international human rights institutions protect democratic institutions and guarantee their ability to respect human rights.

Thus, just as international and domestic human rights law complement each other and are in productive tension, their interpreting institutions should be understood as situated in a joint, albeit complementary, interpretative endeavour and not as mutually exclusive interpretative authorities. This is confirmed by the fact that institutional and procedural standards for the implementation and monitoring of human rights are developed internally in cooperation among democratic states, transnationalised and then internationalised from the bottom up and then imposed from the top down again as external constraints on domestic institutions and procedures. International institutions and procedures

[71] See e.g. Neuman, note 40 above at 1873–4.
[72] See Buchanan, 'Reciprocal legitimation', note 48 above.
[73] *Ibid.* See also Hessler, note 45 above at 45ff.

are incomplete without domestic ones, but the latter are organised so as to work in tension with the former. One may think, for instance, of the development of conventional review in European democracies that did not know of constitutional review before ratifying the ECHR. Conversely, one should mention the 2009 introduction within the ECHR regime of an infringement procedure, based on domestic authorities' experiences with the implementation of their own human rights decisions.

This normative account of the mutual interpretative authority of domestic and international human rights institutions fits current human rights practice and the ways in which potential interpretative conflicts are handled,[74] and in particular the principle of *subsidiarity* that characterises that practice.[75] International human rights institutions only intervene once domestic remedies have been exhausted and domestic authorities have had a chance to specify, allocate and interpret human rights duties in context. One may refer to this as procedural or jurisdictional subsidiarity. Further, they are usually very reluctant to question domestic institutions' interpretations and specifications of human rights in the specific political context. This may be described as material or substantive subsidiarity. International human rights institutions respect domestic institutions' 'margin of appreciation' in most cases.[76] Finally, they usually impose obligations to reach a result through judgment or decision, but leave the choice of means to domestic authorities. This is referred to as remedial subsidiarity.

The only limit on that international institutional subsidiarity, however, is the existence of a *consensus* among most democratic states going in a

---

[74] See Neuman, note 40 above at 1880ff.

[75] See Besson, '*Erga omnes* effect', note 53 above. See also D. Shelton, 'Subsidiarity and human rights law', 27 *Human Rights Law Journal* 1 (2006), 4–11; L. Helfer, 'Redesigning the European Court of Human Rights: embeddedness as a deep structural principle of the European human rights regime', 19 *European Journal of International Law* (2008), 125–59.

[76] See C. van de Heyning, 'No place like home: discretionary space for the domestic protection of fundamental rights' in Popelier, van Nuffel and van de Heyning, note 33 above, pp 65–96, especially 87–91; J. Kratochvil, 'The inflation of the margin of appreciation by the European Court of Human Rights', 29 *Netherlands Quarterly of Human Rights* 3 (2011), 324–57; Krisch, *Beyond Constitutionalism*, note 2 above, pp 140–43; Y. Arai-Takahashi, *The Margin of Appreciation Doctrine and the Principle of Proportionality in the Jurisprudence of the ECHR* (Antwerp: Intersentia, 2002); E. Brems, 'The margin of appreciation doctrine in the case-law of the European Court of Human Rights', 56 *Zeitschrift für Ausländisches Öffentliches Recht und Völkerrecht* (1996), 240–314; R. MacDonald, 'The margin of appreciation' in R. MacDonald, F. Matscher and H. Petzold (eds), *The European System for the Protection of Human Rights* (Dordrecht: Martinus Nijhoff, 1993), pp 83–124.

direction different from the one chosen by a given state.[77] Here, the mutual validation and legitimation among democratic states alluded to in the previous section also applies to the level of human rights interpretation and specification. The joint interpretative endeavour of all democratic domestic authorities leads indeed to the gradual constitution of an international interpretation and specification for a given human right, albeit a minimal and abstract one. Once there is such a consensual minimal interpretation among most domestic authorities, it may be recognised by international human rights institutions themselves and thus become consolidated and entrenched at the international level. The evolutionary nature of this joint interpretative process is sometimes referred to as 'dynamic interpretation' of international human rights law.[78] And the joint and mutual process of human rights interpretation among domestic and international human rights institutions is sometimes called 'judicial dialogue'.[79] Once identified, that minimal human rights interpretation can then be reimposed on domestic authorities. This is what is often referred to as the interpretative authority or *erga omnes* effect of an international human rights interpretation or decision.[80]

Importantly, however, those minimal international interpretations can only be more protective and never less protective than the conflicting domestic one; they entrench interpretations to prevent levelling-down but never hinder levelling-up.[81] This is the point of so-called *saving clauses* in

---

[77] See e.g. L. Helfer, 'Consensus, coherence and the European Convention on Human Rights', 26 *Cornell International Law Journal* (1993), 133–65; K. Dzehtsiarou, 'Does consensus matter? Legitimacy of European consensus in the case law of the ECtHR', *Public Law* (2011), 534–53. See also Neuman, note 40 above at 1884.

[78] See e.g. *Tyrer v. United Kingdom* (App. No. 5856/72) Series A (1979–80) No. 26. On the subsidiary nature of its interpretations, see e.g. *Burden v. United Kingdom* (App. No. 13378/05) [2008] ECHR 357, para. 42; *Hatton v. United Kingdom* (App. No. 36022/97) [2003] ECHR 338, para. 97. See also Letsas, note 4 above.

[79] See e.g. Krisch, *Beyond Constitutionalism*, note 2 above, pp 109–52, 126ff.; L. Wildhaber, 'Ein Überdenken des Zustands und der Zukunft des Europäischen Gerichtshofs für Menschenrechte', *Europäische Grundrechtezeitschrift* 36 (2009), 547–53; E. Lambert Abdelgawad, *Les effets des arrêts de la Cour européenne des droits de l'homme* (Brussels: Établissements Émile Bruylant, 1999), pp 331–4.

[80] See e.g. Besson, '*Erga omnes* effect', note 53 above; J. Christoffersen, 'Individual and constitutional justice: can the power balance of adjudication be reversed?' (pp 204–29) and L. Wildhaber, 'Rethinking the European Court of Human Rights' (pp 181–203), both in J. Christoffersen and M. Rask Madsen (eds), *The European Court of Human Rights between Law and Politics* (Oxford: Oxford University Press, 2011).

[81] See, more generally, A. Buchanan, 'Moral progress and human rights' in C. Holder and D. Reidy (eds), *Human Rights: The Hard Questions* (Cambridge: Cambridge University Press, 2012), pp 399–417.

many international human rights instruments (e.g. Article 53 ECHR).[82] Of course, a domestic institution may still disagree about whether some international interpretation provides better protection of a given human right than a domestic one.[83] Here, the judicial nature of the interpretative authority of international human rights decisions implies that judicial distinctions and overruling past decisions may always be possible provided judicial reasoning across institutional levels leads to that result.[84] Furthermore, domestic courts may invoke a change in the transnational interpretative consensus itself. Thus, the interpretative authority of an international human rights institution ought to evolve in step with states' margin of appreciation as a two-way street and not simply oppose it, as some may fear.[85] Moreover, restrictions to human rights may always be justified on important grounds and provided the conditions of democratic necessity are fulfilled.[86] This applies even in circumstances in which there is a transnational human rights consensus, for instance on controversial moral issues,[87] and even when that consensus has been sanctioned with interpretative authority by an international human rights decision

---

[82] See Neuman, note 40 above at 1886–7. See also van de Heyning, note 76 above.

[83] See e.g. Besson, 'Decoupling and recoupling', note 14 above; Buchanan, *Justice, Legitimacy, and Self-Determination*, note 61 above, pp 180–86. Contra: E. Brems, 'Human rights: minimum and maximum perspectives', 9 *Human Rights Law Review* 3 (2009), 343–72.

[84] See e.g. Besson, '*Erga omnes* effect', note 53 above. See e.g. in the United Kingdom, the House of Lords' decision in *R.* v. *Lyons* [2002] UKHL 44, [2002] WLR 1562, 1580, 1584, 1595 that was confirmed later by the ECtHR in *Lyons and others* v. *United Kingdom* (App. No. 15227/03) ECHR 2003–IX. See also *Z and others* v. *United Kingdom* (App. No. 29392/95) ECHR 2001–V, confirming a British decision (*Barrett* v. *Enfield LBC* [1999] UKHL 25, [2001] 2 AC 550) that had been intentionally decided against the European Court's decision in *Osman* v. *United Kingdom* (App. No. 23452/94). Most recently, see also ECtHR, *A* v. *United Kingdom* (App. No. 3455/05) [2009] ECHR 301. See also Besson, 'Reception of the ECHR', note 59 above; Besson, 'Supranational judicial review', note 33 above, p. 129; Krisch, *Beyond Constitutionalism*, note 2 above, pp 134ff.; van de Heyning, note 76 above, pp 91–4; Christoffersen, note 80 above, pp 198–200.

[85] See Wildhaber, 'Ein Überdenken', note 79 above, and 'Rethinking the European Court of Human Rights', note 80 above, pp 215–7 on interpretation at the ECtHR not being a 'one-way street'. See also van de Heyning, note 76 above, pp 90–91; Krisch, *Beyond Constitutionalism*, note 2 above, p. 143; Lambert Abdelgawad, note 79 above, pp 331–4.

[86] On this second meaning of the margin of appreciation in the ECtHR's case law (the first being the equivalent to the material or substantive subsidiarity alluded to before), see e.g. G. Letsas, *A Theory of Interpretation of the European Convention on Human Rights* (Oxford: Oxford University Press, 2008).

[87] See e.g. *Stübing* v. *Germany* (App. No. 43547/08) 12 April 2012, nyr; ECtHR, *A, B and C* v. *Ireland* (App. No. 25579/05) [2010] ECtHR 2032.

or judgment. Finally, if saving clauses and judicial dialogue seem too risky a perspective in view of certain, potential, structural violations of human rights, states have the possibility of devising interpretative declarations or even *reservations* to certain human rights in order to favour their established interpretations when acceding to a human rights instrument.[88] Importantly, however, those may not be devised later, after new interpretations have arisen.

What this means for the idea of alleged pluralism of human rights interpretations in Europe, however, is that legal pluralism alone is not an adequate model to capture the way in which complementary and distinct human rights interpretations relate in case of conflict. The model does perceive the immediate validity and lack of hierarchy among international or European and domestic human rights norms, but misses the mutuality and reciprocal validation and legitimation process at stake. There is much more than judicial politics and dialogue at play, if one is to explain the existing processes of mutual interpretation and reasoning.[89] There are reasons, in other words, behind international or European judges' and domestic judges' cooperation, reasons that go beyond judicial attitudes and strategies and their mutual respect for each other's beliefs.

This does not mean, however, that human rights adjudication is merely about finding the right determination of human rights in each adjudication body and independently of what the other domestic or European/international human rights courts have said, as Letsas argues.[90] There is no right determination of the scope and allocation of human rights duties in circumstances of widespread and persistent moral disagreement and deep indeterminacy about human rights, except for a democratically legitimate one in the community to which belong those members whose rights and duties are at stake. Of course, that democratically legitimate, collective determination may then be questioned in court, and before many different courts including international or European ones. However, as I argued earlier, the democratic dimension of human rights implies that international human rights bodies may only interpret human rights in cooperation with domestic democratic ones. There is therefore a third way that lies between human rights pluralism *stricto sensu* and Letsas's 'harmonic law'.

---

[88] See Neuman, note 40 above at 1888–90.
[89] This is something that the pluralist account of Krisch, 'Open architecture', note 3 above at 215, cannot explain on its own.
[90] See Letsas, 'Harmonic law', note 4 above.

2.4. Human rights in response to legal pluralism in Europe

Besides European human rights' own legal pluralism, human rights are also related to European legal pluralism in a second and distinct way. This is the role human rights are seen to play in the judicial settlement of normative conflicts that stems from the legal pluralism prevailing in other areas of European law.

Increasingly, human rights are used as common standards for adjudicating normative conflicts in the EU. They allegedly provide a basis for the common 'identity' or 'equivalence' of the overlapping legal orders in Europe and enable those legal orders to 'communicate' on that basis.[91] Evidence of this may also be found in European judicial decisions that refer to the equivalence of human rights guarantees stemming from the different legal orders applying in an actual case.[92] The argument seems to be that, if the legal orders from which the conflicting legal norms stem entail equivalent human rights norms, the prima facie normative conflicts may no longer need to be regarded as conflicts.

Renewed references to human rights as the solution or part of the solution to legal pluralism in Europe do not come without difficulties, however. First,the multilevel and multisourced guarantees of human rights have given rise to what I have referred to before as human rights plurality. And that plurality is in the way of a settlement of normative conflicts themselves generated by a plurality of legal norms. To start with, when different legal orders overlap, usually their respective human rights guarantees also overlap. The EU legal order is a case in point with ECHR rights, EU fundamental rights and domestic fundamental rights overlapping. Even when overlapping legal orders do not contain their own human rights legal regime because some of them are specialised, human rights are usually interpreted differently from one political context and from one judicial body to the next. The ECHR is an example: its

---

[91] See e.g. the chapters by Maduro, by Champeil-Desplats and by Azoulai, in Dubout and Touzé, note 5 above.

[92] See e.g. Case C–127/07 *Arcelor Atlantique* [2008] ECR I–9895; Case C–213/07 *Michaniki AE* [2008] ECR I–9999. See also, for the latest example of the corresponding practice of domestic courts, e.g. the German Federal Constitutional Court case, *Lissabonvertrag*, 2/08 BVerfGE 5/08, para. 340. See also Kumm, note 4 above; Maduro, 'Three claims', note 2 above. Authors (e.g. Azoulai, note 5 above) usually also include the ECtHR's equivalence presumption in *Bosphorus* (*Bosphorus* v. *Ireland* (App. No. 45036/98) ECHR 2005–VI; confirmed in *Michaud* v. *France* (App. No. 12323/11) ECHR 2012–VI). As I will argue, however, the equivalence test used in *Bosphorus* is of another kind and ought not to be conflated with the *Arcelor* and *Lissabonvertrag* tests.

interpretation varies depending on the context of application and the jurisdiction. Finally, within the same legal order, human rights often have many sources without clear hierarchies between those sources. This is the case in the EU where EU fundamental rights find their sources in general principles of EU law, in EU primary law and in EU secondary law. It is still unclear, however, which of these should take priority in cases of conflict (see e.g. Article 6(3) TEU; Article 53 Charter).

Second, even when it is clear which human rights apply within each legal order and one finds the same human rights within different overlapping legal orders, it would be wrong to assume that they are equivalent norms that can be compared and hence be deemed equivalent. Human rights are not like other abstract legal norms, and their legal guarantees at different legal levels do not have the same function.[93]

On one hand, human rights, when they are legally recognised, are not legal norms like any other. To start with, they are non-functional norms in that they cannot be said to fulfil the same function in every legal order. Their function differs from one domestic legal order to another. They are indeed an essential part of the mutual recognition of political equality among members of the polity, but because polities differ, the exact function of human rights varies accordingly.[94] In this respect, human rights cannot be described as multi-source equivalent norms (MSENs)[95] the way the principles of proportionality or non-discrimination could.

Furthermore, legal human rights cannot even be regarded as legal norms *stricto sensu*, at least in the abstract. A human right exists *qua* moral right when an interest is a sufficient ground or reason to hold someone else (the duty-bearer) under a (categorical and exclusionary) duty to respect that interest *vis-à-vis* the right holder.[96] For a right to be recognised, a sufficient interest must be established and weighed against other interests and other considerations with which it might conflict in a particular social context.[97] Rights, in this conception, are intermediaries

---

[93] On the specificities of legal human rights, see S. Besson, 'Human rights: ethical, political, . . . or legal? first steps in a legal theory of human rights' in D. E. Childress III (ed.), *The Role of Ethics in International Law* (Cambridge: Cambridge University Press, 2011), pp 211–45.

[94] *Ibid.*

[95] Y. Shany and T. Broude, 'The international law and policy of multi-sourced equivalent norms' in Shany and Broude (eds), *Multi-Sourced Equivalent Norms in International Law* (Oxford: Hart Publishing, 2010), pp 1–18.

[96] J. Raz, 'On the nature of rights', 93 *Mind* (1984), 194–214 at 195.

[97] *Ibid.*, at 200, 209.

between interests and duties.[98] It follows, first of all, that a right may be recognised and protected before specifying which duties correspond to it.[99] Once a duty is specified, it will correlate to the (specific) right, but the right might already exist in the abstract without its specific duties being identified. The relationship between rights and particular duties is justificatory therefore, and not logical.[100] As a result, determining who bears the duty in relation to a right and the exact content of that duty are not conditions for the existence of a moral right.[101] A right, secondly, is a sufficient ground for holding other individuals as owing all the duties necessary to protect the interest, regardless of the details of those duties.[102] It follows that a right might provide for the imposition of many duties and not just one. Rights actually have a dynamic nature and, as such, successive specific duties can be grounded on a given right depending on the circumstances.[103] In short, it is only in local circumstances that the allocation and specification of duties may take place.

What this means is that legal human rights only give rise to duties in a specific context. It is only then that one may say there is a human rights norm at work. As a result, they cannot be compared abstractly and cannot be deemed equivalent before they apply to a specific case. For instance, even if a human right is protected both *qua* EU fundamental right and *qua* domestic fundamental right, it will only bear duties in a domestic context once applied to a specific case and there will only be one normative requirement as a result. This actually explains why it is difficult to know in practice when an ECHR right is better protected by EU law than by the ECHR or when an ECHR right 'corresponds' to a domestic or an EU fundamental right along the lines of Article 53 ECHR or Articles 52(3) and 53 Charter.[104]

On the other hand, another difficulty with the idea of human rights equivalence is that human rights' legal guarantees do not have the same function at different legal levels, as I argued earlier. International and

---

[98] *Ibid.*, at 208.

[99] See N. MacCormick, 'Rights in legislation' in P. M. S. Hacker and J. Raz (eds), *Law, Morality and Society: Essays in Honour of H. L. A. Hart* (Oxford: Oxford University Press, 1977), p. 201.

[100] See *ibid.*, pp 199–202; Raz, note 96 above at 196, 200.

[101] See also J. Tasioulas, 'The moral reality of human rights' in T. Pogge (ed.), *Freedom from Poverty as a Human Right: Who Owes What to the Very Poor* (Oxford: Oxford University Press, 2007), pp 75–101.

[102] See J. Waldron, 'Introduction' in Waldron (ed.), *Theories of Rights* (Oxford: Oxford University Press, 1984), pp 10–11.

[103] See Raz, note 96 above at 197–9.   [104] See van de Heyning, note 76 above.

national human rights guarantees cannot be deemed equivalent, as a result. The same may be said about regional human rights guarantees such as European human rights. It would be wrong therefore to compare EU fundamental rights, ECHR rights and domestic fundamental rights even when they all apply to the same specific case.

This difference in function between international or European and domestic human rights by reference to their institutional and political role reveals how misguided it would be to assimilate European human rights too readily to domestic fundamental rights.[105] ECHR rights guarantee the minimum requirements to be respected by a European democratic society. They are guaranteed internationally, outside any democratic polity and have to be transposed into European democratic legal orders. By contrast, EU fundamental rights are the rights of a democratic polity albeit of a post-national and complex nature. This explains their hybrid nature: they play an external, minimal role of the kind the ECHR plays in domestic legal orders, but they also have a municipal dimension that pertains to the EU democratic polity. Their multiple sources and bottom-up nature reflect that hybrid nature.[106] This difference in nature among European human rights explains in turn why the relationship between the interpretations of ECHR rights and domestic rights cannot be the same as that between interpretations of EU fundamental rights and domestic rights, nor, as a result, between interpretations of ECHR rights and EU fundamental rights, the latter being doubly subsidiary to the former.[107]

In view of those arguments, it would be wrong to assume that European human rights may be equivalent across the domestic, the EU and the Council of Europe legal orders, not only in an abstract way but also in a specific case. And even if they were, it remains unclear why this would be of any relevance to the relationship between norms stemming from different legal orders.

In this latter respect, there are two categories that are usually conflated in discussions of the equivalence of European human rights.[108] In the first instance, the normative conflict may be a conflict between human

---

[105] In this sense, I differ from Letsas, *A Theory of Interpretation*, note 86 above. See also Besson, '*Erga omnes* effect', note 53 above.

[106] See Besson, 'Decoupling and Recoupling', note 14 above.

[107] See e.g. Besson, 'Supranational judicial review', note 33 above. For confirmation of the interpretation of Art. 53 of the EU Fundamental Rights Charter (that it should not be interpreted along the lines of the saving clause in Art. 53 ECHR), see Case C–399/11 *Melloni*, nyr, para. 60; and Case C–617/10 *Åkerberg Fransson*, nyr, para. 29.

[108] See e.g. Letsas, 'Harmonic law', note 4 above.

rights guarantees themselves. It may be a conflict between two or many human rights stemming from different legal orders or, most commonly, one between incompatible interpretations of the same human rights or restrictions to the same human rights. This is the kind of case in which the relationship between EU fundamental rights and ECHR rights has been raised and for which the equivalence presumption in *Bosphorus* was first elaborated.[109] These are the cases I discussed in the previous section. In the second category, which is the most common, the normative conflict is not about human rights, but the latter are invoked as part of its resolution. This category corresponds to the vast majority of cases in which the relationship between EU law and domestic fundamental rights has been raised, and for which the equivalence test developed by the German Federal Constitutional Court in the wake of *Solange II*,[110] and by the ECJ/CJEU in its *Michaniki* or *Arcelor* decisions were put forward.[111]

Clearly, the idea of human rights equivalence is different in those two categories of cases. In the former, it is a judicial test aimed at allocating jurisdiction over certain parts of EU law. In the latter case, while it is also a judicial test, it is not directly aimed at allocating jurisdiction and does not pertain solely to monitoring human rights, but at testing the legitimate authority of EU norms and their primacy over domestic law, including constitutional rights. *Qua* test of legitimacy, human rights equivalence is not about 'communication' between legal orders,[112] therefore. It is about authorising the immediate validity and the primacy of EU law within the domestic legal order including its primacy over domestic human rights. This explains why it would be wrong to conflate too quickly the *Solange II* equivalence test with the presumption of equivalence used by the ECtHR in *Bosphorus*. The former is about testing the legitimacy of legal norms that claim immediate validity and primacy within domestic law in an integrated legal order, that of the EU, while the latter is about allocating between two courts jurisdictional power over human rights violations that only partially belong within the jurisdiction of one of them, hence the problem.

In sum, a more careful and informed approach to the function of various human rights guarantees in Europe shows how the reference to human rights as a solution to legal pluralism merely obscures what is

---

[109] *Bosphorus*, note 92 above.   [110] BVerfGE, *Solange II* 73, 339 (1986).
[111] *Arcelor*, note 92 above; *Michaniki*, note 92 above.
[112] On this notion, see Azoulai, note 5 above.

really at stake in circumstances of legal pluralism. This has to do with a misunderstanding of both the function of different European human rights norms and their role in European adjudication.

If human rights play a role in the articulation of legal orders in the EU, it is as part of the basis for a legal order's claim to legitimacy in a given polity. Since the European polity is a complex one that entails many *demoi*, the idea of human rights pluralism reflects its democratic complexity. While human rights are rightly a part of that legitimacy test, they are not the only one. This is why the *Solange II* test should be regarded as a much richer one than authors are usually ready to concede.[113] As confirmed by recent revivals of that test in the caselaw of the Czech Constitutional Court, democracy is as important a component of political legitimacy as human rights since the two go hand in hand.[114]

3. European legal pluralism *redux*

Following the above considerations about the relationship between human rights and democracy, it is interesting to return to the question of European legal pluralism in order to assess it from an angle more sensitive to human rights *cum* democracy.

Legal pluralism in both meanings discussed in the first section, i.e. *qua* plurivalidity and *qua* heterarchy, should not too readily be ascribed across the board, to all relationships between legal orders and to all legal orders. Issues of legal validity and of rank between legal orders are not contingent matters of fact, and ought to reflect key positions on the legitimacy of legal orders and norms. It is only by distinguishing more carefully between the conditions for legitimacy of international, European and national law, and between questions of validity and rank, that we can propose a convincing model of the relationship between legal orders in the EU.

While pluralism may be the right model to capture the integrated nature of the EU legal order,[115] I would like to argue that it is not to the right model for the relationship between international law and European law or

---

[113] *Solange II*, note 110 above.
[114] Czech Constitutional Court, *Sugar Quota Regulation II*, judgment of 8 March 2006, Pl US 50/04 or *European Arrest Warrant*, judgment of 3 May 2006, Pl US 66/04. See most recently, Czech Constitutional Court, *Landtova*, judgment of 14 February 2012, Pl US 5/12. For a confirmation, see the reasoning of the German Federal Constitutional Court in *Lissabonsvertrag*, note 92 above.
[115] See Besson, 'How international', note 1 above, pp 12–15.

between international law and domestic law. Legal validity is shorthand for a claim to legitimacy and ought to entail the possibility for that claim to obtain.[116] The autonomy of a legal order is not a merely legal phenomenon, but the reflection of a political reality: the polity's self-determination. As a result, not all legal orders can be deemed as equivalent and likewise their relationships cannot be organised in a comparable fashion, especially when their subjects are individuals and states, or just individuals.

The very refined *demoi*-cratic regime that was developed within the European legal order during the past thirty years can account for the legitimacy of EU law.[117] It justifies a pluralist relationship between domestic and EU law within the European legal order.[118] Democratic inclusion might be best guaranteed, depending on the cases, at the European level and this may grant certain EU law norms a higher democratic legitimacy.[119] The same may be said about human rights within the EU; EU fundamental rights developed in two stages, first *qua* international and then *qua* transnational human rights, to enable the development of EU democratic credentials and hence to justify EU law's immediate validity within domestic legal orders and its claim to primacy over domestic law. The specificity of their bottom-up sources and the lack of EU human rights competence are characteristic of a form of human rights protection that amounts to more than minimal and external international human rights guarantees while, at the same time, avoids the substitution of an EU set of human rights for the domestic ones. There is a form of EU human rights pluralism, in other words, that backs up the legal pluralism that prevails in the EU legal order *qua* integrated legal order.

[116] See Besson, 'Democratic authority', note 68 above. See also Somek, note 30 above.

[117] See S. Besson, 'Deliberative *demoi*-cracy in the European Union: towards the deterritorialization of democracy' in S. Besson and J. L. Martí (eds), *Deliberative Democracy and its Discontents* (Aldershot: Ashgate, 2006), pp 181–214.

[118] See Besson, 'How international', note 1 above; Besson, 'European legal pluralism', note 2 above.

[119] See for an illustration of the link between fundamental rights and democracy, on one hand, and of the relations between different levels of democratic government, the rich test one may find in the reasoning of the Czech Constitutional Court in the 2006 *Sugar Quota Regulation II* or in the 2006 *European Arrest Warrant* (both note 114 above). It is particularly striking when contrasted with the *Solange I* or *II* tests used by the German Federal Constitutional Court: the latter focus only on fundamental rights and conceive of the national polity as the only source of democratic legitimacy.

Of course, the emergence of a third stage in the EU human rights regime *qua* municipal human rights regime after Lisbon currently questions this status quo.[120] This is why one may argue, as I have in the previous section, that the relationship between domestic fundamental rights and EU fundamental rights is now organised in an increasingly different fashion than that between domestic fundamental rights and ECHR rights, for instance. Unsurprisingly, this development has occurred alongside the development of the principle of political equality in EU law (Article 9 TEU); as always, democracy and human rights develop hand in hand and, with the consolidation of the EU Fundamental Rights Charter, the special kind of *demoi*-cracy we have had in Europe in the past is clearly turning into a more municipal albeit federalist kind of democracy.

This is not (yet) the case at the international level, however. Not only is international human rights protection deficient, but it does not serve the same function as fundamental rights protection within the EU. More importantly, international lawmaking lacks the democratic dimension necessary to back a claim to immediate validity and to constitutional rank within the European legal order.[121] Paying due attention to that democratic requirement appears even more essential in an integrated legal order where validity in EU law also implies immediate validity within Member States' national legal orders and democratic polities.

So, while European legal pluralism could be defended as the model of the relationship between domestic and European law that can best be justified on grounds of democratic legitimacy, that very legitimacy also explains why it cannot constitute the most legitimate model for the relationship between European (and domestic) law and international law. One cannot rule out, of course, the possibility that the international legal order, or the UN regime at least, might at some time develop into an internal legal order with transnational dimensions on the model of the European legal order. This would, however, require accepting even deeper changes within national democracies than what has taken place in the EU since 1957.[122] This is why the ECJ was right not to follow

---

[120] See Besson, 'Decoupling and recoupling', note 14 above. See also the CJEU's decision in *Melloni* (note 107 above).

[121] See my critique of the Advocate General's opinion in *Kadi* (note 15 above) in this respect: Besson, 'How international', note 1 above, pp 12–17.

[122] On those challenges, see S. Besson, '*Ubi ius, ibi civitas:* a republican account of the international community' in S. Besson and J. L. Martí (eds), *Legal Republicanism: National and International Perspectives* (Oxford: Oxford University Press, 2009), pp 205–37;

Advocate General Maduro in the *Kadi* case;[123] there is more at stake in the relationship between international law and EU law in terms of political legitimacy than in the relationship between EU law and domestic law. And neither can the *Solange II* test be applied to that relationship simply by analogy with what prevails in the relationship between EU law and domestic law.[124]

Interestingly, international law includes the ECHR regime. The ECHR remains indeed a regional albeit international law regime and distinct from the integrated legal order of the EU and its Member States. As a result, and as I argued earlier, the relationship between EU law and ECHR rights cannot be described only along the strict lines of the legal pluralist model. Nor can that between ECHR rights and EU Member States' legal orders. Of course, European human rights, like international human rights, are legitimised through reception and contextualisation as domestic or municipal human rights within the domestic or municipal legal order. And this turns their validity and rank into a constitutional matter, as discussed previously. All this, and what was presented in previous sections about the respective nature and role of different human rights guarantees depending on the level of guarantee, explains why the relationship between human rights norms is a special case, compared to that between other legal norms stemming from different legal orders and hence from legal pluralism as it has been understood so far.

One should emphasise that the relationship between the ECHR and EU fundamental rights will now go through a process of reconfiguration in the context of the EU's accession to the ECHR. While one might be tempted to see accession as marking the continuation of the *Bosphorus* test, the argument made in this chapter has hopefully demonstrated that it will toll that test's knell.[125] The negotiations aiming at the EU's accession to the ECHR have awakened the sore question of the Union's human rights

S. Besson, 'Institutionalizing global *demoi*-cracy' in L. H. Meyer (ed.), *Justice, Legitimacy and Public International Law* (Cambridge: Cambridge University Press, 2009), pp 58–91.

[123] AG Maduro, *Kadi*, note 15 above; Case T–315/01, *Kadi* v. *Council and Commission* [2005] ECR–II 3649. See also Case T–85/09 *Kadi* v. *Commission* [2010] ECR II–5177. The dualism between international law and EU law has been confirmed by Case C–366/10 *Air Transport Association of America*, nyr.

[124] See my critique of the Advocate General's opinion in *Kadi* (note 15 above, para. 22ff.): Besson, 'How international', note 1 above, pp 12–17.

[125] See also O. de Schutter, 'L'adhésion de l'Union européenne à la Convention européenne des droits de l'homme: Feuille de route de la négociation', 21 *Revue trimestrielle des droits de l'Homme* 83 (2010), 535–72 at 544, 565. See also the ECtHR's decision in *Michaud*

competence precisely because it implies a shift from the current, hybrid, human rights regime that applies in the EU towards a more municipal model of human rights.[126] And this also means entering a new stage in the political and democratic development of the EU. In this context, the relationship between the EU legal order and its Member States' legal orders will change, but so will that between the CJEU and the ECtHR pertaining to human rights as a result. The CJEU's human rights review of domestic law will have to become bolder and more coherent, while the ECtHR's human rights review of EU law will have to come closer to the subsidiary review it ought to be applying in its relationship to domestic courts and hence less subsidiary than it has been since the *Bosphorus* presumption was adopted.

4. Conclusion

Domestic legal orders match domestic political communities. This realisation affects their autonomy and hence their relationship to other legal orders, whether domestic and hence democratic or regional and international.

Trying to understand and handle European legal pluralism by abstracting from normative political theory and without taking into account the political differences between those orders is doomed to fail. Recent attempts to do this by reference to values instead of democracy, and through human rights equivalence and judicial comity only, are evidence of that failure. While human rights adjudication is a privileged point of contact between norms stemming from different European legal orders, it is not the only one. And it can only perform its role if one takes into account the institutional and political context of the norms and institutions European judges are monitoring.

With respect to human rights more specifically, I hope to have shown how complex those legal norms are and how little we are in fact saying when we refer to 'human rights pluralism'. European human rights guarantees are both plural and complementary at the same time: their plurality gives rise to a richer form of pluralism than that between other

(note 92 above). More generally on the accession negotiations, see http://hub.coe.int/en/what-we-do/human-rights/eu-accession-to-the-convention/.

[126] See Besson, 'Decoupling and recoupling', note 14 above; S. Besson, 'The human rights competence in the EU – the state of the question after Lisbon' in G. Kofler, M. P. Maduro and P. Pistone (eds), *Human Rights and Taxation in Europe and the World*, The 5th GREIT Conference (Amsterdam: IBFD, 2011), pp 37–63.

legal norms, i.e. a kind of pluralism that is characterised by mutuality, both in validity and legitimation, and not by equivalence and competition. The reasons have to do with the political function and the democratically legitimating role of human rights. It is those reasons we need to focus on now, since they are channeling the future of democracy and human rights protection in the EU, but we also might one day need to focus on them in our international relations.

8

Rethinking justice for the EU

SIONAIDH DOUGLAS-SCOTT

This chapter discusses the problem of justice for the EU, suggesting that, for too long, the notion of justice has been overlooked as a necessary conceptual tool for analysing EU problems.[1] Human rights, democracy or accountability tend to have been preferred. Yet the events of the first decade of the twenty-first century – the threat from terrorism, the financial crisis – have forced justice onto the agenda for the EU in a way that might have seemed inconceivable in the 1990s, when some commentators were forecasting, somewhat smugly, in the wake of the fall of the communist bloc, an 'end of history', as if the west had emerged into a Kantian age of perpetual peace.[2]

Analysing the EU's actions in terms of justice highlights their impact on its peoples, and accentuates its imbalances of power. This chapter considers some particular examples in which it is suggested that the EU has not added value but caused injustice. They present particularly intractable problems for the EU and raise singular challenges for justice – partly because some of these very injustices are attributable to the *sui generis* nature of EU law.

I argue that some solution to the problem of justice in the EU may be found in the particular relation of justice to law, in a concept I name critical legal justice, bearing in mind the crucial role that legal integration has played for the development of the EU. However, justice is not confined to legal justice. Therefore, I suggest that, while justice in this broader sense

---

[1] I have also pursued some of the ideas in this chapter in two further articles: in S. Douglas-Scott, 'The problem of justice in the EU' in J. Dickson and P. Eleftheriadis (eds), *The Philosophical Foundations of EU Law* (Oxford: Oxford University Press, 2012) I focus on the rule of law dimensions of justice; and in S. Douglas-Scott, 'Pluralism and justice in the EU', *Current Legal Problems* 65 (2012), 83–118, I pay particular attention to the relationship of pluralism to justice and injustice. I also consider the issue of justice within and outside law at some length in S. Douglas-Scott, *Law After Modernity* (Oxford: Hart Publishing, 2013).
[2] See e.g. F. Fukuyama, *The End of History and the Last Man* (New York: Harper Perennial, 1993).

may be so elusive as to be an ideal or utopian, it is the diagnosis of *injustice* that is itself crucial, as justice is more likely to move people in its absence, rather than as an academic or rhetorical exercise that fails to convince. It is injustice that motivates and propels action, and the highlighting of injustice does its own work.

1. Injustice

1.1. Instances of injustice

The first part of this chapter details examples of injustice that, it is suggested, may be attributable to the EU. This section will be largely descriptive: a critique of EU actions, an attempt to illustrate why I believe the EU has become a source of injustice. At this stage, I am not suggesting that we should understand justice in any particular sense, thick or thin, substantive or procedural; rather, that it is a value the importance of which is immediately recognisable in some sort of Dworkinian 'pre-interpretive' sense,[3] and should surely be acknowledged by an EU that wishes to proclaim its values. But I am also working in the light of my conclusions – that it is injustice that propels action, and so we should be clear-eyed about identifying injustice.

1.1.1. Crisis of the Eurozone

The financial crisis within the Eurozone provides examples of injustice within the EU *par excellence*. Part of the problem has been that the original legal arrangements for Economic and Monetary Union (EMU) failed to provide explicit mechanisms to deal with a debt crisis, because the premise for EMU was that there should be no debt and no deficit within EMU Member States and hence no need for bailouts.[4] Therefore the EU has had to remedy this situation by further action, especially since 2010. The EU's response to the crisis has been ad hoc and reactive, rather than principled. It has involved a raft of new measures on economic governance that have tended to institute austerity through enforced limits on public spending and mandatory changes to labour market policies requiring greater flexibility and lower wages. These dramatic changes have been advanced speedily and without great transparency, under the pretext

---

[3] See R. Dworkin, *Law's Empire* (Cambridge, MA: Harvard University Press, 1986).

[4] Indeed, Art. 122 TFEU, the provision that was used as a partial basis to deal with the Greek bailout, refers to 'severe difficulties caused by natural disasters or exceptional occurrences' beyond a Member State's control, rather than financial or economic crisis.

of restoring stability in the Eurozone. It is important to highlight that the Eurozone crisis is as much a crisis of *governance* as of economics or monetary policy. The institutional arrangements and structures for monetary union have proved inadequate. Recognition of the governance aspects of the Eurozone crisis is essential,[5] as is the need for human rights and public lawyers to focus on the crisis, in order that its injustices and its costs in human rights terms be highlighted.

Moving on to the details of EU action, it is evident that the scope of measures taken in the attempt to solve the Eurozone crisis is considerable. The conditions set by the Greek bailout in 2010 provide a good example (although similar conditions have also been imposed in later bailouts for Portugal and Ireland). These required Greece to end its deficit by adopting measures (described by one author as 'the most drastic intervention in a Member State's economic and social policy ever decided by the EU'[6]) including, for example, to reduce pensions; a large-scale privatisation programme; the reduction of public investment; and a reform of wage legislation in the public sector.[7] Forty-five measures in all were required and Greece was given until December 2011 to implement them.[8]

If we review what has happened since the Greek bailout, there follows a rapid and confusing series of attempts by the EU to deal with the crisis. In

---

[5] For commentaries that focus on the governance aspect see M. Maduro, *A New Governance For The European Union And The Euro: Democracy And Justice* (Fiesole: European University Institute Policy Papers, 2012); K. Tuori, *The European Financial Crisis: Constitutional Aspects and Implications* (Fiesole: European University Institute Working Papers, 2012); see also K. Anderson, 'The Eurozone crisis is also a governance crisis – isn't it?' *Opinio Juris* (2011), available at http://opiniojuris.org/2011/11/25/the-eurozone-crisis-is-also-a-governance-crisis-isnt-it/.

[6] R. Bieber, *Observer, Policeman, Pilot: On Lacunae of Legitimacy and the Contradictions of Financial Crisis Management in the EU* (Fiesole: European University Institute Working Papers, 2011).

[7] Council Decision (EU) 2010/320 addressed to Greece with a view to reinforcing and deepening fiscal surveillance and giving notice to Greece to take measures for the deficit reduction [2010] OJ L145/6 (as amended by Council Decision (EU) 2010/486 [2010] OJ L241/12), respectively Arts. 2(1)(e), 2(1)(n) and 2(2)(d).

[8] Further measures in Decision 2010/320, *ibid.*, included a law to reform the wage bargaining system in the private sector, which should provide for a reduction in pay rates for overtime work, enhanced flexibility in the management of working time and allow local territorial pacts to set wage growth below sectoral agreements (Art. 2(3)(d)); and a reform of employment protection legislation to extend the probationary period for new jobs to one year, reduce the overall level of severance payments and ensure that the same severance payment conditions apply to blue- and white-collar workers, raise the minimum threshold for the rules on collective dismissals to apply, especially for larger companies, and facilitate a greater use of temporary contracts (Art. 2(3)(e)).

May 2010, a European Financial Stabilization Mechanism (EFSM)[9] and European Financial Stability Facility (EFSF)[10] were established under which further bailouts were made to Ireland and Portugal. Yet more measures followed, namely a permanent European Stability Mechanism (ESM),[11] established by a treaty between Eurozone Member States, which replaces the EFSF and EFSM, and is also to provide financial assistance under strict conditions. At the time the ESM was negotiated, a 'Euro plus pact' was concluded in March 2011,[12] requiring Member States to monitor labour law and wages to ensure competitiveness, and stipulating that regard to 'sustainability of pensions, health care and social benefits' should be the primary means of ensuring 'sound public finances'. However, as the Euro plus pact does not include strong enforcement measures, even more action was needed, and a range of binding provisions in a package of six legislative measures on economic governance (sometimes referred to colloquially as the 'six-pack') was adopted later in 2011.[13] This 'six-pack', consisting of five regulations and one directive, was approved by all 27 Member States and the European Parliament and represents the most comprehensive reinforcement of economic governance in the EU and the Eurozone since the launch of the EMU. From 2012, the European Parliament and Commission will have the power to scrutinise national budgets before even national parliaments have the chance to do so. If Member States fail to reduce their debts or refuse budgetary suggestions from Brussels, they can be subject to enforcement measures, which can lead to fines of up to 0.5 per cent of GDP. The most serious breaches are those of the reinforced Stability Pact's two requirements (to keep deficits below 3 per cent of GDP and debt below 60 per cent).[14] Further,

---

[9] Council Regulation (EU) 407/2010 establishing a European financial stabilization mechanism [2010] OJ L118/1.

[10] Terms of Reference of the Eurogroup, European Financial Stability Facility, Luxembourg, 7 June 2010; European Financial Stability Facility Framework Agreement, Execution Version, 7 June 2010.

[11] Treaty establishing the European Stability Mechanism, 11 July 2011. The ESM Treaty was subject to legal challenge in Case C–370/12, *Pringle* v. *Ireland*, nyr, discussed further below.

[12] 'The Euro Plus Pact: stronger economic policy coordination for competitiveness and convergence', annexed to European Council Conclusions, EUCO 10/1/11 REV 1.

[13] For details see Council Press Release of 8 November 2011, available at www.consilium. europa.eu/uedocs/cms_data/docs/pressdata/en/ecofin/125952.pdf.

[14] The Stability and Growth Pact concluded by the European Council in December 1996 lays out the rules for the budgetary discipline of the Euro Member States and binds all parties to engage in the prompt implementation of the 'Excessive deficit procedure' should any of them fail to meet the agreements of the Pact. The procedure is enforced when a Member State runs a public deficit of over 3 per cent of its GDP in any year, and, additionally,

Member States will only be able to avoid fines or other sanctions if a qualified majority in the Council vote against these, a procedure that might be seen as amounting to 'semi-automatic' sanctions. To add to all of this, yet another crisis measure was adopted,[15] this time taking the form of an international agreement on a 'reinforced economic union' (often referred to as the 'Fiscal Compact Treaty' 2012)[16] that raises further serious issues of democratic accountability, not to mention this projected treaty's relationship with, and compatibility with, EU law.

The details above are necessary to bring home the extent and scope of the EU's actions within the field of EMU; yet all of these measures were adopted with little debate and a minimum of public awareness. Most Europeans have little idea that such changes, involving such inroads into their governments' economic sovereignty, have taken place.

In the light of these measures, the warnings of those, such as Alex Callinicos, who counselled against the original adoption of the single currency ('the introduction of this currency, the euro, in present circumstances is likely to have a devastating effect on the jobs, wages, and collective consumption of the European working class')[17] seem prescient. The EU and its Member States' response to the crisis of its currency has been characterised by a continuous flurry of untransparent and undemocratic measures, which impose conditions of severe austerity on Member States, distancing economic governance from the control of elected governments and national parliaments, in an extremely complex and confusing melée of arrangements of EU law and international agreements between the states.

The concerns about the somewhat haphazard way in which these measures dealing with the Eurozone crisis have been adopted by the EU, and

---

governments may not allow total government debt to exceed 60 per cent of GDP. The 'six-pack' measures reinforce its provisions.

[15] This Treaty is an intergovernmental treaty, signed by all members of the EU except the Czech Republic and the UK, on 2 March 2012. In a referendum held on 31 May 2012, the Irish voted in favour of the Fiscal Compact Treaty, which came into effect on 1 January 2013 for the sixteen signatories that had ratified it by this date.

[16] Although, strictly speaking, 'Fiscal Compact' should only apply to Title III of the Treaty, which is formally entitled the 'Fiscal Compact', and is probably the most widely discussed aspect of the Treaty on stability, coordination and governance in the Economic and Monetary Union.

[17] See A. Callinicos, 'Europe: the mounting crisis', *International Socialism* 75 (1997). A critique of the euro and the EU's handling of the euro crisis that goes well beyond those commenting from a socialist perspective. For a recent critique of the imposition of austerity through untransparent Eurozone measures see e.g. F. Scharpf, *Monetary Union, Fiscal Crisis and the Preemption of Democracy* (Cologne: Max Planck Institute for the Study of Societies Discussion Paper, 2011).

their impact for justice and the rule of law, are neatly encapsulated in the *Pringle* litigation before the CJEU.[18] Pringle, an Irish MP, brought a constitutional challenge in the Irish courts, opposing the Irish government's ratification of the ESM Treaty. In the course of these proceedings the Irish Supreme Court made a preliminary reference to Luxembourg. The facts of the case are complex but in essence the CJEU was called upon to determine how the amended Article 136(3) TFEU and ESM Treaty might fit into the existing EU Treaty framework on Eurozone governance, especially given the specific 'no-bailout' clause in Article 125 TFEU. More particularly, the issues were that adoption of the ESM Treaty could violate provisions in the EU Treaties on EMU and confer on EU institutions powers that are incompatible with their functions under the EU Treaties, and also that the amendment of Article 136 TFEU by Decision 2011/199 (to provide a legal basis for the ESM) constituted an unlawful change to the TFEU as it has not been adopted by the European Council according to the appropriate Treaty revision procedure.

Pringle's argument was that setting up the ESM through an intergovernmental treaty rather than as an EU Treaty not only would directly encroach on the EU's competence in monetary policy but also would impose on states obligations incompatible with EU Treaty law. He also asserted that the ESM Treaty is incompatible with the general principle of effective judicial protection and with the principle of legal certainty, and that the ESM would operate outside democratic and constitutional restraints usually imposed by the national laws of Member States or by EU law. These arguments raise concerns over the consequences for the EU of a departure from the rule of law, which is a fundamental constitutional principle enshrined in Article 2 TEU.

The CJEU applied its expedited procedure to hear the case quickly,[19] because of the exceptional circumstances of the financial crisis surrounding the conclusion of the ESM Treaty. The case was heard before the full Court (all twenty-seven judges), which is extremely unusual. The CJEU held that the provisions of the TEU and the TFEU do not preclude the conclusion and ratification of the ESM Treaty, and that, if strict conditions were imposed to ensure assistance does not reduce the recipient state's

---

[18] *Pringle*, note 11 above. Separate challenges to the ratification of the ESM Treaty were also brought in the German Federal Constitutional Court (Bundesverfassungsgericht: BVerfGE) Case No. 2 BvR 1390/12 et al. of 12 September 2012, and a constitutional challenge was rejected by the Supreme Court of Estonia, (*Riigikohus*, Case No. 3–4–1–6–12 of 12 July 2012).

[19] Pursuant to Art. 23a of the Statute of the Court of Justice and Art. 105 of the Rules of Procedure of the Court of Justice.

incentive 'to conduct a sound budgetary policy', no EU law problems arise. The CJEU also rejected Mr Pringle's challenge to the European Council's decision amending the TFEU.

The CJEU's decision may be ultimately unsurprising, given the urgent need to provide an effective legal mechanism to deal with the Eurozone crisis. However, the Court's confirmation that the ESM may be established outside the framework of EU law legitimises a situation in which ESM decision-making processes are beyond the influence of the European Parliament. So also are the Charter and other applicable fundamental rights, given that the ESM is an international treaty, and not a measure falling within the scope of EU law. To this we may add the situation already described, in which the budgetary autonomy of participating states has been limited by externally imposed targets, as well as some troubling jurisprudence of the EU General Court, which has denied requests for access to the European Central Bank (ECB) documents on which further EU actions were based (a decision that underlines the ECB's lack of accountability).[20] All of these elements combine to undermine the legitimacy of economic policy in recipient states, which now is by and large determined by EU institutions, as well as the legitimacy of the EU's own actions in this field.[21]

Regrettably, the Eurozone crisis has been too easily characterised as the product of profligate, peripheral EU countries. As Fritz Scharpf comments, 'it is indeed unfortunate that worries about the euro were triggered by the Greek solvency crisis – which was initially seen as the self-inflicted result of fiscal profligacy'.[22] However, this analysis (while only partially accurate for Greece) is a complete misrepresentation of the problems in

---

[20] See Case T–590/10, *Thesing* v. *ECB*, nyr.

[21] However, it should be noted, perhaps as a counter to these rather pessimistic conclusions, that AG Kokott (perhaps somewhat surprisingly) suggested that 'a broad interpretation of Article 125 TFEU would be incompatible with the concept of solidarity', even if it could 'not be inferred from the concept of solidarity that there exists a duty to provide financial assistance of the kind that is to be provided by the ESM', Opinion of AG Kokott in *Pringle*, note 11 above, paras 142–3.

[22] Scharpf, note 17 above, p. 32:

> If Greek governments had not engaged in reckless borrowing, it is now widely argued, the euro crisis would not have arisen, and if the Commission had not been duped by faked records, rigorous enforcement of the Stability Pact would have prevented it. So even though the more 'virtuous' member states are now unable to refuse help to the 'sinners', such conditions should never be allowed to reoccur ... A major factor seems to have been a particularly pronounced inability or unwillingness to collect taxes. According to OECD figures, Greek tax revenue declined from 37.8 percent of GDP in 2000 to 32.6 percent in 2008.

many other Eurozone countries that had not exceeded EMU rules on public spending prior to the world financial crisis. For example, 'budgetary discipline alone, no matter how rigidly enforced, would not have prevented the crises in Ireland and Spain – where the steep rise in public-sector deficits was clearly a consequence, rather than a cause, of the financial and economic crisis.'[23] Yet, as Scharpf argues, the profligacy analysis 'still dominates debate about the crisis in the "rescuer" countries, and it frames the approach to reforming the EMU regime'.[24] In this way, austerity measures may be more readily justified as the price for bailouts, and solidarity between EU states is sapped.

A further, glaring feature of these measures is their incompatibility with the EU's treaties and proclaimed values, and, more specifically, human rights. Article 3(3) TEU sets the objective that the EU be 'a highly competitive social market economy'. Yet the measures detailed above are incompatible with a social market economy. Nor are they compatible with the provisions of Article 9 TFEU, which requires that, '[i]n defining and implementing its policies and activities, the Union shall take into account requirements linked to the promotion of a high level of employment, the guarantee of adequate social protection, the fight against social exclusion, and a high level of education, training and protection of human health'. Furthermore, it could hardly be said that measures that impose unilateral cuts on wages, pensions, public spending and restrict collective bargaining enhance the objective of social justice set out in Article 3 TEU. Nor do the conditionality clauses in the bailout agreements, imposing restrictions on the availability of collective bargaining, show much in the way of concern for the special status of the social partners recognised by Article 152 TFEU, which states '[t]he Union recognises and promotes the role of the social partners at its level, taking into account the diversity of national systems. It shall facilitate dialogue between the social partners, respecting their autonomy,' or with the freedom of association recognised in both the ECHR and the EU Charter of Fundamental Rights.[25]

---

[23] *Ibid.*   [24] *Ibid.*

[25] Further, all twenty-seven EU Member States have ratified International Labour Organization (ILO) Convention No. 154 on promotion of collective bargaining and ILO Convention No. 87 on freedom of association. Greek trade unions complained to the ILO about the imposition of bailout conditions, and in particular restrictions on collective bargaining. In this context, the CEACR (2011 Report of the Committee of Experts on the Application of Conventions and Recommendations) of the ILO held that 'restrictions on collective bargaining should only be imposed as exceptional measures and only to the extent necessary, without exceeding a reasonable period' (Report, p. 83).

The handling of the Eurozone crisis also reveals a very serious deficit of democracy in the EU. Elected politicians (prime ministers, in the cases of Greece and Italy) have been forced out of office, to be replaced by unelected bureaucrats, or 'economic experts,' without any electoral mandate. National budgets will become the property of EU institutions as much as of national governments and parliaments. This is hugely troubling. Many of the Eurozone crisis measures might be regarded as a travesty of democracy. Since the EEC was founded, it has been prone to charges of a democratic deficit that have never been satisfactorily resolved. The existence of a democratic deficit is not necessarily an example of injustice, although some theorists have challenged any essential difference in nature between democracy and justice in the EU,[26] or have proposed the substituting of discourse on the democratic deficit with that of transnational justice.[27] Although this approach is not followed here, and the discussion in this chapter is confined to justice, it is acknowledged that justice and democracy can be related, that the injustice of a measure may be caused, or increased, by the fact that one had no ability to participate in or influence its adoption.

The injustices of the Eurozone crisis may be summarised in the following way. Certain of these measures directly contradict the EU's avowal of social justice in Article 3 TEU, and also infringe human rights, such as those of collective bargaining and freedom of association in the EU Charter of Fundamental Rights. It is also important to emphasise that the Eurozone crisis is a crisis and result of supranationalism, of a failure to perceive the dangers of integration at one level (monetary union) without integrating in other areas (namely economic, or fiscal union) as well as being a crisis of governance. Yet few Member States desire the deeper union and central control of a fiscal union. So common, principled action is hard to achieve, and it is just this asymmetrical, unbalanced integration that is the cause of some of the injustice.[28]

1.2. The area of freedom, security and justice

It might be thought that an institution proclaiming the term 'Justice' in its title would be a good place in which to examine the EU's capacity

---

[26] E.g. R. Forst, 'Transnational justice and democracy', *Cluster of Excellence*, Goethe University, Normative Orders Working Paper 4 (2011).

[27] J. Neyer, 'Justice, not democracy: legitimacy in the European Union', 48 *Journal of Common Market Studies* 4 (2010), 903–21.

[28] That is, EMU assumes a level playing field. But states are not equal in this union. Conditions that work for Germany do not work for Greece or Ireland.

to deliver justice. In 1997, in the context of the Treaty of Amsterdam, the EU created an 'Area of Freedom, Security and Justice' (AFSJ). This was supposed to make the EU citizen feel closer to the EU and more included by it. Within the scope of the AFSJ, the EU is able to adopt all sorts of measures that people have not traditionally associated with EU action, including measures on terrorism, migration management, visa policies, asylum, privacy and security, the fight against organised crime and criminal justice.

Unfortunately, it has become almost a commonplace to state that, in the context of the EU's AFSJ, Freedom and Justice have been sacrificed to the needs of Security. This means, among other things, that important human rights are sacrificed. Although, since the Lisbon Treaty came into force on 1 December 2009, the EU's Charter of Fundamental Rights at last has binding force, the EU has generally been slow to adopt measures on rights,[29] and too quick to adopt more coercive and potentially rights-violating measures such as the European Arrest Warrant (EAW), or the extremely broad EU definition of terrorism.

The AFSJ now takes up a large part of Council meeting time, and there is no sign that the pace is slowing. The nature of all of this activity undermines the claim made by some theorists that legitimacy of EU action should not be of primary concern because the EU lacks the competences of a traditional state and its powers are mainly economic. Andrew Moravscik, for example, has suggested that any perceived democratic deficit is of less concern in the EU context because the EU still falls far short of what a nation state can do – it has very little coercive power and does not tax and spend: 'Of the 5 most salient issues in most west European democracies – health care provision, education, Law and order, pension and social security policy and taxation – none is primarily an EU competence.'[30]

---

[29] A draft Procedural Rights Framework Decision under discussion for some years had not been adopted at the time of writing, although there have been recent attempts to revive it – see Council Resolution 295/01 on a Roadmap for strengthening procedural rights of suspected or accused persons in criminal proceedings (OJ 2009 C295/01). See, however, Parliament and Council Directive (EU) 2010/64 on the right to interpretation and translation in criminal proceedings (OJ 2010 L280/1). A Council Framework Decision 2008/977 on the protection of personal data processed in the framework of police and judicial cooperation in criminal matters (OJ 2008 L350/60) was adopted in 2008 after years of discussion, as well as a Council Framework Decision 2008/913 on combating certain forms and expressions of racism and xenophobia by means of criminal law (OJ 2008 L328/55), which renders criminal intentional public acts designed to incite violence or hatred, or that trivialise genocide and similar atrocities.

[30] A. Moravscik, 'In defence of democratic deficit: reassessing legitimacy in the European Union', 40 *Journal of Common Market Studies*, 4 (2002), 603–24.

Yet within the scope of the AFSJ are matters that are crucial, areas that have been considered core state powers – the provision of security, the development of public values, the relation between the individual and public authorities – indeed almost at the heart of constitutional law. The evolution of the AFSJ has been likened to the creation of a 'European Public Order'.[31] Bradley and Ewing refer to constitutional law in general as 'one branch of human learning that helps make life in today's world more tolerable and less brutish that it might otherwise be'.[32] However, a significant question is whether, in the context of the EU, life has actually been made less 'brutish'. It is crucial that, if the AFSJ is to be further developed, this be as a space of hope, rather than what J. G. A. Pocock has called a 'Machiavellian moment'[33] (i.e. an attempt to remain stable by any means in the face of a stream of irrational events).

A more precise pinpointing of specific examples of injustice within the AFSJ, namely those associated with the EAW and with data collection and retention in the EU, provides further evidence of this alleged deficit of justice, although the treatment of these areas in this chapter is not intended to be comprehensive but rather illustrative.

The EAW, which was adopted by the EU in 2002,[34] is used to secure the arrest and surrender of an individual for the purpose of conducting criminal proceedings against them in another Member State. The merits of the request are to be taken on trust and traditional exceptions for political, military and revenue offences have been abolished. For many offences, the EAW removes the principle of double criminality, i.e. the usual requirement that the act in respect of which extradition is sought is recognised as criminal in both the requesting and the surrendering states. Based on the principle of mutual trust, the EAW was intended to reinforce the fight against serious cross-border crimes. There has, however, been repeated criticism of the manner in which the EAW has functioned in concrete cases.[35]

---

[31] Paper by A. Vitorino, 'Towards a single treaty for the delivery of the Area of Freedom, Security and Justice', European Convention Working Group X Freedom, Security and Justice Working Document 14 (2002).

[32] A. Bradley and K. Ewing, *Constitutional and Administrative Law* (Harlow: Longman, 2007), p. 4.

[33] J. G. A. Pocock, *The Machiavellian Moment: Florentine Political Thought and the Atlantic Republican Tradition* (Princeton, NJ: Princeton University Press, 2003).

[34] Council Framework Decision 2002/584 on the European Arrest Warrant and the surrender procedures between Member States (OJ 2002 L190/1), as amended by Council Framework Decision 2009/299 (OJ 2009 L81/24).

[35] As well as challenges brought in national constitutional courts and in the ECJ/CJEU.

This criticism must be taken seriously. Human rights organisations are worried about the disproportionate arrests, violations of procedural rights and the impossibility in some countries for an innocent person to appeal against a decision to be surrendered. (Some of these cases are now pending before the European Court of Human Rights in Strasbourg.) These problems have increased with the increase in the number of EAWs – there are now an average of more than 1,000 per month, the overwhelming majority of which relate to minor crimes.

In particular the 2013 *Melloni* case raises concerns.[36] In *Melloni*, the CJEU held that Spain could not refuse to execute a European Arrest Warrant on the basis of Article 53 of the Charter of Fundamental Rights (which states that nothing therein is to be interpreted as restricting or adversely affecting human rights and fundamental freedoms as recognised, *inter alia*, by the Member States' constitutions). The Spanish Constitutional Court had asked the CJEU whether the EAW Framework Decision allowed the Spanish courts to make the surrender to Italy of Mr Melloni (who had been convicted in Italy *in absentia*) subject to the possibility of judicial review of his conviction, as required under Spanish Constitutional law – so it might have seemed that Article 53 Charter would be applicable. However, the CJEU held that to make the surrender of Melloni subject to such a condition, a possibility not provided for under the Framework Decision, would cast doubt on the uniformity of the standard of protection of fundamental rights as defined in the EAW decision, and undermine the principles of mutual trust and recognition which that decision purported to uphold and would, therefore, compromise its efficacy. Yet, by this rather abrupt response to the first ever reference made to the CJEU by the Spanish Constitutional Court, the efficacy of Article 53 Charter itself appears compromised, and such a strong insistence on a uniform EU fundamental rights standard as a ceiling – in spite of the explicit protection granted to Member States' own standards in Article 53 – threatens the possibility of mutual trust and dialogue between the EU (including the CJEU) and its Member States (including their constitutional courts).

The human rights safeguards in EAW procedures need to be increased. In 2010 an EU directive was adopted on the right to interpretation and translation in criminal proceedings.[37] Hopefully this will result in improvements. The Stockholm programme suggests review of the EAW and, where appropriate, 'to increase efficiency and legal protection for

[36] C–399/11 *Melloni*, nyr.   [37] Directive 2010/64, note 29 above.

individuals in the process of surrender'. This review is urgently needed, although efficiency should not be at the expense of rights.

Data collection provides another illustration of the nature and import of the flurry of activity by the EU – and why we should be concerned about it. The EU has long considered control and exchange of information to be a necessary weapon in the fight against terrorism. There are diverse EU-wide databases in existence. For example, states exchange immigration and crime-related information through the Schengen Information System. Crime-related information is also exchanged through the Europol, Eurojust and Customs Information Systems. More specifically, fingerprints and DNA data can be exchanged through the Prüm Treaty decision, and EU law also requires biometric information in passports and visas, and passenger name records to be collected and passed to national authorities by airlines.

Such extensive surveillance and data storage raises considerable questions of privacy rights. At the very least, such actions should be matched by countervailing data protection measures by the EU.[38] All sorts of further issues arise as to how and by whom these huge flows of information are to be controlled, indeed as to who owns the data, who is to be held accountable and responsible for exchange and passing of data (given that private companies are often involved), whether it can be sold and how it can be tracked. A surely crucial question is whether there is any quantifiable benefit from this immense collection and retention of data and biometrics (at, it should not be forgotten, great financial cost)? More information is not necessarily preferable. Is it necessary? Is it proportionate to any threats we face? Can it help anticipate or prevent dangerous activities? Does it make us more secure? Or does it invade our privacy and increase the surveillance of individuals without promoting individual and collective safety? Does it increase suspicion, and undermine social cohesion? One might conclude by borrowing the ironic comment from the cartoonist, Edgar Argo, that 'Justice may be blind but she has very sophisticated listening devices . . . '

1.2.1. The AFSJ's incoherence and undue focus on security

There is hope that the changes of the Lisbon Treaty, as well as the proposals of the EU's five-year Stockholm Programme, which sets out the EU's

---

[38] After several years of debates within EU institutions, Council Framework Decision 2008/977, note 29 above, was adopted. This is a step forward, if not totally satisfactory in the protection it provides.

priorities for the AFSJ for 2010–14, may improve the prospects for freedom and justice in the EU. The Lisbon Treaty dissolved the EU's former three-pillar structure and now the Community method and co-decision will apply for most cases, thus 'normalising' the AFSJ, and the powers of the CJEU and European Parliament (and national parliaments) have been strengthened. This gives the AFSJ a tighter constitutional character, removing it from the Third Pillar connotations of intergovernmentalism and executive dominance. However, the 'Communitisation' of the AFSJ is undermined by the wide range of flexibility and Enhanced Cooperation measures under Lisbon.[39] The Stockholm Programme now ambitiously asserts the EU as 'A Europe of Law and Justice . . . ' and that its focus should be 'on the interests and needs of citizens'. It also asserts that '[t]he area of Freedom, Security and Justice must, above all, be a single area in which fundamental rights and freedoms are protected . . . '[40]

So, is there cause for optimism? I would like to think so, but fear not. This is partly because the idea of the AFSJ is itself incoherent, thereby undermining its ability to deliver, in particular, on justice. Although much has been written about the measures taken under the AFSJ, and there are many books devoted to it, there is surprisingly little about the notion of the AFSJ itself. A little analysis, however, reveals its confused and disjointed nature.

The AFSJ covers very diverse *subject matter* – namely, the control of human mobility, regulation of migration, crime control and cooperation in the field of civil justice. It does not form a coherent policy area. The packaging together of crime control with migration is contentious, given that there is no necessary connection between migration and crime. Its *geographical* scope is also unclear, due to the fact that it is an area of shared competence with Member States, which gives rise to the usual problems of determining the competence of the EU, as well as of opt outs, opt ins, and possible enhanced cooperation. It cannot always be predicted with certainty which measures will apply to which states. This weakens the orderly, unifying and controlling connotations of the use of the term

---

[39] See TFEU Part VI and Title II as well as the arrangements for opt-outs and variable geometry. Protocols exclude the UK, Ireland and Denmark from the application of most of Title V (although they may choose to opt in) and a Protocol also stipulates that the Charter of Fundamental Rights shall not be used as a basis to create newly justiciable rights in the UK and Poland. There is also a mismatch between EU membership and the area of Schengen free movement. So this remains an area of complexity and exceptionalism.

[40] Council of the European Union, 'The Stockholm Programme – An open and secure Europe serving and protecting citizens' (OJ 2010 C115/1–38), at 4.

'Area'. The AFSJ's relation to the values of the EU set out in Article 2 TEU is also unclear. Is 'Freedom' in the context of the AFSJ supposed to have the same meaning as 'Freedom' in Article 2? Further, what is the relationship of the EU's stated aim to 'promote peace' in Article 3 TEU and 'Security' in the AFSJ? Is the 'Justice' that is to prevail under Article 2 the same as 'Justice' in the AFSJ? There are no clear answers to these questions.

The AFSJ's constituent elements have also been undertheorised. Much of the discussion has been about the need to strike a balance between these constituent parts, and in particular the need to ensure that security does not dominate. But security has dominated, particularly since the Hague Programme.[41] Again, it seems that part of the problem is a failure of supranationalism. Are freedom, security and justice actually goods that the EU is capable of delivering? What is it that the EU may do specifically to sustain them, which its Member States may not? What is it about them that requires their realisation at EU level? And is there sufficient consensus at EU level about what they might mean? There has been very little reflection on this. It is the concept of security that appears most liable to require EU action – for it is here that there seems to be the greatest agreement that the EU can, indeed, add value, at least if Eurobarometer polls are to be believed.[42] Unfortunately, the overwhelming focus has been on security as a means of crime control, which is a limited and thin notion, rather than a deeper understanding of it as a social and political good enabling both individual and societal well-being and welfare,[43] which might also require the nurturing of freedom and the realisation of justice. Instead, freedom is perceived as unattainable without a concomitant focus on security. Indeed, the result is that freedom of movement for some individuals

---

[41] For example:

> However, if we compare the guiding common values of the Tampere and Hague Programmes, the latter seems to shift the balance between 'freedom' and 'security' in a very critical way. There has been a significant change in the values on which the EU's AFSJ is being built. In fact, the 'shared commitment to freedom based on human rights, democratic institutions and the rule of law', as set out at Tampere, is not a cornerstone of its successor.

T. Balzacq and S. Carrera, 'The Hague Programme: the long road to freedom, security and justice' in Balzacq and Carrera (eds), *Security Versus Freedom?: A Challenge for Europe's Future* (Aldershot: Ashgate, 2006), p. 5.

[42] E.g. European Commission, Special Eurobarometer, 'Opinions on organised, cross-border crime and corruption' (2006).

[43] See L. Zedner, 'The concept of security: an agenda for comparative analysis', 23 *Legal Studies* 1 (2003), 153–75; A. Williams, *The Ethos of Europe: Values, Law and Justice in the EU* (Cambridge: Cambridge University Press, 2010).

becomes its reverse, associated instead with detention, data collection (fingerprints and biometrics), criminalisation of undocumented entries and sanctions for carriers, leading to hostility against migrants.

Moreover, the interpretation given to justice in the context of the AFSJ has been a narrow one, focused on the administration of justice. Such an interpretation is also supported by the use of wording in some language versions of the EU treaties. The Dutch and German versions, for example, use the word *Recht,* which does not have the same associations as 'Justice' in English or in French, but rather connotes a narrower concern for law and order. The EU's 1998 Vienna Action Plan asserted the need to '[bring] to Justice those who threaten the freedom and security of individuals and society'[44] and therefore a need for crime control, for justice to be administered, for judicial cooperation. Justice is perceived as a means of dealing with those who threaten society. However, even this narrower, instrumental understanding of justice was threatened by the weak judicial mechanisms that operated in the past under the Third Pillar, in which the ECJ's power of judicial review was extremely limited. Access to justice was limited. This understanding leaves little room for any richer sense of justice. Justice in the context of the AFSJ is elided and impoverished in meaning.

So, overall, a notable lack of clarity. Many years have now passed since the AFSJ's inception, and we might expect greater lucidity on these points. Prospects for justice are not enhanced by such incoherence. Also, the lack of clarity lends support to the view that the AFSJ is not a serious notion, that insufficient thought has been given to it, and that its prime importance lies with the symbolic, with the rhetorical. Furthermore, in order for there to be a more balanced AFSJ, in which freedom and justice are not dominated by security, it is essential that fundamental rights be adequately protected. It will also be necessary for states to have greater trust in each others' criminal justice provisions, so that mutual recognition, such as that operating under the EAW, can function adequately. Yet it is a formidable task to create such trust, because EU states do not offer equivalence in human rights protection, nor deliver uniform standards of justice. As in the case of the Eurozone, not all Member States are equal, and cracks appear in the system. A dominant emphasis on security (i.e. automatic surrender) is at the expense of justice (protection of rights). Integration is unbalanced, and although an internal market in security

---

[44] Action plan of the Council and the Commission on how best to implement the Treaty of Amsterdam on an area of freedom, security and justice (OJ 1999 C19/01).

may be in the process of being created, this is at the expense of progress in human rights, freedom or justice.

1.3. Social justice

Article 3 TEU states that the EU 'shall promote social justice'. Yet what possible meaning can be given to 'social justice' as an aspiration for an EU that has focused for so long on market-driven ideology? Admittedly EU law, and ECJ/CJEU case law, have resulted in some benefits in the field of the equal treatment of men and women. However, for the most part these benefits have been driven by the market, by the need to secure a level playing field in an area of free movement, rather than by a freestanding concern for equality. For many years of the EU's existence, equal treatment law failed to extend beyond the employment field and beyond the equal treatment of men and women to discrimination of other sorts, e.g. on grounds of sexual orientation, or race.

However, it would be unfair to accuse the EU of actively opposing social justice in the form of a redistribution of wealth. The situation is rather that a common, harmonised, redistributive social policy remains an impossibility for the EU when its Member States will not give it such a competence because they are divided over whether social welfare should be market-driven or redistributionist and welfarist (although the Eurozone crisis now seems to have imposed austerity throughout the EU). In contrast to the AFSJ, where there appears to be a consensus among both peoples and governments in Europe that the EU should play an active role in the fight against terrorism and organised crime, there exists no such consensus as to the desirability of a redistributive EU social policy. Indeed, if anything, there exists a mutual mistrust, as illustrated by polarised reactions to the Lisbon Treaty, with some states seeing earlier drafts as too free market and Anglo-Saxon in approach, or by the squabbles over how to deal with the financial crisis of the euro. In such an environment, EU joint action is restricted to low minimum standards acceptable to all states, or the very limited redistributive functions in the fields of regional development policy and the varying budgetary contributions of its Member States.

Given these circumstances, as Fritz Scharpf has asserted, European integration has created a constitutional asymmetry between policies promoting market efficiencies and policies promoting social protection and equality. National welfare states are legally and economically constrained by European rules of economic integration, liberalisation and competition law, while efforts to adopt European social policies are politically impeded by the diversity of national welfare states, differing not only in levels of economic development and hence in their ability to pay for social transfers and services but, even more significantly, in their normative aspirations and institutional structures.[45]

One area of great concern has been the CJEU's willingness to assert the equivalence of fundamental market freedoms and fundamental rights (and more particularly social rights) with no positive outcome for fundamental rights. The basis of the claim in both *Viking Line* and *Laval* was that the applicant undertakings' market freedoms had been restricted by trade union collective action.[46] Although the right to take such action was at least acknowledged by the Court as a 'fundamental' one, in both cases it was interpreted as a 'restriction' on a fundamental market freedom. The Court took a broad approach to the application of EU law, holding that collective action could restrict market access. It then went on to weigh the freedom to provide services against this fundamental right to strike, in effect interpreting the right to strike as a *restriction* on the market freedom. The Court found that the right to strike must be exercised proportionately. Yet such reasoning is antipathetic to fundamental rights and has been strongly criticised,[47] especially in its application of a proportionality test to the concept of fundamental rights themselves. Normally, as in the test applied by the ECtHR, it is the *restrictions* on fundamental rights that must satisfy a proportionality test. As has so often been the case in the EU, the Internal Market lies at the centre of things, and proportionality's essential function is to ensure that market integration is not too greatly compromised. In such a mindset,[48] social justice will always be compromised.

To some extent one could argue that in *Viking* and *Laval* the Court was caught in a bind. If national labour standards in the host state are too high (in the context of posted workers) this renders market penetration

---

[45] F. Scharpf, 'The European social model: coping with the challenges of diversity', 40 *Journal of Common Market Studies* 4 (2002), 645–70.

[46] Case C–438/05 *Viking Line* [2007] ECR I–10779; Case C–341/05 *Laval* [2007] ECR I–11767.

[47] See e.g. C. Barnard, 'Social dumping or dumping socialism', 67 *Cambridge Law Journal* 2 (2008), 262–4; D. Nicol, 'Europe's *Lochner* moment', 2 *Public Law* (2011), 307–28 at 308.

[48] Also, see e.g. F. Scharpf, *The Double Asymmetry of European Integration – Or why the EU cannot be a Social Market Economy* (Cologne: Max Planck Institute for the Study of Societies Working Papers, 2009); C. Joerges '*Rechtstaat* and social Europe: how a classical tension resurfaces in the European integration process', 9 *Comparative Sociology* 1 (2010), 65–85.

from a posting state, with lower labour standards, impossible – thus retarding market integration. On the other hand, with degrading labour standards in the host state, the risk of social dumping arises. Therefore, how the CJEU balances economic fundamental rights with social fundamental rights is critical and, with respect, it is submitted that the court failed to achieve that sensitivity in *Viking* owing to its particularly harsh proportionality test.[49]

In an attempt to address the problems posed by the *Laval* and *Viking* rulings of the ECJ, the European Commission proposed the so-called 'Monti II' regulation (named after Italian Prime Minister Mario Monti, who drafted a similar clause while he served as commissioner for the Single Market)[50] on the exercise of the right to take collective action within the context of the freedom of establishment and the freedom to provide services. The proposal would have required that economic freedoms must respect social rights, and vice versa, with no priority given to either. However, the draft regulation was subject both to criticism that it remained inadequately protective of social rights,[51] and also that it infringed the principle of subsidiarity. The European Commission was forced to withdraw the draft regulation in September 2012, after the parliaments of twelve countries adopted reasoned opinions arguing that it violated the subsidiarity principle of the EU Treaty.

---

[49] AG Trstenjak suggested a more nuanced approach in Case C–271/08 *Commission* v. *Germany (Occupational Pensions)* [2010] ECR I–7091 – critical of *Laval* and especially *Viking*, arguing that they 'sit uncomfortably alongside the principle of equal ranking for fundamental rights and fundamental freedoms' (para. 183) – arguing the test for balancing market and social rights to be symmetrical in nature, although neither she, nor the Court, actually applied such a test in the case at hand. See also Opinion of AG Cruz Villalón in *Santos Palhota* (Case C–515/08, [2010] ECR I–9133, para. 53) suggesting that, since the Lisbon Treaty, when 'working conditions constitute an overriding reason relating to the public interest justifying a derogation from the freedom to provide services, they must no longer be interpreted strictly'. However, the Court did not address this argument. See also P. Syrpis, 'Reconciling economic freedoms and social rights – the potential of *Commission* v. *Germany*', 40 *Industrial Law Journal* 2 (2011), 222–9.

[50] Proposal for a Council Regulation on the exercise of the right to take collective action within the context of the freedom of establishment and the freedom to provide services (COM(2012) 130 final).

[51] See e.g. K. Ewing, 'The draft Monti II Regulation: an inadequate response to *Viking* and *Laval*', *Institute of Employment Rights Briefing* (2012), available at www.ier.org.uk/resources/draft-monti-ii-regulation-inadequate-response-viking-and-laval; N. Bruun and A. Bücker, *Critical assessment of the proposed Monti II regulation – more courage and strength needed to remedy the social imbalances* (Brussels: European Trade Union Institute Policy Briefs, 2012).

In any case, it is difficult to see how the EU can promote itself as the sort of social market community urged, for example, by Jürgen Habermas,[52] when so many of its members would veto such a role for it, and when the austerity measures taken in the wake of the Eurozone crisis undermine social justice. In the absence of such a common policy, developments in the social law field have been incremental, ad hoc, tangential to free movement concerns, rather than comprehensive in nature, and inevitably also derived from litigation before the ECJ/CJEU, which has had other motivations (usually enjoyment of free movement, such as in *Viking Line* and *Laval*) as its immediate inspiration. The real worry is that, while the EU lacks its own redistributive social justice policy, for the reasons already outlined, it nonetheless interferes with Member States' social policies, depriving them of an ability to regulate. This results in asymmetrical and unbalanced integration.

1.4. The nature and quality of EU law

There is another way in which the EU contributes to injustice. This derives from its very nature as a transnational legal community, and a living example of legal pluralism. The transfer of certain competences from the state to the EU, with a concomitant decrease in democratic scrutiny, and increase in complexity and untransparent lawmaking, has often seemed to undermine the very justice of the legal process itself. The Eurozone crisis measures are a good illustration – with their mixture of intergovernmental agreements, EU measures, variable geometry and even 'gentlemen's' agreements,[53] they are highly confusing. Before Lisbon, law making under the Third Pillar lacked many of the safeguards of democratic and legal accountability that existed within that Pillar. Neither the European Parliament, nor EU courts, nor the national parliaments or courts, had any great input in their generation or review. One might hope that the reforms of the Lisbon Treaty and communitisation of the

---

[52] See e.g. J. Habermas, 'Why Europe needs a constitution', 11 *New Left Review* (2001), 5–27.
[53] For example, how is the proposed Treaty on Stability, Coordination and Governance in the Economic and Monetary Union for Eurozone countries to apply a reverse Qualified Majority Voting (QMV) procedure, whereby measures are adopted unless a qualified majority of ministers vote against them, without changing the existing EU Treaty, which would be an interference with the EU *acquis* and the autonomy of EU law (see Art. 7 Fiscal Compact Treaty)? It would seem that participants would agree to behave as if the reverse QMV rule existed – i.e. a gentlemen's agreement without real enforcement provisions.

Third Pillar could improve things. However, there is still too much scope for flexibility and abnormal law-making, such as those of the Treaty of Prüm, or agreements within the G6,[54] meetings that take place usually in secret, in an utterly untransparent, impenetrable way, but that often end up informing, or even penetrating, EU criminal justice actions.[55]

More generally, the European legal field is one of segmented authority, overlapping jurisdictions and multiple loyalties, carrying with it the risk of constitutional crisis and of officials being compelled to choose between their loyalties to different public institutions. It is impossible to categorise such complex legal landscapes by a neat, self-contained conception of law, such as those associated with various theories of twentieth-century legal positivism. EU law throws up untidy conflicts and apparently irresolvable dilemmas. In recent decades, legal pluralism has become a popular paradigm,[56] and it is not a paradigm that I wish to challenge, or at least not if pluralism is taken as a statement of fact or description of the contemporary legal landscape.[57] Legal pluralism describes a state of affairs in which two or more legal orders occupy the same legal space, sometimes peacefully coexisting but sometimes in direct competition with each other.[58] Pluralism is extolled by its adherents as a model that more genuinely captures the legal world than monism or legal positivism, and there is often an assumption that it is less oppressive than earlier, unifying, modernist paradigms, less silencing of voices and other ways of doing things.

---

[54] The EU G6 ministers (i.e. from the UK, Germany, France, Italy, Spain and Poland) have discussed their joint response to terrorism, illegal immigration and organised crime. For a critical account of the G6, see e.g. United Kingdom House of Lords, Select Committee on the European Union, 'Behind closed doors: the meeting of the G6 Interior Ministers at Heiligendamm', 40th Report of Session 2005–6.

[55] The Treaty of Prüm, for example, was signed by a group of eight EU Member States in order to further closer cooperation and the exchange of information, including DNA profiles, fingerprints and vehicle registration data, and later incorporated into the EU's *acquis communautaire* in 2007 by EU decision.

[56] For more general theories of pluralism see e.g. S. Falk Moore, 'Law and social change: the semi-autonomous social field as an appropriate object of study', 7 *Law & Society Review* 1 (1972), 719–46; S. Merry, 'Legal pluralism', 22 *Law & Society Review* 5 (1988), 869–96; J. Griffiths, 'What is legal pluralism?', 24 *Journal of Legal Pluralism* (1986), 2–55. For the particular relevance of legal pluralism in the EU and in international law, see also N. MacCormick, *Questioning Sovereignty: Law, State and Nation in the European Commonwealth* (Oxford: Oxford University Press, 1999), p. 78; N. Krisch, *Beyond Constitutionalism: The Pluralist Structure of Postnational Law* (Oxford: Oxford University Press, 2010).

[57] As will become apparent, I am concerned by, and critical of, legal pluralism when it is presented as a normative model, i.e. not only as a description of legal affairs but also as a desirable model for them.

[58] For further commentary on pluralism, see Tuori in Chapter 1 of this volume.

Yet against this optimistic view should be set the fact that legal pluralism also brings a host of its own problems, which have too often been ignored. For example, the complex legal pluralism of the EU carries increased risks of a lack of accountability, of self-regulating institutions or localised laws being captured by special interests, and of 'a fragmented and impotent polity in which the public interest is emptied of meaning'.[59] Accountability can be very weak in this pluralistic landscape, and institutional design and effective tutelage become ever more important. An example of this was provided by the transfer of criminal law competences from Member State to EU level, resulting (at least before Lisbon) in a change from national parliamentary control to a situation of intergovernmental legislation by the Council of Ministers, with very little, if any, parliamentary control. There is also the example provided by Eurozone measures, which now give the unelected Commission the power to scrutinise national budgets prior to national parliaments doing so. Furthermore, relationships of authority can be difficult to trace because what might appear to be strictly hierarchical relationships in fact involve mutual incorporation or mutual influence. How may motive or agency be attributed where injustice is fragmented, systemic and impersonal? How are conflicts to be settled, and by which standards? How will we identify those 'like' cases that are to be treated alike? How will we treat persons with equal concern and respect if there is no uniform system? How may law be legitimate? Does the overwhelming complexity of the legal world diminish the prospects for justice?

I suggest that justice is *a crucial* issue for law in the era of legal pluralism. Rather than, or at least in addition to, questions of ordering or interpreting pluralism,[60] we should ask how is justice achievable, given this complexity? Ultimately, therefore, how is justice possible?

1.5. Conclusions on injustice in the EU

The first part of this chapter has detailed various ways in which the EU is capable of producing injustice. The EU's role as a *transnational* actor has been identified as exacerbating injustice – should we therefore look to repatriate the EU's powers, to cease the project of EU integration, to do

---

[59] P. Nonet and P. Selznick, *Law in Society: Toward Responsive Law* (New York: Harper & Row, 1978), p. 103; cf. T. Lowi, *The End of Liberalism: The Second Republic of the United States* (New York: W. W. Norton, 1969).

[60] See e.g. M. Delmas-Marty, *Ordering Pluralism* (Oxford: Hart Publishing, 2009).

away with the EMU, with the AFSJ, as so many eurosceptics might wish? But this will not do. First, the EU's Member States are not themselves paragons of justice and democracy. Second, the EU's transnational integration represents an imperative drive of a particular sort, paradigmatic of our era. The growth of a preoccupation with security, typical of both the EU and its Member States, singularly illustrates this.

For the social theorist, Zygmund Baumann, this focus on security is a key attribute of late modernity, something that has come about as a result of certain shifts and passages in the way governance is conducted, such as a separation of power from politics to a more uncontrolled private or global sphere and capricious market forces.[61] The consequence has been that traditional political institutions appear less relevant. Therefore, globalisation, the transnational pluralism of laws and, indeed, some of the very circumstances that gave rise to the Eurozone crisis (namely, reckless, volatile financial institutions, global markets) play their part in a perceived growing need for security. This has been accompanied by the gradual, consistent withdrawal of welfare state mechanisms – of communal state insurance against individual failure – *a fortiori* in a post-financial crisis world of spending cuts. Increasing deregulation, flexibility and the multiplicity of forms of governance, indeed legal pluralism, have in fact made us more insecure. The withdrawal of much state social subsistence has sapped social solidarity and community, resulting in alienation and anomie, as well as distrust and fear of migrants, of the other.

As a result of these passages and shifts, suggests Baumann, although, in a certain sense, some of us are more free than we have ever been, (in the sense of more money and time and less drudgery – certainly more freedom to consume, a feature that the EU's Internal Market encourages) this freedom comes at a price – insecurity, anxiety or a more complex *Unsicherheit* – often felt most strongly by those who have the most wealth. Indeed, in a transformation of roles and values, security has itself become seen as the primary freedom. At the same time, this has been accompanied by rising expectations that insecurity is something that can be solved by technology – in that a life free from fear can be assured by expensive technical expertise. Yet this is inadequate – computer technology cannot stand in for humans, nor can biometrics and database profiles predict future behaviour; data become uncontrollable and security is not increased.

[61] Z. Baumann, *Liquid Fear* (Cambridge: Polity Press, 2006).

The state sees itself as having found a valid role – that of the security state. The state cannot compete with a powerful global elite, having lost much of its autonomy, particularly in economic matters to global financial markets. One option is that of regional integration, the Internal Market and EMU – and these bring their own problems and crises. Another way in which states seek to compensate for their lack of power, and to legitimise themselves, is by declaring states of emergency, issuing continual warnings of terrorism threats and enacting repressive measures. This in turn justifies the taking of exceptional measures going beyond ordinary state policies.[62] Yet this merely increases the climate of fear and the state cannot compensate for its citizens' insecurities owing to the very fact that we live in an era of globalisation and increased mobility of persons, provision of security is no longer something that the state can provide by its own efforts alone. Commercial enterprises and security firms are involved. International or regional cooperation is necessary. So the legal orders of the west are now in transition from constitutional criminal law to a transnational security order,[63] of which the AFSJ is a very good example. International securitisation has been given further justification by the lifting of internal border controls in the context of the EU's Internal Market programme, which also increased the free movement of criminals, this in turn giving rise to a further perceived need for EU cooperation in criminal justice matters.

Yet such a move to transnational security brings with it considerable adverse consequences, as this chapter attempts to demonstrate. It wreaks injustice. It removes many of the constraints of the democratic state. It creates a democratic deficit of worrying proportions in the context of great intrusions into individual liberty by biometric regulation, exchanges of data and automatic surrender of suspects without complementary protection of their rights. These measures need to be underpinned with structures that protect the rule of law and human rights, and make provision for accountability.

In such a society what happens to mutual trust and mutual recognition? Anyone is liable to become a potential suspect. For laws to be acceptable and function effectively, there must be reciprocity and participation by

---

[62] Such exceptional measures are not confined to the field of terrorism. The whole raft of Eurozone crisis measures might be described as one great assemblage of exceptional measures.

[63] See K. Günther, 'World citizens between freedom and security', 12 *Constellations* 3 (2005), 379–91.

all in their making, engagement and dialogue of citizens, not mutual suspicion and lack of trust. Fuller, in his account of the rule of law,[64] stressed the reciprocity between citizen and law creator involved in making good law. Yet engagement and dialogue has not been greatly in evidence in the twenty-first-century security frenzy within the EU. Indeed, there has been a failure of reciprocity and mutual recognition as an underpinning of EU criminal law, as evidenced by reactions to the EAW and a reluctance to trust other Member States' criminal laws and to treat them as equivalent to domestic ones. The same applies in the Eurozone, where a lack of solidarity has been evident.[65] It is suggested that the Eurozone bailouts hardly provide examples of solidarity between Member States. Who benefits from these 'solidarity' measures, undertaken with reluctance by states, and only under conditions of extreme austerity? It would seem to be indebted banks, or creditors in other Member States, rather than the citizens of the states in difficulty, who must face years of shrinking wages, unemployment and shrivelling of public services and welfare. Indeed, the result would seem to be that these EU measures actually sap solidarity between Member States, causing resentment and weakening relations between EU members.

In conclusion, it must be stressed that supranationalism, and some-times pluralism, are capable of fostering injustice – most particularly when they function as regulatory failures. The austerity and hardship prevalent in the Eurozone might not be attributable solely to the EU – undoubtedly international financial markets, the banking crisis and the profligacy or irresponsibility of some states' actions all have their part to play. But the existence of a monetary union without a financial union has also wrought its own crisis, which subsequent ill-conceived and undemo-cratic measures have not ameliorated. A further imbalance of injustice has been produced by a highly integrated internal market capable of infring-ing or overriding Member States' social policies, with no commensurate EU social policy able to step in and allay hardship. *Ergo*, there is a vicious circle of injustice and insecurity. The state, inadequate and powerless in the face of global forces seeks transnational solutions. However, it is these same transnational solutions that wreak yet more insecurity and injustice.

---

[64] For this, see L. Fuller, *The Morality of Law* (New Haven, CT: Yale University Press, 1964) and Art. 125(1) TFEU.

[65] Notably, Art. 125(1) TFEU, which could be seen as a 'no solidarity clause'. It was necessary to introduce new measures, notably the ESM, in order to make provision for future loans to troubled Member States, as well as to engage the IMF in the bailouts.

So this is the nature of the problem. Here, the critical part of this chapter ends. Indeed, I believe that this part of the argument may stand as it is, without any further, positive or more constructive, elements. The matters it describes are sufficiently important for the critique to do its own job. As Bertholt Brecht wrote, '[n]othing but *ad hominem* abuse; that's better than nothing' (*'Nichts als Beschimpfungen, das ist mehr als nichts'*).[66]

2. The problem of justice in the EU

2.1. The omission of justice

I start this section by highlighting a significant omission. Notably, justice is not presented as one of the EU's founding values in Article 2 TEU. We are told that justice 'should prevail' in this society but not that justice is one of its values. Why not? Surely, in the many years in which the EU has interrogated itself, its identity and its ambitions, it must have acknowledged the crucial importance of justice. If it does not set justice as a fundamental value then what is its worth? What might we say of any society or legal entity that would not embrace justice as a founding value, especially one such as the EU, which has, from its earliest days, set a premium on 'integration through law'[67] (law and justice of course being intimately related, as I elaborate below)? One might believe it possible to infer justice as a value for the EU from the sum total of all the other values, aims, objectives and principles that it embraces. Yet this seems unsatisfactory – one should not have to extract or distil justice as a value from a range of clauses and provisions – its salience surely renders its importance free-standing. For after all, as John Rawls stipulated, 'justice is the first virtue of social institutions'[68] – a suggestion to be taken very seriously, even if one does not concur with the actual substantive theory of justice that Rawls proposed. Furthermore, as noted earlier in this chapter, in the context of the AFSJ the focus has been on the administration of justice, of 'bringing to justice' those who threaten society, on a perceived need for crime control, for justice to be administered. Justice is interpreted as a means of dealing with those who threaten society. So this is the first problem, or obstacle, for justice in the EU – the omission of justice as a stated value.

---

[66] B. Brecht, *Schriften zur Politik und Gesellschaft 1919–56* (Frankfurt: Suhrkampf, 1974), p. 311.

[67] See e.g. M. Cappelletti, M. Seccombe and J. Weiler (eds), *Integration through Law* (Berlin: Walter de Gruyter, 1986).

[68] J. Rawls, *A Theory of Justice* (Cambridge, MA: Harvard University Press, 1971), p. 3.

2.2. The elision of justice

In *The Ethos of Europe: Values, Law and Justice in the EU*,[69] Andrew
Williams castigated the EU for lacking any coherence in its values, or
ethos, and for the absence of a clear moral purpose, suggesting that the
EU's ethos has been technical rather than ethical, with the requirements of
the market providing a 'value surrogacy'. It has not taken justice seriously.
Williams' suggested solution to the EU's failure to take justice seriously
is to propose a concept of justice centred on human rights – one that
understands human rights primarily as a response to suffering. I agree
with much of Williams's argument. Human rights are crucial and should
play a vital role in European integration. In particular, collective rights,
which have a presence (albeit a rather slim one[70]) in the Charter of
Fundamental Rights, can enable justice to be done. But human rights
are not identical to justice, although they may be an essential part of an
understanding of justice. Yet not every situation of injustice can be framed
in terms of human rights.[71] This is not to belittle the role of human rights
in any way – indeed, I have written elsewhere, urging the importance
of their full recognition in the EU and in the wider European context,[72]
but to regret that, too often, human rights now occupy the full terrain
of moral discourse. For the remainder of this chapter, rather than eliding
justice into human rights, I seek to focus more directly on the concept
of justice itself, as a free-standing concept, to engage more deeply with
what particular form it might take in the EU, given the peculiarities and
singularities of the EU legal order.

2.3. The substance of justice in the EU

Yet one must also engage with the nature of the EU itself. Some have
questioned the possibility of a workable, overarching concept of justice
for the EU. Pluralism, soft law, governance, networks, supranationalism,
the democratic deficit – all recognisable aspects of the EU legal space –
create particular problems for the provision of justice.

[69] Williams, note 43 above.
[70] See e.g. the somewhat qualified provisions on 'Solidarity' in Title IV of the Charter of
Fundamental Rights of the European Union.
[71] For example, Rawls's 'Difference Principle', which permits redistribution of wealth in order
to benefit the least well-off in society, is not based on human rights principles.
[72] E.g. S. Douglas-Scott, 'Europe's constitutional mosaic: human rights in the European legal
space – utopia, dystopia, monotopia or polytopia?' in N. Walker, J. Shaw and S. Tierney
(eds), *Europe's Constitutional Mosaic* (Oxford: Hart Publishing, 2011), pp 97–134.

It will be noted that I have not yet suggested that the concept of justice should be given any specific meaning or interpretation. It is also clear that attaining justice in the supranational and pluralist EU raises very complicated issues. Confronting the nature of justice for the EU raises justice in all of its manifold forms – substantive and procedural, distributive and corrective. For example, the question of securing social justice in the EU raises very thorny issues of distributive justice, while the problems of the AFSJ will often turn on issues of corrective justice, which raise different concerns, but may be equally problematic for a transnational community. Also, different parties within the EU – states, EU institutions, private parties – may clearly have different obligations of justice.

The very nature of the EU itself causes problems – it is unfinished, inchoate and there exists no consensus as to its nature. Should we conceive of it as an international organisation, as evolving into some sort of 'superstate', or as a *sui generis* organisation? Clearly, the ways in which we conceive the EU will colour impressions of its capacity for justice. If we believe it is becoming something more state-like in nature, then we may require it to generate affective bonds and the type of solidarity necessary for a more substantial concept of justice.

Further, as I have suggested in Part I, some of the examples of injustice in the EU have been generated by the EU's very nature as a supranational project. Unless the EU becomes a superstate, a role almost no one would wish for it, it will always have competences in some areas and very limited powers in others. Its institutions will lack the full institutional capacities of national governments and parliaments. They will not be democratic or accountable in the way that states may be, and indeed, might not seem democratic at all. Yet those areas in which the EU's powers are strong will inevitably cause spillover problems that are beyond the capacity of functionalist theories to solve. But the urgency of moments of crisis – 9/11, Eurozone – will require swift solutions, which, however, the EU will be perceived as lacking the full legitimacy to dispense. So there is a sense in which injustice (and not just the inefficiency bemoaned by some EU commentators) is built into the very nature of the EU itself. Yet an end to, or reversal of, integration provides no obvious solution. A vicious circle exists. The imperatives of globalisation – global financial markets, security threats – render cooperation necessary, and with it the injustices rendered by the failures and imbalances of integration.

The complexity of the EU does not end the investigation, however, for it is necessary to take account of the pluralism and contested nature of the concept of justice itself.

2.4. The perplexing nature of justice

Justice appears all-encompassing. It is hard to imagine that any community, however large, might escape its remit. It is a necessary part of our moral landscape.[73] According to Michael Walzer, nothing can be omitted, 'no feature of our common life can escape its scrutiny'.[74] Yet justice may seem so elusive as to be a utopian ideal. There is no one determinate way of interpreting it. It may be understood in a rich, substantive sense, or as a complex of fair procedures. It may be deemed to be closely tied to particular circumstances, or proclaimed as a universal good, for all times. Justice is clearly related to law, but nonetheless justice also importantly acts as an external standard by which we evaluate law. Jacques Derrida captures the perplexing nature of justice by interpreting it as a complex of aporia – demanding immediate action, yet infinite time, knowledge and wisdom in order to do 'justice'. According to Derrida,[75] justice is unquantifiable, it is 'deconstruction' but not, unlike law, deconstructible. Indeed, Costas Douzinas and Adam Gearey find it to be somewhat of a philosophical failure, given that no society or ideology has yet developed a determinate and accepted theory of justice, and it is probably fair to assume that no such theory can be developed.[76]

In these circumstances, namely the existence of multiple and conflicting conceptions of justice, Danny Nicol argues, contra Jürgen Neyer, that justice is not an adequate replacement for democracy in the EU. The EU's democratic deficit cannot be eased away by ensuring that the EU observe a particular, shared, notion of justice, because there can be no agreement on such a notion of justice. Indeed, for Nicol, democratic means – argument, contestation, voting and representation – are needed to settle these very questions of justice.[77]

---

[73] W. Sadurski, 'Social justice and legal justice', 3 *Law and Philosophy* 3 (1984), 329–54.

[74] M. Walzer, *Spheres of Justice: A Defense of Pluralism and Equality* (New York: Basic Books, 1983).

[75] J. Derrida, 'Force of law: "the mystical foundation of authority"' in D. Cornell, M. Rosenfeld and D. G. Carlson (eds), *Deconstruction and the Possibility of Justice* (New York: Routledge Chapman & Hall, 1992).

[76] C. Douzinas and A. Gearey, *Critical Jurisprudence* (Oxford: Hart Publishing, 2005), pp 227–302.

[77] Neyer, note 27 above; D. Nicol, 'Can justice dethrone democracy in the European Union: a reply to Jürgen Neyer', 50 *Journal of Common Market Studies* 3 (2012), 508–22; also the riposte to Nicol by J. Neyer, 'Who's afraid of justice? A rejoinder to Danny Nicol', 50 *Journal of Common Market Studies* 3 (2012), 523–9.

It might even appear that justice is a surrogate for value in the modern, post-metaphysical, 'valueless' world, extending a hope or promise of what is right, but always to come; never to be achieved in the here and now; a utopian ideal. We live in a shockingly unjust world but cannot agree on justice. Gilles Deleuze and Felix Guattari, in their writings about Kafka, present a similar interpretation. For them, justice represents the desire for what is lacking in our life, what we yearn for in an empty, valueless world; for them, 'justice is desire and not Law'.[78] Not only continental post-structuralism makes this point, however, but also the English common law. In a negligence action, concerning the disastrous loss of life at the Hillsborough football stadium, the UK House of Lords dispensed the same wisdom. According to Lord Steyn, a respected judge (now famous for his depiction elsewhere of Guantanamo Bay as 'a black hole of injustice'): 'In an ideal world all those who have suffered as a result of the negligence ought to be compensated. But we do not live in Utopia: we live in a practical world . . . This results of course in an imperfect justice but it is by and large the best the common law can do.'[79]

Justice, it seems, raises an inexorably postmodern, ironic question – how we may do justice to justice? The discussion of justice so far raises a quandary for legal theory, and more particularly for a theory of justice for the EU. What direction should legal and political theory of the EU take if it is, on one hand, keen to avoid an impossibly uniform and constricting account of justice, on the other also wary of postmodern theories that decry grand narratives and embrace a plurality of justices that seem unworkable in a fixity with the ideal, and in their pessimism about the actual legal world. Justice is understood as desire, as what is lacking, what will always be lacking, in the EU, as in the world at large.

Therefore, the problem of justice for the EU is considerable and may be summarised in the following ways:

1. Justice is undervalued in that it is not specifically named as a value for the EU in Article 2 TEU (although more indirectly referenced). It is also undervalued in that its interpretation in the context of the AFSJ has been reductive – to that of the 'administration of justice' and therefore instrumentalised into something for the provision of security.

---

[78] G. Deleuze and F. Guattari, *Kafka: Toward a Minor Literature* (Minneapolis, MN: University of Minnesota Press, 1986), p. 43.
[79] *White* v. *Chief Constable of South Yorkshire Police* [1999] 2 AC, para. 491.

2. Justice as a concept tends to have been overtaken and overshadowed by human rights, indeed often elided into human rights. It is also very often linked with questions of democracy in EU scholarship.
3. There are specific problems in generating a sense of justice for the EU – namely, how to agree such a concept in a transnational context where there is no shared culture, or sense of solidarity, or indeed agreement as to what the EU itself is or should become. Transnational law, pluralism and integration wreak particular injustices, yet a reverse of integration does not seem feasible.
4. Justice is itself subject to plural interpretations and contested.

Taken together, these points might seem almost to amount to a counsel of despair, causing a resigned pessimism on the issue of justice in the EU. Nonetheless, there is also the sense that we inhabit an unjust world, and there is a need for some sort of ethics, or moral order. And yet what might that justice be?

This chapter continues with two suggestions for taking the debate further. First, it examines what sense may be made of a specific justice *within* law, in particular that which I name critical legal justice. Then it concludes with some thoughts on the inchoate and unfulfillable demands of justice, advocating a politics of resistance.

3. Two notions of justice

In the light of the discussion so far, I suggest that it is unrealistic (at least at present) to expect the EU to be capable of realising a substantive, redistributionist theory of justice. The circumstances of the EU (namely a lack of consensus among its Member States as to the desirability of EU redistributive social welfare policies, and lack of solidarity among Member States[80]) render achievement of a substantive justice particularly difficult. Further, the EU's present lack of an effective public sphere, and its democratic deficit, render it structurally incapable of providing

---

[80] For lack of consensus among political philosophers as to the possibility of justice at the international or transnational level, see e.g. J. Rawls, *The Law of Peoples: With, The Idea of Public Reason Revisited* (Cambridge, MA: Harvard University Press, 2001); T. Nagel, 'The problem of global justice', 33 *Philosophy and Public Affairs* 2 (2005), 113–47 at 115. Others disagree, e.g. for theories of justice applied to the international level, see T. Pogge (ed.), *Global Justice* (Oxford: Blackwell Publishing, 2001); D. Held, *Democracy and the Global Order: From the Modern State to Cosmopolitan Governance* (Cambridge: Polity Press, 1995).

the strong democratic structures necessary to sustain such a substantive concept.[81]

This state of affairs inevitably results in continued injustice in the EU – in imbalances of rich and poor in the absence of every Member State implementing equivalent redistributive policies of their own, and *a fortiori*, in the present climate of austerity. This is a regrettable state of affairs. Nor am I denying the desirability of social justice. It remains a crucial aspiration. I merely assert its unlikely achievement by EU law at present and focus instead on what is possible and sometimes ignored. In the context of the EU, a quest for the possibility of a richer, more substantive justice, has utopian elements. The better way, I argue, is to focus on *injustice* as motivational, and a call to action.

Yet I believe that there does exist a sufficient consensus (perhaps even of an overlapping, Rawlsian form) for the realisation of another notion of justice in the EU. The core of my argument is that, in addition to prioritising the fulfilment of human rights, the EU should seek to achieve *legal* justice through robust adherence to the rule of law. It is just this type of justice, that assured by the rule of law, that has been notably absent in EU activities (and not only in the EU, but in many other legal environments, given the current attachment to flexibility and reflexivity in lawmaking, and a turn toward pluralism overall). However, this seemingly more limited aspiration for a 'legal' justice should by no means be taken as a counsel of despair. A great deal may still be achieved by working with a more formal concept of justice that is still very ambitious in nature, given the problems of the EU.

3.1. Legal justice?

I first want to explore the notion of a 'legal' justice. Law and justice have a very close relationship, a special affinity. It is not by accident that judges take the title 'Justice', that government departments are named ministries of 'Justice'. People go to law because they feel some sense of injustice, which they hope law will address. Law presents itself as a form of governance that is distinct from power and from personal rule, as an institution that can make legitimate demands on citizens, and it holds out the prospect of

---

[81] The German Constitutional Court's *Lisbon Treaty* judgment examines and discusses the various ways in which the Court considers that the EU is at present inadequate as a representative democracy. See BVerfGE, 2 BvE 2/08, 30 June 2009, paras 209–10, 212–13, 250, 268–70, 280–86.

justice. Justice is seen as a peculiarly legal virtue. It plays its part in what Talcott Parsons referred to as 'the Hobbesian problem of order' – namely, that law is perceived as a preferable approach to organising society than private vengeance.[82] Further, law also possesses what Leslie Green has described as its 'aptness for justice'.[83] Law may not be alone in this regard but legal systems are undoubtedly apt for appraisal as just or unjust in the way that other practices, such as carpentry, cookery or rock climbing, are not. Law may not always be just but it is always possible and indeed, often necessary to ask whether it is actually just.

One, or indeed perhaps the most, salient question of legal philosophy focuses on the relationship between law and justice. The long pedigree of the natural law tradition holds that there exists a *necessary* connection between law and justice. Other accounts also see law and justice as necessarily linked – Aristotle isolated a specific concept of 'legal justice', which is distinct from other aspects of justice, such as distributive and retributive justice.

However, law and justice remain connected without insisting on some intrinsic connection. Justice is also perceived as an external standard by which law may be assessed, as an ideal to which law should aspire. One may locate such a view in the Christian tradition whereby justice is seen as realisable not within the City of Man but in the City of God.[84] Christianity proffers an eschatological perspective, with a promise of divine law, of justice in a world yet to come, in contrast to the inadequate, unjust, existing one. Yet the distancing or 'diremption' of law from justice is by no means limited to a religious, dualist perspective. It has been highlighted as a feature of the modern and postmodern era by theorists who view justice as an ideal contrasted to the nihilism of law,[85] as well as by legal positivists. John Austin famously claimed that the existence of law was one thing, and its merit or demerit another, a succinct illustration of the legal positivist's insistence on the separation of law and morality.

Therefore, the relationship between law and justice gives rise to an essential ambiguity – for is justice essential and intrinsic to law, or an

---

[82] See C. Douzinas and R. Warrington, *Justice Miscarried: Ethics and Aesthetics in Law* (London: Harvester Wheatsheaf, 1994), p. 137.

[83] L. Green, 'Positivism and the inseparability of law and morals', 83 *New York University Law Review* 4 (2008), 1035–58.

[84] E.g. in the works of St Augustine.

[85] See e.g. Douzinas and Warrington, note 82 above; G. Rose, *Mourning Becomes the Law: Philosophy and Representation* (Cambridge: Cambridge University Press, 1997).

external measure by which we assess law? Or, perhaps, can it be both, depending on how we understand justice? This vexed relationship between law and justice involves the issue of what Lon Fuller termed 'the Law in quest of itself.'[86] Philip Selznick captures the complexity of the situation in this way:

> It is important to preserve the distinction between Law as an operative system and Justice as a moral ideal. But clear distinctions are compatible with – indeed they are important preconditions of – theories that trace connections and reveal dynamics. Law is not necessarily just, but it does promise Justice. We must look to the theory of Law and Justice to understand why that promise exists and under what conditions it may be fulfilled or abridged.[87]

This statement captures the nature of the relationship between law and justice, and is the basis of my argument in this chapter – law is not necessarily just but it does promise justice. Law is an entity that, in Green's words, is 'justice apt'.[88] There are many diverse and hidden dynamics in the rich relationship between law and justice. They do not give rise to one dominant conception of justice or one way in which the law can realise justice, but there is one particularly salient account of legal justice that may aid our investigation here.

The rule of law is what is very often understood by the concept of 'legal justice', importantly acknowledging it as a form of justice. For many it is also seen as playing a key role in the legitimacy of law – such legitimacy itself being somewhat of a holy grail of modern jurisprudence as well as of EU constitutional theory. There exists a strong intuition that power, position and status should not corrupt, or 'maim' justice, and the rule of law functions to constrain and control the abuse of power. The rule of law has traditionally been seen to require laws to rest on legal norms that are general in character, relatively clear, certain, public, prospective and stable, as well as recognising the equality of subjects before the law.[89] Some would add to this the protection of fundamental rights.[90] It stresses the fixed

---

[86] L. Fuller, *The Law in Quest of Itself* (Chicago: The Foundation Press, 1940).

[87] P. Selznick, *The Moral Commonwealth: Social Theory and the Promise of Community* (Berkeley: University of California Press, 1992), pp 443–4.

[88] Green, note 83 above, at 1050.

[89] See both J. Raz 'The rule of law and its virtue', 93 *Law Quarterly Review* (1977), 195–211 at 196; and Fuller, *The Morality of Law*, note 64 above, who both give similar but not identical accounts to this.

[90] See for example, T. Bingham, *The Rule of Law* (London: Allen Lane, 2010); also German constitutional theory on the rule of law in which constitutional review for breach of

and stable enforcement of general principles – legitimate expectations, formal rights of access to the courts, equality before the law. Its benefits can be stated simply. Observance of the rule of law enhances certainty, predictability and security both among individuals, and between citizens and government, as well as restricting governmental discretion. It restricts the abuse of power. Thus it has both private and public law functions – an attraction in the world of growing legal pluralism. Citizens are able to interact together, knowing in advance what rules will regulate conflicts, should there be any.

3.1.1. Critical legal justice

I therefore argue that the rule of law should be recast as critical legal justice,[91] which adheres strongly to the *values* that the rule of law protects – looking to its spirit, rather than overly focusing on the forms that it has taken in various contexts. A belief in the rule of law does not commit one to a consequent belief in law as rules or in law as a strongly bounded, autonomous discipline. Neither does it commit one to the legal theory of legal positivism – nor to any other legal theory for that matter. Further, I also argue that the rule of law does not violate substantive equality, nor is it blind to difference, because of its apparent focus on a philosophy of neutral, formal equality. To do all of this (naturally no small order) it is necessary to reclaim the rule of law and to reimagine it. That is why I prefer to recast this concept as critical legal justice, in order to distinguish it in perception from discredited understandings of the rule of law.[92] I also wish to identify it more clearly with *justice*, rather than with the bland identification of the rule of law as a value in Article 2 TEU, the content of which is empty and undefined.[93]

---

fundamental rights is closely associated with the rule of law: R. Grote, 'Rule of law, *Rechtstaat*, and *état de droit*: the origins of the different national traditions and the prospects for their convergence in the light of recent constitutional developments' in C. Starck (ed.), *Constitutionalism, Universalism and Democracy – A Comparative Analysis* (Baden-Baden: Nomos, 1999), p. 269.

[91] See also, for further argument on the nature of critical legal justice, Douglas-Scott, 'The problem of justice in the EU' as well as Douglas-Scott, *Law After Modernity*, both note 1 above.

[92] Namely, those understandings of the rule of law that have been perceived as overly formalist and blind to difference.

[93] Notably, the rule of law is nowhere defined in the EU Treaties and different Member States have different understandings of it, according to their diverse legal traditions – i.e. *état de droit* in France, *Rechtstaat* in Germany, and so on. See also L. Pech, '"A union founded on the rule of law": meaning and reality of the rule of law as a constitutional principle of EU law', 6 *European Constitutional Law Review* (2010), 359–96, for further elucidation.

There exists no single model for the Rule of Law.[94] Yet this should not mean that its value is lessened, nor that it may be dismissed as incoherent or essentially contested. Rather, I believe it suggests that we should acknowledge that there exist different ways of furthering the values it serves. What are these values? Surely at its base lies the opposition to unrestrained, despotic power, to be achieved through the accountability of power, and correlative emphasis on freedom and equality that are enhanced by restraining power. In order to reclaim the rule of law, it is necessary to focus on these values rather than on specific, contingent, historical practices that have sometimes been used to further these values, otherwise there is a danger of believing that contingent practices are in fact the essence of the rule of law – a fault that A. V. Dicey might be said to have committed by identifying the rule of law with its rather singular form under Victorian constitutional law.[95]

The rule of law has its classical connotations – it brings to mind order, regularity, proportionality and equality, and there is something geometric or architectonic about it. This appears to be in sharp contrast to the 'chaos of surfaces' and 'rhetorical fronts'[96] of postmodernity – and seemingly the reverse of the chaotic trajectories and vortices of much contemporary law. The rule of law requires that law consist of standards, sometimes even described as 'rules'. This may seem challenging in a legal world where 'the model of rules' may no longer be clearly applicable. And yet, the very fact of complex trajectories and perspectives might suggest a reason why this structural component is needed more than ever – as a bulwark against, a counterpoint to, injustice, a means of containing the chaos of the legal universe. It does not require that actual, substantive laws form rule-like systems, but rather that certain structural components be applied to shore up laws, or even eject them, where necessary.

The rule of law has too often been lacking in the EU. Proceduralism and the rule of law have been associated with 'integration through law' in the EU, principally through the actions of the ECJ/CJEU, and the pressing of free movement principles that ignore policy and social market interests. Yet the *lack* of a rule of law has been glaring and damaging in areas of EU

---

[94] Selznick makes this point; see M. Krygier, 'Philip Selznick: incipient law, state law and the rule of law' in H. van Schooten and J. Verschuuren (eds), *International Governance and Law: State Regulation and Non-State Law* (Cheltenham: Edward Elgar Publishing, 2008), pp 31–55.

[95] A. V. Dicey, *The Law of the Constitution* (London: Macmillan, 1961).

[96] See P. Goodrich, 'Postmodern justice' in A. Sarat, M. Anderson and C. O. Frank (eds), *Law and the Humanities* (Cambridge: Cambridge University Press, 2009), p. 188.

affairs: for example, in the lack of access to courts in the criminal law pillar
of the EU (at least until the Lisbon Treaty); or in the lack of institutional
balance that has granted too much power to unelected, unaccountable
agencies such as Eurojust and Europol or to Member State executives in
the Council; in less than transparent, almost secretive lawmaking[97] – this
suggests an *absence* rather than the presence of the rule of law. This is also
evident in the field of EMU, of which one author recently commented:

> the EU's economic governance rules fail the test of transparency, because
> of their near-total complexity and unreadability, scattered across a dozen
> primary, secondary and soft-law sources, with more to come. This might
> be justifiable if the subject-matter of these rules were a technical issue
> like chemicals regulation, but it is hardly acceptable that the basic rules
> on the EU's coordination and control of fundamental national economic
> decisions are essentially unintelligible.[98]

Further, the experience of actions taken in the course of the 'war on terror',
such as the willingness of some EU states to accept landing of US flights in
the course of 'extraordinary rendition',[99] and the unwillingness of the EU
to take any action against those states under Article 7 TEU, also suggests
that the rule of law, along with human rights, has been lost in a search for
'expedient' measures.

3.1.2. An impoverished theory of justice?

However, one critique derides formal justice and formal or thin versions
of the rule of law as 'morally impoverished', 'the shabby remnant of the
sum total of virtues that was once called Justice' where now 'only a *minima
moralia* remains'.[100] Naturally, as I do not wish to be associated with a
'morally impoverished' theory of justice for the EU, this critique must be
addressed.

The first point to make is that I am not suggesting critical legal justice as
a complete theory of justice but rather as a theory of legal justice, capable of
complementing other notions of justice such as social justice. But critical

---

[97] See e.g. Case C–345/06 *Gottfried Heinrich* [2009] ECR I–1659. Also the Treaty of Prüm, and G6 as discussed earlier.

[98] S. Peers, 'Analysis: draft agreement on reinforced economic union (REU Treaty)', *State-watch* 21 (2011).

[99] For which now see the application lodged against Poland, *Al Nashiri* v. *Poland* (App. No. 28761/11), in the European Court of Human Rights, in which it is alleged that Poland hosted a secret CIA prison at a military intelligence training base in Stare Kiejkuty where the applicant was held incommunicado and tortured.

[100] A. Heller, *Beyond Justice* (New York: Basil Blackwell, 1987).

legal justice can be defended on its own terms. For example, Lon Fuller did not believe the rule of law to be morally impoverished. He stressed the link of the rule of law with freedom, describing his eight canons or principles of legality as 'the inner morality of law'[101] – and argued for their intimate association with a moral view of the relation between citizen and authorities, and with their ability to support normative grounds for believing that citizens have a moral obligation to obey the law. He believed that they indicated and mandated an element of reciprocity between government and citizen, established by the observation of certain types of rules. The building of such reciprocity is very important if the EU is to work toward establishing a European identity and the growth of solidarity necessary for developing social justice. Although, in the context of the Hart–Fuller debate, Hart famously suggested that Fuller's 'inner morality of law' consisted of no more than principles of efficiency, which could be 'compatible with very great iniquity',[102] Fuller vehemently denied this criticism. Fuller believed that compliance with 'the inner morality of law' increases the capacity of law to become *good* law, and that it is extremely difficult, if not impossible, for a regime bent on immoral or unsavoury ends to achieve them through the rule of law.[103] He gave Nazi Germany as an example, which, he felt, far from using formally viable laws to achieve substantively immoral ends, had actually failed to produce 'Law' at all,[104] due to its near-complete lack of consistency, publicity, clarity and coherence.

Note that I am not here committing to critical legal justice as thick or thin, formal or substantive justice. However, I believe these responses to the impoverishment critique are persuasive indications that even thin versions of the rule of law do not just produce an impoverished, diminished justice. It suggests that the values that the rule of law serves are variegated or levelled – on one hand, a 'cynical' aspect requiring the simple function of constraining power and its abuse; on the other, a more aspirational one of enabling individuals to plan their lives productively

---

[101] Fuller's 'inner morality of law' basically follows the key tenets of the rule of law. L. L. Fuller, 'Positivism and fidelity to law – a reply to Professor Hart', 71 *Harvard Law Review* 4 (1958), 630–72 at 660.

[102] See e.g. H. L. A. Hart, *Essays in Jurisprudence and Philosophy* (Oxford: Oxford University Press, 1983), p. 207.

[103] Fuller, 'Positivism and fidelity', note 101 above.

[104] An opinion that was shared by F. Neumann in *Behemoth: The Structure and Practice of National Socialism* (New York: Harper Torchbooks, 1966); H. Arendt, *The Origins of Totalitarianism* (Cleveland, OH: World Publishing, 1958).

and securely in the context of a transparent, reciprocal administration of law.

Franz Neumann, an anti-Nazi labour lawyer and legal theorist working in the conditions of Weimar Germany,[105] sought to rehabilitate the rule of law and ascribe an ethical function to it. In his writings on Weimar Germany, Neumann crucially noted growing anti-formalist trends in business law, which appeared to reduce capitalism's traditional reliance on stable, predictable laws, its traditional 'elective affinity' with formal law. Large monopolistic enterprises were able to manipulate the creation and application of law, and by their economic power produce measures that suited their needs rather than general laws applicable to all. Neumann acknowledged, along with many others, that in Weimar Germany there existed a crisis of the rule of law but, unlike many of his contemporaries such as Carl Schmitt, he thought that the solution to this crisis could be found in the rule of law itself, which he believed had unfulfilled potential to support democracy. Neumann asserted (and here his thinking was very much in line with traditional liberal theorists, Locke and Bentham) that ambiguous laws present a danger to democracy, because they could be used to advance the needs of social elites.[106] Therefore, for Neumann it was essential to preserve formal law as an element of the liberal democratic heritage. In this way, Neumann's approach provided a more optimistic prognosis for rescuing, reinventing and rendering more robust the rule of law, and may be contrasted with the pessimism of other members of the Frankfurt School, such as the melancholy of Adorno and Horkheimer's *Dialectic of Enlightenment*, or Marcuse's revolutionary approach.

Contemporary EU law possesses anti-formal trends similar to those noted by Neumann – often being flexible and discretionary with vague clauses and general principles (the 'fundamental freedoms' in the EU Treaty are prime examples of this). Cases such as *Viking Line* and *Laval*, for all that they have been vaunted as examples of an over-strenuous 'integration through law', of relentless application of the rule of law as rule of free trade, are not examples of the application of the rule of law; for they present an unpredictable, slanted application of a principle (i.e. free movement of goods) in favour of business. What will constitute a 'restriction' on trade, what restrictions will be proportionate, becomes ever more uncertain, except in the favouring of business over anything else. Is not the classification of a fundamental right as a restriction on trade

---

[105] See e.g. Neumann, *ibid.*   [106] *Ibid.*

surely a wrong turning in EU law's cohabitation with capitalism rather than the predictable application of clear law? The failure to take Article 7 TEU seriously and to suspend the membership of those states that do not take fundamental rights seriously as it requires, the less-than-transparent integration of specific treaties such as that of Prüm into the EU *acquis*, the proliferation of a comitology so Byzantine as to lack transparency, the extremely untransparent and undemocratic measures taken in the wake of the Eurozone crisis, are other examples. What we see are ad hoc, discretionary trends rather than traditional virtues associated with the rule of law. Neumann's analysis illustrates how dissatisfaction with law's links with capitalism, as well as concern over legal indeterminacy, need not lead to rejection of the rule of law, deconstruction, nor the trashing of law, but instead to a recasting and rethinking of the rule of law. In this way, the injustice provoked by a relentless EU integration, by its imbalances and fault-line, may at least be minimised by a regard for careful, transparent lawmaking.

The rule of law, in its elements of public, prospective law, rights to equality of treatment, an independent judiciary, a fair assessment of evidence and rights of appeal, is affirmative of many crucial elements of justice within law, an illustration of how law may demonstrate an aptness for justice and aspire to make good on its proclaimed ideals. Furthermore, fundamental rights, in spite of their apparent indeterminacy, can also be meaningful and achieve change when they function within the legal structures of the EU, even if their 'juridification' is liable to deaden some of their initial, emancipatory promise. However, with regard to law's more practical duties, they function as important weapons against injustice, going some way to fulfilling law's identification as a concept and practice that is 'justice-apt'. The application of critical legal justice involves, at its best, a remorseless and pervasive holding to account, and attention to the detail of lawmaking and transparency. This is not to argue that the rule of law exhausts justice, but rather that it is an essential element of it.

3.2. Injustice and demanding justice

Nonetheless, the Rule of Law, however recast, is inadequate to surmount the feelings of lack we experience at injustice, the desire for something more.[107] It is unlikely that any revolutions will be ignited in the name of

---

[107] Some of the ideas in this last section are explored in much greater depth in Douglas-Scott, *Law after Modernity*, note 1 above, pp 175–214, 287–328, 383–96.

critical legal justice. Therefore, we turn to the ideal of justice outside of the law.

The point I wish to make is this. As I have already argued, it is extremely difficult to agree upon a theory of justice in the abstract. This contrasts with the readiness with which we experience injustice, with the immediacy of emotion that injustice provokes. The world that we inhabit is violently unjust. Douzinas and Gearey refer to the 'great paradox' in which 'we are surrounded by injustice, but we do not know where justice lies . . . We know injustice when we come across it . . . but when we discuss qualities of justice both certainty and emotion recede . . . Justice and its opposite are not symmetrical.'[108] As they also note, justice is far more likely to move people in its breach, than as an academic exercise or 'piece of rhetoric that fails to convince or enthuse',[109] concluding that justice is therefore something of a philosophical failure. It is injustice that motivates and propels action.

However, several things follow from the observation that we have a keenly felt sense of injustice that may be distinguished from attempts to formulate coherent theories of justice. First, it may provoke pessimism, or even despair or nihilism. There exists a large gulf between a keen awareness of injustice and a perception that liberal democracy is not in good shape, and that there is little that can be done to improve it. Institutions of the Establishment are permeated with scandal, whether it be politicians fiddling expenses, bankers gambling away millions and still claiming huge bonuses, the press engaged in illegal phone-hacking with the complicity of the police or EU states lurching from summit to summit in their efforts to solve the Eurozone crisis. Politics fails to motivate, and philosophical attempts to reach a coherent theory of justice are unlikely to reassure a sceptical public. There exists both a moral and a motivational deficit.[110] In these circumstances, law is experienced as coercive or regulatory, but not as internally binding. A respect for law, or political institutions, is not part of the mindset, nor part of the disposition of our subjectivity.[111] In these circumstances, some populations identify themselves, and seek coherence, by turning inward, towards some atavistic, racist, xenophobic self-identifications, a move sadly on the increase, and encouraged by certain elements of the media. Others turn inward in a different way, to a sort of passive nihilism, what Nietzsche described as a 'European

---

[108] Douzinas and Gearey, note 76 above, p. 28.   [109] *Ibid.*, p. 109.
[110] S. Critchley, *Infinitely Demanding* (New York: Verso Books, 2007), Ch. 1.   [111] *Ibid.*

Buddhism', away from political or active life, to a focus on the self, and individualist concerns.

Where does this leave justice? Perhaps we should acknowledge that, in the twenty-first century, justice is somewhat of a philosophical failure. Yet it is still a powerful intuition, and injustice provokes strong emotion. Although the notion of justice presents problems of incredible complexity for the EU, this does not mean that we can have no aspirations for justice.

Perhaps justice is best envisaged as a discourse of absence, something that does not belong to the order of being, is always desired, to come, unachieved. There is an excess of demand over need. As an object of our fantasies, the content of justice is always subjective and indeterminate. We are left with a sense of *injustice* as a motivator, a call to resistance, instilling us with a sense of responsibility to some sort of action, in Amartya Sen's words, 'a matter of actualities, of preventing manifest injustice in the world, of changes, large or small, to people's lives – the abolition of slavery, improvement of conditions in the workplace – realisation of an improvement in the lives of actual peoples'.[112]

This, I think should be the response to the injustice of the EU – one of resistance and action: of scepticism, scrutiny and critique – to look closely at each legal measure adopted by the EU and to resist greater infringements of our liberty in the name of security, to demand transparency and to resist measures taken under EMU that violate human rights and 'values' proclaimed at the forefront of the EU's treaties. It is necessary to ensure that the EU's inadequate governance arrangements do not operate to create further injustices, nor stifle any reactions to such injustice through the imbalances of its governance structures. But it is also necessary to work on our imagination, and to aspire to something better for the EU – rather than agonising over a finely tuned theory of justice.

---

[112] A. Sen, *The Idea of Justice* (London: Allen Lane, 2009), pp 131–54.

9

Legitimacy without democracy in the EU?

Perspectives on the constitutionalisation of Europe through law

CHRISTIAN JOERGES

1. Guiding questions, theoretical framing and structure

The state of the European Union is deplorable. The need to understand the reasons for the current crises is obvious, and a new debate on the prospects of the integration project is urgent. The challenges that this situation entails for legal scholarship are to a considerable degree determined by the specifics of its conceptual legacy. In the formative era of the then European (Economic) Community the study of European integration was essentially in the hands of legal academics who were confident that European integration would essentially rely upon, and be promoted by, law.[1] This kind of confidence has been weakened. For quite some time now, political science has clearly dominated European studies and the quest to take the law seriously does not find much resonance in that discipline.[2] With the failure of the integration-through-law project its major *lacunae* became apparent. At present the most important *lacuna* is the difficulty in coming to terms with the political economy of an ever-more-diverse Union and the benign neglect of 'economy and society' in European constitutionalism: the failure to consider the societal embeddedness and the political dimensions of 'the economic'

I would like to thank Rainer Forst, Jürgen Neyer, Kaarlo Tuori and above all Chris Thornhill for their comments on an earlier version of this essay and Lennart Lutz for his assistance in the production process.

[1] See the seminal series of studies by M. Cappelletti, M. Seccombe and J. Weiler (eds), *Integration through Law. Europe and the American Federal Experience* (Berlin–New York: Walter de Gruyter, 1985–7).

[2] C. Joerges, 'Taking the law seriously: on political science and the role of law in the process of European integration', 2 *European Law Journal* (1996), 105.

and to address the preconditions for a democratic striving for social justice.[3]

1.1. New challenges

This has led to a stunning silence amongst legal researchers in face of the current crisis, and it is not yet apparent when and how European law scholarship will move beyond the paralysis that this crisis has caused. This chapter strives for a reorientation. Its focus will be on the role of law in the integration project, on its accomplishments and its failures. The chapter's analyses and deliberations will operate on three levels. They will be historical in that they seek to understand legal developments as responses to the dynamics of the integration process; they will build upon political science and economic sociology in the reconstruction of this process; the legal conceptualisations and normative suggestions will try to take these historical contexts and theoretical assumptions adequately into account. The argument is an exercise in critical legal thought of a specific kind.

1.2. Discourse theory of law and conflicts-law constitutionalism

> [W]e are accustomed to consider law, the rule of law, and democracy as subjects of different disciplines: jurisprudence deals with law, political science with democracy, and each deals with the constitutional state in its own way – jurisprudence in normative terms, political science from an empirical standpoint.[4]

Jürgen Habermas explains how this schism came about – and then raises objections to it on both normative and theoretical grounds. In the constitutional state as we know it, he argues, a separation of the rule of law from democracy has become inconceivable; an 'internal relation' between the two has been established that 'results from the concept of modern law itself'.[5] Habermas's discourse theory of law and democracy

---

[3] C. Joerges, 'Rechtsstaat and social Europe: how a classical tension resurfaces in the European integration process', 9 Comparative Sociology (2010), 65.

[4] J. Habermas, 'On the internal relation between the rule of law and democracy' in Habermas (ed.), The Inclusion of the Other. Studies in Political Theory (Cambridge: Polity Press, 1999), p. 253.

[5] Ibid., at 254.

seeks to respond to the disciplinary schism between legal and political science. He anchors his constitutionalism in historical reconstructions and seeks to defend these accomplishments in the European post-national constellation.

In all of these methodological and theoretical dimensions, the following deliberations and arguments are indebted to Habermas's discourse theory of law; this also holds true in principle with respect to his defence of democratic accomplishments in the debate on the constitutionalisation of Europe. However, we will have to depart from the Habermasian vision in our analyses of the crisis *problématique* and the rescue of Europe's commitments to democracy, the rule of law and the legacy of the welfare state. In that respect, Habermas seems to take the socio-economic background of Europe's current malaise too lightly, and to fall prey to his normative commitments when claiming that this crisis should and could generate a new constitutional moment.[6] The counter-vision of our 'conflicts-law constitutionalism' is much more cautious. The questions that we pose and address are: do Europe's crises require moderation of integrationist and federal or quasi-federal ambitions? Does the socio-economic diversity of the old Europe and of the enlarged Europe militate in favor of stronger European powers, as the proponents of an ever-stronger Europe assume? Or would Europe be better advised to institutionalise fora that would address the conflict constellations that Europe's diversity is bound to produce, foster the generation of fair responses to its diversity that abstain from the one-size-fits-all philosophy that underlies the 'integration-through-law' project and reject the 'pretence of knowledge' that the quest for centralised European governance implies? To substantiate these concerns: European integration has departed from an equilibrium between the opening of national borders and commitments to democracy and social justice in a small community of homogeneous states. With its internal market project it has established a 'market without a state'; with Monetary Union it has seriously curtailed political powers and degraded the 'Masters of the Treaties' to 'States without markets'.[7] Now we seem to be witnessing a new quality of market governance in which the 'states operate as servants of the markets'.

---

[6] See, e.g. J. Habermas, 'The crisis of the European Union in the light of a constitutionalization of international law', 23 *European Journal of International Law* (2012), 335.

[7] See C. Joerges, 'The market without a state? States without markets? Two essays on the law of the European economy' (San Domenico di Fiesole: EUI Working Paper Law 1/96, 1996).

If there is a kernel of truth in these observations, we need to consider whether it is precisely the deepening of integration, the striving for 'ever more Europe' that jeopardises Europe's commitments to democracy and the rule of law. Conflicts-law constitutionalism, as we immodestly claim, provides an adaptation of the discourse theory of law to the post-national constellation.

2. The structure of the argument

Our argument will be developed in four distinct steps.

In the first (in section 2.1.1), we will draw renewed attention to the conventional distinction between 'domestic justice' and 'justice between' autonomous orders. This is not to argue that the Member States of the Union still remain, or should once again become, independent ('sovereign') entities. This distinction is nevertheless of topical importance for the debates on justice and solidarity in the Union. To illustrate this, the chapter will provide brief reconstructions of two classic positions: it will recall Friedrich Carl von Savigny's conceptualisation of 'justice under private international law' (*internationalprivatrechtliche Gerechtigkeit*), and Hermann Heller's theory of the 'social state' (*Sozialstaat*).

The second step of the argument (in section 2.1.2) will address the threefold challenges posed by the process of Europeanisation. That is, it will address, first, the need to abandon justice as defined under private international law as a model to govern the relations between the Member States of the EU; second, the erosion of the social state as envisaged by Heller in the integration process; third, the ensuing efforts to cope with these transformations in a new synthesis.

One attempt by this author to create such a synthesis was undertaken in collaboration with Jürgen Neyer.[8] There are better than merely biographical reasons to discuss Neyer's recent plea for a shift from democracy to justice in the legitimation of European supranationalism,[9] and contrast this with a defensive move towards conflicts-law constitutionalism. Both perspectives are certainly distinct. But they also share important elements. These affinities will become apparent in section 4 of this chapter where

---

[8] C. Joerges and J. Neyer, 'From intergovernmental bargaining to deliberative political processes: the constitutionalisation of comitology', 3 *European Law Journal* (1997), 273.

[9] See J. Neyer, *The Justification of Europe. A Political Theory of Supranational Integration* (Oxford: Oxford University Press, 2012).

we will discuss the present unruly state of two classic paradigms of legal integration theory, each of which attempted, in its own way, to establish the legitimacy of European governance 'without democracy'.

The concluding part (section 5) will restate the methodological and theoretical implications of the conflicts-law approach, namely a radical turn to proceduralisation and an understanding of European law as a *Recht-Fertigungs-Recht*, that is, as a law of law production, which provides orientation both for resolution of conflicts within the European Union and for the machinery of transnational problem-solving, which it is bound to establish.

2.1. The legacy of classical legal and political thought: two distinct worlds of justice

The divide between 'domestic justice' and the normative objectives of the various legal disciplines that deal with the international system is very firmly established. To exemplify different sides of this divide, we will treat in the following, first, a post-classical constitutional theory, namely, Heller's notion of the social state, and then, second, deal with von Savigny's classical theory of justice in private international relations.

2.1.1. Social justice in constitutional democracies

'Can the welfare state survive European integration?' This query has figured prominently both on the agenda of European politics and in legal circles for more than a decade. Political unrest was particularly disquieting during the campaigns accompanying the French referendum on the European Convention's Draft Constitutional Treaty. In the proceedings of the Convention, Foreign Ministers Joschka Fischer and Dominique Villepin had sought to respond to anxieties about the neo-liberal bias of the integration project by proposing a 'Contribution to the Convention', which sought to anchor the notion of the 'social market economy' in the Draft Constitutional Treaty.[10] The notion of the social market impressed the Convention, and it was thereafter included in the Treaty of Lisbon. However, its impact on the 'real-life' European polity was much less significant. Neither the broader political public nor the academic community of European constitutionalists knew, in any great detail, about the legacy

[10] See CONV 470/02.

of Germany's social market economy (*soziale Marktwirtschaft*).[11] They knew far less about the tensions between this notion and the social legal state (*sozialer Rechtsstaat*). The unspecified public scepticism nevertheless had its *fundamentum in re*, and the same applies to the difficulties encountered by Europe's legal academia in integrating the concern about the problematic question of the social state into their discourses on the constitutionalisation of Europe.

The reference point for analysis of the social market in German domestic constitutional debate is the social-state clause contained in Article 20(1) of the Basic Law, which is protected against amendments by the eternity clause of Article 79(3). What kind of positive validity can such constitutional commitments to social justice claim, and what orientation do they provide? The first grand constitutional debate in postwar Germany, now possessing legendary status, addressed these issues. At the centre of this was an argument between Ernst Forsthoff (a conservative disciple of Schmitt) and Wolfgang Abendroth (a constitutional lawyer, on the left of the Social Democratic party). In an influential essay, Forsthoff argued that it was simply impossible to reconcile the promise of social justice with the requirements of the rule of law.[12] Abendroth countered this by asserting that the Basic Law's commitment to the welfare state (*Sozialstaatsgebot*) had the status of a binding legal principle.[13] The debate is regularly recalled to this day.[14]

The debate brought to the fore a fundamental tension that has again become visible in Europe's present crisis management. Economic stability and social justice require manifold political activities that cannot be predetermined by substantive rules. This is why Heller insisted on *democratic procedures and legislative autonomy*. Social justice, for Heller, is not predefined by the constitution. Rather, democracy entails a mandate to define social justice and a chance of accomplishing politically defined objectives. On this reading, Heller paved the way for a proceduralised notion of justice in constitutional democracies.

---

[11] C. Joerges and F. Rödl, 'The "Social Market Economy" as Europe's social model?' in L. Magnusson and B. Stråth (eds), *A European Social Citizenship? Preconditions for Future Policies in Historical Light* (Brussels: Lang, 2005), p. 125.

[12] E. Forsthoff, 'Begriff und Wesen des sozialen Rechtsstaats', 12 *Veröffentlichungen der Vereinigung der Deutschen Staatsrechtslehrer* (1954), 8.

[13] W. Abendroth, 'Zum Begriff des demokratischen und sozialen Rechtsstaates im Grundgesetz der Bundesrepublik Deutschland' in A. Herrmann (ed.), *Festschrift Ludwig Bergsträsser* (Düsseldorf: Droste, 1954), p. 279.

[14] Joerges, '*Rechtsstaat* and Social Europe', note 3 above.

2.1.2. Justice under private international law among civilised nations in international law

If we conceive of social justice as an outcome of democratic processes, it will be shaped by political contest, historical experience and contingent events. How, then, should a comprehensive 'European Social Model' come into being? A difficulty for all those indebted to the legacy of Heller's constitutionalism stems from the linkage between social justice and democratic processes. This problematic question has even older and deeper roots than the technocratic, as opposed to democratic, foundational moment of the European Economic Community. It originates in the categorical difference between internal and external affairs: that is, in the taming of 'the political' by nation-state constitutionalism, on one hand, and the unruliness of the state of nature in the international system, on the other. The legal disciplines involved have conceptualised these differences quite rigidly. Beyond its recognition of commitments undertaken in international treaties, international law was far from enthusiastic about affirming interference in the economic and social affairs of the sovereign entities that constituted it. Private international law became considerably more ambitious with von Savigny's seminal treatise of 1849.[15]

In what has been praised as a Copernican turn, von Savigny developed the vision of a truly transnational legal order of private law relations that depended, not on uniformity of substantive rules, but on the readiness of courts in all spheres of jurisdiction to apply the legal order in which these private legal relationships were situated. Private international law was not intended to strive for 'substantive' justice but for uniformity of decision making, which would be generated by the acceptance of rules able to identify the 'seat' of a legal relationship. This is the distinctive character of the 'justice' that the discipline of private international law seeks to promote: von Savigny's concepts were both revolutionary and realistic. They were revolutionary in their principled separation of private law from the state and its public policy. They were realistic in their delimitation of the scope of the new principles. The mutual respect of foreign legal orders, their equal treatment, and the toleration of diversity were premised upon an understanding of private law as a non-political order that was

---

[15] F. von Savigny, *System des heutigen Römischen Rechts* (Berlin: Veit & Comp., 1849) Vol. VIII.

not permeated by public policies. This meant that application of a foreign order would not affect the policies and interests of a particular state in any significant way.[16]

Von Savigny's premises seem clearly outdated today. But his vision of an autonomous, transnational ordering of private-law relationships continues to resurface in constantly new variations. In the EU, this vision was advocated with particular strength after the collapse of the Soviet Union.[17] The plea for a 'return of the private-law society and its legal order' was expressly based upon neo-liberal premises and a restatement of notions of justice that reject any positive commitment to social justice on the part of constitutional democracies. We will refrain here from any closer analysis of this. It suffices to underline the exemplary importance and topicality of the two reference points of this section – Heller and von Savigny – and so to rephrase our understanding of the problematic question of social justice and democracy in the EU. As long as the Member States continue to exist and operate, be it as Masters or Servants of the Treaties, any European synthesis of social justice and democracy presupposes a twofold transformation. In other words, any synthesis of social justice and democracy in the EU presupposes a reconceptualisation of horizontal relations and commitments between Member States, and it presupposes embedding this transformation into a democratisation of the Union's institutional architecture.

To rephrase this challenge: on one hand, 'private international law justice' would be a very meagre response to concerns for justice among Europe's citizens, and it would mark a retreat from the accomplishments of the national constitutional social state. On the other hand, social justice, as Heller's democratic constitutionalism envisages it, presupposes societal and political conditions beyond the commitments of the Member States and beyond the powers that the Member States have conferred on Brussels, Luxembourg and Strasbourg. What kind of justice, then, can European citizens expect from the integration project? Is some sustainable European synthesis of 'private international justice' and the 'domestic social justice' of constitutional democracies conceivable? If so, how could that be accomplished?

---

[16] K. Vogel, *Der räumliche Anwendungsbereich der Verwaltungsrechtsnorm*, (Frankfurt am Main: Metzner, 1965), at 215.

[17] E.-J. Mestmäcker, 'Die Wiederkehr der bürgerlichen Gesellschaft und ihres Rechts', *Rechtshistorisches Journal* 10 (1991), 190.

3. Justice, not democracy? Jürgen Neyer's reconceptualisation of Europe's legitimacy *problématique*

According to many well-meaning protagonists of the integration project, a resolution of the conflict between social justice within constitutional democracies and the ordering of the international system that has inscribed itself so deeply in legal disciplines is conceivable only through the establishment of a state-like European entity. This unlikely event, Neyer submits, does not deserve the kind of attention that it has attracted.

3.1. European justice and domestic democracy: complementarities?

Neyer argues that democratic legitimacy as we know it from constitutional states is unattainable in the EU. The usual search for a cure to the Union's democratic deficits is focused on incorrect and ill-conceived issues. Instead of this, the EU has the means to promote transnational justice among its Member States and to defend its legitimacy upon the basis of this potential.[18]

Neyer's argument modifies the position proposed under the heading 'deliberative supranationalism'.[19] We suggested that European law had a particular vocation to cure a structural deficit of nation-state democracies: we perceived this deficit as stemming from the fact that nation states failed to include in their internal political processes persons who were externally affected by their policies, so that these persons were, as a consequence, unable to understand themselves as the authors of the acts to which they were exposed. European law, we concluded, needed to be understood and practised with a view to curing this deficit. It needed to perceive itself as deriving its legitimacy from this potential, and so to structure its interventions accordingly. Neyer continues to defend these ideas – in fact, he seeks to complement and substantiate them. On Neyer's conception, the regulative idea and leitmotif of the ordering of relations among the Member States of the Union is 'justice'. Justice is meant here, not in the sense of some supranational distributive arrangement, but in the sense of a 'right to justification' (*Recht auf Rechtfertigung*), which European law has institutionalised along with other provisions that further the compensation of nation-state failures and cooperative problem-solving. The right to justification can be invoked by individual citizens against

---

[18] Neyer, *The Justification of Europe*, note 9 above, at p. 73ff.
[19] Joerges and Neyer, 'Comitology', note 8 above.

restrictions on their autonomy. This right is not just an individual one. On the contrary, it is a right that encompasses the duty of the community to produce the material conditions under which individual freedom can exist, and it is required to govern the relations between the Member States of the Union. On this basis, supranationalism needs to be understood and reconceptualised, not as a hierarchical command, but as a horizontal bond between Member States. With its two dimensions – as a right of European citizens to insist on justification and as a commitment by Member States to respect foreign concerns and to engage in cooperative problem-solving – Neyer's right to justification ensures compliance with European criteria that place restrictions on national autonomy. This type of restraint, however, can be understood as a democratic command: 'transnational justice' and 'national democracy' will then complement one another. Transnational justice is a distinct form of justice. It is not the type of justice that Heller's social state can accomplish through majoritarian democratic will-formation. It is nevertheless a move far beyond Savigny's model of 'justice under private international law' because it is not focused on spheres of private autonomy but engages national polities comprehensively.

3.2. Transnational and domestic justice: a complication

Conflicts-law constitutionalism as sketched out in section 5 can subscribe in principle to these suggestions but underlines two difficulties.

The first is Neyer's insistence on the reconstructive quality of his project. This same claim was indeed a foundation of 'deliberative supranationalism'. Conflicts-law constitutionalism has become more sceptical. Neyer's trust in the prudence of the CJEU and in the normative quality of its doctrines is, or has become, too benevolent in light of the Court's more recent performance.[20] Even the *Cassis de Dijon* case,[21] which we have cited as our prime example of a just compromise between German, French and European concerns, rests on highly questionable constitutional assumptions. To be sure, the Court has institutionalised a right to justification on behalf of European citizens and corresponding duties on the Member States. But its conception of this obligation subjects the political autonomy

---

[20] Suffice it here to point to the recent decisions on labour law critically discussed in C. Joerges and F. Rödl, 'Informal politics, formalised law and the "social deficit" of European integration: reflections after the judgments of the ECJ in *Viking* and *Laval*', 15 *European Law Journal* (2009), 1.

[21] C–120/78 *Rewe-Zentral AG v Bundesmonopolverwaltung für Branntwein* [1979] ECR 649.

of Member States to enormous restriction, as they can only invoke those reasons that the ECJ/CJEU has enumerated. By the same token, the Court has assigned to itself wide discretionary powers as a constitutional court above national authorities. Similar reservations, unfortunately, need to be added to our defence of comitology as a model of 'deliberative supranationalism'. The way we envisaged the constitutionalising of this institution has not proved to be the road taken in the institutional development of European social regulation.[22]

The second premise that has turned out to be highly problematic concerns the compensatory function of European law in the control and correction of external effects. In particular in the context of management of the current crisis, external effects are being controlled by undemocratic means.[23] Such interventions must not claim any 'democratic' legitimacy.

It seems, finally, that Neyer's turn to justification, his objections to the validity of expert rule notwithstanding,[24] neglects somewhat the intricacies of cooperative problem-solving, which are increasingly 'resolved' in technocratic ways.

All of these issues, however, look more like family quarrels when contrasted with our reservations regarding two competing traditions that seek to define Europe's legitimacy without democracy. To these we now turn.

4. Non-democratic responses in legal integration theory: technocratic legitimacy and economic constitutionalism

Technocratic planning prevailed at the beginning of the European Economic Community. Equally important was the economic project of opening still-national economies. 'Technocratic rationality' and 'economic rationality', the two paradigms of legal integration theory that we will discuss in this section, thus appear as concepts with a historical and political foundation.

[22] M. Weimer, 'Democratic legitimacy through European conflicts-law? The case of EU administrative governance of GMOs', (Florence, EUI PhD thesis, 2012), p. 153ff.
[23] See C. Joerges and M. Weimer, 'A crisis of executive managerialism in the EU: no alternative?' (2012), Maastricht Faculty of Law Working Paper No. 2012–7, available at http://ssrn.com/abstract=2190362.
[24] Neyer, *The Justification of Europe*, note 9 above, at pp 96–7.

4.1. Two different strategies and their common failure

In the present context, the responses of both traditions to the cleavage of (domestic) social from transnational justice ('justice under private international law') deserve particular attention.

4.1.1. Europe's technocratic legacy

'Executive power', 'executive federalism', 'functional constitutionalism', 'transnational administrative power'[25] – ever since its inception, and in constantly changing variations, terms of this kind have been used to characterise the integration project as bureaucratic machinery. The path-breaking initiator of this tradition was Hans Peter Ipsen, the influential founding father of European law as a new legal discipline in Germany. Ipsen's sensitivity regarding the precarious legitimacy of the European system and his search for a type of rule having validity that did not depend on democratic legitimacy are certainly impressive. With his understanding of the European Communities as organisations oriented towards functional integration (*Zweckverbände funktionaler Integration*), Ipsen at once rejected positions endorsing more far-reaching federal ambitions and earlier interpretations of the Community as a mere international organisation. He characterised Community law as a *tertium* between federal or state law and international law, and he described it as an order constituted by its 'objective tasks' and assuming adequate legitimacy through its ability to provide solutions to these tasks.

4.1.2. Economic constitutionalism

Ipsen represented the public-law department of the new discipline, which was to become, in German universities and elsewhere, the natural haven, so to speak, of European law. For historical and political reasons, Germany was destined to favour – with particular emphasis – the private- and economic-law dimensions of the European project, and to conceptualise its juridical nature as an 'economic constitution'. The theoretical basis of this notion was formed by Germany's ordo-liberal tradition, which reached back to the beginnings of the Weimar Republic and was to gain a semi-official status in the new German democracy and even to provide a

---

[25] See respectively D. Curtin, *Executive Power of the European Union. Law, Practices and the Living Constitution* (Oxford: Oxford University Press, 2009); P. Lindseth, *Power and Legitimacy: Reconciling Europe and the Nation-state* (Oxford: Oxford University Press, 2010).

transdisciplinary (legal and economic) foundation for the 'social market economy'. Among the core messages of ordo-liberalism were the fundamental human-rights dimension of private autonomy, the economic benefits of a system of undistorted competition, the indispensability of law as a means to establish such an order and to protect its functioning, and restriction of discretionary state interventions in a society founded on private law. The proponents of ordo-liberalism were fully aware of the strength of Germany's corporatist traditions and the collusion of economic and political actors in its history of 'organised capitalism'. Such anxieties surely exercised influence on the (ordo)-liberal 'turn to Europe'. The European level of governance promised to ensure stronger barriers against Germany's not-so-liberal traditions and its political opportunism in economic affairs than could be expected from the domestic institutional pillars of Germany's *Ordnungspolitik*.[26]

4.1.3. The common democratic deficit

Both conceptualisations of the EEC – that is, its perception as an essentially functional entity and its interpretation as an economic constitution – imposed on the Member States a broad set of commitments, which included wide areas of public law and policy. But this move was not expected to erode, let alone overrule, domestic social entitlements. This is easy to understand as far as the technocratic project is concerned, with its explicit limitations of transnational governance and its abstention from distributional politics. The ordo-liberal project of an economic constitution of supranational validity is more ambivalent in that respect. To be sure, postwar ordo-liberalism had sought to come to terms with simultaneous commitment, on one hand, to the idea of an 'undistorted system of competition' and, on the other, to the promise of social justice and security, in Germany's model of a 'social market economy'. The ordo-liberals sought to resolve the conceptual tensions between these commitments through institutionalising specific orders: that is, a legally structured order of industrial relations and of social security (*Arbeits- und Sozialverfassung*) along with the legally guaranteed economic ordo, the 'economic constitution' (*Wirtschaftsverfassung*). The tensions were thereby understood as a sustainable interdependence.

---

[26] See for more detailed analysis, see C. Joerges, 'What is left of the European Economic Constitution? A melancholic eulogy', 30 *European Law Review* (2005), 461.

4.2. Retractions

We refrain here from any detailed reconstruction of the well-known further development of the integration project, its successes and crises, and the many efforts to adapt Europe's institutional configuration to its various transformations. Instead, we focus on responses of exemplary importance for the present state of the Union from within the two paradigms.

4.2.1. Technocracy without efficiency? Giandomenico Majone's sceptical turn

The importance of the technocratic tradition in the practical reality of the integration project can hardly be overestimated. Its weight was bound to increase with the involvement of the European Community in an increasing number of regulatory policies, which were to be organised at transnational levels without being supported by a consolidated democratic order. How could the European Community hope to ensure acceptance of its involvement in ever more problem-solving activities if not through an 'objective' and expertise-based conceptualisation of its enormous tasks? By far the most interesting and influential work to have renewed and refined the technocratic legacy is that of Majone. It is unique not only in its clarity and coherence, but also in the precision and subtlety of its reflections on the options for an alternative to the democratic constitutionalism of the Member States of the European Union. Majone's famous conceptualisation of Europe as a 'regulatory state', which operated essentially through non-majoritarian institutions, was conceived as a way of ensuring the credibility of commitments to, in principle, uncontested policy objectives.[27] Welfare policies pose additional, and categorically different, problems, he argued. The Union's failure to institutionalise a comprehensive social policy is explained by Majone by reference to the 'reluctance of the Member States to surrender control of a politically salient and popular area of public policy'. Equally important is the factual difficulty and political impossibility of replacing the variety of European welfare-state models and traditions with an integrated European scheme. On one hand, Majone respects the primacy of constitutional democracies. On the other hand, he underlines (with increasing urgency) that the integration project has, in a fallacious manner, become comprehensively subject to its 'operational code' (the principle 'that integration has priority over

---

[27] G. Majone, 'The European Community as a regulatory state', *Collected Courses of the Academy of European Law* (The Hague: Martinus Nijhoff, 1996) Vol. 1, p. 321.

262   CHRISTIAN JOERGES

all competing values'),[28] and he also identifies the camouflage strategies that he calls 'integration by stealth'.[29] This is an alarming retreat from his earlier trust in the problem-solving potential of the European project. However, his warnings cannot in any way be taken to reflect a change in his theoretical premises. Majone continues to underline that Europe does not have legitimate authority to pursue the type of distributive policies that welfare states have institutionalised. He does not retract his plea for regulatory efficiency. Instead, his critical turn is motivated by the inefficiencies that he observes in the Union's operations. His quest for more modesty in Europe's ambitions – expressed in the phrase '*Geht's nicht eine Nummer kleiner?*' (Can't we content ourselves with a smaller size?)[30] – summarises these observations. His adaptation of the 'unity in diversity' formula is a consequence of these insights, to which we will return in the concluding section.

4.2.2. Delegalised economic governance in the financial crisis

Most proponents of ordo-liberalism know all too well of the tensions between their visions and the *Realpolitik* operative at all levels of governance. To what degree did Germany's social market economy represent a society founded in private law (*Privatrechtsgesellschaft*)? Is there a grain of truth in Maurice Glasman's assertion that to characterise Germany as a 'freely competitive capitalist economy' is a 'most fundamental fallacy', so that we need to stop even calling it a market economy?[31] Can Walter Eucken's recognition of the specific features of the agricultural sector really be interpreted as a conceptually sound basis for establishment of the Common Agricultural Policy?[32] How did the defeat of the ordo-liberal philosophy of competition law at European level, the so-called 'modernisation' of European competition law and the move towards a 'more economic approach', affect the life of the economic constitution? Is the deletion of the 'system of undistorted competition' from Article 3

---

[28] G. Majone, *Europe as the Would-be World Power. The EU at Fifty* (Cambridge: Cambridge University Press, 2010), p. 1.

[29] G. Majone, *Dilemmas of European Integration: The Ambiguities and Pitfalls of Integration by Stealth* (Oxford: Oxford University Press, 2005).

[30] Majone, *Europe as the Would-be World Power*, note 28 above, p. 170.

[31] M. Glasman, *Managing Market Utopia* (London: Verso, 1996), p. 56.

[32] W. Eucken et al., 'Agrarpolitik in der sozialen Marktwirtschaft. Gutachten des Wissenschaftlichen Beirats beim Bundeswirtschaftsministerium vom 30.10.1949' in Der Wissenschaftliche Beirat beim Bundeswirtschaftsministerium für Wirtschaft (ed.), *Sammelband der Gutachten von 1948–1972* (Göttingen: Verlag Otto Schwartz & Co, 1973).

TFEU (previously Article 2 EU) truly insignificant because this notion has survived in Protocol 27?

Hence, it seems quite daring to reconstruct the European project in ordo-liberal terms. But only in one, albeit important, instance, namely, the adoption of the Treaty of Maastricht with its substantial broadening of European policies and the recognition of constitutional commitments to non-economic objectives, did prominent exponents of the ordo-liberal tradition indicate that their allegiance to the European project might be exhausted.[33] The conceptual implications of the present financial turmoil have not yet been spelled out. The ordo-liberal contribution to its emergence is both tragic and ironic. Ordo-liberal warnings about the intrusion of discretionary politics into the edifice of the economic order were placated by the establishment of a European legal framework, which promised to establish the primacy of law over politics. This occurred through an insulation of monetary policy, its dedication to price stability, the establishment of the European Central Bank as a fully independent institution outside the European constitutional order and completion of this regulatory straitjacket by the Stability Pact. When the German Constitutional Court, in its Maastricht judgment,[34] designated economic integration a non-political phenomenon occurring autonomously outside the Member States, and interpreted the whole construction as a constitutional imperative for other, albeit insignificant, reasons, the otherwise extremely critical academic community remained silent.[35]

By now, the failures running through the whole construction of Monetary Union have become obvious. They have led to hectic activities, opaque bargaining and a treatment of the rule of law that seemed to be far beyond the power of juridical imagination. A noble normative reason – namely, solidarity, understood as a valid legal principle and duty in the EU – is invoked to justify this readiness to take the letter of the law very lightly. We have to refrain here from detailed analysis.[36] In the present context one dimension of the ongoing transformation of Europe's constitutional settlement deserves particular attention, namely responses to the

---

[33] M. Streit and W. Mussler, 'The economic constitution of the European Community. From "Rome" to "Maastricht"', 1 *European Law Journal* (1995), 5.

[34] *Brunner* v. *European Union Treaty* (1994) 1 CMLR 57.

[35] See, most prominently, J. Weiler, 'Does Europe need a constitution? Reflections on *demos, telos* and the German Maastricht decision', 1 *European Law Journal* (1995), 219.

[36] But see C. Joerges, 'Europe's economic constitution in crisis', Zentra Working Papers in Transnational Studies No. 06/2012, available at http://ssrn.com/abstract=2179595; Joerges and Weimer, 'A crisis of executive managerialism', note 23 above.

ever-increasing awareness of the interdependence of Europe's economies and societies, an interdependence, however, which is not embedded in an 'ever-closer Union' but is instead generated by an ever-wider socio-economic divergence. The notion of solidarity has emerged as the new common reference point for the new constellation, albeit one that is interpreted in diametrically divergent ways. The noble version reads solidarity as a duty to share the burdens that the financial crisis so asymmetrically imposes on the societies of the Union.[37] The *praxis* of Europe's crisis management is different. Its response to Europe's socio-economic divergence is a quest for austerity of the weaker periphery that is understood as the price to be paid for the credit and transfers it receives from the stronger north.[38] Europe's most important courts have by now given their judicial blessing to the practice of conditionality that has been institutionalised in ever more sophisticated regimes.[39] Objections against both the actuality and the validity of Europe's crisis management abound.[40] The dilemma that the most important proponents of the noble version of solidarity face is their quest for an ever-stronger Europe and their inability to show how this strength can be established and tamed democratically. Rather than elaborating this critique in any detail here,[41] we are now moving towards presentation of an alternative to the normative failures of Europe's ever-more authoritarian managerialism on the one hand and the practical weaknesses of the proponents of its democratic transformation on the other.

5. The alternative: conflicts-law constitutionalism

A robust basis exists for rejecting not only the current European *praxis* but also the proponents of a federal or quasi-federal transformation. For

---

[37] J. van der Walt, '*Timeo Danais Donna Ferre (sic)* and the constitution that Europeans may one day have given themselves', (ms. Luxembourg, 2012) available at http://papers.ssrn.com/sol3/papers.cfm?abstract_id=2127087.

[38] For a particularly clear statement, see C. Calliess, 'Treue und Solidarität', *Frankfurter Allgemeine Zeitung*, 30 June 2011.

[39] BVerfGE, 2 BvR 1390/12, judgment of 12 September 2012, (incomplete) English translation available at: www.bundesverfassungsgericht.de/entscheidungen/rs20120912_2bvr139012en.html; Case C–270/12, *Thomas Pringle* v. *Republic of Ireland*, judgment (full court) of 27 November 2012, nyr.

[40] Joerges and Weimer, 'A crisis of executive managerialism', note 23 above.

[41] Among the most outspoken critics is G. Majone, *Has European Integration Gone Too Far – Or Not Far Enough?* (Cambridge: Cambridge University Press, 2014, forthcoming); his reasoning is compatible with the plea for a turn to conflicts-law constitutionalism.

quite some time, certainly since enlargement, it has become essential to take Europe's diversity seriously. In light of the very different histories and historical experience of the European states, the deepening of variations in their socio-economic constellations, their uneven potential to pursue objectives of distributive justice and to respond to economic and financial instabilities, it has become increasingly inconceivable that European publics will converge in their political perspectives. In particular, it has become inconceivable that a magic formula might be found and endorsed that is capable of institutionalising a pan-European system ensuring social justice. Hence, the search for a 'third way', lying between a defence of the nation state, on one hand, and federalist ambitions, on the other, seems to be the order of the day.

5.1. Conflicts-law justice

The idea of conflicts-law constitutionalism has been presented quite often and at some length.[42] It should suffice in the present context to restate briefly the basic analytical premises of this approach and its normative premises. These premises are as follows: for compelling historical reasons, European nation states have established a Community that, in its foundational period, was meant first of all as a response to their 'bitter experiences', but that also sought to foster the well-being of the Community's citizens. This latter rationale has developed an enormous independent dynamic. It has deepened interdependencies and produced irresistible demands for cooperation between Member States. The response that the conflicts-law approach advocates is to tolerate and to take seriously the fortunate motto of the otherwise unfortunate Draft Constitutional Treaty. That is to say, the principle 'unity in diversity' needs to be read as Europe's vocation.[43] Moreover, it needs to be viewed as a challenge to transform what may be perceived as a precarious constellation into a stable and sustainable cooperative venture.

Strong normative reasons exist why conflicts-law constitutionalism proposes itself as the legal basis and framework for this venture. Europeanisation has opened a constantly increasing gap between decision makers and those who are affected by decision making. This schism is widely

---

[42] For an elaboration and discussion see C. Joerges, P. Kjaer and T. Ralli, 'A new type of conflicts law as constitutional form in the postnational constellation', *Transnational Legal Theory* 2 (2011), 153.

[43] Article I–8 Draft European Constitutional Treaty (OJ C 310/1, 16/12/2004).

perceived as a characteristic of European-level decision making that affects European citizens profoundly but does so in non-transparent ways that admit few opportunities for holding the decision makers accountable.[44] The schism is a normative challenge to democratic orders in which citizens can interpret themselves as the authors of the rules with which they are expected to comply. However, the schism is also one that is inherent in nation-state government. Increasingly, constitutional states are unable to guarantee inclusion of all those upon whom their policies and politics in internal decision-making processes have an impact. The conflicts-law approach offers a way out of this dilemma, turning the debate on the European democratic deficit upside down. It reconceptualises European law as a means of compensating for the democratic failure of nation states, and suggests that it is precisely from this potential that European law can derive its legitimacy.[45]

It seems simply obvious that responses to Europe's complex conflict constellations need to break radically with the legacy of 'methodological nationalism' inherent in jurisdiction-selecting rules of private international law. By the same token the very nature of these constellations militates against any hierarchical structuring of the European polity. Europe needs to strive for both: compensation for the structural democratic deficits of the nation state *and* constructive responses to its increasingly interdependent, regulatory tasks and problems. It has to reconstitute, within Europeanised frameworks, the 'geology of the law' of constitutional democracies, the need for problem-oriented 'special' legislation, the development of a regulatory machinery with specific institutional infrastructures, inclusion of non-governmental actors in regulatory tasks and supervision of the governance arrangements within which such cooperation can take place. There is no space here to go into the complex details of such efforts.[46] Instead, we will focus on our guiding normative question: in what way can this type of conflicts law affect or, as we propose, accomplish, a new synthesis of social and transnational justice?

---

[44] See J. Habermas's very first essay on European integration, 'Staatsbürgerschaft und nationale Identität' (Zurich: Erker, 1991); the English translation of this essay was published as Annex II to *Between Facts and Norms, Contributions to a Discourse Theory of Law and Democracy* (Cambridge, MA: MIT Press 1999), 491–516.

[45] See Joerges and Neyer, 'Comitology', note 8 above.

[46] C. Joerges, 'The idea of a three-dimensional conflicts law as constitutional form' in C. Joerges and E-U. Petersmann (eds), *Constitutionalism, Multilevel Trade Governance and International Economic Law*, 2nd edn (Oxford: Hart Publishing, 2011), p. 413.

5.2. Reconstructing justification

The conflicts-law approach operates without a substantively predefined *finalité* and without a system of doctrinal recipes. The conflict constellations to which European law is required to respond are simply so multifaceted and unpredictable that a prefabricated system of rules able to provide orientation for 'just' solutions is simply inconceivable. However, the deeper normative reason for this type of legal indeterminacy resides in the need to elaborate new answers in the search for a proper balancing of European and national concerns. Conflicts-law solutions must build upon a 'discovery procedure of practice'. They must be generated in a process that aspires to what Rudolf Wiethölter has called *Rechtfertigungsrecht* (the Law of Just-ification): a process becomes evident that reveals the mysterious potential of law to transform social contexts, to extract socially adequate legal concepts from these social contexts, and, both at the same time and in the same move, to give legitimacy to this law production.[47] Wiethölter's visionary notion is adequately deciphered as the 'dual self-justificatory and juridification tendencies of all law within society'.[48] It is an attempt to renew the 'proceduralisation of the category of law' that Wiethölter had already conceptualised in the 1980s, at the same time as, or even before, Habermas systematically elaborated this notion as a bridge or mitigator between facts and norms.[49] More openly and strongly than Habermas's later concept, Wiethölter's idea of *Rechtsverfassungsrecht* [law formed through the constitution of law] underlines its societal sources, a message that the title of his essay – 'Just-ifications of a law of associations' (*Recht-Fertigungen eines Gesellschafts-Rechts*) – captures in highly condensed form.

The conflicts-law approach is always susceptible to the question: how can we be sure that a law finds the envisaged justification? We are not counting on some invisible hand guiding Europe behind its citizens' backs. However, it is possible to reconstruct the contexts that generate their competing claims. It is possible to examine the factual and normative reasons held by the pertinent contenders. It is finally possible to expose

---

[47] R. Wiethölter, 'Just-ifications of a law of society' in O. Perez and G. Teubner (eds), *Paradoxes and Inconsistencies in the Law* (Oxford: Hart Publishing, 2005), p. 65.

[48] M. Everson and J. Eisner, *The Making of the EU Constitution: Judges and Lawyers Beyond Constitutive Power* (Milton Park, Oxon: Routledge-Cavendish, 2007), at 41.

[49] See R. Wiethölter, 'Proceduralisation of the category of law' in C. Joerges and D. Trubek (eds), *Critical Legal Thought: An American-German Debate* (Baden-Baden: Nomos, 1989), p. 501.

the responses by decision-making bodies to the crucial question on what grounds they may 'deserve recognition'.[50] There is no guarantee available for the success of that vision – and no conceivable alternative way by which Europe might realise its 'unity in diversity'.

[50] Habermas uses this formula quite often. See J. Habermas, *The Postnational Constellation. Political Essays* (Cambridge, MA: The MIT Press, 2001), p. 113.

PART III

The Law's Divisions

10

Rethinking the public/private divide

HANS-W. MICKLITZ

Felix Frankfurter: Old pictures of a political and legal scene remain current long after it has been dramatically altered.[1]

Walter van Gerven: The division between public and private law serves only pedagogical purposes in the training of undergraduate students.[2]

Kaarlo Tuori: What we call today legal hybridity is a sign of our conceptual confusion: new conceptual and systemizing grids are needed, but our legal mind-set is still in many respects attached to the state-sovereigntism of the black-box model and the distinctions of traditional systematization.[3]

Harm Schepel: Standards hover between the state and the market; standards largely collapse the distinction between legal and social norms; standards are very rarely either wholly public or wholly private, and can be both intensely local and irreducibly global.[4]

I would to thank the Centre of Excellence at the University of Helsinki and its two directors Kaarlo Tuori and Pia Letto-Vanamo for hosting me so generously in their inspiring intellectual environment in spring/summer 2012.

[1] F. Frankfurter, 'The Final Report of the Attorney-General's Committee on Administrative Procedure. Foreword', 41 *Columbia Law Review* 4 (1941), 585–8 at 585, quoted by M. Taggart, 'From "parliamentary powers" to privatisation: the chequered history of delegated legislation in the twentieth century', 55 *University of Toronto Law Journal* 3 (2005), 575–627 at 625.

[2] Quotation from J. Stuyck, Professor at the University of Leuven, who is one of his disciples and who was confronted with this wisdom as an undergraduate student.

[3] K. Tuori, 'On legal hybrids' in H-W. Micklitz and Y. Svetiev (eds), *A Self-sufficient European Private Law: A Viable Concept* (Fiesole: European University Institute Working Papers, 2012), p. 73.

[4] H. Schepel, *The Constitution of Private Governance: Product Standards In the Regulation of Integrating Markets* (Oxford: Hart Publishing, 2005), p. 3.

1. Approximations: on hybrids, hybridisation and perspectivism – how to couch what we conceive but cannot define

Researchers around the world, whether they are working on private law or on public law, at the national, supranational or international level, are united in the conviction that the dividing line between public and private law is vanishing away. They do not look at the intermingling of the public and private primarily in their national legal orders, where the *Veröffentlichrechtlichung des Privatrechts* – the intrusion of the public into the private – constituted one of the major battlefields in national private/public law during the debate on the rise of the welfare state in Europe in the 1970s and after. The shift in focus beyond the nation state continues a fifty-year-old debate on the relationship between the state and the private. Perhaps the most well-known and widely debated area of the public/private divide today is European law. Transnational law entered the arena later, but nowadays it is here we find the most outspoken dicta on the vanishing divide.

1.1. On the phenomenon

There is certainly a common understanding of what European law is. For the sake of argument it might be important to recall that thirty years ago European law was a subdiscipline of public international law; only European competition law received the necessary attention, which within the circle of competition lawyers was linked to the ordo-liberal school and the idea of the European legal order as an 'economic constitution'.[5] Until the early 1980s most EU law fitted best into the category of 'administrative law' – *Wirtschaftsverwaltungs-Recht*.[6] The second step then was the 'constitutionalisation of the European legal order', through the ECJ in *Les Verts* 1986.[7] The 2002 White Paper on Governance triggered an overall debate on constitutional pluralism and the feasibility of a European Constitution. Europeanisation of private law started with consumer law after adoption of the Single European Act in 1986, but only in the twenty-first century was it equated with a nation state understanding

---

[5] J. Drexl, 'Competition law as part of the European constitution' in A. von Bogdandy and J. Bast (eds), *Principles of European Constitutional Law* (Oxford: Hart Publishing, 2010), pp 659–98; C. Joerges, 'A renaissance of the European Economic Constitution' in U. Neergard, R. Nielsen and L. Roseberry (eds), *Integrating Welfare Functions into EU Law* (Copenhagen: Djøf Publishing, 2009), p. 29.

[6] Think of J. Schwarze, *Droit Administratif Européen* (Brussels: Établissements Émile Bruylant, 2009).

[7] Case 294/83, *Parti écologiste 'Les Verts' v. European Parliament* [1986] ECR 1339.

of private law in the highly debated and highly debatable project on a European civil code. In all three areas we may identify the public/private as being closely interconnected.[8]

The notion of transnational law goes back to Philip Jessup's lecture at Yale Law School in 1956.[9] Over the last fifty years transnational law has had an amazing career, and today it is the most dynamic, and intellectually one of the most fascinating, fields of legal research and legal theory. Its *ratio materiae* reaches from classical private law issues between two parties, to debates over new forms of cooperation between the executive and the private, to the interaction between states themselves – provided a cross-border/transborder 'beyond the state' element exists.[10] What exactly transnational law means, what the 'trans' implies,[11] how it is related to national law and to what extent it is distinct from supranational and international law, is the subject of controversy. The discipline of transnational law invokes private law, international private law, administrative law, international administrative law and public international law, thereby bringing together theories on international private law, on transnational private law, comparative law, administrative law and constitutional law. Transnational law is a playground for curious researchers interested in combining legal practice with all sorts of legal and non-legal theories to cope with the interaction of the public and the private. For my purposes I will use the circumscription provided by Kaarlo Tuori.[12] I deliberately

---

[8] N. Reich, 'The public/private divide in European law' in F. Cafaggi and H-W. Micklitz (eds), *European Private Law after the Common Frame of Reference* (Cheltenham: Edward Elgar Publishing, 2010), p. 56; L. Azoulai, 'Sur un sens de la distinction public/privé dans le droit de l'Union Européenne', 46 *Revue trimestrielle de droit européen* 4 (2010), 842–60.

[9] P. Jessup, 'Transnational law', 66 *Yale Law Journal* 5 (1956), 813–16.

[10] R. Michaels and N. Jansen, 'Private law beyond the state? Europeanization, globalization, privatization', 54 *American Journal of Comparative Law* 4 (2006), 843–90.

[11] K. Nuotio, 'Criminal law of a transnational polity' in H. Müller-Dietz, E. Müller, K-L. Kunz, H. Radtke, G. Britz, C. Momsen and H. Koriath (eds), *Festschrift für Heike Jung* (Baden-Baden: Nomos, 2007), pp 685–98.

[12] See Tuori, note 3 above at 71:

> In effect, the very idea of transnational law is an epitome of legal hybridization. Transnational law is law beyond the dichotomy of nation-state law and international law which has emerged as a reaction to the spatial and temporal shortcomings of the black-box model in front of the cultural and social changes often enough examined under the notion of *globalisation* or – to use a less pretentious expression – *de-nationalisation*. The distinctive features of transnational law can be attached to either norm-formation or norm-application. Transnational norm giving assumes other forms than bi- or multilateral treaties between nation states. In norm-application, in turn, the establishment of dispute-solving or sanctioning bodies beyond the control of nation states suggests the emergence of transnational law.

use circumscription as it seems rather difficult to give a definition. The ever-growing literature is full of discussion of the public/private divide, providing examples and case studies across the fields of law.

Whether European law or transnational law is involved, the most fashionable term to determine the interplay between public and private is to speak of *hybrids*, usually without clarifying what is meant.[13] The message is that law in action is a composite law, bringing together bits and pieces of various legal orders. Hybrids may be found in substantive or procedural law, in institution building, in the lawmaking and law enforcement mechanism. All in all, the term means – in a rather diffuse, phenomenological way – the congregation of the private and the public in a particular legal domain (preferably in European and/or transnational law), usually with the undertone that it becomes ever-more difficult to separate the private from the public – or vice versa, in European law as well as in transnational law. This observation deserves to be emphasised. Correctly speaking, we have to separate two phenomena: *identifying the hybrids in public/private;* and the *vanishing of the public/private distinction.* The first is getting to grips with what hybrids are and whether we can find a concept that allows us to categorise and define them. The second concerns the process of hybridisation. If the public/private divide is vanishing – where is it vanishing to? What kind of legal order is the result once the process comes to a halt, or is the idea of a process already wrong as it suggests that there is a means to an end? What does a legal order with no distinction between the public and the private look like? Is this the reason why legal historians enter the arena claiming the 'renaissance' of medieval times in law? Is it a kind of *romanticism* in which medieval times are seen through rose-tinted glasses?[14]

Felix Frankfurter reminds us of how our mindset is stamped by categories in which we have been educated. If the public/private divide is really just a tool, a teaching device, if Walter van Gerven is correct, then it is an ambiguous tool as it hides deeper theoretical uncertainties. Understood as a pedagogical tool, the public/private divide might help law students to organise the vast and not very accessible subject of the law. Kaarlo Tuori would have to insist on the search to understand legal hybrids and to develop a deeper theoretical meaning.

---

[13] See, for such an attempt, *ibid.*

[14] See, for example, B. Hall and T. Bierstecker (eds), *The Emergence of the Private Authority in Global Governance* (Cambridge: Cambridge University Press, 2002); with followers, N. Jansen, *The Making of Legal Authority* (Oxford: Oxford University Press, 2010).

The starting point for getting to grips with the claim that the public/private divide is vanishing could be the classical division between 'public' and 'private' law, the first referring to the relationship between citizens and the state, the second to the relationship between citizens. '*Publicum ius quod at statum rei Romanae spectat, privatum quod at singularum utilatem*', as the Roman jurist Ulpian said.[15] This model is based on a separation between the state arena, in which political prerogatives prevail, and the private sphere in which autonomous persons interact according to their own preferences, a separation that, at least in the continental tradition, permeates the division of legal disciplines and court competences. In one sentence we find condensed two thousand years of struggle between the 'public political sphere' and the 'private intimate and the private economic sphere', the struggle over the building of political institutions in their relationship and function to the 'individual'.[16]

Does this Roman distinction suffice? Is this the nightmare Walter van Gerven refers to, which undergraduate law students have to confront when they embark on the adventure of studying the law: providing a rather handsome technical definition, that allows for and facilitates 'orientation'? Do we have to go into the history of the distinction? Do we have to go into political and moral philosophy to understand where the distinction comes from and why it is such a powerful device?[17] I think to a certain extent we have to, although my focus is the public/private divide in *law*, not the public vs. the private *good* or the public vs. the private *realm*. But even in such a more comfortable, narrower perspective, we have to ask: where is the public in private (law) and – less discussed – the private in public (law)? We cannot escape the question of what lies behind the public/private 'divide', which is said to be vanishing. Postulating a distinction is often the first step in an argument against a spillover between the two realms.[18] This is equally true for denying a distinction, which can turn into an argument in favour of the vanishing of the public/private divide.

---

[15] Ulp. Dig. 1,1,1,2 as cited by K. Larenz and M. Wolf in *Allgemeiner Teil des Bürgerlichen Rechts*, 8.A., 1997, § 1 Fn. 20.

[16] Reich, note 8 above.

[17] H. Arendt, *The Human Condition* (Chicago: University of Chicago Press, 1958), pp 22–78.

[18] C. Michelon, 'The public nature of the private law' in G. Clunie, C. MacCorkindale, C. Michelon and H. Psarras (eds), *The Public in Law* (Aldershot: Ashgate Publishing, 2011), p. 200, referring to R. Geuss, *Public Goods, Private Goods* (Princeton, NJ: Princeton University Press, 2001), p. 109.

Claiming that the dividing line between the statutory and the private sphere is vanishing has deep implications for our understanding of the political and the private, the role and function of public and private law. Is 'vanishing' a factual/sociological/empirical or a conceptual/philosophical/normative claim, or both? Is overcoming the divide 'good' in that the public interferes in the private and the private the public? Or is it 'bad' in that autonomy and liberty are restricted? Is there a price to pay for the amalgamation? Far from being able to provide an answer to all these questions, I will start by clarifying the two elements that are enshrined in rethinking the public/private divide: the determination of hybrids and the process of hybridisation.

1.2. On legal hybrids

The famous quote from Ulpian catches precisely our own mindset, the way in which we lawyers are trained, not only in Europe, but obviously beyond. We learn to distinguish between the public and the private sphere. Admittedly the distinction is diffuse as there is no common conception of the state as a legal concept, just as we do not share a common understanding of what the private sphere is, let alone what the role and function of the law in the private sphere is or should be. Despite all these uncertainties, it seems safe to argue that, in the European context, at least since the French Revolution, we associate the public with the state and the state with the existence of a constitution and the private with the shaping of legal relations between private parties, with the existence of a national private-legal order, codified or not. Thus two branches of the law can easily be linked to the public/private distinction. Each of the two has its particular perception of the public/private divide, defence of the distinction or its critique factually and normatively and therefore also its perception of legal hybrids.

Hybrids can be identified mainly in the area between the constitutional (the Constitution) and the private (the Civil Code). I will draw no distinction between the common and civil law systems here. The form might differ, but the substance is similar.

My first hypothesis is that this distinction is still very much alive and that it leads to an *inward*-looking analysis of the public/private divide, often in a rather defensive way, shielding the purity of the public against the private and vice versa. By inward I understand a focus on the respective discipline, the existence of a national constitution in its interaction between other constitutions – public international law; or of a national private-legal order in its interaction with other, international private-legal orders – the international private-legal order. An *inward* perspective keeps the constitution and the private legal order distinct from one another. Hybrids are alien to such an understanding. What is in between? Is there an *outward* interaction between the public and the private and if so, where does it take place – within the public as it is affected by the private-legal order and/or in the interface between the public and the private legal order? *Outward*, then, refers to opening up the perspective, to engaging in an unbiased dialogue between the public and the private.

My second hypothesis starts from the premise that the major candidate for the area in which the interaction is most visible and most obvious is *administrative law*. Administrative law is older than the state, at least as reconstructed in the concept of a national constitution. If we again take the French Revolution as a starting-point, the state changed its outlook considerably, first through the emergence of the regulatory state and later through the welfare state.[19] The way in which the European integration process operated fully consists with such a distinction, as European integration was promoted first and foremost through administrative law. It has certainly contributed to the rise of transnational law, in which the interaction between the executive and the private holds a prominent position. What is meant, is nicely caught in Harm Schepel's research on standardisation, a field in which the congregation of the public and the private is well established over hundreds of years – in fact it goes back to the Greeks and the Romans who discovered standardisation as an efficient means to build their warships[20] – a field which seems to be of paradigmatic importance for an understanding of the public/private

---

[19] On the distinction between the regulatory and the welfare state in a historical perspective, see C. Torp, *Die Herausforderung der Globalisierung: Wirtschaft und Politik in Deutschland 1860–1914* (Göttingen: Vandenhoeck & Ruprecht, 2005).

[20] See also, for a comprehensive analysis of the history, P. Marburger, *Die Regeln der Technik im Recht* (Tübingen: Mohr Siebeck, 1979); J. Falke, *Internationale Normen zum Abbau von Handelshemmnissen – Analyse der Abkommen und normungspolitischen Diskussion* (Bremen: Zentrum für Europäische Rechtspolitik, 2001); H. Schepel and J. Falke, *Legal Aspects of Standardisation in the Member States of the EC and EFTA: Vol. 1: Comparative Report, Vol. 2: Country Reports* and *Vol. 3: Rechtliche Aspekte der Normung in den EG-Mitgliedstaaten und der EFTA* (Luxembourg: Office for Official Publications of the European Communities, 2001).

HANS-W. MICKLITZ

divide. Understood this way administrative law is the most prominent field in which to find legal hybrids. Maybe such an understanding of administrative law would require the area to be renamed as something like 'private administrative law'.[21]

The three domains of law, constitutional, private administrative and private, broken down into inward- and outward-looking, is no more than a first approximation to the public/private divide. This rather rough and static categorisation will then be combined with four levels of legal hybrids. Kaarlo Tuori proposes to distinguish

1. the level of individual phenomena,
2. the level of fields of law
3. the level of legal orders and systems, and
4. hybrid legal spaces, which might emerge when legal orders and systems compete for authority.

What remains to be clarified is the relationship between the four levels. As it stands, the distinction suggests a kind of developing logic; an individual phenomenon may become the trigger for establishing first a legal field and then a legal order. The idea of a linear relationship seems to be confirmed if combined with the inward/outward-looking perspective in the three branches of the law, constitutional, administrative and private. The higher the level of legal hybrid (1–4), the more difficult it seems to shield constitutional and private law against the existence of such hybrids. An individual phenomenon may be singular and contained within one branch of law. If the phenomena multiply, this might indicate the emergence of a new field of law that in itself then raises the question of the interrelationship between 'new' and 'old' legal systems and orders. But if this is correct, what are the reasons behind such a development? Is that development over the four different levels really linear? A closer analysis of the four levels of hybrid will help us to explain the logic in more detail, if there is any.

In combining the three domains of the law with the four levels, we have a tool that can be used to develop a more concrete picture of where to find legal hybrids and how they can be identified.

---

[21] In German this could be associated with Verwaltungsprivatrecht, which is used to cover statutory activities through private law means. However, the way in which I use the term is broader.

Table 10.1 *Levels of legal hybrids in constitutional, administrative and private law*

	Individual phenomena	Field/branches	System/order	Hybrid legal space
Public constitutional law	Typically cases *Bürgschaftsurteil*	Property rights Social rights	Economic constitution Many constitutions	Constitutional pluralism
Private administrative law	Administrative practice	Labour, consumer law Telecom, energy, transport, financial markets European regulatory private law	Sectoralisation Administrative enforcement of private law	Transnational law
Private law	Fundamental rights before private law jurisdiction	Constitutionalised private law	Private law society Private law as economic law	Pluralism of private legal orders

1.3. On perspectivism

Legal categories, however defined, are static. This results from the fact that thinking in categories implies the need to define demarcation lines between what belongs within a particular field of law and what does not. This is true for all the categories here presented: constitutional, administrative and private law. Hybridisation suggests a dynamic as it insinuates the existence of change, whether thought of as a linear process or as a loop. Whether dynamic or static, however, all categories used to get to grips with the public/private divide have in common that each and every distinction is the result of a particular conceptual and systematising framework.[22] This is true for the three law dimensions, constitutional, administrative and private, and it is equally true for the four levels of legal hybrid that we have identified. This can be demonstrated in the way the three disciplines look at their own field and the way in which they interact or do not interact.

Constitutional law research focuses on the changing role and function of the nation state and statehood in a post-Westphalian world order,

---

[22] Tuori, note 3 above, p. 67.

seeking the response either in 'global constitutionalism' or in 'constitutional pluralism'.[23] Administrative law research argues that the new world order is being built on rules that emerge from what Ulrich Beck termed as early as 1986 'Weltinnenpolitik'.[24] In such a perspective the emphasis is put on the executive around the world, which cooperates in topic- and sector-related matters.[25] Private lawyers revitalise their arsenal of legal theories, the revival of *lex mercatoria*, the fine-tuning of transnational law in the definition by Philip Jessup,[26] or international private law as a means to cope with the growing pluralism of legal sources.[27] Private law research hovers between law and economics and social science research. Transnational private law research concentrates on the growing space for private parties beyond the nation state.[28] A bulk of social science theories are mobilised to structure empirical research, mainly in the field of administrative law,[29] a smaller mass in private law,[30] to justify wide-ranging theoretical conclusions.

Despite the largely common set of social science theories standing behind legal theoretical discourse on the blurring line between the public

---

[23] M. Avbelj and J. Komarek (eds), *Constitutional Pluralism and the European Union and Beyond* (Oxford: Hart Publishing, 2012).

[24] U. Beck, *Risikogesellschaft, Auf dem Weg in einer andere Moderne* (Frankfurt: Suhrkamp, 1986), in English: *Risk Society: Towards a New Modernity* (London: Sage Publications, 1992).

[25] See the Global Administrative Law project at New York University. The most prominent contribution is B. Kingsbury, N. Krisch and R. Stewart, 'The emergence of global administrative law', 68 *Law & Contemporary Problems* 15 (2005), 15–61.

[26] G-P. Calliess and P. Zumbansen, *Rough Consensus and Running Code: A Theory of Transnational Private Law* (Oxford: Hart Publishing, 2011); F. Cafaggi, 'New foundations of transnational private regulation', 38 *Journal of Law and Society* 1 (2011), 20–49.

[27] C. Joerges and F. Rödl, 'Zum Funktionswandel des Kollisionsrechts II: Die kollisionsrechtliche Form einer legitimen Verfassung der post-nationalen Konstellation' in G-P. Calliess, A. Fischer-Lescano, D. Wielsch and P. Zumbansen (eds), *Soziologische Jurisprudenz: Festschrift für Gunther Teubner zum 65.Geburtstag* (Berlin: De Gruyter, 2009), p. 767; H. Muir Watt, 'Private international law beyond the schism', 2 *Transnational Legal Theory* 3 (2011), 347–428.

[28] This is the heading of the well-known article by Michaels and Jansen, note 10 above at 843; see also the two volumes published under the same title by the same authors, *Beyond the State: Rethinking Private Law* (Tübingen: Mohr Siebeck, 2008).

[29] This is true for the Global Administrative Law Project, but see in particular O. Dilling, M. Herberg and G. Winter (eds), *Transnational Administrative Rule-Making: Performance, Legal Effects and Legitimacy* (Oxford: Hart Publishing, 2011).

[30] Calliess and Zumbansen, note 26 above, provide two case studies; Cafaggi, note 26 above focuses on supply chains.

and the private,[31] the three legal disciplines vary considerably in how they look at legal hybrids: constitutional law on private law, private law on constitutional law, administrative law on constitutional and private law and so on. Perspective matters. Shifting from legal hybrids to the process of hybridisation implies a change in focus from a rather static approach to the dynamism behind the vanishing of the public/private divide. This is first and foremost a shift in perspective.

In my effort to rethink the public/private divide through the categories of legal hybrids (the concept) and hybridisation (the process), I would like to pinpoint the crucial role of perspectivism, what Nietzsche called subjective perspectivism:[32]

> In so far as the word 'knowledge' has any meaning, the world is knowable; but it is interpretable otherwise, it has no meaning behind it, but countless meanings.
>
> – 'Perspectivism.'
>
> *It is our needs that interpret the world; our drives and their For and Against* [emphasis added]. Every drive is a kind of lust to rule; each one has its perspective that it would like to compel all the other drives to accept as a norm.
>
> Friedrich Nietzsche; trans. Walter Kaufmann, *The Will to Power*, §481 (1883–8)

This means that my attempt to rethink the public/private divide is not meant to claim that I have found the 'truth' behind that divide, or even worse, that I can predict where the development will lead us. What is needed is to constantly ascertain and question the perspective from which I will look at the public/private divide. The truth can be no more than the ensemble of the different perspectives, as Akira Kurosawa so masterly demonstrated to us in *Rashomon*.[33] Each of the four actors involved in the killing has their own version of the truth. Akira Kurosawa visualised this consequence in demonstrating how convincing each of the four stories is, as long as it stands by itself. This is the perfect realisation of *inward*-looking

---

[31] E.g. K. Polanyi, *The Great Transformation: The Political and Economic Origins of Our Time* (Boston, MA: Beacon Press, 1944); F. Scharpf, 'Monetary Union, fiscal crisis and the preemption of democracy', *LEQS* Paper no. 36 (2011); G. Teubner, *Global Law without the State* (Farnham: Ashgate Publishing, 1997).

[32] 'Perspectivism' in *Wikipedia: The Free Encyclopedia* at http://en.wikipedia.org/wiki/perspectivism.

[33] See http://en.wikipedia.org/wiki/Rashomon.

perspectivism. We find four truths through four different perspectives. It is only in the interaction between the four levels that we might gain an *outward*-looking perspective, which allows us to understand the relativity of what we see and identify.

Perspectivism directs us into the search, not only for concepts and theories, but for *facts*. This might explain why all research revolving around the public/private divide so desperately depends on 'evidence', on examples and case studies, on 'concrete circumstances' in which the divide/non-divide crystallises.[34] Akira Kurosawa teaches us that the search for facts, for evidence in identifying legal hybrids, may increase our knowledge considerably, but putting the facts together does not automatically give us the full picture or some sort of objective truth. We need to understand not only the relativity of the facts, but also why facts are limited in their self-explanatory messages. This is not meant to downgrade facts or the search for facts, but to stress that their importance in the understanding of the public/private divide is relative.

Perspectivism equally explains why even the most ambitious attempts to conceptualise the public/private divide, as is being done in transnational law, end up in legal methodology, without offering a particular legal theory. These theories are united in analysing the phenomenon from a particular angle, from the perspective of global administrative law, from *lex mercatoria*,[35] or from international private law.[36] Legal methodology and legal techniques will bridge the gap between the phenomena that we can identify in real life and the reasons behind the transformation process. I would like to invite the reader to understand the bringing together of the

---

[34] As proof for my argument I could quote nearly each and every article and book on transnational law I am referring to. For a more theoretical perspective, see Kennedy, note 102 below at 1357; L. Azoulai, note 8 above at 842.

[35] See Calliess and Zumbansen, note 26 above; G-P. Calliess and M. Renner, 'Between law and social norms: the evolution of global governance', 22 *Ratio Juris* 2 (2009), 260–80, who both understand their conceptual considerations to get to grips with the distinction of social norms and legal norms as a particular methodology.

[36] Muir Watt, note 27 above: at the very end of her paper Muir Watt looks into 'Methodological approaches: an historical reminder'. In this context she presents her plea for unilateralism:

> In the heyday of positivism – during the long era of the closet – there was always a dissident, pluralist-compatible methodology present in the 'unofficial portrait' of private international law ... The unsung song of private international law – counterintuitively named unilateralism – was a project for the open-ended articulation of diverse claims to govern, based on mutual defence and balancing, rather than exclusiveness and hierarchy.

Table 10.2 *The constitutional law perspective*

	Individual phenomena	Field/branches	System/order	Hybrid legal space
Public Constitutional	Typically cases *Bürgschaftsurteil* of the Gulf Cooperation Council Bank charges Case of the UK Supreme Court	Property rights Social rights Environmental rights Consumer rights	Economic constitution Many constitutions	Constitutional pluralism Conflicting rights
Perspective	Inward	Inward	Outward	Outward

two dimensions, analysis of legal hybrids and analysis of hybridisation, as a first attempt to provide what might be called a theoretical explanation. This does not mean that my perspective is neutral or objective. Perspectivism always contains a subjective element, as is so convincingly shown in *Rashomon*.

1.4. How the argument flows

I will first look into the various forms of legal hybrid, thereby combining constitutional, administrative and private-law thinking with the four levels of hybridisation. This step is meant to give a much clearer picture of the phenomenon of legal hybrids. It builds on the distinction between the inward, discipline-oriented perspective and the outward one, looking across disciplines. The emphasis on the interaction between the different hybrids, the turn to the changing interrelation, hybridisation, leads us directly to the question whether the public/private *divide* should be understood and read as a *process* or as a *loop*.

2. On legal hybrids

2.1. Inward- and outward-looking

Constitutional law is *inward*-looking, starting from the nation state constitution, first and foremost in the western democratic version. In this perspective, the widely recognised transformation of the nation state is perceived as a 'threat' to national constitutionalism. By contrast, the *outward*-looking perspective advocates constitutional pluralism or a global constitution.

In both perspectives the 'constitution' is preserved as an idea and as a concept. It is a state-centred debate and does not keep an eye on the public/private divide. The state is 'public'. Seemingly, the EU constitution, whether with a small 'c' or a big 'C',[37] does not fit into that picture, as it is open to debate whether the European legal order can be regarded as a constitutional project and if so, in what sense: as an extended version of the nation-state constitution; as a new device that could function as a blueprint for regional legal orders; or as a misconception?[38] There is definitely a strong element of a legal hybrid here, in the form of pan-national, hybrid, constitutional space. My focus, however, is the public private/divide. The constitutional discussion does not aim to create a bridge to debates within global administrative law or within transnational private law.

It is plain that administrative law can be, and has been, regarded as the experimental field for the development of constitutional principles.[39] The deeper link between the 1985 New Approach on Technical Standards and Regulations and the elaboration of the Single European Act underpins the correctness of such thinking in the European context.[40] I understand the Global Administrative Law project (GAL) as exactly fitting into that perspective. Global administrative law has its origin in the first Technical Barriers to Trade Agreement (TBT) concluded in the aftermath of the 1973 Directive on low voltage. The 1994 WTO Sanitary and Phytosanitary Measures (SPS) mechanism combines elements of the EU 1985 New Approach, the 1986 Single European Act and the 1991 Directive on Product Safety.[41] However, the two strands of discussion largely fell/fall apart. Constitutional law looks at administrative law as a kind of a subdiscipline

---

[37] N. Walker, 'Big "C" or small "c"', 12 *European Law Journal* 1 (2006), 12–14.

[38] M. Maduro, 'Europe and the Constitution: what if this is as good as it gets?' in M. Wind and J. H. H. Weiler (eds), *Constitutionalism Beyond the State* (Cambridge: Cambridge University Press, 2003), pp 74–102.

[39] The wording is attributed to Otto Mayer, one of the founding fathers of German administrative law. I have used this formula and the deeper background behind in my search for the foundations of a 'right to safety', which mutated from administrative law into a constitutional principle.

[40] Joerges has used his research in the field to build his theory on deliberative supranationalism. It is by no means a coincidence that the ECJ started using constitutional language from 1986 onwards; see *Les Verts*, note 7 above.

[41] H. Schepel, 'The empire's drain: sources of legal recognition of private standardisation under the TBT Agreement' in C. Joerges and E-U. Petersmann (eds), *Constitutionalism,*

of public law; European or global administrative law is struggling with its constitutional outlook.[42]

Even less satisfying is the non-existent discourse between global constitutional/constitutional pluralism and transnational private law. A striking though paradigmatic example is a conference organised by the Venice Commission, the Centre of Excellence in Foundations of European Law and Polity (COE) at the University of Helsinki and the International Association of Constitutional Law on 'Constitutional Design', held in Helsinki on 21 and 22 May 2012. The Venice Commission is designing rules and using self-established rules as a benchmark in evaluating the degree to which democracy and human rights are realised in countries outside the EU. In private law the 'design of rules' by state and non-state actors stands at the forefront of the discussion, at least since the emergence of the state in the post-Westphalian world.[43] Combing the two strands of experience would allow for dialogue and instigate a mutual learning process.

Neglect of the private law domain dominates even European constitutional discourse, in which the link to private law might and should be more obvious than at the international level. The book on *The Past and Future of EU Law: The Classics of EU Law Revisited on the 50th Anniversary of the Rome Treaty*, edited by Miguel Maduro and Loïc Azoulai,[44] looks into twelve classic European law judgments, but none of the contributions treats their private law dimension, although the EU is first and foremost about alcohol, cars and cosmetics. If they ever discuss the economic freedoms, European constitutional lawyers do so only with regard to their constitutional implications, not with regard to their impact on private law.[45]

If at all, constitutional law is building links to what is called the 'economic constitution', which was developed by the ordo-liberals largely during the Second World War, and made its way into the deeper

---

Multilevel Trade, Governance and International Economic Law (Oxford: Hart Publishing, 2011), p. 397; H-W. Micklitz, *Internationales Produktsicherheitsrecht* (Baden-Baden: Nomos, 1995).

[42] Joerges was at the forefront of those who understood European administrative law as enshrined in the New Approach and the comitology procedure to be a form of constitutionalisation.

[43] Jansen, note 14 above.

[44] M. Maduro and L. Azoulai (eds), *The Past and Future of EU Law: The Classics of EU Law Revisited on the 50th Anniversary of the Rome Treaty* (Oxford: Hart Publishing, 2010).

[45] This is left to private law. If any, see V. Kosta, 'Internal market legislation and the private law of the Member States: the impact of fundamental rights', 6 *European Review of Contract Law* 4 (2010), 409–36. Even in private law, however, the link between the two domains is all too often neglected.

theoretical if not cultural foundations of the German legal system,[46] from which it was transferred to Europe,[47] and to international economic law.[48] Private law is very much regarded as being distinct from constitutional law; the debate is limited to the question whether and to what extent constitutional law and constitutional principles could equally be applied within private relations. This is what Mattias Kumm termed 'total constitution', the quest for hegemony of constitutional law over all other areas of the law, including private law.[49] Again, what matters is not whether Mattias Kumm is right or wrong, but that he looks from constitutional law 'downwards' to private law.

2.2. On the four levels of legal hybrids

The starting point for hybrids is at individual phenomena (level 1) enshrined in 'cases', such as the so-called *Bürgschaftsurteil* (private securities) of the *Bundesverfassungsgericht* (German Constitutional Court). In the case at issue, the public and the private clash, in concrete terms – the constitutional decision in the German Basic Law (*Grundgesetz*) is that private economic liberties are subject to constitutional social restrictions. Similar developments may be reported from other Member States or more generally from states that have empowered a constitutional court to overlook economic activities as well, such as India or Brazil.[50]

---

[46] See D. Gerber, 'Constitutionalizing the economy: German neo-liberalism, competition law and the "new" Europe', 42 *American Journal of Comparative Law* 25 (1994), 25–84.

[47] In particular, E-J. Mestmäcker, 'Macht – Recht – Wirtschaftsverfassung', in H. K. Schneider and C. Watrin (eds), *Macht und ökonomisches Gesetz. Verhandlungen auf der Tagung des Vereins für Socialpolitik Gesellschaft für Wirtschafts- und Sozialwissenschaften in Bonn 1972, Erster Halbband*, (Berlin: Duncker & Humblot, 1973), pp 183–99, and for an adapted version in English: 'Power, law and economic constitution', 10 *Law and State* (1974), 117–31.

[48] See the Petersmann–Alston debate: E-U. Petersmann, 'Time for a United Nations "global compact" for integrating human rights into the law of worldwide organizations: lessons from European integration', 13 *European Journal of International Law* 3 (2002), 621–50; P. Alston, 'Resisting the merger and acquisition of human rights by trade law: a reply to Petersmann', 13 *European Journal of International Law* 4 (2002), 815–44; Petersmann responding, 'Taking human dignity, poverty and empowerment of individuals more seriously: rejoinder to Alston', 13 *European Journal of International Law* 4 (2002), 845–51.

[49] M. Kumm, 'Who is afraid of the total constitution? Constitutional rights as principles and the constitutionalization of private law', 7 *German Law Journal* 4 (2006), 341–69; O. Gerstenberg, 'Private law and the new European constitutional settlement', 10 *European Law Journal* 6 (2004), 766–86.

[50] N. Bryner, 'Brazil's green court: environmental law in the Superior Tribunal de Justica (High Court of Brazil)', 29 *Pace Environmental Law Review* (2012), 470–537.

If constitutional courts have to engage in more and more cases that contain a link to private law matters, a new field of law (level 2) may emerge, such as the domain of constitutionalised property rights, constitutionalised social rights of workers, environmental rights or consumer rights. So far the phenomenon still dominates the national level. The breadth and depth depends on the conditions under which individuals may invoke constitutional rights before national (constitutional) courts.[51] In countries that do not have a constitutional court, the highest court in the country may take on an equivalent function. This is true of the UK Supreme Court (the former House of Lords)[52] which decided a much-debated bank charges case quite differently from the German Constitutional Court.

The establishment of a particular, new field of law within the constitutional branch may trigger a debate on the relationship between 'the' constitution and the new field or branch of law that claims its own 'constitutional system or order' (level 3). Here the perspective changes from inward to outward. The debate is not really new, as the discussion on the social constitution and the economic constitution in the 1930s demonstrates. However, constitutions tend to proliferate. For a German lawyer, it makes perfect sense to speak of an '*Unternehmensverfassung*' (company constitution), '*Finanzverfassung*' (financial constitution), '*Umweltverfassung*' (environmental constitution), '*Privatrechtsverfassung*' (private law constitution) and '*Verbraucherrechtsverfassung*' (consumer law constitution). The wording contains the message. Whoever argues in favour of a '*Umwelt-* or *Finanzverfassung*' claims the existence and the applicability of constitutional principles and rights that frame the laws, regulations, statutes and standards governing that respective field of law (in my example *Umwelt* (environment) or *Finanzen* (finance)).[53] What is then needed is a concept and a theoretical understanding of how the different 'constitutions' are interlinked and how the conflict is decided. This is particularly true if the 'economic constitution' clashes with the 'social constitution'

[51] See on the differences O. Cherednychenko, *Fundamental Rights, Contract Law and the Protection of the Weaker Party: A Comparative Analysis of the Constitutionalisation of Contract Law, With Emphasis on Risky Financial Transactions* (Munich: Sellier European Law Publishers, 2007); C. Mak, *Fundamental Rights in European Contract Law. A Comparison of the Impact of Fundamental Rights on Contractual Relationships in Germany, the Netherlands, Italy and England* (Alphen aan den Rijin: Kluwer Law International, 2008).

[52] *Office of Fair Trading* v. *Abbey National plc and Others* [2009] UKSC 6.

[53] For a discussion, see K. Tuori, 'The many constitutions of Europe' in K. Tuori and S. Sankari (eds), *The Many Constitutions of Europe* (Farnham: Ashgate Publishing, 2010), pp 3–30.

or the environmental constitution with the private law constitution. Formally, the public/private divide is abrogated since the conflict is absorbed by the constitution. Materially, however, the public/private divide has only changed clothes. What was a conflict between different legal orders has been integrated into the inner logic of the constitutional order.

The hybrid legal space (level 4) may show up at all three levels. We may find authorities competing over cases. Here the outward-looking perspective becomes more prominent. Competition may be the result of Member States' conflicting decisions, but also of national courts in conflict with the CJEU or the ECtHR. The integration of the Charter of Fundamental Rights into the European legal order paves the way for a new wave of constitutionalisation of rights that stem from a 'lower' legal order, be it national law below the constitution or a national constitutional right challenged before the CJEU or the ECtHR. Equally, the sheer number of potential conflicts in the triangle between national courts, the CJEU and the ECtHR may rise. Looking through the lenses of the public/private divide, it is amazing to see that not only the CJEU but also and in particular the ECtHR, now even the ICJ,[54] are becoming increasingly involved with conflicts that are deeply anchored in private law or in private law relations. The more cases are decided in the hybrid legal space the more imminent will become the question how the different systems are linked together; the national legal system, the European legal order and the European Convention on Human Rights. Here we suffer from a severe lack of empirical research that would inform us on the areas in which these conflicts emerge and on whether there is already an emerging pattern that allows mention of conflicting systems and orders.

2.3. Inward- and outward-looking (on the global level)

In transnational and global 'private' administrative law, we find a similar, *inward*-looking perspective, although the subject matter to be analysed is necessarily more open to links with constitutional law and private law. A selection of articles and books dominating the field of global

---

[54] *Ahmadou Sadio Diallo (Republic of Guinea v. Democratic Republic of the Congo)*, Preliminary Objections, Judgment of 24 May 2007, ICJ Reports 2007, p. 582 (compensation owed by the Democratic Republic of the Congo to the Republic of Guinea).

Table 10.3 *The administrative law perspective*

	Individual phenomena	Field/branches	System/order	Hybrid legal space
Private administrative	Administrative practice	Labour, consumer law Telecom, energy, transport, financial markets European regulatory private law	Sectoralisation Administrative enforcement of private law	Global administrative law Transnational law
Perspective	Inward/outward	Inward/inward	Outward	Outward

administrative law focuses on a standard set of practical examples,[55] thereby setting aside the distinction between rules with which public authorities have been involved, and those in which private initiatives stand at the beginning of the process.[56] In the first group belong rules on forests and fisheries (e.g. Forest Stewardship Council, FSC),[57] labour practices and codes,[58] corporate social responsibility,[59] global finance (the

[55] I would like to thank Chantal Bratschi for an evaluation of the literature, largely inspired by the Global Governance Programme workshop (European University Institute, 23 and 24 May 2011) on transnational business governance interactions coordinated by Stepan Wood (EUI/York University), Fabrizio Cafaggi (EUI), Ken Abbott (Arizona State University), Julia Black (London School of Economics and Political Science), Burkard Eberlein (York University) and Errol Meidinger (University at Buffalo).
[56] For the purposes of this argument, the difference between the two in actuality is not important.
[57] G. Auld and J. Green, 'Unbundling the regime complex: the effects of private authority', paper presented at the Workshop on Transnational Business Governance Interactions at the European University Institute, May 2011; T. Bartley, 'Legality, sustainability, and the future of transnational forest governance', Working Paper, Department of Sociology, Ohio State University (2012); L. Gulbrandsen, 'Dynamic governance interactions: evolutionary effects of state responses to non-state certification programs', *Regulation & Governance*, DOI: 10.1111/rego.12005 (2012).
[58] D. Doorey, 'Polycentric governance, cooperation, and tensions in supply chain labour practices', paper presented at the Workshop on Transnational Business Governance Interactions at the European University Institute, May 2011; F. Cafaggi, *The Architecture of Transnational Private Regulation* (Fiesole: European University Institute Working Papers, 2011).
[59] Cafaggi, *ibid.*; Calliess and Zumbansen, note 26 above; L. Fransen, 'Multi-stakeholder governance and voluntary program interactions: legitimation politics in the institutional design of corporate social responsibility', 10 *Socio-Economic Review* 1 (2012), 163–92;

International Accounting Standards Board, IASB,[60] the International Organization of Securities Commissions, IOSCO,[61]) standardisation (ISO 26000 on corporate social responsibility),[62] the *Codex Alimentarius* Commission, environmental standards,[63] product safety standards,[64] copyright and intellectual property,[65] and security. In the second group belong *lex digitalis* (ICANN),[66] trade and *lex mercatoria*,[67] and *lex sportiva* (UEFA and FIFA, the Olympic Games, World Anti-Doping Agency).

Hybrids are the direct result of delegated lawmaking.[68] The prime responsibility may lie with international organisations such

---

K. Webb, 'ISO 26000: bridging the public/private divide in transnational business governance interactions', Osgoode CLPE Research Paper 21 (2012).

[60] L. Cunningham, 'Private standards in public law: copyright, lawmaking and the case of accounting', 104 *Michigan Law Review* (2005), 2–54.

[61] J. Biggins and C. Scott, 'Extending and contracting jurisdictions in a transnational private regulatory regime: efficiency, legitimacy, ISDA and the OTC derivatives markets', University College Dublin Working Papers in Law, Criminology & Socio-Legal Studies Research Paper 51 (2011); T. Porter, 'Transnational business governance interactions and technical systems in global finance', Osgoode CLPE Research Paper 19 (2012); J. Conley and C. Williams, 'Global banks as global sustainability regulators? The equator principles', 33 *Law & Policy* 4 (2011), 542–575.

[62] C. Ruwet, 'Towards democratization of standards development? Internal dynamics of ISO in the context of globalization', 5 *New Global Studies* 2 (2011), 1–28.

[63] R. van Gestel, 'Self-regulation and environmental law', 9 *Electronic Journal of Comparative Law* 1 (2005), 1–25.

[64] Cafaggi, *Architecture of Transnational Private Regulation*, note 58 above; Calliess and Zumbansen, note 26 above; M. Herberg, 'Global governance and conflict of laws from a Foucauldian perspective: the power/knowledge nexus revisited', 2 *Transnational Legal Theory* 2 (2011), 243–69.

[65] L. Dobusch and S. Quack, 'Strategizing institutional interactions: conflicts over transnational private regulation in the field of copyright', paper presented at the Workshop on Transnational Business Governance Interactions at the European University Institute, May 2011.

[66] Calliess and Renner, note 35 above; Cafaggi, *Architecture of Transnational Private Regulation*, note 58 above.

[67] Calliess and Zumbansen, note 26 above, in which they discuss the new *lex mercatoria*; A. Fischer-Lescano and G. Teubner, 'Regime-collisions: 'the vain search for legal unity in the fragmentation of global law', 25 *Michigan Journal of International Law* 4 (2004), 999–1046; P. Schiff Berman, 'Global legal pluralism', 80 *Southern California Law Review* (2007), 1155–240; and R. Wai, 'The interlegality of transnational private law', 71 *Law and Contemporary Problems* (2008), 106–27.

[68] Prominent and forceful, Taggart, note 1 above; for the EU with regard to the *Meroni* doctrine see T. Tridimas, 'Community agencies, competition law, and ECSB initiatives on securities clearing and settlement', 28 *Yearbook of European Law* 1 (2009), 216–307.

as the WTO/SPS, WTO/TBT/International Standards Organization/
Electrotechnical Commission Standards or FAO/*Codex Alimentarius*, in
which a tight legal framework exists, or in the EU within the comitology procedure, the *Lamfalussy* procedure, to a lesser extent via the open
method of coordination. The link to constitutional law is obvious, as
delegated lawmaking procedures raise deep questions about the degree
to which lawmaking via the executive in cooperation with private parties
requires parliamentary guidance and approval and how the legitimacy of
the process can be ensured. The history of the comitology procedure in
the EU provides ample evidence of the power struggle between the Parliament and the European Commission for suzerainty in the lawmaking
process. The preliminary outcome is the development of a thin version
of constitutional principles such as participation and accountability,[69]
for the development of which the USA has paved the way in mimicking
parliamentary legislation.[70] Despite these links between administrative
law and constitutional law, I would still claim that here, as with constitutional lawyers, is a strong tendency towards an *inward*-looking perspective, which connotes a specialised field of law only open to experts
belonging to the respective 'club'.

   Much less attention is given to the genuine private law perspective,
which I associate with the outward-looking perspective; this means with
the role and function of private actors in the making of the rules in
close cooperation with public authorities, national agencies, ministries
and/or official (*Codex Alimentarius*) or semi-official (IASB; IOSCO) international bodies.[71] The various issues that constitute the empirical core
of transnational administrative private law provide for strong relations
to private law issues because private actors, business organisations and
NGOs are heavily involved in the making of those rules, though to a lesser
extent in their monitoring and supervision.

   No administrative lawyer ever claimed 'total' administrative law in the
sense of the supremacy of administrative law over constitutional or private law. There is no counterpart to Mattias Kumm in this domain. In

---

[69] See Kingsbury, Krisch and Stewart, note 25 above.
[70] Taggart, note 1 above; S. Sassen, *Losing Control? Sovereignty in an Age of Globalization*
(New York: Columbia University Press, 1996), who said the same, nearly ten years earlier,
in 1996.
[71] Of course there are exceptions: K-H. Ladeur, 'The evolution of general administrative law
and the emergence of postmodern administrative law', Osgoode CLPE Research Paper 16
(2011).

practice, however, private actors and private organisations are down-graded to suppliers of the necessary expertise to what is then ennobled (upgraded) through being integrated into the public law body. Administrative law very much focuses on the relevant procedure and on responsibilities. There is only a limited understanding of the subject matter involved. This is why expertise is needed. In his comparative analysis of the history of delegated powers in the common law system – UK, Canada, Australia, New Zealand, accomplished in 2005 – Michael Taggart comes quite close to claiming statutory superiority in delegated law making:

> Behind all the delegated legislation and (although more in the shadows here [Taggart refers to e.g. standardisation]) quasi-legislation is the state. Yes the state, that much-maligned concept, supposedly too small to deal with global problems and too big to deal with local ones, under attack from globalisation from without and privatization from within. The literature of other disciplines is full of phrases like the hollowing-out state, the shadow state, the reinvented state, and the virtual state. Much of this otherwise welcome intra-disciplinary influence has led some scholars away from the state, particularly many of those doing cutting edge work on regulation and socio-legal studies.[72]

While this comes relatively close to claiming the dominance of administrative law over private law, I would like to assert that the role of bodies making private law bears a particular, private law dimension that can only be taken into consideration from an outward-looking perspective that goes beyond Taggart's claim.

2.4. On the four levels of legal hybrids (private administrative law)

It is striking to recognise how well established legal hybrids are in the field of private administrative law; I dare say not just recently, but for more than two hundred years. In contrast to the constitutional law perspective, the inward/outward distinction is less developed in administrative law. We might already find early elements of the 'vanishing divide' at the first two levels, although still with an inward focus.

Individual phenomena (level 1) exist, but they are much less accessible in administrative law than in constitutional and private law. This owes to the fact that administrative practice and administrative decisions are not

---

[72] See Taggart, note 1 above at 626; in his footnote at the end of the passage quoted M. Taggart refers to his own contribution in T. Jones, 'Administrative law, regulation and legitimacy', 16 *Journal of Law and Society* 4 (1989), 410–25.

automatically made public, in contrast to court decisions. Accessibility largely depends on the tradition and culture of nation states as regards granting access to information generated within public authorities. The United States and the Scandinavian countries are at the forefront in disclosing information on the inner world of administrative bodies.[73] In the Nordic countries, open access to the administration dates from the seventeenth century. The EU has managed to adopt common access standards only with regard to environmental protection issues but not with regard to financial services or consumer protection issues. Therefore information on legal hybrids largely depends on empirical research undertaken in particular countries by researchers who build relations with the respective agencies. A good example of a hybrid administrative practice is the preparedness of UK agencies in the area of regulated markets not only to take measures to correct market failures (the public law aspect) but also to push for compensation of private parties who have suffered from illegal practices (the private law aspect).[74]

More obvious is the overall tendency (level 2) over the last hundred years to establish a mixture of public and private law rules to govern the relationship between employee and employer (labour law) and supplier and consumer (consumer law). Today labour law is an established field of law in which the public/private divide is a mere fiction. Individual and collective labour law is the result of a well-established mechanism of rules that cuts across the boundaries of private and public law and that has enabled the emergence of a field of law somewhere between private and public law. A similar development has taken place in the field of consumer law, with the rise of the consumer law society. The majority of states have adopted a special consumer law code that usually combines public and private law rules in a way that fits neither traditional administrative nor traditional private-law thinking. These new areas are not really integrated into the administrative law body. They remain somewhere between the two, thereby facilitating the emergence of a club mentality: only experts have access.

Less obvious is the development triggered via liberalisation and privatisation of former public services such as telecommunications, postal

---

[73] E. Gurlit, *Die Verwaltungsöffentlichkeit im Umweltrecht. Ein Rechtsvergleich Bundesrepublik Deutschland – USA* (Düsseldorf: Werner-Verlag, 1989); H-W. Micklitz (ed.), *Informationszugang für Verbraucher in Europa und den USA: Recht und Praxis* (Baden-Baden: Nomos, 2009).

[74] C. Hodges, *The Reform of Class and Representative Actions in European Legal Systems: A New Framework for Collective Redress in Europe* (Oxford: Hart Publishing, 2008).

services, energy, transport and financial services. The widely agreed policy to establish competitive markets led in practice to a combination of public and private law rules, which can hardly be separated from each other. New fields of law have emerged in which experts govern lawmaking and law enforcement. Quite often, however, the experts involved focus on the technical intricacies of the respective fields but are not aware of the fact that in practice they interfere in private law relations or in an even more far-reaching manner shape private law relations via administrative rules.[75]

Administrative law is first and foremost associated with procedural mechanisms to guarantee access to courts and judicial review for those affected by administrative decisions. Seen through the lenses of the public/private divide, this dimension of administrative law takes a backstage role. What is much more interesting is the ongoing tendency towards sectoralisation (level 3). The former fields and branches of private administrative law are turning steadily into densely regulated sectors governed by their own procedural rules and their own substance and values, largely disconnected from traditional administrative and traditional private law. That is why the law on regulated markets can no longer be equated with a mere field or branch of private administrative law, but has to be understood as a holistic system merging the public and the private in an indivisible amalgam of rules.

Hybrid legal spaces (level 4) are not so much the result of conflicting individual rights (as in constitutional law), but of transnational, organised rulemaking and rule enforcement. This may take two forms: sectoral lawmaking either regionally (energy, postal services) or internationally (telecoms, transport, financial services, health and safety regulation) and/or horizontal lawmaking, meaning development of rules that are equally applicable across the various sectors (corporate social responsibility, ISO 26000). Different rulemaking bodies may very well compete over authority within the same field/branch or within the same system/order. A prominent example is the attempt to use the WTO/SPS rules against private initiatives to define standards higher than those agreed upon in the *Codex Alimentarius* Commission.[76]

---

[75] A. Ottow, 'Intrusion of public law into contract law: the case of network industries', The Europa Institute Utrecht Working Paper 2 (2012).

[76] J. Wouters, A. Marx and N. Hachez, 'In search of a balanced relationship: public and private food safety standards and international law', Leuven Centre for Global Governance Studies Working Paper 29 (2009).

Table 10.4 *The private law perspective*

	Individual phenomena	Field/branches	System/order	Hybrid legal space
Private	Fundamental rights before private law jurisdiction	Constitutionalised private law European regulatory private law	Private law society Private law as economic law	Pluralism of private legal orders Transnational private law
Perspective	Inward	Inward	Outward	Outward

2.5. Inward- and outward-looking (traditional private law)

The counterpart to the *inward*-looking, state-focused, constitutional perspective is what I would like to call the 'traditional private law' perspective. Here the focus is laid entirely on the private sphere in the sense Ulpian gave the term, in which autonomous citizens pursue their economic activities, establish firms and interact via contracts, and in which injuries and damages are balanced via tort law. This is what the ordo-liberals termed *Privatrechtsgesellschaft*,[77] again, a concept that made its way up to the European level.[78] The 'private law society' – strictly speaking the term '*Privatrechtsgesellschaft*' is untranslatable as it is a concept and not just a verbal composition – is inherently linked to the economic constitution. The role of the state is to adopt competition law rules to tame private power and guarantee liberty to the private sphere, staying away from regulatory interventions. In such a perspective there is no place for legal hybrids. Regulatory intervention, in particular via policy regulation largely linked to and identified with administrative law, is rejected as interference in the private sphere. Constitutional law has to shield the private sphere against politicisation through politically minded intervention.

I do not claim that the concept *Privatrechtsgesellschaft* is universal; in fact, it is not even widely recognised in Europe. However, the concept is paradigmatic for the separation of private from public law functions, though to a different degree in all market-based, democratic, legal orders.

---

[77] F. Böhm, 'Privatrechtsgesellschaft und Marktwirtschaft', *ORDO Jahrbuch für die Ordnung von Wirtschaft und Gesellschaft* 17 (1966), 75–151.
[78] E-J. Mestmäcker, 'Die Wiederkehr der bürgerlichen Gesellschaft und ihres Rechts', *Rechtshistorisches Journal* 10 (1991), 177–84; H. Collins, 'The European economic constitution and the constitutional dimension of private law', 5 *European Review of Contract Law* 2 (2009), 71–94, with contributions from J. Rutgers and H. Eidenmüller.

Traditional, national, private legal orders have emerged and are deeply rooted in the state-nation and nation-state building process of the eighteenth and nineteenth centuries in continental Europe. The starting point is private autonomy; freedom of contract, *la liberté de la volonté*. Interaction between different, nation-state, private legal orders is governed by the concept of private international law, which is based on a strict distinction between the public and the private.[79] Traditional private law is still alive. I would say it dominates the mindset of private lawyers in just the meaning that Walter van Gerven gave to it. The now-more-than-ten-year-old debate about the feasibility of a European Civil Code provides ample evidence for its vibrancy.[80]

The shift in focus from traditional private law to regulatory private law has accompanied private law from the early days of codifications, beginning with the French civil code that was adopted in 1804. The rise of labour law in the first half, and of consumer law in the second half, of the twentieth century led to conceptual irritations and even clashes between the now gradually emerging camps of private law, those interested in and focused on traditional private law and those specialised in what I call regulatory private law. The conceptual means to avoid changing perspective in the dominant private law research and doctrine is *either* to single out all sorts of laws that intervene in the private sphere and denominate these as public or administrative law that has to be kept distinct from the 'holy grail', *or* more recently to reintegrate regulatory private law through a process of scientification and depoliticisation.[81] Both strategies pursue an *inward*-looking perspective. The first keeps the traditional private law system intact by excluding all matters that do not fit into the traditional perspective, the second aims at reintegration without raising the question whether and to what extent reintegration deprives the respective subject matter of its particular legal and political context.

However, there has always been a different understanding of private law, in the sense of a political project that can be equated with an

---

[79] See the powerful reconstruction by Muir Watt, note 27 above.

[80] The official start might be dated to the Communication of the European Commission, although the European Parliament had been advocating a European Civil Code since the early 1990s.

[81] H-W. Micklitz, 'The expulsion of the concept of protection from the consumer law and the return of social elements in the civil law – a bittersweet polemic', 35 *Journal of Consumer Policy* 3 (2012), 283–96.

outward-looking perspective. Here private law is understood as economic law,[82] covering more than just contract and tort, or systematically speaking the continental codifications, but also public and private regulation of the economy. The regulatory law at that time mainly comprised labour and social laws, which were kept outside continental codifications. The German BGB, just like its counterparts the Codice Civile or the Code Civil, provided only a basic set of rules on contracts for services, the so-called *Dienstverträge*, setting aside the social concerns of labour lawyers who were already fighting for better protection of the legal position of dependent workers during the late nineteenth century. Today's regulatory private law cuts across all sectors of the economy and across policies. It lies in particular at the heart of service contracts for financial services, telecommunications, energy (electricity, gas), for (increasingly privatised) health care services, increasingly on educational services and last but not least on transport. Services amount to 70 per cent of gross income in the EU. The driving force behind all these rules that aim mainly at opening up markets, at establishing competition, at liberalising former public services, at promoting privatisation in former areas of public services, is undoubtedly the EU and international institutions. This finding seems to confirm Michael Taggart's forceful statement on the role of states. However, that conclusion might fall short as it does not take into account the changing pattern of the nation state and the EU which serves as a blueprint for this transformation, being interpreted elsewhere as a change from the nation state to the market state.[83]

The understanding of private law as economic law leads to a dramatic change in perspective, from *inward* to *outward*, from national private legal orders in their interaction between each other and with non-state law.[84] Suddenly the way is free to look at traditional private law in its interaction with public regulation, be it at national, European or international level. Just as regulatory private law emigrated from the national to the European

[82] H-D. Assmann, G. Brüggenmeier, D. Hart and C. Joerges (eds), *Wirtschaftsrecht als Kritik des Privatrechts: Beiträge zur Privat- und Wirtschaftsrechtstheorie* (Frankfurt: Athenäum, 1980).

[83] H-W. Micklitz and D. Patterson, 'From the nation state to the market: the evolution of EU private law' in B. van Vooren, S. Blockmans and J. Wouters (eds), *The EU's Role in Global Governance: The Legal Dimension* (Oxford: Oxford University Press, 2013), pp 59–78.

[84] See, for a revival of international private law as a discipline that reaches beyond scholastic exercises in solving the applicability of different legal systems and including the public policy domain, Joerges and Rödl, note 27 above, Muir Watt, note 27 above.

level in the 1990s in order to escape the tight grip of traditional private law, we can observe a shift to the international level, this time – at least seen through the lenses of a continental European private lawyer – to establish a new discipline of transnational private law which is said to have its roots in the *lex mercatoria*. This transnational private law constitutes the mirror image of global administrative law, at least as long as the subject matters listed above involve private parties, business organisations and NGOs in the making of the rules and in their enforcement. But it reaches beyond, as it is not bound and limited to cooperation within a public law framework of recognised, delegated lawmaking. Co-regulation is just one variant of transnational private law. Mere self-regulation within organisations, like *lex sportiva, lex digitalis* or the FSC, or in free-standing institutions like IOSCO or GLOBALG.A.P (Good Agricultural Practice),[85] belongs to the emerging field of transnational law. A new field of research has been opened up by Fabrizio Cafaggi in the Hague Institute for the Internationalisation of Law (HiiL) project on transnational private regulation, where he himself looks *inter alia* into contract governance.[86] Facts-based research analyses the way in which multinational companies introduce public policy commitments into their supply chains upwards to the producer – if they operate as buyers – or downwards to the consumer, if they operate as sellers.

2.6. On the four levels of legal hybrids (national private law and fundamental/human rights)

The level 1 type of issue is particularly prominent in the relationship between national private law and constitutional or European fundamental/human rights. The more advanced the constitutionalisation of private law, the more often the 'constitutional defence' might be raised before 'normal' courts. The civil courts then have to embark on a discussion of the constitutional implications of private law litigation. In countries like Germany, individual litigants are even entitled to argue that the national court has not respected the constitutional law and that

---

[85] See www.globalgap.org/uk_en/; N. Hachez and J. Wouters, 'A glimpse at the democratic legitimacy of private standards – democratic legitimacy as public accountability: the case of GLOBALG.A.P', 17 *Journal of International Economic Law* 3 (2011), 677–710.

[86] F. Cafaggi and P. Iamiceli, *Private Regulation and Industrial Organisation* (Fiesole: European University Institute Working Papers, 2012).

therefore the decision taken is 'unconstitutional'. The German constitutional complaint – called the *Verfassungsbeschwerde* – is often made by private parties, although successfully only to a very limited extent. If a particular procedural remedy such as a constitutional complaint is available, information on the interrelationship between the two legal orders is easily accessible. More complications arise when the national court does not address the tensions between legal orders in the written judgment, which makes decisions difficult to analyse. This form of hybrid plays a major role in the interrelation behind national law and European fundamental rights, where level 1 hybrids strongly interrelate with the hybrid legal space (level 4). It would be a marvellous research project to analyse the arguments of national courts that decide not to refer a case to Luxembourg. So far we have only limited, if not merely anecdotal, evidence.[87]

The level 2 hybrids in private law mirror those in constitutional and administrative law. What matters is the difference in perspective. The first field is constitutionalised private law. From a constitutional perspective there is no conceptual resistance to the intrusion of constitutional law into private law. From a private law perspective, there is conceptual resistance that might result from different values enshrined in the two legal orders. A perfect example to demonstrate the different perceptions is the litigation on the legality of Benetton advertising. The same legal question twice made its way to the Supreme Court and the German Constitutional Court.[88] The second field is labour and consumer law, to which could be added the law of regulated markets. Again, the perspective makes the difference. Administrative law looks very much into procedure, into the way in which the law is made and by whom and under what conditions, while private law focuses on the content of the rules, the rights and obligations established and the values enshrined. At least continental private lawyers would look for ways and means to systematise the various fields and whether common denominators tie the fields together. Understanding European regulatory private law as an emerging field, in which public and private domains/orders(?) merge, undermines such a way of thinking.

---

[87] House of Lords in *Director-General of Fair Trading* v. *First National Bank plc* [2001] UKHL 52; see on this H-W. Micklitz, 'Reforming European Union unfair terms legislation in consumer contracts', 6 *European Contract Law Review* 4 (2010), 347–83.

[88] See the analysis in H-W. Micklitz, J. Stuyck and E. Terryn (eds), *Cases, Materials and Text on Consumer Law (Ius Commune Casebooks for the Common Law of Europe)* (Oxford: Hart Publishing, 2010), p. 80ff.

Legal hybrids materialise only in a holistic approach in which procedural and substantive elements are combined – which is usually not the case.

Private law struggles hard to reconcile traditional private law with private law understood as economic law (level 3). This implies the recognition that private law as economic law is a viable concept that unites traditional private law concepts with regulatory private law. The ever-stronger existence of a hybrid legal space in which regulatory law is intertwined with European and international/transnational law/rules increases the difficulties with how the two systems of private law could be looked at from a holistic perspective. The problem is not new, but the ever-stronger impact of 'external' rules on national private legal systems has increased the tension. Seen this way, the level 3 conceptual question of the link between traditional private and emerging mixed private/public order is closely tied to the handling of the hybrid legal space at level 4. As the settled means of handling conflicts between conflicting legal orders international private law fails to grasp private law as economic law, under which the public and the private are no longer kept distinct.[89] We can observe diagonal conflicts between national and European/international legal rules, which require rethinking the role and function of international private law.[90] In being confronted with a multitude of legal orders, private law and constitutional law face comparable problems. Private law discusses legal pluralism, a dimension of legal thinking inherent to private law, the only major problem being the distinction between formal and informal authority in making private law.[91]

3. The three law perspectives read together – first interim thoughts

In taking the inward- and the outward-looking perspectives together, it seems possible to distinguish two levels of discussion, one more conceptual (level 3) and the other more thematic (level 2). We can set aside individual phenomena as they only matter in so far as they reach the second and the third level. The hybrid legal space (level 4) cuts across the boundaries of the different levels. They become more visible the more advanced the legal hybrids are. There is a steady increase from an

---

[89] Muir Watt, note 27 above.   [90] Joerges and Rödl, note 27 above.

[91] N. Jansen, 'Legal pluralism in Europe: national laws, European legislation, and non-legislative codifications' in L. Niglia (ed.), *Pluralism and European Private Law* (Oxford: Hart Publishing, 2013), pp 109–32.

individual phenomenon (level 1) over establishment of new fields (level 2) towards aggravating tensions between different systems (level 3).

3.1. Concepts, systems and orders

The conceptual layer is to be found in constitutional law and in traditional private law. Each of the two is largely defending its own self-portrait,[92] constitutional law focusing on 'the constitution', thereby setting aside what is called private law society (*Privatrechtsgesellschaft*), private law limiting itself to the private sphere, in which autonomous persons (citizens) interact according to their own (economic) preferences. Each of the two worlds remains hermetically sealed. Interaction is possible only in the cross-discipline, which means comparative constitutional law, constitutional pluralism or public international law. The same holds true for such an understanding of private law. Here communication is with other, national, private legal orders, their comparison and the relationship between national private legal orders, and international private law.

Both disciplines differ in the degree to which they turn their perspective from inward to outward, from constitutional law to private law, or from private to constitutional law. Constitutionalisation of private law ranks high on the research agenda. For the good or the bad private law research is drifting – this is subject to a fierce debate on the foundations of private law – into accepting the need to discuss the constitutional impact on private law. This should not be confounded with acceptance of the impact itself. However, an important disclaimer must be made. Most of the discussion turns around the impact of the *national* constitution on *national* private law.[93] The closet – I borrow this telling metaphor from Horatia Muir Watt (it comes close to what is called in German *Kästchendenken* – thinking in categorical boxes)[94] – is enlarged from the *national* private legal order to the *national* constitutional order, but there is no research on the cross-border impact of the national constitutionalisation of national private law on the constitution/private legal order of another (Member) State.

---

[92] M. de S.-O.-l'E. Lasser, 'Judicial (self-) portraits: judicial discourse in the French legal system', 104 *Yale Law Journal* 6 (1995), 1325–1410.

[93] See Mak, note 51 above; Cherednychenko, note 51 above.

[94] Muir Watt, note 27 above, where she uses 'closet' to demonstrate and to analyse the insularity or the seclusion of the system of international private law in mainstream nineteenth- and twentieth-century legal thinking. In German 'closet' sounds like *Klosett* (toilet), which is less intriguing.

The *Bürgschaftsurteil* of the German Constitutional Court recognised the structurally inferior position assigned to consumers (*strukturelle Unterlegenheit des Verbrauchers*) and declared family guarantees under certain conditions as violating the German constitution.[95] How could a conflict between constitutionalised private law and the non-constitutionalised common law in Germany be resolved?[96] Does the constitutional 'upgrading' of consumer rights in Germany affect the choice of jurisdiction and/or the choice of law? It is commonly agreed that it is for the parties' discretion to invoke the choice of jurisdictions/conflict of laws. Can the UK Supreme Court simply reject the argument of the consumer that he is better protected in his own country? How far does the autonomy of the consumer reach to choose the applicable law?[97] Do constitutionalised private law positions meet the requirements of Article 6 (2) or even Article 9 of the Rome I Regulation?[98] In case substantive law is fully or partly harmonised, is there now an *ex officio* obligation on the national court in charge,[99] let us assume the Supreme Court of the UK, to investigate the applicability of Article 6(2) and Article 9 Rome I Regulation for the benefit of the German consumer who is defending his

[95] *Entscheidungen des Bundesverfassungsgerichts* (Collection of the judgments of the German Constitutional Court volume) 89, 214.

[96] This is not far-fetched; for the divergence between the bank charges judgment of the UK Supreme Court and the position of the German Supreme Court (not constitutional court), see H. Kötz, 'Schranken der Inhaltskontrolle bei den Allgemeinen Geschäftsbedingungen der Banken: Entscheidung des britischen Supreme Court vom 25. November 2009', *Zeitschrift für europäisches Privatrecht* 2 (2012), 332–50.

[97] J. Smits, 'A radical view of legal pluralism' in Niglia, note 91 above, pp 161–71.

[98] See Regulation (EC) No 593/2008 of the European Parliament and of the Council on the law applicable to contractual obligations (*Rome I*) (OJ 2008 L177, pp 6–16), Arts 6(2) and 7.

[99] In Case C–618/10 *Banco Español*, nyr, the CJEU extended its *ex officio* doctrine to Regulation (EC) No 1896/2006, thereby imposing on the national authority in charge of issuing the payment order the obligation to find out whether the contract in question contains unfair terms that might jeopardise the rights of the consumer. Para. 53:

> In that context, it must be stated that such a procedural arrangement, which completely prevents the court before which an application for order for payment has been brought to assess of its own motion, *in limine litis* or at any other stage during the proceedings, even though it already has all the legal and factual elements necessary for that task available to it, whether terms contained in a contract concluded between a seller or supplier and a consumer are unfair where that consumer has not lodged an objection, is liable to undermine the effectiveness of the protection intended by Directive 93/13 (see, to that effect, Case C–473/00 *Cofidis* [2002] ECR I–10875, para. 35).

See also D. Bureau and H. Muir Watt, *Droit international privé* (Paris: Presses Universitaires de France, 2007).

German-constitutionalised, private rights before an English court? We know even less whether the reference point for national private law is not a national constitutional order, but the European Charter of Fundamental Rights or the European Convention on Human Rights,[100] not to mention the lack of attention constitutional lawyers devote to this development. In sum, what is needed is a much deeper analysis of the link between constitutional and private legal orders. Two whole systems of law have to be interconnected. The case law of the courts, national and European – meaning the reality, the facts – is far ahead of the theoretical/doctrinal reflection on the growing interplay between constitutional law and national private law.

3.2. Themes, fields and branches

The thematic layer can be identified in the interplay of administrative private law and private law. Here the interpenetration of the two fields of law is much more advanced. Kaarlo Tuori calls transnational law 'the true El Dorado of legal hybrids'.[101] By thematic layer I mean first and foremost that private lawyers and administrative lawyers discuss the same set of issues, mainly based on some sort of co-regulation. This means neither that the two perspectives have merged, nor that the two disciplines communicate or even are able to communicate. This is just another variant to catch legal hybrids beyond individual phenomena.

Even if administrative and private lawyers discuss the same set of issues, e.g. standardisation, their perspectives differ. Administrative lawyers focus on the *process* of lawmaking, the rules and procedures to be applied, as well as on enforcement via statutory agencies. Private lawyers concentrate on the *substance* of standards and their impact on contract and tort. Administrative lawyers working in this area are specialists. Private lawyers using contract and tort as analytical devices are generalists. The result of this form of perspectivism is a mutual claim of incompetence. As a participant in numerous conferences in the field and having done empirical research myself on technical standardisation, on health and safety standardisation and on the elaboration of technical rules in the financial sector, I have

---

[100] This is a black box on which research has to be directed. See on the impact of the right to be heard, Art. 6 ECHR, on jurisdiction clauses in family matters, H. Muir Watt, 'Conflict and resistance – the national private law response' in H.-W. Micklitz and Svetiev, note 3 above, pp 115–18.
[101] Tuori, note 3 above.

realised the enormous difficulties in finding a common approach and a common language for the same object of research. The common theme (standardisation) constitutes the joint intersection of two different perspectives. There is no such thing as holistic research in that area. The closet remains closed despite a joint theme and joint interest.

3.3. Closing and opening – a plea for the search for the new

Thematic-bound empirical research produces its own limitations. In the light of the so far rather limited set of identified hybrids, there is pressure to chase after new phenomena. Looking into facts produces a particular form of addiction. Ever more facts are needed to support the identification of level 2 hybrids. Two options are working in opposite directions. The first option is reintegration into separate systems. This option leaves the public/private divide largely unaffected at the expense of eradicating what is 'new', what is unknown, what is as yet unexplainable. The other option is to focus on 'newness', to make the 'newness' explicit and to interconnect the various fields (level 2) that are subject to research either in administrative or private law. It is my strong conviction that administrative and private lawyers have to find a common theoretical framework that takes both sides into consideration. The new law between private and administrative law might contain what we cannot yet put into words: an emerging new legal order, which unites elements of public and private in a truly innovative way, representing what is so far enshrined in catchphrases like postmodern society, postmodernism and the like. I suggest that we are in search of a new theory, a new model, a new toolbox, which allows us to understand ongoing developments. What is needed is a holistic theoretical framework that could serve as the starting point for developing a joint research methodology. It seems indispensable to keep theory and methodology distinct. Mere methodology cannot replace missing theory.

4. The public/private divide – process or loop – an outlook

Bringing together the analysis of the different levels of legal hybrids and the process of hybridisation, we may find first and foremost a strong need to take Akira Kurosawa seriously, to leave our thinking in legal boxes behind us and to engage in a dialogue that will not find the 'objective truth', but relativise our own position, including that of this author.

It is in this spirit that we should try to identify 'what we conceive but cannot couch in terms'. The foregoing analysis has focused on trying to understand what lies behind the public/private divide and what kind of hybrids we might find in law, public or private, national, European or international. It is more than a snapshot of where we stand, as it combines an analysis of hybrids with the process of hybridisation. This is enshrined in the distinction between the four levels that suggests the existence of a process.

What I have not yet done so far is to discuss the process itself, who or what lies behind the process and where the process of hybridisation might lead to. Is it a *linear* process that requires a new understanding of the public and the private or is it a *loop*, around which the vanishing of the public/private divide might trigger restoration of the public against the private or the private against the public? Duncan Kennedy rejected any attempt to get to grips with the public/private divide by thinking of it as a linear process that could be caught in categories such as 'intermediate terms (hybrids)', 'collapse (distinction is useless)', 'continuumization' or 'stereotypification'.[102] He advocated *loopification* as the appropriate change of approach with which to comprehend the public/private divide. 'One's consciousness is loopified when one seems to be able to move by a steady series of steps around the whole distinction [between public/private], ending up where one started without ever reversing direction'.

Transferred to our findings, we locate the public/private divide in post-Westphalian times. The result would be that the division between public and private in the seventeenth and eighteenth centuries might be substituted by legal hybrids in the nineteenth and twentieth centuries. A possible next step would then lead to re-establishing the public/private divide in the twenty-first century. This is exactly what Duncan Kennedy catches by 'loopification'. Loopification of the public/private divide comes near to the understanding that in Europe we are currently moving backwards towards the Middle Ages. Quite opposite to loopification, the idea of history as a process suggests that postmodern society will yield a new understanding of the public and the private.

In my previous research I have looked into the process under the formula of transformation of the state, from state nation to nation state to market state, and its impact on private law. The changing role and function of the state has been at the forefront of an abundant literature for more

---

[102] D. Kennedy, 'The stages of the decline of the public/private distinction', 130 *University of Pennsylvania Law Review* (1982), 1349–57 at 1354.

than a decade.[103] There is agreement that the state is changing, but there is disagreement as to how and in what direction it is developing. Translated to the distinction between state nation, nation state and market state, I would link the emergent state nation in the seventeenth and eighteenth centuries to the rise of the public/private divide, the nation state of the nineteenth and twentieth centuries to the early development of hybrids in all variations and the twenty-first century to the full development of the market state in which the vanishing of the divide is open-ended and the future of the divide uncertain, since it requires redefinition of the role of the state and the functions of the private.

What is needed and what goes beyond the scope of this chapter is to discuss who and what triggers 'transformation' of the public/private divide, transformation of the state but also of the private. 'Transformation' is not a self-triggered process. In my search for the drivers behind 'transformation', I come to the conclusion that it is possible and feasible to identify three major parameters: economy, technology and civil society. These drivers would then have to be linked to the public/private divide as here enshrined in the process of hybridisation of constitutional, administrative and private law. This will be the next step in my research.

---

[103] P. Bobbitt, *The Shield of Achilles: War, Peace and the Course of History* (New York: Knopf, 2002); Sassen, note 70 above.

11

Private law in a post-national society

From *ex post* to *ex ante* governance

JAN M. SMITS

1. Introduction

The focus is on the field of private law in this contribution to the cooperative search for interpretative and normative grids needed in charting our contemporary legal landscape.[1] My aim is to show that we can only understand the main changes caused by globalisation and Europeanisation in this field if we turn away from substantive law and analyse the changing role of law itself. I claim that, as a result of increasing economic globalisation and technological progress, the power of state-made law to govern relationships among private parties is decreasing and that, as a result, private actors increasingly turn towards different types of arrangement that as far as possible avoid applicability of (default) state-made law. I term this a development from *ex post* to *ex ante* governance of private relationships.

It is clear that this shift is only one of many developments caused by the increasing Europeanisation and globalisation of private law. The rise of transnational law is also reflected in changes in substantive law (though mostly limited to European influence owing to a lack of meaningful global institutions in this field),[2] in perceptions about the role of social justice,[3] in the erosion of the public/private distinction,[4] and in a turn towards a more instrumental private law (related to, but not limited to,

---

[1] See Tuori in Chapter 1 of this volume.

[2] See for a recent overview R. Zimmermann, 'The present state of European private law', 57 *American Journal of Comparative Law* 2 (2009), 479–512.

[3] See e.g. Study Group on Social Justice in European Private Law, 'Social justice in European contract law: a manifesto', 10 *European Law Journal* 6 (2004), 653–74 and P. Zumbansen, 'Law after the welfare state: formalism, functionalism, and the ironic turn of reflexive law', 56 *American Journal of Comparative Law* 3 (2008), 769–808.

[4] Cf. the contribution of H-W. Micklitz to this book and e.g. M. Freedland, 'The evolving approach to the public/private distinction in English law' in M. Freedland and J-B. Auby

the European Union).[5] Although these developments are important, they do not fully grasp the real influence of increasing transnationalisation. In my view, the most important aspect of denationalisation of law is that *the law itself* is being increasingly replaced by other mechanisms to achieve similar goals. This contribution puts 'delivering legality' – as Marc Galanter famously said[6] – beyond the law at the centre of attention. It may be argued that this development can be particularly noticed in the field of private law because of its relatively low quantity of mandatory rules and the freedom it thus leaves actors to shape their relationship in the way they prefer.[7] However, as we shall see in the following, the move away from law towards alternative modes of governance is certainly not limited to facilitative rules. Mandatory rules may stand in the way of achieving the 'legality' that actors prefer, and this is precisely the fact that is likely to lead to a desire to circumvent existing national laws.

From a methodological viewpoint, the only way to draw conclusions about the changing role of law is by adopting a perspective that is external to the law itself. The method used in this contribution is therefore a functional one: the assumption is that private law performs certain functions and that the way in which these functions are achieved not only develops over time, but can also differ from one place to another.[8] This

---

(eds), *The Public Law/Private Law Divide: Une Entente assez Cordiale?* (Oxford: Hart Publishing, 2006), pp 93–108, and F. Bydlinski, 'Kriterien und Sinn der Unterscheidung von Privatrecht und Öffentlichem Recht', *Archiv für die Civilistische Praxis* 194 (1994), 319–51.

[5] Cf. H-W. Micklitz, 'The visible hand of European regulatory private law', 28 *Yearbook of European Law* 1 (2009), 3–59. See for these, and other, developments R. Michaels and N. Jansen, 'Private law beyond the state? Europeanization, globalization, privatization', 54 *American Journal of Comparative Law* 4 (2006), 843–90; N. Jansen and R. Michaels, 'Private law and the state: comparative perceptions and historical observations', 71 *Rabels Zeitschrift* 2 (2007), 345–97, and the special issue 56 *American Journal of Comparative Law* 3 (2008), 527–844.

[6] M. Galanter, 'Delivering legality: some proposals for the direction of research', 11 *Law & Society Review* 2 (1976), 225–46.

[7] See also H. Dagan, 'Autonomy, pluralism, and contract law theory', *Law and Contemporary Problems* (2013), 19–38. Dagan claims that private law is about offering people a repertoire of multiple and sufficiently diverse institutions for structuring their interpersonal relationships.

[8] For a similar effort in the field of constitutional law, see J. Dunoff and J. Trachtman, 'A functional approach to international constitutionalization' in Dunoff and Trachtman (eds), *Ruling the World? Constitutionalism, International Law, and Global Governance* (Cambridge: Cambridge University Press, 2009), pp 3–35. I realise that the functional approach ultimately requires a definition of what amounts to law in a global society. See on this question and how it relates to functionalism W. Twining, *General Jurisprudence: Understanding Law from a Global Perspective* (Cambridge: Cambridge University Press, 2009), p. 88ff.

approach allows us to see the law as only one possible alternative way to achieve a specific societal goal or a desire held by private actors. This is also the reason why terms such as 'transnational law' and 'global law' can be misleading:[9] in so far as they suggest a departure from what William Twining calls 'black box theories' based on the coexistence of territorially differentiated, national, legal orders,[10] they only refer to a change in *the law itself*, not in the function that law has in a post-national society. I therefore prefer the term 'transnationalisation' or 'denationalisation.'

My focus is on what are arguably three essential functions of private law: rulemaking, enforcement and dispute resolution. These are functions that play a role not only in the core areas of contracts, tort and property, but also in related fields such as intellectual property law, corporate law, environmental law, competition law and cyberlaw – and arguably also outside private law, broadly understood.[11] All these fields face similar problems of rulemaking (including identification of the 'right' substantive legal norm), of effective enforcement and of dealing with (potential) conflicts. It will be shown that our legal thinking about all three functions is still state-centred and that there is a need to rethink them in view of globalisation and technological development. Even though this is obviously no easy task – our way of thinking about law is so much shaped by the division of societies along nation-state lines that this is often seen as the natural way to organise things[12] – it is possible to make an effort.

2. Rulemaking: the turn towards private regulation and choice of law

The relationship between rulemaking and private law is an interesting one. Unlike the case in, e.g., administrative law and criminal law, in principle parties are free to decide how they want to shape their two-way relationship. This is reflected in the nature of most private law rules

---

[9] Cf. Jessup's (too limited) definition of transnational law as 'all law which regulates actions or events that transcend national frontiers'. P. Jessup, *Transnational Law* (New Haven, CT: Yale University Press, 1956), p. 2.

[10] W. Twining, *Globalisation and Legal Theory* (Cambridge: Cambridge University Press, 2000), p. 8.

[11] I make no attempt to define private law further than that it is about governance of the relationship between private actors. On the various ways to define private law, see Michaels and Jansen, 'Private law beyond the state?', note 5 above at p. 846ff.

[12] Cf. A. Wimmer and N. Schiller, 'Methodological nationalism and beyond: nation-state building, migration and the social sciences', 2 *Global Networks* 4 (2002), 301–34 at 304.

provided by national lawmakers: to a large extent these rules contain only default law, meaning that parties can deviate if they prefer to do so. It is true that this freedom is restricted by national legislatures' public policies, but these only rarely concern external social values.[13] It is commonly accepted that the primary aim of the core areas of private law is not to pursue redistribution of wealth or some other policy goal.[14] This may be different if the legislature aims to pursue specific regulatory goals – as is usually the case at the European level[15] – but the great majority of national private laws do not have this ambition. This implies that, unlike fields in which the public interest is of overriding importance, the national lawmaker produces rules to facilitate private actors for reasons at least partly different from those prompting regulation in other areas of the law.

The reasons why a national legislature is suited to provide rules on private law seem to be threefold. First, to codify or create rules at the level of national states can provide these rules with democratic legitimacy through the availability of a parliamentary procedure. Even though historically many rules of private law derived their legitimacy from the fact that they were accepted in practice,[16] in the nineteenth century legislative intervention was seen as necessary to provide a more formal underpinning to their applicability. Second, national rulemaking can serve to unify previously divergent laws, with a view not only to pursuing equality among citizens and to satisfying economic needs (creation of a market), but also to contributing to nation building.[17] In the civil law tradition codification traditionally performs both functions.[18] The third function of rulemaking is arguably even more important: it is to provide information about the law in such a way that it is easily accessible and predictable, thus contributing to legal certainty and through this to the stability and rationality of

[13] Cf. H. Dagan, 'The limited autonomy of private law', 56 *American Journal of Comparative Law* 3 (2008), 809–33 at 823.

[14] Cf. C. Fried, *Contract as Promise* (Cambridge, MA: Harvard University Press, 1981), p. 106; see, however, Study Group on Social Justice, 'Manifesto', note 3 above at 653.

[15] Cf. H-W. Micklitz and Y. Svetiev (eds), *A Self-sufficient European Private Law: A Viable Concept* (Fiesole: European University Institute Working Papers, 2012).

[16] See N. Jansen, *The Making of Legal Authority* (Oxford: Oxford University Press, 2010).

[17] See recently J. M. Smits, 'What do nationalists maximise? A public choice perspective on the (non-)Europeanisation of private law', 8 *European Review of Contract Law* (2012), 296–310.

[18] Cf. J. Maillet, 'The historical significance of French codifications', 44 *Tulane Law Review* (1969–70), 681–703.

the law.[19] In the civil law tradition, codification is the most important way to realise this, but in both the common law and the Nordic legal traditions national rulemaking (by the highest courts through the system of precedent and through specific statutes) fills the need for a more accessible, more certain law.

The question is whether these functions of providing legitimacy, uniformity and accessibility, and legal certainty are still satisfied today in the best possible way through national rulemaking. I have argued elsewhere that, for normative reasons, this is no longer necessarily the case within the (Member States of the) European Union.[20] But the argument also applies on the global level. If we take for example the important function of providing accessibility to and certainty of the law, it is clear that national states are no longer able to guarantee this. If one is to describe by which rules the rights and obligations of private actors are influenced in today's world, national law only plays a limited role. Relevant rules are increasingly found in the products of European and international lawgivers (both legislatures and courts), but also in private regulation.[21] Moreover, the core element of economic globalisation is that parties are increasingly active in a global market through which use of their 'own', default, national law often becomes obsolete, either because they physically move to another country or because they are able to make use of enhanced possibilities for choice of law.

The focus in this chapter is not on these normative consequences of the change in relative importance of national rulemaking, but on what it means for the behaviour of private actors. My claim is that if the demand for legal certainty or for an accessible law can no longer be met by national states for the reasons set out above, parties are inclined to shy away from state law and to turn towards privately created orders instead. These orders include not only large functional systems such as the international law merchant (*lex mercatoria*) and transnational sport law (*lex sportiva*),[22] but

---

[19] See in more detail J. M. Smits, 'Codification without democracy? On the legitimacy of a European (optional) code of contract law' in C. Joerges and T. Ralli (eds), *European Constitutionalism without Private Law – Private Law without Democracy?* (Oslo: ARENA Centre for European Studies, 2011), pp 127–40.

[20] See J. M. Smits, 'Democracy and (European) private law: a functional approach', 2 *European Journal of Legal Studies* (2009), 26–40.

[21] Cf. G. Teubner, 'Breaking frames: the global interplay of legal and social systems', 45 *American Journal of Comparative Law* 1 (1997), 149–69 at 157.

[22] Cf. Michaels and Jansen, 'Private law beyond the state?', note 5 above at 869ff.

also the use of general conditions in business-to-consumer transactions and private rulemaking in certain types of trade.[23] These private regimes offer what a national legal system is not able to provide: a set of rules that is not territorially limited and that allows actors to be easily informed.[24] Alternatively, parties can still make use of state law, but not necessarily that of their own jurisdiction applicable by default. Instead, they are able to choose a foreign law to apply to some specific aspect of their activities.[25] In both cases, provision of the public good of legal certainty is highly influenced by the proactive attitude of private actors. This means that, in order to avoid the automatic and *ex post* (after the relevant event took place) applicability of default national law, *ex ante* actors replace this law with rules to their own liking that better meet their demands. This implies that the role of law changes fundamentally: instead of relying on rules provided by the national, democratic lawgiver, (non-mandatory) default law is seen as just one possible set of rules that can be set aside if needed. This development can be easily explained: if the supply side (the state or other legislature at whatever geographical level) is no longer able to provide an accessible or sufficiently certain set of laws because of increasing plurality of sources, the demand side (consisting of private actors) is likely to search for alternatives and to escape state law as far as possible.

One aspect of this development towards private regulation and choice of law deserves special attention: the role of information. At present, not every party has the possibility to replace *ex post* reliance on default laws with an *ex ante* choice of a private legal regime or a foreign law, simply because it lacks the information needed to make that choice. In practice only companies and wealthy individuals are able to engage in

---

[23] The diamond industry is a well-known example: see L. Bernstein, 'Opting out of the legal system: extralegal contractual relations in the diamond industry', 21 *Journal of Legal Studies* 1 (1992), 115–57.

[24] See also G. Calliess, 'The future of commercial law: governing cross-border commerce' in S. Muller, S. Zouridis, M. Frishman and L. Kistemaker (eds), *The Law of the Future and the Future of Law* (Oslo: Torkel Opsahl Academic EPublisher, 2011), p. 235, and V. Gessner, 'Towards a theoretical framework for contractual certainty in global trade' in Gessner (ed.), *Contractual Certainty in International Trade* (Oxford: Hart Publishing, 2008), pp 3–27.

[25] The classic reference is E. O'Hara and L. Ribstein, *The Law Market* (Oxford: Oxford University Press, 2009). For empirical evidence on the extent to which parties opt out of their own laws, see the Oxford Civil Justice Survey, available at http://denning.law.ox.ac. uk/iecl/ocjsurvey.shtml.

this type of conduct. Jeremy Bentham lamented in the late eighteenth century that English law was only accessible to a small group of people, leading him to argue in favour of codification and the 'cognoscibility' of law that this would bring with it.[26] One might well argue that the present situation is not very different: even if people have some idea of their own national law, they are agnostic as to the possibilities of opting out of it. I agree with Richard Susskind that this calls for making available 'straightforward, no-nonsense, online legal guidance systems' that inform people about the law.[27] Technology can play an important role in making these systems. In my view, they should not just limit themselves to providing legal information but should also allow users to compare different national jurisdictions and private regimes with each other in much the same way as is already possible today on websites for comparing and reviewing products.[28] This calls for development of criteria for comparison and ranking of entire jurisdictions and of specific parts thereof.

The development of such criteria is no easy task. A well-known method, used by the World Bank,[29] is to assess jurisdictions on the extent to which they are suited to the needs of business. However, the methodology of this ranking is highly criticised.[30] Other rankings consider the extent to which a jurisdiction complies with the requirements of the rule of law.[31] We need more ranking methods that also include other criteria, including the satisfaction of actual end-users (consumers, citizens or firms) of the specific jurisdiction. A major problem in developing this method is that these end-users, when assessing the quality of a jurisdiction, are not always able to identify the elements specific to the law. For example, when a party is asked how it assesses the quality of a substantive rule that governs a dispute, the outcome of the dispute is likely to blur its judgement.

---

[26] Cf. J. Bowring (ed.), *The Works of Jeremy Bentham* (Edinburgh: William Tait, 1843), vol. IV, p. 454, and R. van Caenegem, *Judges, Legislators and Professors: Chapters in European Legal History* (Cambridge: Cambridge University Press, 1987), p. 161.

[27] R. Susskind, *The End of Lawyers? Rethinking the Nature of Legal Services* (Oxford: Oxford University Press), p. 234; cf. J. M. Smits, *Private Law 2.0: On the Role of Private Actors in a Post-National Society* (The Hague: HiiL and Eleven International Publishing, 2011).

[28] See e.g. www.pricerunner.co.uk and www.kelkoo.com (comparison) and e.g. www.epinions.com and www.booking.com (review).

[29] See World Bank Doing Business 2012, available at www.doingbusiness.org.

[30] An extensive account of the methodology used can be found in M. Faure and J. M. Smits (eds), *Does Law Matter? On Law and Economic Growth* (Cambridge: Intersentia, 2011).

[31] S.-E. Skaaning, 'Measuring the rule of law', 63 *Political Research Quarterly* 2 (2010), 449–60.

3. From state enforcement to self-enforcement

The second traditional function of the state is that it facilitates enforcement of the applicable private law. In a Westphalian view, the state has a
monopoly on both drafting substantive rules and enforcement of those
rules through the national courts. While the first monopoly is rapidly
eroding (as we just saw), the second still largely exists: enforcement of
law essentially remains in the hands of national state institutions (or,
in some specific fields, of European agencies entrusted with this task by
Member States). This can easily be understood: while today's problems
may be increasingly global, our institutions are not. It is even inherent
to enforcement that it takes place through state institutions, either at the
initiative of the state itself or by private actors initiating proceedings in
its courts.[32] Thus private actors and other international rule-setters still
need to rely on the teeth of national courts to enable their addressees to
claim their rights.

This age-old jurisdictional approach, based on the territorial division
of competences, makes enforcement complicated in cross-border cases.
A party active in the European or global market would wish to be able to
enforce its rights by addressing only one court that gives a decision that
binds the entire market in which it is active. However, this is generally not
the case. Despite attempts to overcome the territorial limitations of the
traditional approach through techniques of private international law,[33]
at the end of the day this does not provide a very attractive solution. While
the European legislature is now competent to act in the field of civil justice,
and can for example broaden the international jurisdiction of national
courts and enhance mutual recognition, this is much more difficult to
achieve at the global level since it requires each individual state to change
its own laws on a purely voluntary basis. Litigation of an international case
in a national court is therefore often seen as 'unproductive'.[34] Arbitration
and mediation (as discussed in the next section) do not offer a real solution
for this enforcement problem because these dispute settlement techniques

---

[32] I am not concerned here with the question of what is the optimal mix of public and private
enforcement, as discussed in particular in (European) competition and consumer law.

[33] In the European Union in particular through the Rome I, Rome II and Rome III Regulations on (respectively) contractual obligations (593/2008/EC), non-contractual obligations (864/2007/EC) and divorce and legal separation (1259/2010/EU).

[34] See M. Scheltema, 'Does CSR need more (effective) private regulation in the future?' in
Muller, Zouridis, Frishman and Kistemaker, note 24 above, Vol. II (The Hague: Torkel
Opsahl Academic EPublisher, 2012), pp 389–99.

are still dependent on state courts when it comes to enforcement of an arbitral award or a mediation agreement.

It is therefore much more likely that, as a result of transnationalisation, a similar phenomenon will occur to that we just identified in the field of rulemaking. If the demand for effective enforcement cannot be met by state law, parties will turn towards other (non-legal) types of enforcement or adopt devices that allow them to completely avoid enforcement. One important mechanism (*ex ante* reliance on reputation instead of *ex post* addressing the law in case things go wrong) prevents a party from entering into a transaction at all and will be discussed in the next section. My focus here is on the use of 'self-enforcing' agreements.[35] What one would expect to happen in the absence of a meaningful global enforcement mechanism by way of law is that a party decides for itself whether it wants to take the risk of initiating or continuing a relation with other parties and will design its own practical mechanisms to ensure that it does not need to make use of the law in case things go wrong. This could mean that one party will only perform if it has received pre-payment, or some other type of security guaranteeing that the other party will in fact carry out its obligations. This was recently confirmed in empirical research on relationships among commercial parties in the software industry carried out by Thomas Dietz.[36] Dietz shows that parties tend to agree to deliver and pay in instalments matched to the progress of the project. Once the last milestone is completed and a party is still dependent on the other party to cure possible faults, it tends to delay the last payment for as long as possible (until it knows performance was correct), or decides to place a new order with the same party in order to keep the latter dependent. Dietz concludes that '[parties] design the exchange in such a way that contracts are fulfilled without outside intervention'.[37]

It must be noted that this self-enforcement mechanism is not available under all circumstances. It plays a larger role in relational transactions and where parties already know each other (as in franchising, distribution and agency agreements) than in one-shot exchanges between parties at

---

[35] The foundations of these can be found in L. Telser, 'A theory of self-enforcing agreements', 53 *The Journal of Business* 1 (1980), 27–44.

[36] T. Dietz, 'Contract law, relational contracts, and reputational networks in international trade: an empirical investigation into cross-border contracts in the software industry', 37 *Law and Social Inquiry* 1 (2012), 25–57 at 43 and 47.

[37] *Ibid.* at 54.

arm's length (as in a single contract of sale).[38] However, in these cases self-enforcement does offer a viable alternative to legal enforcement through the state. In a way like that in which *ex post* reliance on default laws is replaced by private regulation or by choice of law (as was seen in section 2), the very possibility of having to enforce an agreement in the courts can be minimised by the mechanism of self-enforcement.

4. From dispute resolution to reliance on reputational networks

Dispute resolution is the third function of state law previously identified as an essential element of a well-functioning system of private law. Effective access to justice is not only guaranteed in most national constitutions, it is also laid down in Article 6(1) of the European Convention on Human Rights. Although this does confirm the great importance attached to this principle, one cannot say that national states provide private actors with an attractive form of dispute resolution, particularly not in a cross-border situation. It is a familiar refrain that, despite the globalisation of trade, of environmental concerns, of competition among companies, etc., there is no such thing as an effective global trade law, consumer sales law, environmental law or competition law. This absence is felt in particular when it comes to effective dispute resolution. Gralf-Peter Calliess makes this point in the following way: 'state courts are slow (e.g. stages of appeal), inflexible (e.g. with regard to language), partial (so-called home-state bias *vis-à-vis* foreigners), too expensive (e.g. with regard to small claims), unreliable (e.g. regarding enforcement of foreign judgments), or even corrupt (e.g. in low developed countries)'.[39]

These deficiencies of the state court system are gradually leading to two different shifts. The first is a development from the use of state courts in resolving disputes towards forms of private justice. These include arbitration, mediation and other types of alternative dispute resolution.

---

[38] Cf. D. North, *Institutions, Institutional Change and Economic Performance* (Cambridge: Cambridge University Press, 1990), p. 55:

> The most likely and indeed empirically observable state in which contracts are self-enforcing is that in which the parties have a great deal of knowledge about each other ... Under these conditions, it simply pays to live up to agreements. In such a world, the measured costs of transacting are very low because of dense social networks interaction. Cheating, shirking, opportunism, all problems of modern industrial organization, are limited or indeed absent because they do not pay.

[39] Calliess, note 24 above, p. 236.

The development that is probably most related to the globalisation of commerce is the rise of online dispute resolution. Not only are quick and effective dispute resolution schemes offered by eBay and other Internet companies popular;[40] they also lead to initiatives by official institutions to create 'cyber-courts' themselves in order to remain competitive in the market for civil justice. In particular in contractual disputes between consumers and traders, online out-of-court resolution is seen as a good alternative to the slow and expensive state court system.[41] Indeed, this makes a lot of sense: in particular if the contract itself was concluded by electronic means, often with a buyer located in a different country than the seller, it is ineffective to have a national court decide a potential dispute.

The second shift is in my view even more important. This is the gradual development from dispute resolution to dispute avoidance. Private actors prefer to address the challenges of globalisation by replacing their *ex post* reliance on courts (or other external providers of justice) for an *ex ante* avoidance of possible disputes. Again, as with rulemaking and enforcement, if national law is no longer in demand and global law does not exist, alternative mechanisms are sought to order the relationship. These mechanisms allow a party to assess the risk of default by the other party before even entering into the transaction.

It is no surprise that social networks traditionally play an important role in this process of alternative arrangements. David Charny wrote in 1990:

> One key to effective reputational controls is a system for transmitting relevant information to market participants... Collective reputational enforcement should work well... in markets limited to small numbers, homogenous groups of individuals who are in frequent contact and thus can share relevant information. These markets are, of course, relatively rare. Conversely mass markets based on reputational bonds are feasible only with technology that conveys information cheaply to a large group of transactors.[42]

The most interesting aspect of this view is that what Charny considered impossible in 1990 has become possible today: owing to the rise

---

[40] See http://resolutioncenter.ebay.com and e.g. www.modria.com and www.e-court.nl. On this development in general: Susskind, note 27 above, p. 217ff.

[41] See also the recent European Commission's Proposal for a Regulation on online dispute resolution for consumer disputes (Regulation on consumer ODR), COM (2011) 794 final.

[42] D. Charny, 'Nonlegal sanctions in commercial relationships', 104 *Harvard Law Review* 2 (1990), 373–467 at 373.

of the Internet, reputational networks need no longer be based on close social contacts. Perfect strangers are often able to assess the reliability of other parties through websites that give information about their previous behaviour. Put differently: the trust needed among people who do not form part of a small, homogeneous group, and thus do not know each other, is not necessarily created by the law. It can also come into existence by the reputational networks that new technologies help to create. In turn, in the absence of a global law, the rise of transactions in cyberspace increases the need for trust-creating devices.[43] These range from implementation of domain-name registration and dispute resolution through private bodies such as the Internet Corporation for Assigned Names and Numbers (ICANN) and encryption and digital certificates,[44] to websites that identify bad payers,[45] parties willing to pay bribes,[46] or parties not acting in conformity with codes of corporate social responsibility.[47] These new trust-creating devices come next to the more traditional ways in which parties can assess the reliability of another (foreign) party. In the case of larger companies, reliability may be judged on the basis of information from professional standardisation bodies (such as ISO), but it is more likely that a party simply carries out a reliability check itself by scrutiny of the company's website or a physical visit.[48] On the other hand, consumers considering buying products from unknown professional sellers on the Internet are also likely to carry out an initial web search in order to retrieve information about the reputation of the other party, or alternatively rely on safety certificates issued by associations

---

[43] Cf. G. Hadfield, 'Delivering legality on the internet: developing principles for the private provision of commercial law', 6 *American Law and Economics Review* 1 (2004), 154–84 at 155: 'How does one trust an entity that may lack any physical location or reside outside the jurisdiction of local law enforcement to protect credit card numbers, or deliver quality goods or services?'

[44] *Ibid.* at 156ff.   [45] See https://creditorwatch.com.au.

[46] See www.ipaidabribe.com.

[47] See www.business-humanrights.org and www.rankabrand.com.

[48] How this can work is illustrated by Dietz, note 37 above at 39ff., in an interview with a German company considering doing business in Romania:

> If someone invests a certain amount of money to build up a business, he shows that he will be serious. It is the same with the companies in Romania. Usually after I am contacting them, who are you, how many employees do you have, 70, ok. You have an office? 'Yes.' That is why we have such a nice office; we have video cameras outside, all kinds of good networks. This is an investment of two million Euros. If I put so much money in the environment, that means that I have the capability to do such a good job.

of e-commerce retailers.[49] Online feedback mechanisms such as those available on eBay, encouraging buyers and sellers to rate one another, are also an important source of knowledge about the reliability of the other party.[50]

It must be emphasised that, although the given examples could suggest otherwise, there is nothing new about reputational networks ensuring an alternative form of arrangements for private actors. Economist Avner Greif has convincingly shown that the origins of long-distance trade lie in efforts to overcome the problem of lack of trust among people who are at a distance from each other.[51] Traders have always tried to overcome the problem of the absence of a well-functioning legal system by informing themselves about potential partners before entering into the transaction and by trading in the shadow of excluding the other party from future transactions. Law is of extreme importance in a political society sanctioned by organised force,[52] but the present, territorially fragmented, globalising society can hardly be qualified as such. This does not change the substance of the law to any great extent, but it does lead to a fundamentally different role that law plays: the 'space' it covers gradually decreases.

5. Conclusions: the importance of 'legality' without law

This chapter sheds some light on how the role of law is changing as a result of globalisation and technological progress. It shows how the traditional view of law as being produced by different nation-state legal orders, each claiming exclusive jurisdiction over a limited territory, is gradually making way for alternative types of arrangement. *Ex post* reliance on the law to provide appropriate rules, enforcement and effective dispute resolution is replaced by a situation in which actors proactively minimise the need to make use of national laws and institutions. I believe that this

---

[49] See e.g. the Dutch label www.thuiswinkel.org and the French label www.fevad.com.

[50] See C. Dellarocas, 'The digitization of word of mouth: promise and challenges of online feedback mechanisms', 49 *Management Science* 10 (2003), 1407–24.

[51] A. Greif, P. Milgrom and B. Weingast, 'The merchant gild as a nexus of contracts', E-90–23 (1990), Working Papers in Economics, The Hoover Institution; and A. Greif, 'Contract enforceability and economic institutions in early trade: the Maghribi Traders Coalition', 83 *American Economic Review* 3 (1993), 525–48.

[52] J. Dator, 'Communication technologies and the future of courts and law' in Muller, Zouridis, Frishman and Kistemaker (eds), note 34 above, pp 211–21.

development towards delivering 'legality'[53] without law is much more important in understanding the denationalisation of law than concrete efforts by European and supranational organisations to create rules deemed fit for the European or global market. Any attempt to chart our contemporary legal landscape should recognise this.

[53] See Galanter, note 6 above, at 226.

12

Transnational public law in Europe

Beyond the *lex alius loci*

GIACINTO DELLA CANANEA

1. Variations on a given theme

My task in this chapter is mainly a theoretical one. It is an attempt to verify whether transnational thoughts about the law make sense in the field of public law, with specific regard to administrative law.[1] This, however, should not be taken to suggest that it is concerned essentially with abstractions. Indeed, after a short explanation of the reasons why, until a few years ago, such an attempt would probably have been regarded by some scholars as implausible, the analysis is based on the ordinary material of public law, including positive norms and judicial decisions. My aim is precisely to try to use this material to call into question some traditional, if not received, ideas, about public law, considered as a province of the state.[2]

This is a revised version of a paper presented at the EUI conference on Transnational Law in 2011. Later drafts were presented at two seminars organised by the Universities of Florence and Rome 'La Sapienza' (convened by Bernardo Sordi, and Fabio Giglioni and Angelo Clarizia, respectively). My thanks to Remo Caponi, Leonardo Ferrara, Miguel Maduro, Bernardo Sordi, Alec Stone Sweet and Kaarlo Tuori for their comments. The usual disclaimer applies.

[1] Although 'transnational' and 'supranational' processes are connected in the cases examined in this chapter, analytically they must be kept distinct: the former 'transcend the limits of the states', as pointed out by P. Jessup, *Transnational Law* (New Haven, CT: Yale University Press, 1956), p. 3, while the latter imply that two or more states have created another legal entity, whatever the criteria (hierarchy, competence or anything else) that govern their relationships. See also Tuori in Chapter 1 of this volume.

[2] For further remarks, see S. Cassese, 'Administrative law without the state? The challenge of global regulation', 37 *New York University Journal of International Law and Politics* 4 (2005), 663–94, arguing that global principles of law are emerging and J. B. Auby, *La Globalisation, le Droit, l'État* (Paris: Montchrestien, 2011), observing that globalisation does not imply less public law, but a new one. See also E. Schmid-Assmann, 'The internationalization of administrative relations as a challenge for administrative scholarship', 9 *German Law Journal* (2008), 2061–80, calling for new theories of administrative law.

For this reason, the legal material examined deals with a set of issues that not even a traditional public lawyer might consider as exotic, despite the expression used to designate it, that is to say the *jus poenitendi*, or the power to modify or cancel the effects of a previous act. With specific regard to public authorities, what is at issue is, for example, whether an administrative agency that possesses licensing power also carries the authority to revoke, withdraw or suspend licences. While a detailed comparative analysis of this issue largely encompasses the goals and limits of this chapter, it ought to be stated at the outset that this kind of administrative power is neither an Italian nor a French peculiarity. For example, in Germany it was codified by Article 48 of the Administrative Procedure Act and in US law the power to revoke or suspend a licence is recognised, and there are safeguards for its exercise.[3]

In this respect, two cases are examined over time: the *Algera* case before the European Court of Justice and a ruling of an Italian administrative court, the Tribunale di giustizia amministrativa di Trento. While *Algera* is a dispute that occurred in the 1950s within the first phase of integration, that of the European Coal and Steel Community (ECSC), the other case was decided only a few years ago. In both cases, the judge came to the conclusion that the initial measure taken by the administrative authority was unlawful and that, therefore, it had to be withdrawn. But what matters more, for our purposes, is that both courts 'found' the relevant norms governing the exercise of administrative power beyond their own legal system.

2. An overview of the paradigm of administrative law as an exclusive province of the state

Since in this chapter I propose and test a theory of public law that differs from the traditional paradigm, especially as far as administrative law is concerned, it is helpful to begin with the latter. Reduced to bare essentials, this paradigm relies on three factors that are interdependent in their effect.[4]

---

[3] *Garris* v. *Governing Bd of the SC Reinsurance Facility*, 319 SC 388 (1995). For a different kind of withdrawal, see C. Wheatley, 'Withdrawals under the Federal Land Policy Management Act of 1976', 21 *Arizona Law Review* (1979), 311–28.

[4] For a further elaborated account of this paradigm, as well as for an alternative perspective, see G. della Cananea, 'Administrative law in Europe: a historical and comparative perspective', *Italian Journal of Public Law* 1 (2009), 162–211.

The first factor is the recent birth and growth of administrative law, seen both as a field of law and as a scholarly field. Unlike private law, which has thousands of years of history, administrative law is essentially a product of the state in the Weberian sense, or the modern state, which differs from all previous polities.[5] Whatever its driving force, a combination of political authority and social demand for public goods, administrative law increasingly extends its scope of application into new areas, not just within those that were previously regulated only by private law.

The second factor is a consequence of the first. Since administrative law is a product of the state,[6] of each state, not only its main features but also its very existence is bound by its national environment. This theory was brought to its extreme conclusions by very different theorists such as Albert Venn Dicey and Massimo Severo Giannini. Dicey, the most eminent constitutionalist of Victorian England, drew an antithesis to affirm that a divide existed between England, which was subject to the rule of law, and those continental countries that were instead subject to *droit administratif*.[7] This method had famous forerunners, including Alexis de Tocqueville,[8] but it was heavily criticised by contemporaries, such as the American lawyer Frank Goodnow,[9] and one of the most eminent French academics, Maurice Hauriou.[10] However, it had a profound and

---

[5] See M. Weber, *Wirtschaft und Gesellschaft* (Tübingen: Mohr Siebeck, 1922), Ch. 7, §2, observing the connection between the monopoly over legislation and that over enforcement.

[6] See, for example, S. Romano, 'Prime pagine di un manuale di diritto amministrativo' in S. Romano (ed.), *Scritti Minori, Vol. II* (Milano: Giuffrè, 1950), p. 425, in which Romano affirmed that administrative law was a 'branch' of the law of the state. The question thus arises whether this remark was incoherent with Romano's earlier pluralist vision: for an excellent account of Romano's works, see A. Sandulli, 'Santi Romano and the perception of public law complexity', *Italian Journal of Public Law* 1 (2009), 21–48.

[7] It is the well-known *incipit* of A. V. Dicey's *Introduction to the Study of the Law of the Constitution* (London: Palgrave Macmillan, 1959), Ch. 12.

[8] A. de Tocqueville, *De la Démocratie en Amérique* (Brussels: Louis Hauman, 1835). On Tocqueville's comparative goals, see L. Cohen-Tanugi, *Le Droit sans l'Etat: Sur la Démocratie en France et en Amérique* (Paris: Presses Universitaires de France, 1985).

[9] F. Goodnow, *Comparative Administrative Law: An Analysis of the administrative Systems, national and local, of the United States, England, France and Germany* (New York: G. P. Putnam's sons, 1893), p. 6 observing that Dicey 'did not mean . . . to deny the existence of an administrative law in the true continental sense, but simply the existence of his conception of *droit administratif*. For a recent reappraisal, see P. Craig, 'Dicey: unitary, self-correcting democracy and public law', 106 *Law Quarterly Review* (1990), 105–33.

[10] For a bird's-eye view of the shift from the legal theories of the state prevailing in the nineteenth century to those of the twentieth, see J. Rivero, *Droit Administratif* (Paris: Dalloz, 1987), p. 28.

long-lasting impact, not only on English theories about public law, but also elsewhere. One century after the first edition of Dicey's *Law of the Constitution*, Giannini, perhaps the most influential Italian administrative lawyer of the twentieth century, still affirmed that there were countries with administrative law and countries in which public administrations were subject to a body of principles or rules essentially common to that regulating the relationship between citizens.[11]

Regardless of either the intellectual soundness of this antithesis or of its adequacy after the phenomenon that John Maynard Keynes called the end of *laissez faire*,[12] it heavily influenced legal theories and methods. Administrative law was regarded as a province of the state, much more than private law and trade law. This explains why the conjecture that administrative law may be a field of inquiry from a transnational perspective would have been regarded by most scholars as implausible. Even use of the comparative method (*Rechtsvergleichung*) was less frequent than in the field of private law. In particular, whatever its intellectual and empirical soundness, the concept of 'legal families' was based on private law institutions.[13]

From all that has just been said, it should be clear enough that the traditional paradigm of administrative law as a national enclave was shared by some leading intellectual figures and had profound implications. As often happens when a paradigm is established, people tend to work within it for reasons that are no longer properly articulated nor, most of all, justified.[14] As a result of this, the risk arises that only problems that are set within this framework are viewed by the legal community

[11] See M. S. Giannini, *Istituzioni di Diritto Amministrativo* (Milano: Giuffrè, 1981), pp 8 and 9. See also S. Cassese, *Culture et Politique du Droit Administratif* (trans. M. Morabito) (Paris: Dalloz, 2008) for the thesis that Italian legal culture was heavily influenced by German public law doctrines.

[12] See J. M. Keynes, *The End of Laissez-faire* (London: L. & Virginia Woolf, 1926), pp 5 and 6, for the thesis that the rights of property and of free trade, as conceived during the eighteenth century, 'accorded with the practical notions of conservatives and of lawyers' and that 'a change [was] in the air' after the end of the *belle époque*.

[13] See R. David and C. Jauffret, *Les grands Systèmes de Droit* (Paris: Dalloz, 1985). See also J. Merryman, *The Civil Law Tradition: An Introduction to the Legal Systems of Europe and Latin America* (Palo Alto, CA: Stanford University Press, 1969). For a bird's-eye view of the two main Western legal traditions, see D. Fairgrieve and H. Muir Watt, *Common Law et Tradition Civiliste* (Paris: Presses Universitaires de France, 2006).

[14] See T. Kuhn, *The Structure of Scientific Revolutions* (Chicago: University of Chicago Press, 1970), arguing that the evolution of scientific theory does not emerge from the straightforward accumulation of facts, but rather from a change in the set of beliefs shared by a group. For further remarks from a legal perspective, see M. Loughlin, *Public Law and*

as worth considering by scholars. Other problems, by contrast, may be marginalised because they are considered either as less important or as too distant from reality. This explains why we need to begin with an analysis of reality, in order to see whether the traditional paradigm is still adequate to explain the legal phenomena of our world.

3. From national administrative laws to the administrative law of the European Community

3.1. A stateless administration

Before considering *Algera*, its institutional context ought to be taken into account. When Dicey wrote his treatise, some international administrative unions already existed, although they were neglected by public lawyers, with the notable exception of Georg Jellinek.[15] After 1950, an unprecedented change occurred, when a plan proposed by the French foreign minister Robert Schuman was accepted by five other European countries and gave birth to the first European Community, established in 1952 by the Treaty of Paris.

At the heart of the new organisation stood the High Authority.[16] It was a stateless administration, since it was created by the six founding countries and acted beyond the borders of each of them. As a transnational administration, it was also 'apatride', according to its critics, particularly General Charles de Gaulle. The High Authority was entrusted with significant powers. First, it could take 'general' decisions. Second, even a quick glance at the Treaty, and especially at the volumes of the official

Political Theory (Oxford: Oxford University Press, 1992), p. 31. See also J. Bell, 'Comparative administrative law' in M. Reimann and R. Zimmermann (eds), *The Oxford Handbook of Comparative Law* (Oxford: Oxford University Press, 2006), p. 1268, observing that 'leading administrative law jurists in liberal democracies have always been aware of development... Often this has served as a benchmark to assess the quality of national administrative justice and to raise questions about areas that need reform.'

[15] See G. Jellinek, *Die Lehre von den Staatenverbindungen* (Berlin: O. Hearing, 1882) and, for further remarks on Jellinek's essay, Schmid-Assmann, note 2 above at 2062. See also E. Stein, 'International integration and democracy: no love at first sight', 95 *American Journal of International Law* 3 (2001), 489–534, pointing out the unprecedented growth of intergovernmental organisations after 1950.

[16] For further analysis, see S. Cassese and G. della Cananea, 'The Commission of the European Economic Community: the administrative ramifications of its political development' in E. Heyen (ed.), *Early European Community Administration* (Baden-Baden: Nomos Verlagsgesellschaft, 1992), p. 75, pointing out the initial importance of French influence on the organisation and functioning of European administration.

journal of the ECSC, shows that most rules of the Community were rules of administrative law. Those rules entrusted the High Authority with powers traditionally exercised by national authorities, including limits on imports, tariffs and sanctions, although legal scholars were reluctant to recognise their importance. Third, as established by the Schuman Plan,[17] these measures had direct binding effects on private undertakings. As a result, the traditional, exclusive relationship between the state and the administration was broken, with the further consequence that individuals were subject to measures taken by a public authority that differed from the state.

Precisely because the new administration was entrusted with vast and potentially intrusive powers, a system of judicial review was necessary. Since the High Authority could not be subject to the jurisdiction of national courts, a Court of Justice was set up, with evident similarities to the French Conseil d'État (grounds of illegitimacy, the advocate general). Its legal importance was strengthened by the fact that the European Court of Justice (ECJ) constructed a set of general principles of public law, both written and unwritten, capable of sustaining economic integration under the guidance of the High Authority, thus enriching the Community legal framework.[18]

3.2. The Algera case

Since the early years of the Community, staff disputes have been an ideal field in which to elaborate and test new judicial doctrines. Although the staff was regulated by a specific piece of legislation, following the French model, the Court did not hesitate to integrate it with general principles and rules. The Algera case, adjudicated by the ECJ in 1956, is particularly helpful in shedding light on this.

---

[17] In this respect, the Schuman Plan affirmed that '[p]ar la mise en commun de production de base et l'institution d'une Haute Autorité nouvelle, dont les décisions lieront la France, l'Allemagne et les pays qui y adhéreront'. Few perceived the innovative character of the new institution, beyond the rhetoric of supranationalism: see E. Haas, *The Uniting of Europe: Political, Social and Economic Forces, 1950–1957* (Palo Alto, CA: Stanford University Press, 1958).

[18] See E. Stein, 'Lawyers, judges, and the making of a transnational constitution', 75 *American Journal of International Law* (1981), 1–27, at 1, affirming that '[f]rom its inception a mere quarter of a century ago, the Court has . . . established and obtained acceptance of the broad principle of direct integration of Community law into the national legal orders of the member states'.

Mrs Algera and several other employees of the Common Assembly of the ECSC brought an action against the decision by which the Assembly's General Secretariat had withdrawn some financial benefits. The questions that thus arose were, a) whether such power did exist, either as a sort of inherent power or as one that existed only in the circumstances provided by law, and, if so, b) how that power could be exercised and under what kind of constraints and, c) whether, in order to challenge the exercise of that power, the affected private party had to prove that the action of the administration was illegal and unreasonable.

The first question, that is to say whether the administration could withdraw an unlawful measure, posed a delicate problem for the Court, since neither the Treaty nor the specific regulation expressly provided such power. The applicants argued, therefore, that such a power simply did not exist. Faced with the problem of a *lacuna* in the legal system created by the Treaty, the Court resolved it in an ingenious way. It acknowledged that there was no textual basis for the exercise of *jus poenitendi*.[19] However, it declared the following:

> unless the Court is to deny justice, it is therefore obliged to solve the problem by reference to the rules acknowledged by the legislation, the learned writing and the case-law of the member countries.[20]

It thus carried out an accurate comparative study of the laws of the Member States. Within the latter, an administrative measure conferring benefits on individuals could not in principle be withdrawn, if it was a lawful measure. By contrast, if it was an unlawful measure, it could be revoked or withdrawn under the laws of all the Member States. Accordingly, the Court stated, following its Advocate General Lagrange, that 'the revocability of an administrative measure vitiated by illegality is allowed in all Member States'.[21] The question thus arose under what conditions and constraints the *jus poenitendi* could be exercised. The Court examined French law,

---

[19] Joined cases 7/56, 3/57 to 7/57 *Algera et al.* v. *Common Assembly of the ECSC* [1957] ECR 81, in which the Court observed that 'the possibility of withdrawing such measures is a problem of administrative law, which is familiar in the case-law and learned writing of all the countries of the Community, *but for the solution of which the Treaty does not contain any rules*' (emphasis added).

[20] *Ibid.*, para. 19.

[21] *Ibid.* See also the Opinion of Advocate General Lagrange (at ECR 80). He did not simply hold that 'this solution, which meets the need to ensure the stability of legal relationships, and which, in the realm of unilateral public law relationships, corresponds to the effects of a contract in multilateral relationships, is common to the principles of the law of all six member countries', but also provided extensive quotations from case law and doctrine.

which allows withdrawal within a short period of time. It then observed that the laws of the Benelux countries seemed to follow the same general rule, despite 'certain small differences'. When it turned to German and Italian law, it observed that there was no specific time limit for the exercise of *jus poenitendi*, although measures that had produced effects for a long time should be kept in force according to widely shared doctrines (*treu und glauben* in the former and the necessary stability of established facts, or *fatti di lunga data*, in the latter). It thus came to the conclusion that:

> whereas this principle is generally acknowledged, only the conditions for its application vary. [Consequently, it accepted] the principle of the revocability of illegal measures at least within a reasonable period of time.[22]

This also provided a solution for the last question mentioned earlier, that is to say whether the affected private parties had to prove that the action of the administration had been unreasonable. The Court conceded that radically modifying or withdrawing an administrative measure after a long time would have infringed the principle of reasonableness. However, it found that this had not occurred in this case.

3.3. A common legal substratum

We do not need to emphasise again that, in phrasing its ruling, the Court had effectively conferred a new power on the European administration. Rather, appropriate emphasis must be placed on two aspects: denial of justice and the significance of the Court's reasoning from the point of view of transnational approaches to the study of law.

When confronted with the problem of a *lacuna*, as the French administrative lawyer Jean Rivero observed, the Court reasoned as if its own legal system was based on the principle that is laid down in Article 4 of the French civil code.[23] The French code prohibited any denial of justice, so frequent under the *ancien régime*. Once the Court rejected the applicant's argument on these grounds, and thus affirmed its duty to act, it made at the same time a fundamental choice, recognising itself as having the power to find the applicable rule elsewhere, if not to create it.

---

[22] *Ibid.* For a more recent ruling applying this principle, see Case 54/77 *Herpels* v. *Commission* [1978] ECR 585.

[23] Art. 4 provides that '[l]e juge qui refusera de juger, sous prétexte du silence, de l'obscurité ou de l'insuffisance de la loi, pourra être poursuivi comme coupable de déni de justice'.

Since it could not anchor the administration's power in the Treaty, it had to find ways to fill the *lacuna*, and therefore looked at national laws. This was certainly not the first time. However, in other cases the Court had referred only implicitly to national laws, for example in order to interpret the notion of 'common interest' (*intérêt commun*) used by Article 3 of the Treaty of Paris.[24] In this case, it had to take a step further, by looking at the general principles of law common to the laws of the Member States, in order to find the applicable rule.

Even a quick comparison with the legal framework applicable to its international predecessor, the International Court of Justice, shows at least two distinctive features. First, within the international legal order, the existence of unwritten general principles was codified in 1945, by Article 38 of the Statute of the International Court of Justice.[25] By contrast, the Treaty of Paris lacked a similar norm. Only in 1957 did the Treaty of Rome introduce it, with regard to the non-contractual liability of the institutions of the EC.[26] Second, Article 38 of the Statute of the ICJ considered the 'general principles of law recognized by civilized nations' apart from case law and learned writings. By contrast, the European Court considered legislation, case law and learned writings (*la doctrine*) as authoritative sources for ascertaining whether a general principle common to the laws of the Member States existed and, if so, to specify its content.

That said, the Court did not explain why, if such a general principle was shared by all national administrative laws, it should also be, by virtue of this, a principle of Community law, for which it had to ensure respect. It is clear from the reasoning just illustrated that the Court's 'recognition' of the principle of revocability of illegal measures, at least within a reasonable period of time, was based on an implicit assumption. The

---

[24] J. Rivero, 'Le problème de l'influence des droits internes sur la Cour de Justice de la Communauté Européenne du Charbon et de l'Acier', 4 *Annuaire Français de Droit International* (1958), 295–308.

[25] The best account of general principles common to municipal jurisdictions is still B. Cheng, *General Principles of Law as Applied by International Courts and Tribunals* (Cambridge: Grotius, 1987). See also, for a description of the various doctrinal positions, B. Vitanyi, 'Les positions doctrinales concernant le sens de la notion de "Principes généraux de Droit reconnus par les Nations civilises"', 86 *Revue Générale de Droit International Public* (1982), 46–116 at 48.

[26] For further remarks, see W. van Gerven, 'The emergence of a common European law in the area of tort liability: the EC contribution' in D. Fairgrieve, M. Andenas and J. Bell (eds), *Tort Liability of Public Authorities in Comparative Perspective* (London: British Institute of International and Comparative Law, 2002), p. 125.

assumption was that what was common to the founders of the new organisation was common to that new organisation, even though this was not a state. For our purposes, this is the most significant implication of *Algera*, which provided the Court with one of its first opportunities to elaborate unwritten principles of law.

As Rivero rightly noted, the influence of the French model of administrative justice was appreciable, but it was indirect. The French tradition had spread across Europe, well after 1815. It had influenced the evolution of the other continental legal systems. Although Belgium had followed the English constitution, its system of administrative law was deeply influenced by the French model. A similar influence emerged within the Italian administrative system, initially with regard to the organisation of administrative institutions and later with regard to the system of remedies.[27] Otto Mayer, in his fundamental treatise on German administrative law, was equally influenced by French doctrines of administrative law, while he thought that the underlying constitutional principles had to be adapted to the German Empire.[28] It was, thus, a '*droit commun*' that was elaborated in the Europe of the Six with regard to the standards of legality. Rivero also added that this elaboration was based on a deeper unity of their legal systems.[29] Since the early years of European integration, the Court has rejected the positivist assumption that the 'law' for which it had to ensure respect under Article 164 coincided with the Treaty and the sources it had created. Rather, the ECJ worked on the assumption that a common legal substratum existed, in the field of public law as in others, and that it could avail itself accordingly. As Advocate General Dutheillet de Lamothe subsequently observed in *Internationale Handelsgesellschaft*, it was one thing to say that the legitimacy of measures adopted by the Community institutions had to be assessed on the basis of European Community law, but it was another to exclude the fundamental principles of national legal systems from having any function in the legal order of the European Community. Quite the contrary, the Advocate General said, these

---

[27] See F. Scoca, 'Administrative justice in Italy: origins and developments', *Italian Journal of Public Law* 1 (2009), 118–61.

[28] See O. Mayer, *Deutsches Verwaltungsrecht* (Leipzig: Dunker & Humblot, 1894). Interestingly, Dicey affirmed that 'the administrative law of France comes nearer than does the *Verwaltungsrecht* of Germany . . . to the rule-of-law as understood by Englishmen': see Dicey, note 7 above, p. 328, fn. 3.

[29] Rivero, note 24 above at 302: 'un droit commun . . . traduction juridique d'une unité plus profonde, qui atteint l'ordre des rapports entre le pouvoir, le droit, et l'homme'.

fundamental principles 'contribute to forming that philosophical, political and legal substratum common to the Member States from which through the case-law an unwritten Community law emerges, one of the essential aims of which is precisely to ensure respect for the fundamental rights of the individual'.[30]

Interestingly, what was at issue in that dispute was whether the European Community system of deposits for the agricultural market infringed the principle of proportionality under which, to borrow again the words of the Advocate General, 'citizens may only have imposed on them, for the purposes of the public interest, obligations which are strictly necessary for those purposes to be attained'.[31] Historically, the idea that there must be at least some minimal 'fit' between a legal action (in this case of the public authority) and its effects on protected interests (those of individuals), or between ends and means, was deeply rooted in German legal culture.[32] However, the Court did not hesitate to follow the advice of its Advocate General and stated that a public authority may not impose excessive obligations on business, where 'excessive' meant not strictly necessary to attain the purpose of the measure adopted by the authority.[33] Once the principle of proportionality was included among the general principles of European Community law, it was only a matter of time before the courts of the other Member States were required to enforce it, as they did. The principle is, therefore, not only at the heart of the system of judicial review of administrative action built by the ECJ, but also a pillar of national systems. Its diffusion is one of the clearest examples of the growth of transnational public law.

---

[30] Opinion of AG Dutheillet de Lamothe, Case 11/70 *Internationale Handelsgesellschaft* [1970] ECR 1125, para. 2. See also Stein, note 18 above, and T. Koopmans, 'The birth of European law at the cross-roads of legal traditions', 39 *American Journal of Comparative Law* (1991), 493–507.

[31] See Lamothe, *ibid.*, pointing out that the question of the source was logically 'prior' to that concerning proportionality.

[32] See A. Stone Sweet and J. Matthews, 'Proportionality, balancing and global constitutionalism', 47 *Columbia Journal of Transnational Law* (2008), 73–165 at 99, describing the evolution of this principle in Germany. See also A. Sandulli, *La proporzionalità dell'azione amministrativa* (Padua: CEDAM, 1998), affirming that a similar concept had been introduced by Giandomenico Romagnosi in Italy, at the beginning of the nineteenth century.

[33] *Internationale Handesgesellschaft*, note 30 above, para. 14. For further remarks on the process of Europeanisation of the general principles of law common to the laws of the Member States, see J. Schwarze, 'The role of general principles of administrative law in the process of Europeanization of national law' in L. Ortega Alvarez (ed.), *Studies on European Public Law* (Valladolid: Lex Nova, 2005), p. 24.

4. Influences between national legal orders

4.1. A case of ordinary administrative injustice

While *Algera* concerned delivery of benefits to public employees, or to use another terminology the exercise of *dominium*,[34] the other dispute is about the administration's use of its powers in order to rule or, to use the same terminology, *imperium*. If during the twentieth century the administration has become ubiquitous, as the American public lawyer Jerry Mashaw has consistently argued, this is particularly evident in our towns. Mashaw observed that the decisions of administrators substantially affect 'the density and architectural character of our neighbourhood', as well as the 'form of our house'.[35]

All this is at the heart of a dispute that arose in Trento, before the Tribunale di giustizia amministrativa di Trento (hereinafter TGAT). The local administration authorised a private applicant to build more than was permitted by its own rules. When a neighbour contested this and asked the administration to withdraw the licence, the latter refused do so.[36] It might have been one of the hundreds of cases in which public administrations exercise their powers without a proper basis and refuse to take into due account all relevant interests.[37]

Even a quick look at the facts as stated in the factual part of the ruling shows that the local authority had behaved arbitrarily.[38] First, after receiving a request from an interested party, it did not carry out a thorough investigation. Second, the licence issued by the administration was manifestly unlawful. As the TGAT observed, the licence permitted the owner to build almost a floor and more than seven hundred square metres more than was allowed by local rules (as if this was not enough, the owner built

---

[34] This terminology is borrowed from T. Daintith, 'The techniques of government' in J. Jowell and D. Oliver (eds), *The Changing Constitution* (Oxford: Oxford University Press, 1994), p. 209.

[35] J. Mashaw, *Due Process in the Administrative State* (New Haven, CT: Yale University Press, 1985), pp 13 and 14.

[36] What was at issue was a withdrawal, not a revocation, which may be justified by a different assessment of the public interest that justified the initial measure: see the ruling of the Consiglio di Stato, VI, 17 March 2010, n. 1554.

[37] See F. Merusi and G. Sanviti, *L'Ingiustizia amministrativa in Italia* (Bologna: Il Mulino, 1986), referring, instead, to the injustice of the system of administrative justice.

[38] TGAT, judgment of 16 December 2009, *Il Foro Amministrativo – TAR* (2010), n. 305. An appeal has been lodged with the Consiglio di Stato.

even more than this, without any control by the local administration).[39] As a result, there is no doubt that the TGAT could have annulled the contested measures on those grounds; but this is not what it did. After noting the substantive and procedural weaknesses of the contested measure, it observed that the most innovative part of the relevant legislative rule, that is to say Article 21-*nonies* of the Italian Administrative Procedure Act (APA), concerns interest balancing. It states that:

> 1. When there exist grounds in the public interest for so doing, an administrative measure that is unlawful in accordance with section 21-*octies* may be annulled *ex officio* by the administrative unit that issued it or by other administrative unit so empowered by law, within a reasonable timeframe and taking account of the interests of the addressees and parties with conflicting interests.

> 2. The possibility of validating voidable measures, when there exist grounds in the public interest for so doing and within a reasonable timeframe, shall remain unaffected.[40]

In this respect, a profound change has occurred with regard to *jus poenitendi*. Traditionally, it was conceived as a manifestation of the government's almost absolute prerogatives. Consider, for example, how *jus poenitendi* was elaborated by Feliciano Benvenuti, another influential Italian public lawyer of the twentieth century. According to Benvenuti, not only had the administration an inherent power to adopt a new measure aiming at re-examining, rectifying or annulling a previous measure, but that power served to ensure the most efficient pursuit of the public interest.[41] The underlying assumption is that the administration's decision did not depend on the conduct of the individuals affected by the exercise of *jus poenitendi*. This was by no means a purely Italian peculiarity. For example, one of the most influential German public lawyers, Ernst Forsthoff, argued that the authority's power to annul or revoke an administrative measure was a sort of inherent power that was limited in some respects.[42]

---

[39] *Ibid.*, §7a. For further details and analysis, see A. Cassatella, 'Una nuova ipotesi di annullamento doveroso', *Il Foro Amministrativo – TAR* (2010), 802.

[40] An English translation of the law is published in issue no. 2/2010 of the *Italian Journal of Public Law* (special editors della Cananea and Sandulli).

[41] F. Benvenuti, 'Autotutela (dir.amm.)' in *Enciclopedia del diritto*, Vol. IV (Milano: Giuffrè, 1959), p. 537ff. On Benvenuti's influential standing, see Cassese, *Culture et Politique*, note 11 above.

[42] E. Forsthoff, *The Administrative Act* (Nicosia: Zavallis Press, 1963), p. 61.

In contrast, the APA calls for transparency and openness. It has been argued that outside interests may not determine the course of administrative policy, but this misses the point. What the law does is to require administrative agencies to allow all interests to be taken into account in the decision-making process, and the basis of the policy choice to be clear. In this respect, it provides an answer to the wide demand for inclusive and open procedures to ensure that all affected interests are allowed a voice, not just those of the addressees of the final measure. Precisely because the legitimacy of the final measure does not depend on the views of administrators insulated from the plurality of interests arising from society, the administrative judge might have focused on this element. We may see in its insistence on the need to carry out a non-formalistic balancing of the interests in the case, an instance of inclusive administrative procedures, which is not far from the American-style 'interest representation' model of modern administration.[43]

4.2. An interpretation of Italian legislation in the light of German judicial doctrines

As observed earlier, although the TGAT could settle the dispute on the substantive and procedural grounds just mentioned, this is not what the court did, instead referring to German judicial doctrines of administrative power. That is precisely the reason why this ruling is so interesting from the point of view of transnational theories of law. The TGAT considered how the administration had dealt with the complainant's request to ensure observance of the law, by withdrawing the contested measure. The Tribunal held that, when there is evidence that an administrative measure is unlawful, it is intolerable that it should produce any effect in the legal world. It observed that this interpretation of Italian law is in line with the German courts' doctrine according to which, in 'schlechthinunerträglich' cases (that is to say intolerably unsound ones), the scope for administrative discretion is not simply more limited, but no longer exists.[44]

The least that can be said is that this was an unusual ruling. For sure, Italian administrative courts have never hesitated to deviate from the positivistic assumptions that have dominated the case law of civil courts.

---

[43] See R. B. Stewart, 'The reformation of American administrative law', 88 *Harvard Law Review* (1974–5), 1667–813 at 1685, distinguishing the 'interest-representation' model from the 'transmission belt'.

[44] TGAT, §7d. The ruling explicitly refers to Joined cases C–392/04 and C–422/04 *i–21, Germany GmbH and Arcor AG & Co. KG* v. *Germany* [2006] ECR I–8559.

Since its creation, in 1890, the Council of State (Consiglio di Stato) has elaborated and refined general principles of administrative law, such as the principle of legality and the right to be heard. In some cases, it has gone so far as to refer openly to principles of natural law. One century on, while precedents from other jurisdictions are rarely mentioned,[45] both the Council of State and the lower administrative courts set up in every region of Italy do not hesitate to enforce EU law and they are quite active in sending requests for preliminary references to the CJEU.

However, even a quick glance at the TGAT reasoning shows that it did not mention ECJ precedents, specifically its ruling in *Arcor*, because the latter had elaborated a principle of German origin, as happened with the principles of proportionality (*Verhältnismässigkeit*) and protection of legitimate expectations (*Vertrauensschutz*). Indeed, in *Arcor,* the ECJ simply said that, if under national law an unlawful administrative measure has to be withdrawn, then the same must be applied to measures that infringe EU law.[46] Otherwise, as the Court has repeatedly observed in its case law, the principles of effectiveness of EU law and of equal protection would be undermined.[47]

The administrative court did not content itself with repeating that the powers conferred by legislation on public administrations must be exercised in a manner consistent with the law. Rather, it interpreted that law in a very unusual way. In Germany it is settled case law, codified by Article 48 of that country's equivalent of the the APA, the Verwaltungsverfahrengesetz (law on administrative procedures, VwVfG), that the administration enjoys a discretionary power in deciding whether an unlawful measure (*Verwaltungsakt*) must be withdrawn. If the act's legal existence is *schlechthinunerträglich* then administrative discretion does not exist (*'Reduzierung auf null'*).[48] Accordingly, the unlawful administrative

---

[45] See A. Sandulli, 'The use of comparative law before the Italian public law courts' in G. Canivet, M. Andenas and D. Fairgrieve (eds), *Comparative Law before the Courts* (London: British Institute of International and Comparative Law, 2004), p. 165. See also M. Gelter and M. Siems, 'Language, legal origins, and culture before the courts: cross-citations between supreme courts in Europe', 21 *Supreme Court Economic Review* (2014, forthcoming).

[46] *I-21 Germany and Arcor*, note 44 above, para. 69.

[47] *Ibid.*, paras 8 and 11, where the Court refers to the preliminary question formulated by the *Bundesverwaltungsgericht*, which affirmed established judicial doctrine, but found that it did not apply in this specific dispute.

[48] See H. Erichsen, D. Ehlers and P. Badura, *Allgemeines Verwaltungsrecht* (Berlin: De Gruyter, 2002), p. 270. See also M. Singh, *German Administrative Law in Common Law Perspective* (Berlin: Springer, 2001), p. 890.

measure must be withdrawn.[49] By contrast, in Italy what the law says is that, if an administrative measure is unlawful, then it 'may be annulled *ex officio*'. There is not, therefore, a duty to withdraw it but, rather, a discretionary power. More precisely, what the public authority is obliged to do is to balance the interests in the case, including both public and private interests. In the light of these remarks, it can be argued that what the TGAT did was not only to refer to a German judicial doctrine, but to boldly read Italian legislation in conjunction with that doctrine, more precisely with the German conception of bound administrative powers.

The questions that thus arise are neither few nor of marginal importance. Before considering them, at least two possible objections to the relevance of this case should briefly be considered. First, we should ask ourselves whether the TGAT's reference to the German judicial doctrine of bound administrative powers was simply an *obiter dictum*, that is to say an element of the court's reasoning that was not essential for resolving the dispute.[50] This was not the case, however. Indeed, it was only by reinterpreting Italian legislation in accordance with that judicial doctrine that the court could annul both the permit to build issued by the administration and its refusal to withdraw that measure.

Second, it should be considered whether a single judgment might provide a sufficient basis for affirming that a new trend is emerging. Chaim Perelman, a renowned expert on judicial reasoning, illustrated this argument with the German words *einmal ist keinmal*.[51] However, my analysis concerns neither the principle of revocability of unlawful administrative measures nor the broader influence exercised by German legal culture. Whether this specific ruling was heavily influenced by the specific cultural environment of Trento, so close to the Austrian and German area, is an intriguing question. However, what is at issue here is whether this case can be regarded as a symptom that even one of the traditional prerogatives of administrative powers is not immune from transnational influences, with intermediation by EU law being either low or none at all.

---

[49] *I-21 Germany and Arcor*, note 44 above, para. 15, in which the Court refers to its ruling in Case C–453/00 *Kuhne & Heitz* [2004] ECR I–837, pointing out that the principle of legal certainty implies that the validity of administrative measures may not be called into question indefinitely. For further remarks on this, see H. Blanke, *Vertrauensschutz in Deutschen und Europäischen Verwaltungsrecht* (Tübingen: Mohr Siebeck, 2001).

[50] For this distinction, see G. Gorla, '*Ratio decidendi*, principio di diritto (e *obiter dictum*)' in G. Gorla, *Diritto Comune e Diritto Comparato* (Milan: Giuffrè, 1981), p. 882.

[51] C. Perelman, *Logique juridique: Nouvelle Rhétorique* (Paris: Dalloz, 1976).

5. Using the law of another land

5.1. *Two normative models:* lex alius loci *and conflict of laws*

Although the ruling of the TGAT raises some doubts that will be illustrated later, its intellectual construction apparently has much to commend it. It is a construction that appears consistent with the increasing weight that European integration has in the interpretation of national legislative provisions. The ruling also suggests that, within this common legal order, doctrines concerning the exercise of authority might be elaborated by analogy to those provisions that better pursue the themes of legality and equality before the law. This is certainly neither novel nor surprising. Indeed, during the last ten centuries European law has been characterised by a variety of exchanges and transplants. But what we are considering is a more specific phenomenon, notably use of the legal rules of another land. In this respect, two main models may be envisaged, which differ remarkably as to both normative basis and methodology. While the first approach is that of *jus commune*,[52] the second is that of modern rules on conflict of laws.

As will be argued later, the first approach is of more than historical interest. It lasted for several centuries because it provided a principled approach for an institutional environment characterised by a high number of polities (kingdoms, duchies, free cities) and a high differentiation of local rules. This approach gave much room for use of *lex alius loci* (law of another land).

In his seminal article on *lex alius loci*, Gino Gorla illustrated the main features of this principle.[53] First, the countries involved were regarded as being, as a whole, a community, though they were not necessarily included in the empire.[54] In this community, when neither the *jura particularia* (that is to say the law of a specific polity) nor the *jus commune* provided a

---

[52] For this concept, see R. van Caenegem, *European Law in the Past and the Future: Unity and Diversity over Two Millennia* (Cambridge: Cambridge University Press, 2002), pointing out that the *jus commune* developed in the faculties of law. It was thus a common 'learned law'. It consisted of two, theoretically distinct but in practice interconnected, elements: the canon law of the Catholic Church and the civil law of Justinian's *Corpus Juris Civilis*. See also A. M. Hespanha (trans. L. Apa), *Introduzione alla storia del diritto europeo* (Bologna: Il mulino, 1999).

[53] G. Gorla, 'Il ricorso alla legge di un "luogo vicino" nel diritto Comune Europeo' (1973) in Gorla, note 50 above, p. 617. The importance of Gorla's studies has been pointed out, in particular, by R. Schlesinger, 'The past and future of comparative law', 43 *American Journal of Comparative Law* (1995) 477–82 at 479.

[54] On this point, see J. Bryce, *The Holy Roman Empire* (New York: Macmillan, 1905).

rule for deciding a new or controversial case, the courts normally used the *lex alius loci* or *extera*. Second, this law was not considered a binding source of law but, rather, as an authoritative doctrine (*doctrina magistralis*). Third, and equally important, what was regarded as the law was not only a text written by a political authority (*gubernaculum*), but also the interpretation given by courts and learned lawyers to those texts. There is no overemphasis in saying that, especially between 1500 and 1750, there was not only a common law, based on Roman law, but also a common legal culture, shared by lawyers, judges and professors.[55] Fourth, it is not clear whether the use of *lex alius loci* was seen as a power or, instead, as a duty of the court. Last but not least, with regard to choice of law, the main criterion was that of proximity (*vicinitas*). This, however, was not regarded as such in spatial terms, but, rather, on the basis of affinities. In both respects, the judges clearly exercised much more than a mere implementing discretion. To take a couple of exemplary issues, both French law in matters of chivalry and the Spanish *ley de las siete partidas* were regarded as *leges alius loci*.

As a consequence, 'reported' judicial opinions formed part of the legal materials and authorities that were regularly consulted by anyone seeking to ascertain the principles and rules that could be applied everywhere. This implied that 'decisions rendered by a court sitting in Italy or Germany, or indeed anywhere in continental Europe' could be relied on by a Belgian, Dutch or French court.[56]

This model gradually lost its importance during the eighteenth century, owing to codifications, although some examples may still be found in the following century. An opposite model took its place. What is usually called either conflict of laws or private international law (though this is a branch of municipal law) is a set of rules that determine which legal system, and the law of which jurisdiction, apply to a given dispute, generally characterised by some 'foreign' element. A typical example is that of a contract agreed by parties located in different countries. Unlike in the *lex alius loci*, first, there is no such thing as a community of countries sharing the same culture, but a variety of sovereigns, each with its own principles (it was in this period that, as Carl Schmitt observed, the idea that the same legal principles were shared was replaced by what he called

---

[55] Gorla, note 53 above, p. 627.

[56] Quotations are drawn from Schlesinger, note 53 above at 478. Schlesinger also raised an important issue, of whether similarities existed between continental *jus commune* and the English common law, arguing that this was not the case (at 480).

the maxim *cujus regio, ejus et oeconomia).*[57] Second, referring to the law of another land is not necessary in order to fill *lacunae* in the domestic legal order. It is on the basis of the criteria adopted by domestic law that the 'external' rule becomes part of the domestic legal order.[58] The fact that the 'law' in this respect is basically, if not exclusively, legislation is still another important distinctive element, as well as the duty of the domestic judge to refer to it. Precisely because legislation is separated from case law, recognition of foreign judgments is seen as a distinct field.

The above is of course only a sketchy illustration of either model. Rather, it serves only to shed some light on a twofold, fundamental difference concerning the normative basis and the methodology. When considering *jus commune,* it ought to be clarified that legal technique operates at the level of the individual case; it devotes considerable importance to the facts. However, this is at the same time a principled approach. The underlying rationale is that principles are shared within countries that are parts of the same community and that these principles are not solely for legislators, or, better, are mainly for the courts. As a result, the methodology is that typical of the judiciary. The general norm or value that underlies modern conflict of norms might be viewed, instead, in regulation of the social order by each national legislator. Both laying down (positive) norms and setting the limits to their sphere of validity, in order to avoid conflicts, is essentially a task for the legislator.

5.2. *The* lex alius loci *within a common legal order*

Contrasting the methodologies that characterise the models of *lex alius loci* and conflict of laws permits us to reconsider the TGAT ruling. In the ruling of the Italian judge there is no reference, even implicit, to the conflict of rules model. Moreover, when establishing an analogy between its interpretation of its own legislation and the German legal order, the TGAT finds that the analogy concerns judicial doctrines, rather than the VwVfG. In other words, it is a case of dialogue between national courts. This raises at least three questions.

The first is whether, through this ruling, we might develop a perspective through which the empirical reality of transnational exchanges and influences is adequately reflected in our attempts to theorise law. We have

---

[57] C. Schmitt, *Der Nomos der Erde im Völkerrecht des Jus Publicum Europaeum* (Cologne: Greven, 1950), using a paraphrase of the maxim *cujus regio, ejus religio.*
[58] Gorla, note 53 above, p. 623.

seen that the conflict of laws model does allow us to address the question at a theoretical level. We may add that this model is undermined by the principles underpinning European integration. Consider, in particular, the principle of equivalence, or mutual recognition, which obliges public authorities to use the rules established by other national regulators since the landmark ruling of the ECJ in *Cassis de Dijon*.[59] Consider, more broadly, the general principles of administrative law elaborated by the Court in *Algera* and several other cases, such as *Factortame* in which, following the opinion of Advocate General Tesauro, the ECJ affirmed that interim measures must be available to national courts even if they are excluded by national rules.[60]

However, it would be naïve to infer from this that European integration has recreated the institutional conditions of the epoch of *jus commune*. Such an inference would fail on both empirical and interpretative grounds. These two dimensions of failure are linked. When considering the empirical side, it soon becomes evident that, although during the last thirty years or so we have witnessed an explosion of judge-made law, our legal systems are still based on a mass of statutes. This is particularly evident in continental countries, where the role of codes cannot be neglected.

This brings us to the other ground, that is to say interpretation. My argument here is that, while positivism fails to provide us with an adequate theory of public law for our epoch, existing positive norms can, and should, be reinterpreted. Consider, for example, Article 12 of the rules that precede the Italian civil code. Unlike its predecessor of 1865, the civil code of 1942 obliged the judge to adjudicate on the basis of the general principles of the legal order of the state. Whatever the legacy of the political doctrines of that period, Article 12 must not be interpreted solely in the light of the constitutional principle according to which the validity of legislation is subordinated to respect for the legal order of the EU. It must also be interpreted in the light of a more specific legislative provision, Article 1 of the APA. Under this provision, action by public administrations must respect the principle of legality, other general

---

[59] Case C–120/78 *Rewe-Zentral* [1979] ECR 649. For a theoretical approach, see J. Weiler, 'The constitution of the Common Market place: text and context in the evolution of free movement of goods' in P. Craig and G. de Búrca (eds), *The Evolution of the EU* (Oxford: Oxford University Press, 1999), p. 349, explaining the *ratio* of equivalence.

[60] Case C–213/89 *Factortame* [1990] ECR I–2433. For further details, see D. Oliver, 'Fishing in the incoming tide', 54 *Modern Law Review* 3 (1991), 442–51. See also, for a comparative analysis, S. de la Sierra, 'Revisiting European courts and European remedies. How do interim measures really function?', 17 *European Review of Public Law* (2005), 1439–80.

principles including transparency and the 'principles of the legal order of the EC'. Both the classic principles of hierarchy and competence thus require, rather than simply justify, a different interpretation of Article 12.

However, while all this explains why the general principles of law common to the laws of the Member States, once recognised by the ECJ, are directly applicable by national courts, it fails to directly confront another part of the empirical reality of law, that is to say transnational exchanges. In other words, once the dualism between Community law and national law is overcome, this does not necessarily entail the laws of the other Member States becoming relevant. A clue for a better understanding has been proposed by Sabino Cassese. He argued that the importance of European integration should not be assessed only from the point of view of the hierarchical relationship between the Union and each Member State, a bilateral one. Rather, European integration has opened each national legal system horizontally, that is to say each towards the others. The 'fact' that the principle of equivalence operates in favour of national rules, rather than EU rules, can thus be conceptualised in these terms.[61] In sum, a fundamental transformation of the law has occurred since 1952 and this requires a reconsideration of the laws of the countries that are part of the same legal tradition.

While, in this perspective, the courts obviously enjoy much more than a mere implementing discretion in the analysis of *affinitas*, a second set of questions arises. When the TGAT uses the German doctrine of withdrawal, it explicitly refers to the concept of *schlechthinunerträglichkeit*, that is to say that it is intolerable that such an unlawful administrative measure produces legal effects. The critical issue, it would appear, is not only that this judicial doctrine clearly deviates from the legislative codification of 2005, but also that such an indeterminate legal concept might leave too much discretion to the courts.

As a variation on the preceding remark, the choice made by the TGAT raises some concern. An obvious reason is the absence of any justification in existing legislation. Another is the dialogue between the courts. One thing is to observe that a more intense dialogue between legal cultures has emerged within the European legal space and that this dialogue is facilitated and stimulated by both more frequent exchanges and a better

---

[61] See S. Cassese, 'Diritti amministrativi nazionali e diritto amministrativo comunitario' in M. P. Chiti and G. Greco (eds), *Trattato di Diritto Amministrativo Europeo* (Milan: Giuffrè, 2007), p. 11. See also A. Padoa Schioppa, 'Il diritto comune in Europa: riflessioni sul declino e sulla rinascita di un modello', 119 *Il Foro Italiano* (1996), 14–21.

knowledge of the legal materials of other countries in the Internet era. Another thing is whether the increasingly frequent and regular meetings of judges from different jurisdictions produce changes that were debated beyond those circles.[62] Finally, the choice of one legal order instead of another should be considered critically. France is, in some respects, the missing part of this story. Under French administrative law the legal framework for exercising *jus poenitendi* differs considerably from that in Germany. It is an established principle of the case law of the French Conseil d'État that annulment is possible, not necessary. Moreover it can be achieved only within two or four months, depending on the content and effects of the previous measure.[63] Last but not least, the procedure for annulment may only be initiated by the administration itself, *ex officio*. There is, in other words, a strong analogy between judicial and administrative annulment. Both are conceived as powers that must be exercised in the light of the public interest. Why, then, did the TGAT choose the latter, instead of the former? If the TGAT thought that it was more appropriate, was it at least obliged to consider whether other national systems might have been even more appropriate? Or did the choice made by the TGAT reflect a sort of general preference for German public law? This would be neither novel nor dangerous in academic works, given that Vittorio Emanuele Orlando, Santi Romano and their contemporaries in the first half of the twentieth century reconstructed Italian administrative law following that model.[64] There is also evidence that new legislation governing the judicial process before administrative courts is following the German model, when individual actions are concerned. Yet, precisely for this reason, it could be argued that this is a choice reserved to the legislature.

6. Towards a theory of transnational public law

The questions raised by the legal material examined in this chapter confirm and justify the doubts initially cast on the traditional paradigm of administrative law as a province of the state. First, not only as a matter of intellectual history, but also as a matter of history of legal events, some

---

[62] See A-M. Slaughter, *A New World Order* (Princeton, NJ: Princeton University Press, 2004).

[63] See the *arrêt* du Conseil d'État, 26 October 2001, affaire *Ternon*, judgment no 197018/2001, stating that the term for withdrawing an unlawful decision is four months.

[64] For further remarks, see G. della Cananea, 'On bridging legal cultures: the Italian Journal of Public Law', 11 *German Law Journal* (2010), 1281–91.

problems obviously arise with the basic claim that public law coincides with positive norms and such norms are inevitably connected with a specific *Volksgeist*. For a long period of time, the law was 'transnational by definition',[65] although *jus commune* coexisted with *jura particularia*. In particular, similarities between the administrative institutions of continental countries under the *ancien régime* were evident to Tocqueville.[66] Obviously that epoch ended long ago and it would be naïve to overlook that the last two centuries were characterised by very different institutional premises and values.

Second, at the level of intuition, it is certainly plausible to claim that 'diversity and pluralism are greatly to be preferred' to uniformity.[67] Moral and political theories that can be employed to support and refine this intuition must be seriously taken into account. However, from a methodological point of view, the fact that these values are asserted as desirable and attractive and those theories are shared by many should not obscure the realities of our epoch. My main claim is not that lawyers should be aware of the intrinsic limitations of the paradigm based on legal positivism and nationalism. It is, rather, that lawyers should be aware of the problems which that paradigm inevitably faces when it confronts the contemporary realities of public law.[68]

These realities, arguably, include law that, as noted by Kaarlo Tuori,[69] does not fit into the dichotomy between municipal and international law. I have argued elsewhere that this dichotomy is not 'natural', corresponding to the '*natur der sache*'. It is, rather, a cultural product, strongly connected with Hegel's doctrine that each state is, in principle, self-sufficient, though it may discretionally decide to self-limit its own legislation.[70] A

---

[65] Van Caenegem, note 52 above, p. 13.

[66] See A. de Tocqueville, *L'Ancien Régime et la Révolution*, Vol. I (Paris: Michel Levy, 1856), Ch. 4.

[67] C. Harlow, 'Global administrative law: the quest for principles and values', 17 *European Journal of International Law* 1 (2006), 187–214 at 207. Note, however, that Harlow argues for pluralism, but recognises the increasing similarity of the solutions chosen by European countries: see also C. Harlow and R. Rawlings, 'National administrative procedures in a European perspective: pathways to a slow convergence', *Italian Journal of Public Law* 2 (2010), 215–58.

[68] The distinction between facts and values, of course, is itself problematic: see Loughlin, *Public Law*, note 14 above, p. 38.

[69] See also Tuori in Chapter 1 of this volume.

[70] See G. della Cananea, 'Minimum standards of procedural justice in administrative adjudication' in S. W. Schill (ed.), *International Investment Law and Comparative Public Law* (Oxford: Oxford University Press, 2010), p. 49, noting the influence played by Hegelian theories on doctrines of public law and particularly the separation between public law

move towards a more comprehensive framework for legal theory requires us to devote proper attention to the realities of public law that cannot be adequately explained within the paradigm of administrative law as a national enclave. Consider, for example, the ruling issued by the Italian administrative court. Its basic argument is not simply that, when a decision maker decides whether its *jus poenitendi* ought to be exercised, the interest of private parties must be balanced with the public interest. It is, rather, that, if the initial administrative measure is intolerably unjust, then it must be withdrawn, according to a principle that is shared by other legal orders, and of which the CJEU is well aware.

Consider also *Algera*. *Algera* is not only a case which shows that creation of the ECSC was not merely a treaty, giving rise to a new system of law, partially distinct from international law, as the ECJ argued later in *van Gend*.[71] In contrast to the approach that prevailed for a long time between both international and national public lawyers, it can be argued that the distinctive element of law within the new Communities was not simply the new kind of bilateral relationship between them and each Member State, but also, on a deeper level, the existence of multiple connections between national legal orders. From this point of view, whatever the intellectual soundness of the theories according to which at the end of the 1960s the ECJ began to refer to fundamental rights only or mainly in an instrumental way, that is to say to protect the EC from criticism raised by some powerful national courts, we should not forget that development of general principles of law began much earlier and with different purposes.[72] The problem was not so much that of strengthening the legitimacy of common institutions. It was, rather, how to shape an effective machinery

internal and external to states. In para. 330 of Hegel's *Philosophy of Law*, the latter is called '*Aussere Staatsrecht*': see 'Grundlinien der Philosophie der Rechts' (1821), in *Werke* 7 (Frankfurt: Suhrkamp, 1989), p. 497.

[71] Case 26/62 *van Gend & Loos* [1963] ECR 1 at 3, where the Court argued that 'the Community constitutes a new legal order of international law for the benefit of which the States have limited their sovereign rights, albeit in limited fields'. For a masterly analysis, see Stein, note 18 above, arguing that the ECJ achieved a quiet revolution.

[72] Until a few years ago, the only general treatise was J. Schwarze, *Europäisches Verwaltungsrecht: Entstehung und Entwicklung im Rahmen der Europaischen Gemeinschaft* (Baden-Baden: Nomos, 1988), soon translated into English and French. His approach, however, was not uncontested: see C. Harlow, 'Changing the mindset? The place of theory in administrative law', 14 *Oxford Journal of Legal Studies* 3 (1994), 419–34 at 431, and P. Cane, 'Review of Schwarze's *European Administrative Law*', 110 *Law Quarterly Review* (1993), 147–64.

of government that is restricted by law, coherently with constitutionalism at the same time. In this sense *Algera* is essentially a case showing that any court with a public law jurisdiction must have an approach that goes beyond interpretation of existing rules, and thus incorporates a doctrine of general principles of law, distinct from custom or equity.

All this does not imply, however, that a different paradigm would not be problematic. It can be argued, rather, that the mark of a grand theory, or a paradigm, is not so much that it produces solutions to perplexing questions, but whether and the extent to which such theory or paradigm provides a fruitful programme for future work, by the author and other scholars.[73] In this sense, following one of Rivero's latest studies, it can be argued that study of general principles common to the laws of European countries provides us with a new 'perspective',[74] if not with a new paradigm. More precisely, a transnational perspective provides a conceptual and normative framework capable of giving significance to processes of recognition, or creation, of general principles of law beyond the borders of the state. Whether, and the extent to which, such general principles of law draw on a common legal substratum are thus a distinctive feature of the European legal space,[75] or are shared within the broader area of Western legal tradition or even elsewhere, is another question that must be analysed not only empirically, but also historically. The risk of unhelpful abstractions is otherwise very high.

---

[73] See Loughlin, note 14 above, p. 258.

[74] See J. Rivero, 'Vers un droit commun Européen: nouvelles perspectives en droit administratif' in L. N. Brown, M. Cappelletti and M. Kohnstamm (eds), *Nouvelles Perspectives du Droit Commun de l'Europe* (Leiden: Sijthoff, 1978), p. 389.

[75] See, again, Rivero, 'Le problème de l'influence', note 24 above at 260, holding that the six founding Member States had 'un fond commun, une éthique identique, un accord sur les catégories fondamentales'.

13

The law of the Internet between globalisation and localisation

ORESTE POLLICINO AND MARCO BASSINI

1. Introduction

If under the label of 'globalisation' it is possible to identify, in the words of Habermas,[1] all those trends capable of modifying that historical constellation that has been characterised, since the end of the Westphalian era, by the convergence, within the same national borders, of state, society and economy, then the Internet could be seen as the pioneer of the new post-national constellation.[2]

It is difficult, in fact, to find in history any expression of a compression of time and space more profound than that which characterises social interaction in cyberspace.[3] With particular reference to space – the territorial element – our main research question is whether this compression has been so extreme as to create a borderless world, 'allergic' to any attempt to regulate it at national and even supranational and transnational levels.

If the answer is positive, then the anarchic nature of the Internet would imply that Internet law has benefited only from the *pars destruens* of the post-Westphalian legal context (globalisation as denationalisation), which has triggered the crisis of the national legal order as a self-contained and

---

Oreste Pollicino wrote section 1; Marco Bassini wrote sections 2 and 3.

[1] J. Habermas, *The Postnational Constellation* (Cambridge: Polity Press, 2001).

[2] In Thomas Friedman's view 'the Internet is going to be like a huge vice that takes the globalization system, and keeps tightening the system around everyone, in ways that will only make the world smaller and faster and faster with each day passing'. See T. Friedman, *The Lexus and the Olive Tree: Understanding Globalisation* (New York: Farrar, Straus & Giroux, 2000), p. 141. More recently, and more broadly, see also A. Hamann and H. Fabri, 'Transnational network and constitutionalism', 6 *International Journal of Constitutional Law* 3, 4 (2008), 481–508 at 482.

[3] At the basis of the well-known definition of globalisation given by D. Harvey, *The Condition of Postmodernity: An Inquiry into the Origins of Cultural Change* (Oxford: Blackwell, 1989).

self-sufficient normative whole.[4] In that hypothesis, the rise of cyberspace would instead be completely immune to the *construens* part (globalisation as multilevel supranational governance). This is also encapsulated in the progressive loss of centrality by municipal law caused by the advent of the new season of transnational law, a law which, as Kaarlo Tuori has pointed out,[5] does not entirely fit within the dichotomy between municipal law and international law.[6]

If, by contrast, the answer to our first question is negative, and consequently we can see combined in Internet law both the *destruens* and the *construens* parts emerging after the crisis of the post-Westphalian legal order, then it might be interesting to explore to what extent and especially at what level of governance a regulatory approach could play its role in cyberspace.

If the latter hypothesis were to be confirmed, then a highly paradoxical scenario would emerge, seeing the area of Internet law, for years considered the most emblematic expression of the limits of national law in facing the challenges of globalisation, prove, by contrast, to be one of the few fields of law still encapsulated in national law, in which not only a global approach but also a transnational approach are likely to prove not quite appropriate.

In an attempt to find reasonable answers to these research questions, this chapter will investigate initial scholarly analysis of the main characteristics of the law of the Internet (in section 1.1), and then focus on

---

[4] The *destruens* element of the process of globalisation finds, in other words, its realisation in the end of the black-box model that was premised, as Tuori in Chapter 1 of this volume notes, on the '(co)existence of territorially differentiated state legal orders, each of them claiming exclusive jurisdiction within their respective, territorially defined, social spaces, and international law, confined to regulating external relations between sovereign states'.

[5] *Ibid.*

[6] According to Calliess,

> Transnational Law identifies a third category of autonomous legal orders beyond the traditional categories of national and international law. Transnational law is created and developed by the law creating powers of global society, it is based on general principles of law and their concretisation in social practice, its application, interpretation and development are, at least primarily, the responsibility of private dispute resolution providers, and it is codified – if at all, in general catalogues of principles and rules, standardised contract forms of codes of conduct which are set up by private rule-making bodies.

> See G. Calliess, 'Transnationales Verbrauchervertragsrecht', 68 *Rabels Zeitschrift für Ausländisches und Internationales Privatrecht* 1 (2004), 244–87 at 254.

how that analysis has influenced, even though only partially, the original case law of national courts regarding identification of the relevant jurisdiction (in section 1.2).

In light of the foregoing, this chapter will highlight how, after some years, the first, radical arguments relating to the presumed anarchic nature of the Internet have started to show their weakness. Consequently, the relevant question is no longer whether it is possible to regulate the Net but, very differently, how to do it. In particular, in the present, second season of cyber law, the issue at the core of current academic, judicial and legislative debate is how to determine and choose the best level to regulate what some years earlier was considered, by definition, to be an a-national phenomenon.

In this respect, we will first try to bring to light the weakest points of the cyber-anarchic approach (in section 1.3) then, from a more practical perspective, underline, by an overview of the relevant case law (in section 2), how far from being an a-national or post-national issue the problem of enforcement jurisdiction over the World Wide Web very often lies at the heart of a state's national identity.

The concluding remarks have a twofold aim. First, we will explore whether, and, if so, how the future evolution of Internet law could find its place in the new era of transnational law, in particular dealing with the relationship between law and technology. Second, special emphasis will be given to the rise of a new fundamental right in the new season of transnational law: the right to access to the Internet.

1.1. The origins: the debate over the feasibility of Internet regulation – the characteristics that make the Internet an atypical environment for legal interaction

At the outset, the engineering of the Internet responded to a notably internal and state-centric priority, that of national security.[7] However, according to the earliest legal scholarship on the subject,[8] the Internet would present an entirely new dimension to the problem of squeezing transnational activities into the national context. In particular, according to these authors, while law and regulation had always been

---

[7] See S. Sassen, 'The impact of the Internet on sovereignty: unfounded and real worries' in C. Engel and H. B. Heller (eds), *Law and Economics of International Telecommunications* (Baden-Baden: Nomos, 2000).

[8] See D. Johnson and D. Post, 'Law and borders: the rise of law in cyberspace', 48 *Stanford Law Review* (1996), 1367–1402.

organised on the assumption that activities are on the whole geographically delimited, the peculiar character of the World Wide Web is its
borderless nature. Thus the Internet, by undermining the criterion of territoriality as a basis for common regulation, would chip away at the state
itself.

More precisely, some authors have described the Internet as a self-
regulating platform, able to develop its own code,[9] while others have
argued that regulation based on geographical boundaries was infeasible
so that applying national laws to the Internet was therefore impossible. In
particular, David Johnson and David Post, two champions of this anarchic
approach to the Web, held that 'events on the Net occur everywhere
but nowhere in particular' and therefore 'no physical jurisdiction has a
more compelling claim than any other to subject events exclusively to its
laws'.[10]

In the cyber-anarchic view, the rise of Internet law would have caused
the disintegration of state sovereignty over cyberspace. That disintegration would have implied the impossibility of applying to the field under
investigation any tool based on the theory of transnational law. How
would it be possible to share either horizontally or vertically a sovereignty
which no longer exists?[11]

How did this approach influence the first judicial attempts to assess the
new kinds of conflicts emerging on the Internet?

1.2. How case law has addressed attempts to emancipate the Internet from legal regulation

The approach of the US courts to problems raised by the seemingly
borderless nature of the Internet has moved away from reconsidering
the criteria they had set forth over time to determine the power of a
court to adjudicate disputes directly or indirectly involving legislation
of two or more jurisdictions. With regard to the most critical matters

---

[9] See P. Baran, *Communications, Computers and People* (Santa Monica, CA: RAND Corporation, 1965) and L. Lessig, *Code and other Laws of Cyberspace* (New York: Basic Books,
1999).

[10] See Johnson and Post, note 8 above.

[11] It is indeed quite paradoxical that one of the most famous and drastic assumptions of
the new, alleged a-national, borderless dimension of cyberspace has used, to assert its
claim, the constitutional (and then consequently national) rhetoric of the fathers of the
US Constitution. See J. Barlow, 'A declaration of the independence of cyberspace' (1996),
available at https://projects.eff.org/~barlow/Declaration-Final.html.

addressed, such as the exercise of freedom of speech, US case law has established the limits of personal jurisdiction in cross-border disputes on the ground of the due process of law clause contained in the Fourteenth Amendment.

It is worth looking at these criteria in order to understand how problems arising from the nature of the Internet have found solutions pretty much consistent with former rulings. In *Pennoyer* v. *Neff* the Supreme Court held that 'the authority of every tribunal is necessarily restricted by the territorial limits of the State in which it is established. Any attempt to exercise authority beyond those limits would be deemed in every other forum ... an illegitimate assumption of power, and be resisted as mere abuse'.[12] According to the *Pennoyer* court, each US state has jurisdiction 'over persons and property within its territory'.[13]

This approach reflected a concept of jurisdiction based exclusively on territorial borders but turned out to be inappropriate as the growth of interstate commerce implied an increase in litigation, while new technologies facilitated the circulation of people and goods. Thus, harm could be inflicted and suffered in one US state though neither the wrongdoer nor the injured party were physically present there.

Therefore, in *International Shoe Co.* v. *Washington* the Supreme Court, even if not explicitly, overruled *Pennoyer* and developed a more flexible test requiring 'minimum contact' between the defendant and the forum state.[14] In particular, the court specified that in any case jurisdiction must not 'offend traditional notions of fair play and substantive justice'.[15] The minimum contact test did not provide a fixed rule, but prompted a specific and in-depth factual inquiry in every case in which jurisdiction over the defendant was at issue. In *Hanson* v. *Denckla,* the Supreme Court further refined the minimum contact test by requiring from the defendant an act constituting 'purposeful availment' of the benefits and protections of the forum state.[16]

An important application of these criteria was made in *Calder* v. *Jones,*[17] in which the court developed an 'effects test'. The plaintiff had filed suit in California against two reporters, living and working in Florida, who had written an allegedly defamatory article published in a newspaper that circulated in California. The Supreme Court found that California had jurisdiction, since 'under the circumstances, petitioners

[12] *Pennoyer* v. *Neff,* 95 US 714 (1878) at 720.   [13] *Ibid.*
[14] *International Shoe* v. *State of Washington*, 326 US 310 (1945).   [15] *Ibid.* at 326.
[16] *Hanson* v. *Denckla*, 357 US 235 (1958) at 253.   [17] *Calder* v. *Jones*, 465 US 783 (1984).

must reasonably anticipate being ha[u]led into court there to answer for the truth of the statements made in their article'.[18] In greater detail, the Supreme Court set out a three-pronged test of the defendant's awareness of three circumstances: first, the allegedly defamatory article circulated in California; second, the plaintiff's residence there; finally, that the allegedly defamatory statements would have harmed the reputation of the plaintiff there.

Adjudicating jurisdiction began to be felt as a key issue, since development of the Internet implied that interactions seemed to take place anywhere and nowhere.[19] What the US courts did in reaction to the development of legal relationships on the Internet was to adapt the principles expressed in case law to this new, apparently borderless environment. Some important 'refinements' were needed.[20] In making these, the judges distanced themselves from the approach of those who had maintained that the Internet could not be subject to legal regulation.

These efforts were carried out through a series of cases in which courts tackled the dilemma of whether websites should be considered either foreign entities attempting to enter national borders or foreign territories that can be visited once users have access to them. Depending on the answer, it could be said that a website is anywhere instead of nowhere, but this seems a merely formalistic exercise. Rather, courts took account of the type of contact required by the case law to assert jurisdiction over operators of websites given the transnational character of the Internet. In this light, they mainly focused on whether the activities carried out on the Internet by defendants constituted a 'purposeful availment' of the benefits and protections offered by the state claiming jurisdiction and thus met the minimum contact test.[21]

---

[18] *Ibid.* at 790.

[19] See J. Goldsmith, 'Against cyberanarchy', 65 *University of Chicago Law Review* (1998), 1199–250.

[20] U. Kohl, *Jurisdiction and the Internet: Regulatory Competence over Online Activity* (Cambridge: Cambridge University Press, 2007).

[21] *Ex multis*, in *CompuServe, Inc.* v. *Patterson*, 89 F.3d 1257 (6th Cir. 1996) the court ruled that the defendant, a Texas resident, purposefully availed himself of the privilege of doing business in Ohio by electronically transmitting shareware software files to CompuServe, which, in turn, advertised and distributed them to its subscribers over the Internet. Contra, the Second Circuit of Appeals in *Bensusan Restaurant Corp.* v. *King*, 126 F.3d 25 (2nd Cir. 1997) said that the simple creation of a passive website did not constitute a purposeful availment, since it permitted users located anywhere in the world to access it. See also *Maritz, Inc.* v. *CyberGold Inc.*, 947 F. Supp. 1328 (ED MO 1996) and *Humphrey* v. *Granite Gate Resorts, Inc.*, 568 NW 2nd 715 (MN 1997).

A first attempt to refine the criteria developed in the foregoing decisions was made in 1997 in the landmark case of *Zippo Manufacturing Co. v. Zippo Dot Com, Inc.*[22] In this case the District Court for the Western District of Pennsylvania developed a 'sliding-scale test' by distinguishing websites according to three levels of interactivity: 'the likelihood that personal jurisdiction can be constitutionally exercised is directly proportionate to the nature and quality of the commercial activity that an entity conducts over the internet'.[23] At the outset, the court focused on subjects operating websites with the purpose of doing business: in these cases, 'if the defendant enters into contracts with residents of a foreign jurisdiction that involve the knowing and repeated transmission of computer files over the Internet, personal jurisdiction is proper'.[24] Second, the court pointed out that passive websites, unlike 'active' ones, are operated with the sole purpose of supplying information and making it available (also) in other countries, so that kind of activity does not provide a sound basis for personal jurisdiction. Last, the court held that 'the middle ground is occupied by interactive Web sites where a user can exchange information with the host computer. In these cases, the exercise of jurisdiction is determined by examining the level of interactivity and commercial nature of the exchange of information that occurs on the web site.'[25] On these grounds the District Court concluded that a Californian corporation had entered into contact via its website with Pennsylvania residents with the purpose of doing business. This 'purposeful availment' was enough to meet the minimum contact test; thus, the court had jurisdiction and could adjudicate the case.

The sliding-scale test has been strongly criticised, however. Among others, Kohl noted that '[a]ssuming its validity, a site which is highly interactive in its design would appear to subject its provider to the personal jurisdiction of every court, and those which are not, of no court at all'.[26] Hörnle, on her part, downgraded the *Zippo* sliding scale to 'only a frequently cited test established by a US District Court' unable to 'overrule or replace the minimum contacts test'.[27] Indeed, in only a few cases have courts referred to *Zippo*.[28] On the other hand, it is useful to quote Justice

---

[22] *Zippo Manufacturing Co. v. Zippo Dot Com, Inc.*,952 F. Supp. 1119 (WD PA 1997).
[23] *Ibid.* at 1124.   [24] *Ibid.*
[25] *Ibid.*   [26] Kohl, note 20 above, p. 86.
[27] J. Hörnle, 'The jurisdictional challenge of the Internet' in L. Edwards and C. Waelde (eds), *Law and the Internet* (Oxford: Hart Publishing, 2009), p. 147.
[28] See, among others, *ALS Scan, Inc. v. Digital Service Consultants, Inc.*, 293 F.3d 7907 (4th Cir. 2002); *Cybersell Inc. v. Cybersell, Inc.*, 130 F.3d 414 (9th Cir. 1997).

Crabb's opinion in *Hy Cite Corporation* v. *BadBusinessBureau.com*, which rejected *Zippo*'s sliding-scale test on the grounds that it

> does not mean that a website's level of interactivity is irrelevant in deciding whether the exercise of jurisdiction is appropriate. The website's level of interactivity may be one component of a determination whether a defendant has availed itself purposefully of the benefits or privileges of the forum state.[29]

US courts are not the only ones to have faced problems of jurisdiction over the Internet. Another landmark case regarding a claim for online defamation was addressed in 2002 by the High Court of Australia. In *Dow Jones & Company, Inc.* v. *Gutnick* the plaintiff filed a complaint for defamation against a financial information firm relating to an article that appeared in its online newspaper.[30] Few of its subscribers were located in Australia, but the High Court heard the case, holding that

> [i]f people wish to do business in, or indeed travel to, or live in, or utilise the infrastructure of different countries, they can hardly expect to be absolved from compliance with the laws of those countries. The fact that publication might occur everywhere does not mean that it occurs nowhere.[31]

It is worth comparing the arguments used by the Australian High Court with the criteria established by US courts. First, the Australian court found that 'harm to reputation is done when a defamatory publication is comprehended by the reader, the listener, or the observer. Until then, no harm is done by it.'[32] Accordingly, it held that:

> [d]efamation is to be located at the place where the damage to reputation occurs... It is only when the material is in comprehensible form that the damage to reputation is done... In the case of material on the World Wide Web, it is not available in comprehensible form until downloaded on to the computer of a person who has used a web browser to pull the material from the web server. It is where that person downloads the material that the damage to reputation may be done. Ordinarily then, that will be the place where the tort of defamation is committed.[33]

Similarly, a UK court heard a defamation case brought by a US citizen against the authors of some articles posted on a website based in California. In *Lewis* v. *King* the England and Wales Court of Appeal addressed

---

[29] *Hy Cite Corporation* v. *BadBusinessBureau.com*, 2004 WL 42641 (WD WI 8 January 2004) at 12.
[30] *Dow Jones & Company, Inc.* v. *Gutnick* [2002] HCA 56.
[31] *Ibid.* at 186.   [32] *Ibid.* at 26.   [33] *Ibid.* at 44.

what should be deemed an attempt at 'forum shopping',[34] very similar to the idea of 'regulatory arbitrage'.[35] Both plaintiff and defendant resided in the USA, and the website on which the defamation occurred was 'located' in California. Nonetheless, the plaintiff brought the suit before a British court, assuming that the defamatory content could be accessed in the UK, thus causing harm to his reputation there. US and British law require different burdens of proof in such cases. Under US law, the plaintiff has to prove that the defamatory statements are false, while under British law it is incumbent on the defendant to bring evidence that those statements are true. Anyway, the court did not care about the forum-shopping argument raised by the defendant and found that it had jurisdiction because defamation, according to British law, occurs when a libellous statement is posted on the Web and becomes accessible in the UK. Accordingly, since the plaintiff had a reputation there, the harmful event was felt in Great Britain and the domestic court's jurisdiction was proper.[36]

Another remarkable judgment was issued in the criminal case *R v. Perrin*,[37] in which the French operator of a website resident in the UK was convicted of having posted contents prohibited under the Obscene Publications Act 1959. He contended that the UK court lacked jurisdiction since the server hosting the website was located outside the UK and thus that British law was not applicable; however, the court rejected this argument, pointing out that, otherwise, if domestic laws were applicable exclusively to content posted from the country of origin, operators would be encouraged to go forum shopping, as also noted by Kohl.[38]

Courts also asserted jurisdiction over online gambling operators targeting users in other states. Gambling law varies considerably from state to state, since it depends on a number of factors such as morality, culture and religion. As many states restrict gambling, the Internet allowed providers to overcome these 'regulatory barriers' in order to target users where gambling was prohibited or restricted. In particular, the Court of Justice of the European Union sought a balance between the economic freedoms guaranteed by the European Union Treaty and the power of states to forbid or limit (online) gambling to safeguard values

---

[34] *Lewis* v. *King* [2004] EWCA Civ 1329.

[35] M. A. Froomkin, 'The Internet as a source of regulatory arbitrage' in B. Kahin and C. Nesson (eds), *Borders in Cyberspace* (Cambridge, MA: MIT Press, 1997), p. 129.

[36] As specifically regards England, for more details see A. Sachdeva, 'International jurisdiction in cyberspace: a comparative perspective', 13 *Computers and Telecommunications Law Review* 1 (2007), 245–58 at 252.

[37] *R* v. *Perrin* [2002] EWCA Crim 747.   [38] Kohl, note 20 above, p. 98.

encapsulated in national constitutions. On the other hand, national courts sought to assert their jurisdiction over the owners of websites that offer Internet gambling without being legally licensed in the country of destination of their services.

These efforts are illustrated by two leading cases. First, in *People* v. *World Interactive Gaming Corp.* the court prohibited two companies headquartered in Antigua,[39] legally licensed in that state, from offering gambling to Internet users in New York, where games of chance are illegal. The respondents contended that the New York court lacked both personal and subject-matter jurisdiction. The court rejected this argument, saying that 'what makes Internet transactions shed their novelty for jurisdictional purposes is that similar to their traditional counterparts, they are all executed by and between individuals or corporate entities which are subject to a court's jurisdiction'.[40] At the outset, the court found it had personal jurisdiction on the grounds that both the *International Shoe* minimum contact and the 'purposeful availment' requirements were met since the respondents were clearly doing business in New York. Then, in reaction to the respondents' argument that New York law does not apply to companies incorporated in Antigua, the court pointed out that 'the act of entering the bet and transmitting the information from New York via the Internet is adequate to constitute gambling activity within New York State'.[41] The Court said that a computer server cannot work as a shield against liability.[42]

Similarly, the US Court of Appeals for the Second Circuit affirmed the judgment delivered by the district court in *United States* v. *Cohen*.[43] The defendant had been convicted of violations under a federal statute which prevented operators involved in the business of betting or wagering from using wire communications facilities (such as the Internet or the telephone) for transmission of bets or wagers in interstate or foreign commerce. As in *People* v. *World Interactive Gaming Corp.*, the company was legally licensed in Antigua, where it had been incorporated, but also targeted US residents via the Internet. At issue was not violation of the law of the state of New York, but compliance with a provision of the Wire Wager Act that forbids using the Internet to bypass prohibitions on land-based activities under national laws.

Some important remarks arise in light of the case law discussed above on jurisdiction over the Internet. As Reidenberg highlighted, '[t]he

---

[39] *People* v. *World Interactive Gaming Corp.*, 714 NYS 2d 844 (1999).   [40] *Ibid.* at 849.
[41] *Ibid.*   [42] *Ibid.* at 850.   [43] *United States* v. *Cohen*, 260 F.3d 68 (2nd Cir. 2001).

maturation of the analysis reflects an evolution from a somewhat naïve view of the Internet to a rejection of the Internet activists' simple denial of law'.[44]

All the cases examined above, as well as many others, clearly pose at least two types of problem. These issues stem in large part from the lack of a common framework of standards that could be shared between states. Especially when we are dealing with values such as freedom of speech, the level and extent of protection guaranteed by national constitutions vary significantly from state to state; so that an expression deemed defamatory or contrary to public moral standards in a given state could, on the contrary, be protected under the law of another.

First, if the Internet makes websites accessible anywhere and jurisdiction proper in any state where harm occurs due to their contents, two paths are feasible: either the contents must comply with all the relevant jurisdictions where the website can be accessed, or access to those contents may be limited to those countries which have not outlawed them.[45] Both these solutions are merely hypothetical: the first would entail the law of the most restrictive state becoming, at least potentially, the law applicable to every form of speech owing to the simple fact that the Internet makes it accessible anywhere. It would be paradoxical that a national law should regulate interaction outside national borders. This point was highlighted in *American Civil Liberties Union* v. *Reno,* in which it was held:

> Web publishers cannot prevent Internet users in certain geographic locales from accessing their site; and in fact the Web publisher will not even know the geographic location of visitors to its site. Similarly, a Web publisher cannot modify the content of its site so as to restrict different geographic communities to access of only certain portions of their site. Thus, once published on the Web, existing technology does not permit the published materials to be restricted to particular states or jurisdictions.[46]

The second solution, which would lead to an opposite result, has long been challenged by operators that dispute the existence of technical

[44] J. Reidenberg, 'Technology and Internet jurisdiction', 153 *University of Pennsylvania Law Review* (2005), 1951–74 at 1956.
[45] See also the case of *CompuServe* that was brought in Germany in 1995. The service provider blocked access to 200 chat groups in order to avoid prosecution under the Bavarian obscenity law. It was unable to ban only local customers from gaining access, so it suspended the groups worldwide. In so doing, it applied the moral standard of Germany across all those countries in which the website could be accessed. Further details in L. Lessig, *Code 2.0* (New York: Basic Books, 2006), p. 39.
[46] *American Civil Liberties Union* v. *Reno,* 217 F.3d 162 (3rd Cir. 2000) at 169.

instruments to target users by reference to their place of origin. Additionally, it would not ensure effective protection of constitutional values, since technological barriers could also be overcome under certain conditions.

The second problem is directly connected with the first. If websites can be accessed anywhere, then their contents might cause harm beyond the borders of the country of origin. Thus, foreign jurisdictions have the power to adjudicate disputes arising out of online activities, but it has to be questioned how judgments delivered in these cases could effectively be enforced.

Both the issues above were evidently involved in the case of *Yahoo!* v. *Licra*, which is relevant to both enforcement issues and to the difficulty of striking a balance on the Internet between freedom of speech and protection of other fundamental rights. An analysis of this case is provided in section 2.1 of this chapter. However, some remarks can be made even at this stage. Yahoo! hosted a website where auctions for the sale of Nazi memorabilia took place. Two French anti-racist organisations sought an order directing Yahoo! to disable the website in France, since sale of those memorabilia is prohibited under the French Penal Code. In the first case, brought before the Court of Paris, the issue was whether technical devices could allow operators to monitor and block access to websites by users from certain places of origin. Considering such a system of control feasible, the court required Yahoo! to prevent the website from being visited in France. Yahoo! had contended that no technical device allowed such monitoring but the court ruled in favour of the petitioners since the offending material was accessed (also) in France and, accordingly, the harm was felt there.[47]

A common denominator can be found amongst the cases described above: they all show that, so long as websites do not target or produce harm to certain individuals or entities, domestic jurisdiction cannot be asserted on the sole ground that website contents do not comply with the laws of that state. In the *Yahoo!* saga the point at issue was definitely whether a French court had the power to issue an order directed to a foreign operator who maintained the website on the ground of violation of the French Penal Code.

---

[47] As noted by M. Fagin, 'Regulating speech across borders: technology vs. values', 9 *Michigan Telecommunications and Technology Law Review* (2003), 395–455 at 429: 'The central mechanism of the French decision is the application of an effects-based analysis for international Internet jurisdiction, employed as a means of imposing the social cost of global Internet communications on content providers'.

1.3. The Achilles' heel(s) of the 'futility' argument: three points overlooked by the anarchic approach

As noted above, since the advent of the new millennium national courts have started to reject the so-called 'futility argument', according to which laws based on geographic borders are not feasible on the Internet. On the contrary, they have begun to require website operators to manipulate the architecture of websites so as to make them recognise or take account of territorial boundaries. In other words, the analysis shows how, even for the most revolutionary global communication technologies, geography and governmental coercion retain fundamental importance.[48]

At least three arguments seem to have been undervalued by the cyber-anarchic approach; as we saw at the beginning, it has been said that 'cyberspace really undermines the relationship between legally significant phenomena and physical location'.[49] The first argument relates to identifying the relevant conception of sovereignty. The second has to do with the paradoxical effect of the evolution of technology. The third is instead connected to the many faces which the notion of jurisdiction can wear.

First of all, taking the conception of sovereignty as a point of reference, this approach considers relevant a granitic and static notion that was already old-fashioned at the beginning of the 1990s, when the Internet acquired a commercial dimension, and thus is even more so today. It is a conception according to which a nation exercises plenary enforcement jurisdiction over persons and property within its border, but little, if any, beyond.[50]

More precisely, this conception could perhaps have been considered current and still valid more than 100 years ago when, in the 1895 case of *Carrick* v. *Hancock*, Lord Russell of Killowen CJ famously declared that 'the jurisdiction of a court was based upon the principle of territorial dominion, and that all the persons within territorial dominion owe their allegiance to its sovereign power and obedience to all its laws and to the lawful jurisdiction of its courts'.[51]

Since then, many things have changed. First of all the absolutist concept of sovereignty and assumptions related to the supposed exclusivity of

---

[48] J. Goldsmith and T. Wu, 'Preface' in Goldsmith and Wu (eds), *Who Controls the Internet? Illusions of a Borderless World* (Oxford: Oxford University Press, 2008).

[49] See Johnson and Post, note 8 above at 1367.

[50] See J. Goldsmith, 'The Internet and the abiding significance of territorial sovereignty', 5 *Indiana Journal of Global Legal Studies* (1998), 475–91.

[51] *Carrick* v. *Hancock* (1895) 12 TLR 59.

control by the sovereign state over everything present in its territory have started to show their lack of adequacy. This happened much earlier than the rise of the Internet, with the development of technology, the growth of international trade and the resulting increase in cross-border movement of persons, goods, capital and services. In particular, even before the advent of the Internet, problems related to regulation of the telephone, television, financial services and pollution, for instance, had brought to light the need for shared sovereignty, or at least, for shared agreement between the country of origin and the country of destination of the transborder content involved.

In this light, if compared to regulation of other transnational activities Internet law does not seem to raise new problems in qualitative terms but rather in quantitative terms, by the exploitation of two elements that play a crucial role in the theoretical framework of transnational law: space and time.

With regard to the territorial dimension, the real jurisdictional novelty of cyber law seems to be, on one hand, that it will more frequently give rise to circumstances in which effects are felt in multiple territories at once,[52] and on the other hand, that it makes it very easy and inexpensive for individuals outside the regulating jurisdiction to send harmful content into the regulating jurisdiction.[53]

With regard to the temporal dimension, one of the most peculiar characteristics of the Internet is that it does not seem to raise new legal issues, but instead can be used to rebut factual assumptions underlying certain already well-known legal regimes. Copyright law, for example, 'relied upon the factual assumptions that reproduction will lead to a loss of quality and that the marginal cost of reproduction and distribution will outweigh the benefits achieved by infringement. However in the digital age, an unlimited number of perfect copies can be made and distributed at minimal cost'[54] and a drastic compression of time. The compression

---

[52] J. Trachtman, 'Cyberspace, sovereignty, jurisdiction and modernism', 5 *Indiana Journal of Global Legal Studies* (1998), 561–81 at 569.

[53] For example, in relation to online defamation it has been said that 'there is nothing very new here, which is, formally, true – but the problems of traditional publishing and defamation are so multiplied when applied to a forum as large, as accessible, as cheap and as transnational as the Internet, that it is not hard to see why there is a perception that the law of libel has been transformed by its application to the new electronic highway.' See L. Edwards, 'Defamation and the Internet' in L. Edwards and C. Waelde (eds), *Law and Internet-Regulating Cyberspace* (Oxford: Hart Publishing, 1997), p. 184.

[54] Kohl, note 20 above, p. 38.

of time in the World Wide Web was clearly underlined by the High Court of Australia in the *Dow Jones* case, where it was stated that 'in the past *The Times* newspaper would have gone to every colony in Australia. It might have got there rather late, but it could have gone ... throughout the whole of that part of the world that was coloured red. I do not see the internet as introducing anything particularly novel; you just get it more quickly.'[55]

In relation to the sovereignty conundrum at the heart of Internet regulation, the only certainty is that there is no monocular vision of the impact of Internet law on state sovereignty. It could be said the Internet is seriously able to undermine the sovereignty of the state, and at the same time, especially in dictatorial regimes, that it represents a privileged tool for enforcing the sovereignty of the people against the regime. Is it not the case that for recent events in Egypt and the other countries involved in the Arab Spring, one of the key phrases has been 'Internet Revolution'?[56]

With regard to the second element noted above, which undermines the claims of a 'borderless' Internet, particular attention has to be paid to the process of innovation in information technology. This process, on one hand, is at the basis of claims advocated by the cyber-anarchic school of thought in order to challenge state jurisdiction, but on the other hand, seems, in a paradoxical way, to have empowered sovereign states to assert their rules on Internet activities.[57]

As in fact we have seen in the analysis of case law, major concerns about multijurisdictional regulatory exposure have been based on the idea that a content provider or Internet service provider with a multijurisdictional presence cannot monitor or control the geographical flow of information on the Internet. As has been correctly stated,[58] this assumption has become weaker with the evolution of digital technology, and especially with more recurrent use of tools of geo-localisation allowing content to be limited by reference to user location.

Against this background, the relevant question today is no longer whether content discrimination is technically feasible, but, as Goldsmith has noted in this respect,[59] how much it costs and what is the desired

---

[55] *Dow Jones*, note 30 above.
[56] See http://internetsgovernance.blogspot.com/2011/02/egypt-crisis-and-internet-revolution-20.html.
[57] See Reidenberg, note 44 above at 1956.
[58] J. Goldsmith, 'Unilateral regulation of the Internet: a modest defence', 11 *European Journal of International Law* 1 (2000), 135–48.
[59] *Ibid.*

degree of its effectiveness. In other words, the technological infrastructure, which has been at the heart of some authors' assault on national jurisdiction, has proved to be one of the most powerful engines to make the Internet 'less transnational'.

In relation to the third element, an important difference too often overlooked by the cyber-anarchic approach is that between prospective jurisdiction and enforcement jurisdiction. Prospective jurisdiction finds its expression in the power of a state to make its law apply to a particular transaction. This is evident, as in this context national law continues to play a crucial role, even where the content source is beyond the reach of the territorial government. The inability of government to stop this content at the border does not mean that the source is beyond local regulation of the harmful effects it has caused.

If it is not possible to intercept content at the border, a nation can take many steps within its territory to indirectly regulate content transmitted from abroad. Generally, this happens through adoption of legal sanctions against the foreign content provider's local assets or agents. This has always worked, for example, with unwanted radio and television content broadcast from one nation to another and, as will be seen in the case of *Google* v. *Vivi Down*, it applies to Internet content as well.

As has been correctly stated, 'the medium by which the harm is transmitted into the regulating jurisdiction – be it economic interdependence, postal mail, wind current or the internet – is not relevant to the justification for regulating it'.[60]

If, in the light of the notion of prospective jurisdiction, the right of sovereign states to establish rules for online activity is undeniable, it seems more problematic for the same state, moving on to enforcement jurisdiction, to enforce all the regulatory claims it is entitled to assert under its prospective jurisdiction. Territorial constraint does not occupy a decisive position with respect to prospective jurisdiction; by contrast, as we have seen in the analysis of case law, that constraint acquires a crucial role in the hand of enforcement. A state, in fact, can enforce jurisdiction only against persons or entities with a presence or assets within its territory.

In this context, the dynamics that characterise the interaction between interconnected legal orders in the era of transnational law become pivotal in order to successfully settle conflicts of law emerging in cyberspace. In particular, the central claim of this section is that in the field of Internet

---

[60] Goldsmith, 'Internet and abiding significance', note 50 above at 479.

regulation, where state intervention is forced to acknowledge its structural limits, national law cannot be replaced, even though some scholars
advocate this,[61] by *ex ante*, 'pre-packed' rules like those implemented
in the area of international public law or even of European law. By contrast, the only practicable solution seems to be a case-by-case approach
that takes place in the no-man's-land between municipal law and international law, in accordance with the rules at the heart of a pluralistic
vision of transnational law. This view, in its normative terms, and in the
words of Tuori, 'advocates discursive treatment of conflicts of authority, search for compatible solutions to such conflicts, mutual learning
processes and inclusion of relevant "foreign" legal orders' perspective in
coherence-seeking reconstructions of law'.[62]

On the other hand, a hierarchical approach encapsulated in an attempt
at top-down harmonisation stemming from international public law or
European hard law does not seem viable with respect to Internet regulation
because it needs to face the unconquerable challenge of the nature of state
interests involved in transnational regulatory issues. Very often, even
paradoxically, in the light of the supposed a-national character of the
World Wide Web, this harmonisation overlaps with the hard core of the
values at the heart of a state's national identity.

A combination of interests and values, those relevant in this context, is
then at the basis of the constituent power of the nation and is by definition
excluded by any process of top-down harmonisation, whether judicial or
legislative, as shown in the dialogue between the constitutional courts of
the EU Member States and the Court of Justice of the European Union.

2. How case law addressed the challenge of the World Wide Web to regulatory barriers

General principles of public policy, protection of morality, human dignity and privacy concerns are only a few of the fundamental values
inspiring legislation adopted in most jurisdictions. Nevertheless, some
of these values are subject to different levels of protection depending
on the community concerned. For example, protections of freedom of
speech and privacy differ substantially from state to state, whether viewed

---

[61] See H. Perritt Jr, 'The Internet as a threat to sovereignty? Thoughts on the Internet's role
in strengthening national and global governance', 5 *Indiana Journal of Global Legal Studies*
2 (1998), 423–42.
[62] See Tuori in Chapter 1 of this volume.

quantitatively or qualitatively, owing to the close link to that state's cultural, moral and religious background. Since the digital era has changed the natural environment in which interactions take place, protection of fundamental rights has become increasingly critical. The following cases will demonstrate that, as most legal interactions take place on the Internet, moving from an exclusive national perspective in regulating them would result in failure; thus, that only a wider approach constitutes a sound basis for regulation, even without exclusion of the national level, which still constitutes an essential stage for the choice of law. Three groups of cases are addressed below in the light of these remarks.[63]

2.1. Hate speech

In the *Yahoo!* v. *Licra* saga, the defendant organisation was sued before the Tribunal de Grande Instance de Paris by two anti-racist organisations seeking an order to disable a website on which auctions of Nazi memorabilia took place.[64] The claim was based on alleged violation of the French Criminal Code. In May 2000, the Court issued an order directing Yahoo! to take 'all necessary measures to dissuade and render impossible any access via Yahoo.com to the Nazi artefact auction service and to any other site or service that may be construed as constituting an apology for Nazism or a contesting of Nazi crimes'.[65] The court of Paris, looking at the effects caused by the website, found that the exercise of jurisdiction was proper, since the harm was suffered in France as a consequence of broadcasting the auction on the Internet. Under its criminal law barring transactions in Nazi paraphernalia, France aimed to protect 'its own internal public order and the dignity of its citizens'.[66]

In response to this order, Yahoo! first argued that the French court lacked jurisdiction, further alleging that the order issued by the court was unenforceable because no technical means could allow Internet service

---

[63] In particular, the first case that will be examined, *Yahoo!* v. *Licra et al.*, demonstrated the growth of the Internet and its ensuing emancipation from US control. Most notably, as argued by Reidenberg, 'the positive impact of the *Yahoo!* decision is that Internet actors will have to recognise varying public values across national borders'. See J. Reidenberg, 'The *Yahoo!* case and the international democratization of the Internet', Fordham University School of Law, Research Paper 11 (2001).

[64] *La Ligue Contre le Racisme et l'Antisémitisme* v. *Yahoo!, Inc.*, Tribunal de Grande Instance de Paris, 22 May 2000.

[65] *Ibid.*   [66] See Fagin, note 47 above at 422.

providers to control and select users having access to a certain website depending on their country of origin.[67] Additionally, Yahoo! contended that, should it be forced to comply with French law, the website would have to be removed altogether, with detrimental consequences for those living in countries in which selling Nazi memorabilia had not been prohibited.[68] In November 2000 the Tribunal rejected Yahoo!'s defences and upheld the decision of the Court of Paris.[69] In response to this judgment, Yahoo! did nothing more than display on the website's home page a warning that it was in violation of the French Criminal Code.

Next, before the US District Court for the Northern District of California, Yahoo! sought a declaratory judgment that the French Tribunal lacked jurisdiction. Yahoo!'s argument was that the court order violated the First Amendment and was therefore unenforceable. It looks to have been a quite paradoxical approach as, before the French court, Yahoo! had seemingly supported regulation sceptics' theories and regarded the First Amendment as a shield ensuring absolute protection.[70] The US court held that:

> [w]hat is at issue here is whether it is consistent with the Constitution and laws of the United States for another nation to regulate speech by a United States resident within the United States on the basis that such speech can be accessed by Internet users in that nation.[71]

The court found that the order issued by the Tribunal conflicted with the First Amendment of the US Constitution: it would have been all the more in breach had a US court issued it, as it was against the Constitution. Nor were international comity concerns taken into account by the court, which articulated the discretionary character of comity as envisaged in *Hilton*.[72] The court said:

---

[67] With respect to this point, it should be noted that, in response to Yahoo!'s claim that no technical device allowed the users accessing a website to be filtered, the Court appointed a panel of experts to ascertain whether it was technically feasible for Yahoo! to determine the origin of cybersurfers.

[68] Many commentators looked at the order of the French court 'as a threat to the exercise of the freedom of speech on the Internet, as a misguided attempt to impose national regulations on the Internet, or as an exercise in futility because of the global nature of the Internet'. See Reidenberg, 'The *Yahoo!* case', note 63 above at 1.

[69] Tribunal de Grande Instance, Paris, 22 November 2000.

[70] See Fagin, note 47 above at 426.

[71] *Yahoo!, Inc* v. *La Ligue Contre le Racisme et l'Antisemitisme*, 169 F. Supp. 2d 1181 (ND CA 2001).

[72] *Hilton* v. *Guyot*, 159 US 113 (1895).

Absent a body of law that establishes international standards with respect to speech on the Internet and an appropriate treaty or legislation addressing enforcement of such standards to speech originating within the United States, the principle of comity is outweighed by the Court's obligation to uphold the First Amendment.[73]

Protection of public order and human dignity in France on one hand and protection of freedom of speech in the United States on the other were therefore at stake.[74] The case showed that a difference in the degree to which fundamental rights are protected can result in conflicts between jurisdictions and problems of enforcement.

However, the defendants appealed the judgment, challenging in turn the jurisdiction that the District Court had assumed. The Ninth Circuit of Appeals reversed the decision, finding that:

France is within its rights as a sovereign nation to enact hate speech laws against the distribution of Nazi propaganda in response to its terrible experience with Nazi forces during World War II. Similarly, LICRA and UEJF are within their rights to bring suit in France against Yahoo! for violation of French speech law. The only adverse consequence experienced by Yahoo! as a result of the acts with which we are concerned is that Yahoo! must wait for LICRA and UEJF to come to the United States to enforce the French judgment before it is able to raise its First Amendment claim. However, it was not wrongful for the French organizations to place Yahoo! in this position.[75]

In particular, the US District Court lacked personal jurisdiction, since the anti-racist organisations had not availed themselves of the benefits and protections of California law and the 'old-fashioned' minimum contact test, applied to the Internet environment, was not met.

In brief, the point at issue in the *Yahoo!* case was twofold. On one hand, the power to enforce a judgment issued by a foreign court was involved; in this light, it should be noted that, because of its discretionary character,

---

[73] *Ibid.* at 1193.

[74] Fagin, note 47 above at 438:

The American allegiance to the First Amendment is as central to the American perception of free speech as the moral imperative and commitment to 'personal dignity' that underlies the French hate speech statute. This variance in approach does not detract from the fact that both are legitimate policies of sovereign democratic political systems. However, in the end, neither the technology of the Internet nor the system of international law gives one a greater claim to legitimacy than the other.

[75] 379 F.3d 1120 (9th Cir. 2004) at 1123.

the principle of judicial comity was significantly undermined in the decision of the District Court. On the other hand, the case clearly illustrates the difficult dialogue between legal orders when courts' decisions affect protection of constitutional values. The reasons why this dialogue is still troublesome today lie with differences between values and the connected degree of protection under national constitutions. Different approaches to freedom of speech, and to public order, result, at the final step, in problems in enforcing judgments issued by foreign courts. If neither state is willing to step back, only mutual recognition of such differences in a supranational perspective could reconcile the transnational character of the Internet with the 'fatal attraction' of legal regulation for nations.

In that light, it seems that Reidenberg's words hit the mark:

> The *Yahoo!* decision can...be seen as both an ordinary case that the French court judged according to basic jurisdictional principles that are also recognized in American law and as an extraordinary case that creates a principle of international democracy and the respect of non-commercial values for the technological infrastructure of the Internet.[76]

2.2. Gambling

In section 1.2 above, we reported some cases concerning jurisdictional issues brought by use of the Internet for cross-border provision of gambling services. On the same matter, the case law of the Court of Justice of the European Union goes far beyond a solely jurisdictional challenge. Indeed, in most of the judgments delivered by the Court, the issue was whether safeguarding certain values encapsulated in national constitutions, such as public order and consumer protection, could be limited for the sake of supranational principles, i.e. the economic fundamental freedoms of the European Union.

Over the last decade, online gambling has provided a special perspective for looking at the relationship between law,[77] intended to protect constitutional values, and technology, intended to make available a borderless environment in which a number of interactions take place. So, one might suppose that harmonisation of substantive rules constitutes the best way to achieve an appropriate legal framework in the transnational context. Harmonisation is usually achieved through international

---

[76] Reidenberg, 'The *Yahoo!* case', note 63 above at 4.

[77] See also B. Maier, 'How has the law attempted to tackle the borderless nature of the Internet?', 18 *International Journal of Law and Technology* 2 (2010), 142–75.

treaties and in the EU context presupposes a transfer of sovereignty to supranational entities from national ones.[78]

However, as the *Yahoo!* case has brought to light, not all parts of different legal orders are well suited to harmonisation, since they reflect the qualitative and quantitative degree of protection afforded to certain values by each legal order. Harmonisation has proved effective for constructing a common legal framework as long as it has been employed to regulate activities that are universally condemned or endorsed. As Uta Kohl points out, the real problems start when we go beyond this core of activities:

> Regulation that would be in the eyes of one State an undue encroachment on the freedom to communicate is in the eyes of another a legitimate curb on that freedom. Substantive harmonisation has not occurred even where the difference of opinion seems rather slight, which is by no means unusual. Most States agree in principle that consumers deserve some protection in their dealing with business or that children should be shielded from pornographic material. But variations in the detail of how much protection there should be and how it should be implemented, and perhaps an inherent resistance to making an external legal commitment, have prevented States from finding a common denominator.[79]

In the European Union context no regulation exists covering online gambling, since Directive 2000/31/EC expressly left such services out of its scope. It goes without saying that gambling fits within the group of activities that are regarded differently across states depending upon different moral, cultural and religious standards.

In the leading case of *Gambelli*,[80] a preliminary proceeding had been brought before the Court of Justice in the course of a criminal trial. Some intermediaries were accused of having violated criminal provisions prohibiting illegal gambling for having established a network of agencies collecting bets on behalf of a British company that lacked the national licence required to operate in Italy. The domestic provisions criminalising the offering of gambling services by operators not granted an Italian licence – but allowed to operate in their country of origin – had been considered by Italian courts a restriction by the European Union justified by the safeguarding of public order, consumer protection and crime prevention.

---

[78] Furthermore, harmonisation can occur 'by deregulation'. See Kohl, note 20 above, p. 262.
[79] *Ibid.*, pp 264–5.
[80] Case C–243/01 *Criminal proceedings against Piergiorgio Gambelli and Others* [2003] ECR I–13031.

The Court said that 'restrictions based on such grounds ... must also be suitable for achieving those objectives, inasmuch as they must serve to limit betting activities in a consistent and systematic manner'. In so holding, the Court developed the 'hypocrisy test': it held that it was for the national courts to determine whether Italian law met such criteria; however it suggested the answer by pointing out that:

> In so far as the authorities of a Member State incite and encourage consumers to participate in lotteries, games of chance and betting to the financial benefit of the public purse, the authorities of that State cannot invoke public order concerns relating to the need to reduce opportunities for betting in order to justify measures such as those at issue in the main proceedings.[81]

The subsequent ruling of the Court of Justice in *Placanica* seemed to mark a point of no return, since the Court found that the Italian law at issue violated the fundamental principles of the European Union: 'that blanket exclusion goes beyond what is necessary in order to achieve the objective of preventing operators active in the betting and gaming sector from being involved in criminal or fraudulent activities'.[82]

In other words, by addressing these cases, the Court of Justice pointed to public order concerns and consumer protection as the only reasons that might justify limitations to the fundamental freedoms of the European Union such as those provided by Italian law, and thereby control of the activities carried out over the Internet by unauthorised operators.[83] These measures, in any case, had to pass the 'hypocrisy test' set forth in *Gambelli*.

The Internet in fact was used in an attempt at striking down the regulatory barriers raised by Italy, but it became clear that a) the restrictions under Italian law were essentially driven by protectionist policies and would have not passed the *Gambelli* test, and b) the desired level of internal protection could also be achieved without curbing the economic fundamental freedoms, since in most cases, operators' countries of origin enact proper systems of protection themselves.

However, a decision delivered in 2009 seemed to reopen the debate.[84] In *Liga Portuguesa de Futebol Profissional* v. *Bwin*, the Court of Justice found that Portuguese law, which had created a monopoly in the gambling

---

[81] *Ibid.*

[82] Joined cases C–338, C–359 and C–360/04 *Placanica and Others* [2007] ECR I–1891.

[83] Italian law also required Internet service providers to block access to websites providing gambling on behalf of non-licensed companies.

[84] Case C–42/07 *Liga Portuguesa de Futebol Profissional* v. *Bwin* [2009] ECR I–7633.

market (no matter whether over the Internet or not) complied with European Union law. The Court held that a monopoly, even though it curbs the freedom to provide services, can be justified on the grounds of maintaining public order and consumer protection, especially in the light of the higher risks caused by use of the Internet for gambling. The fact that other states had implemented less restrictive regulations had no importance in the Court's opinion, since every state has the right, in the absence of any form of harmonisation, to adopt legislation that best reaches the desired degree of protection. In *Liga Portuguesa*, Bwin, a well-known operator incorporated in Gibraltar, had provided betting services over the Internet targeting Portuguese users, and so violating the monopoly in that market.

Two similar judgments were delivered in July 2010 with regard to Dutch law on gambling. In these cases, too, the Court of Justice found that maintaining public order and consumer protection could justify measures restricting the provision of gambling services, such as granting exclusive rights to certain operators for every category of games.[85]

Further, the Italian online gambling saga began another chapter in February 2012, when the Court of Justice decided the case of *Costa and Cifone*.[86] In accordance with its previous rulings, the Court held that no penalties could be imposed against operators excluded from a tendering procedure for the award of national licences in breach of European Union law, even though in the meantime Italy had implemented new provisions to remedy the violations found by the Court in *Gambelli* and *Placanica*. The Court of Luxembourg, in fact, also considered that the new measures by which Italy had launched the new tendering procedure nevertheless did violate European Union law.

The cases above provide an overview of various attempts to strike down restrictions adopted by states, to foster internal protection of con-stitutional values. As the *Yahoo!/Licra* saga brought to light, the most critical issues arise when different ways of thinking and protecting gen-eral principles of public policy confront each other. The Internet, given its transnational character, is the natural environment in which these conflicts might come out. Moreover, where states grant different degrees of protection in different areas of law, these conflicts give rise to the

---

[85] Case C–203/08 *Sporting Exchange* [2010] ECR I–4695 and Case C–258/08 *Ladbrokes* [2010] ECR I–4757. See also Case C–347/09 *Criminal proceedings against Jochen Dickinger and Franz Ömer*, nyr, and Joined cases C–186/11 and C–209/11, *Stanleybet and Others*, nyr.
[86] Joint cases C–72/10 and C–77/10, *Marcello Costa* and *Ugo Cifone* [2012], nyr.

problems focused on in the previous paragraph. In the cases addressed by the Court of Justice, the issue was to what extent states could limit the reach of supranational principles such as the European Union fundamental freedoms by measures allegedly aimed at safeguarding public order and consumer protection. Seemingly, only harmonisation of substantive rules could be a remedy but in the absence of a common denominator for concepts such as public order, this poses a considerable challenge.

2.3. Privacy and data protection

In *Google-Vivi Down*,[87] a criminal proceeding was brought before the Court of Milan against four Google managers who had been charged with defamation and violation of privacy. They were sentenced to imprisonment for having failed to perform information duties arising from data processing in the first instance, but eventually were acquitted by the Court of Appeals.[88] The trial arose out of a case where a user had posted a short video on the UGC platform run by Google showing a teenager with Down's syndrome being bullied by classmates.

One of the main points at issue in the case concerned whether the jurisdiction of the Italian court was proper in the light of the principles regulating data protection in the European Union. Article 5 of the Italian Data Protection Code states that:

> [t]he present Code regulates the processing of personal data, including those held in foreign countries, performed by a controller established in Italy or in a territory however subject to Italian sovereignty.
>
> Also, it applies to controllers from outside the European Union processing personal data that use equipment located within the Italian territory.[89]

On the grounds of the second paragraph of Article 5, Google Italy argued that the Italian Data Protection Code did not apply, since the technical infrastructure (i.e. the server) where the video had been stored was located in the USA, so that no processing of personal data had occurred in Italy. The Court of Milan rejected Google's argument, pointing out that the law

---

[87] Trib. Milan, 24 February 2010, *Foro Italiano*, 5 (2010), vol. II, 279.

[88] For further information on the case, see G. Camera and O. Pollicino, *La Legge è Uguale Anche sul Web* (Milan: EGEA, 2010).

[89] Article 5, Legislative Decree no. 196, 30 June 2003, published in *Gazzetta Ufficiale della Repubblica Italiana*, 29 July 2003, no. 174 – Ordinary Supplement No. 123/L.

requires no correspondence between the place where the server is located and the place where personal data are processed.

Some important rationales seem to underlie the first instance court's opinion. First, the processing of personal data was seen as a process that is anything but instantaneous, so that it had *also* taken place in the United States, but not exclusively there. Second, the Court relied on a comprehensive definition of 'processing', including a long chain of activities (from input through to broadcasting the video). Third, an extensive interpretation was given of 'equipment', in the second paragraph of Article 5: there was technical infrastructure other than the server on which the video was stored that enabled its broadcasting in Italy; in this way processing of personal data (also) occurred outside the United States.

The crucial issue was: did the Italian court have the power to adjudicate the case? In 2006 an Italian citizen had threatened an action against Google Italy for violation of the Data Protection Act. In that case, Google had failed to remove from its cache outdated contents, which continued to be displayed in the search results. Google Italy objected that Italian law was not applicable and contended that the only subject responsible for processing personal data was Google Inc., which had exclusive control of the server and search engines. The Italian Data Protection Authority found that the activities connected with the management of the search engines were carried out only by Google Inc., so that the Italian court lacked jurisdiction over Google Italy.

Moreover, the case law of the European Court of Justice provides that companies operating their business via the Internet have to be deemed to be established in the place where their activities are actually performed. At the same time, in the European context, some clarifications were felt increasingly necessary with respect to cases where the controller in charge of processing personal data was established in a country outside the European Union.

A 'Working document on determining the international application of EU data protection law to personal data processing on the Internet by non-EU based websites' was adopted in 2002 by the Article 29 Data Protection Working Party.[90] It seemed to include in the notion of 'equipment' for processing personal data all the infrastructure used to perform operations such as collection, processing and diffusion of personal data.

---

[90] Article 29 Data Protection Working Party document 5035/01/EN/Final, WP 56, adopted on 30 May 2002.

In this way, the field of application of Directive 95/46/EC would have been significantly extended.

Another important document, the Data Protection Working Party's Opinion 1/2008,[91] focused on search engines. The opinion made clear that, if a company that runs a search engine is located outside the European Economic Area, the European Directive may apply on condition that at least one of the offices of the controller takes part in processing personal data within a Member State and the processing is performed in the context of the activities carried out by that office.[92]

The Court of Milan found this requirement met in *Google-Vivi Down*, and so asserted it had jurisdiction, and proceeded to adjudicate the case. In the appeal proceedings, the Court of Appeals of Milan reversed the convictions, even though the acquittal was based on grounds other than applicability to the defendants of the European Union data protection law (and, accordingly, of the Italian law).[93] In this respect, the appeal court found that the Google Video service had been located in Europe and then in Italy since 2006. Google Italy being established in Italian territory, it was bound by Article 5 of the Data Protection Code.

The Court of Appeals pointed out that, even if the place of establishment could not be determined, Google would nevertheless be subject to the Italian Data Protection Code, as Article 5 paragraph 2 also applies to companies with assets, *even non-electronic ones*, situated in the state's territory. In the court's view, it was undisputed that the company had created an organised structure in Italy that was likely to amount to an 'asset, even non-electronic'.

3. Concluding remarks

3.1. *The unavoidable need for a common ground of values shared among states – what future for constitutional law in transnational governance?*

Beginning the final remarks by reference to the very first assumption of this chapter, it seems to us that the process of globalisation has neither led to a world in which borders are irrelevant, nor, as has been argued,[94] to

---

[91] Article 29 Data Protection Working Party Opinion 1/2008 on data protection issues related to search engines, 00737/EN WP 148, adopted on 4 April 2008.

[92] *Ibid.*, p. 10.

[93] Court of Appeals of Milan, 21 December 2012.

[94] M. Kumm, 'The legitimacy of international law: a constitutionalist framework of analysis', 15 *European Journal of International Law* 5 (2004), 907–31 at 913.

a world in which decisions on how borders are relevant are increasingly made outside the nation's domestic process. In order to give effectiveness to these decisions, the process seems instead to have made crucial the existence of a common, shared, legal ground among the states that are involved in those decisions.

The key question in this regard concerns how to achieve the necessary minimum common ground. It seems evident that a process of hard harmonisation stemming from European or international law is the least suitable method to achieve the goal. It is in fact obvious that, owing to the high degree of vertical transfer of sovereignty required by every process of top-down harmonisation, nation states will be more reluctant to accept a direct limitation of their sovereign powers in those areas that reflect their national identity more closely.

By contrast, it is not surprising that, as an instrument of political and economic integration, a preference for mutual recognition of the national values at stake in Internet regulation appears to be more respectful of diversity and state autonomy.[95] More precisely, in the era of transnational law, on one hand the degree of cooperation shown by each state becomes crucial to a mutual, voluntary recognition of the values characterising each individual nation's legal order, and on the other hand the relationship between the regulatory consequences of mutual recognition and its conception as a form of governance acquires a highly important role.[96]

As has been noted, the recognition of diversity presupposed in mutual recognition actually depends, ironically, on a certain degree of common identity, since only the latter can provide the basis for the mutual trust necessary to implement mutual recognition.[97] This appears even truer in the field of Internet law, as clearly shown by the case law discussed above. The most problematic and irreconcilable issues have arisen in the context of yawning distances between the essential core of the notions of public order held by the different legal orders involved in a single judicial dispute.

The process of mutual recognition still faces two further challenges in proving itself to be the most effective tool to achieve a feasible model for governance of Internet law. First of all, the process of mutual

---

[95] K. Nicolaidis, 'Trusting the Poles? Constructing Europe through mutual recognition', 14 *Journal of European Public Policy* 5 (2007), 682–98.

[96] See M. Maduro, 'So close and yet so far: the paradoxes of mutual recognition', 14 *Journal of European Public Policy* 5 (2007), 814–25 at 817.

[97] *Ibid.* at 814.

recognition is not immune from a necessary, even if partial, limitation of state sovereignty that finds its instantiation in the exercise of public choice.[98] Second, one of the limits of mutual recognition that makes its application to the field of Internet law more problematic is that, until now, it has served to create a more homogeneous (or at least a less hetero-geneous) internal market within the European Union. As we have seen above, however, one of the most crucial issues is the clash between the European and the US conceptions of Internet regulation.

Against this background, a process of mutual recognition of the under-pinning national values at the heart of single-state regulation can only become the most suitable instrument for achieving an effective frame-work of transnational Internet governance if the soft and discretional judicial comity approach (which we saw involved in the *Yahoo!* case)[99] is empowered by an 'injection of legal pluralism', in the terms advocated by Maduro's contrapunctual logic at the heart of the interaction between legal orders and by Tuori's theory of transnational law.[100] In particular, the strengthening legal pluralism should be seen in its normative terms. As Tuori has clarified, this advocates discursive treatment of conflicts of authority, a search for compatible solutions to those conflicts,[101] and sharing of value systems and commitments between legislative and judi-cial powers. States are hard-pressed to realise their regulatory objectives by mutual cooperation, but they can no longer pretend to be regulatory islands.

Before moving on to our second concluding remark, some points have to be highlighted. The first has to do with the notion of so-called 'judicial dialogue', which has also characterised the dynamics of our case law-based analysis; the second is connected with the relationship between

---

[98] *Ibid.*

[99] According to Shany, judicial comity consists in courts in one jurisdiction showing respect and demonstrating a degree of deference to the laws of other jurisdictions, including the decisions of judicial bodies operating in those jurisdictions. See Y. Shany, *The Compet-ing Jurisdictions of International Courts and Tribunals* (Oxford: Oxford University Press, 2003), p. 260. It would not be unfair to recognise, on the other hand, the virtues of the judicial comity approach: 'The principle of comity is important because it alleviates the difficult aspects of jurisdictional competition by encouraging judges to accommodate related procedures; in other words, this principle represents a strategy for soft coordi-nation and harmonization between the entire gamut of jurisdictional configurations'. G. Martinico, 'Judging in the multilevel legal order: exploring the techniques of "hidden dialogue"', 21 *King's Law Journal* 2 (2010), 257–81 at 270.

[100] See M. Maduro, 'Contrapunctual law: Europe's constitutional pluralism in action' in N. Walker (ed.), *Sovereignty in Transition* (Oxford: Hart Publishing, 2003), p. 501.

[101] See Tuori in Chapter 1 of this volume.

state public choice, technology and the role of constitutional law; the third is related to a new kind of collision between interacting legal orders.

With regard to judicial dialogue, the analysis of case law clarifies a stereotype that unavoidably appears every time the judicial globalisation discourse comes close,[102] in the light of the theory of transnational law, to the relationship between the European legal dimension and the dimension of the national constitution.[103]

In our view, it should be noted that the notion of judicial dialogue is nothing but a signal that indicates the presence of something else, often particularly problematic, behind it.[104] It is not, then, a substantive goal in itself but rather a procedural tool to improve a status quo that is not completely satisfactory. If something called global judicial dialogue exists, it very often occurs due to a (real or presumed) risk of collision between the domestic constitutional, European Union, European Court of Human Rights and global levels,[105] especially with regard to the standard of fundamental rights protection.

With regard to the second element mentioned above, our analysis shows that it is crucial, with respect to Internet regulation, that the allocation of jurisdiction to a particular state is not simply considered a technical

---

[102] See C. l'Heureux-Dube, 'The international judicial dialogue: when domestic constitutional courts join the conversation', 114 *Harvard Law Review* (2001), 2049–73; A-M. Slaughter, 'A global community of courts', 44 *Harvard International Law Journal* (2003), 191–219; A-M. Slaughter, *A New World Order* (Princeton, NJ: Princeton University Press, 2004); S. Choudry, 'Globalization in search of justification: towards a theory of comparative Constitutional interpretation', 74 *Indiana Law Journal* 3 (1999), 819–91; C. McCrudden, 'A common law of human rights? Transnational judicial conversations on constitutional rights', 20 *Oxford Journal of Legal Studies* 4 (2000), 499–532; A. Stone Sweet, *On Law, Politics and Judicialisation* (Oxford: Oxford University Press, 2002); A. Stone Sweet, *Governing with Judges: Constitutional Politics in Europe* (Oxford: Oxford University Press, 2000).

[103] V. Skouris, 'The position of the European Court of Justice in the EU legal order and its relationship with national constitutional courts', *Zeitschrift für Öffentliches Recht* 60 (2005), 323ff.; A. Stone Sweet, 'Constitutional dialogue in the European Community' in J. H. H. Weiler, A-M. Slaughter and A. Stone Sweet (eds), *The European Court and National Courts: Doctrine and Jurisprudence: Legal Change in its Social Context* (Oxford: Hart Publishing, 2004), p. 304; F. Lichère, L. Potvin-Solis and A. Raynouard (eds), *Le Dialogue entre les Juges Européens et Nationaux: Incantation ou Réalité* (Paris: Dalloz, 2004).

[104] See F. Jacobs, 'Judicial dialogue and the cross-fertilization of legal systems: the European Court of Justice', 38 *Texas International Law Journal* (2003), 547–56; A. Rosas, 'The European Court of Justice in the context: forms and pattern of judicial dialogue', *European Journal of Legal Studies* 1 (2007), 1–16.

[105] N. MacCormick, 'Risking constitutional collision in Europe?', 18 *Oxford Journal of Legal Studies* (2005), 517–32.

issue, because it necessarily involves distributional or public choice.[106] It follows that the evolution of technology cannot dominate the public choice of states. From this perspective, it should always be the law – the regulatory expression of legislative and governmental public choice – that takes advantage of the presence of technology infrastructure, and not the other way round. As has been observed, to dismiss Internet rules as merely technical standards, would dramatically miss the political and constitutional dimension of the technology.[107]

This means that, as happened in the past for other technological innovations in writing, printing and broadcasting, the law possesses in itself the force to evolve in response to a changing world. As has been correctly stated in this regard, 'while it seems that the Internet is totally new and unprecedented, in many ways it is no more than the epitome of a long standing development towards greater and greater economic globalisation'.[108]

In this context, the relationship between transnational law, public choice and constitutional law assumes crucial importance from two points of view. From the first, much of the literature on transnational governance has shifted from goal-oriented intentional strategy to a design constellation that places its hopes in the ingenuity of the actors involved.[109] In this respect, it must be regarded as essential that governance remain an intentional activity even when it is transnational. As has been argued:

> The transfer of social problems from the constitutionally controlled national space is not a matter of simply following the dictates of technology or the needs of knowledge generation that transcends the national

---

[106] As has been underlined, the technological choice either to filter or not to filter becomes a normative decision by the user's forum state to adopt the 'purposefully avail' standard. See J. Reidenberg, 'Technology and Internet jurisdiction', note 44 above at 1962. For a background on public choice theory, see, e.g., M. Stearns, *Public Choice and Public Law: Readings and Commentary* (Cincinnati, OH: Anderson Publishing, 1997); J. Buchanan and G. Tullock, *The Calculus of Consent* (Indianapolis, IN: Liberty Fund, 1962); D. Farber and P. Frickey, 'The jurisprudence of public choice', 65 *Texas Law Review* (1987), 873–927; W. Eskridge, 'Politics without romance: implications of public choice theory for statutory interpretation', 74 *Virginia Law Review* (1988), 275–338.

[107] See L. Lessig, 'The limits in open code, regulatory standard and the future of the Net', 14 *Berkeley Technology Law Journal* (1999), 759–70: see also G. Calliess and P. Zumbansen, *Rough Consensus and Running Code* (Oxford: Hart Publishing, 2010), p. 136.

[108] Kohl, note 20 above, p. 52.

[109] C. Joerges, 'Constitutionalism and transnational governance: exploring a magic triangle' in C. Joerges, I-J. Sand and G. Teubner (eds), *Transnational Governance and Constitutionalism: International Studies in the Theory of Private Law* (Oxford: Hart Publishing, 2004), p. 368.

state. The lack of national control is often the result of deliberate choices on the part of private actors or even government entities.[110]

The second related aspect is that when a transfer takes place, even a partial one, from the national dimension to a transnational one, precisely because public choice issues do not disappear but are simply transferred, constitutional law could not leave the field entirely to international law. Even where, as happens in the field of Internet law, states cannot fully achieve control over the private sector, they cannot simply turn away their gaze, claiming that no relevant phenomenon is taking place. The consequence, as we have pointed out, would be to accept passively, from a constitutional law perspective, that the allocation of private risk and injustice and so forth are sometimes generated within the borders of constitutionally protected, private autonomy.[111]

Finally, with respect to the third point listed above, it should also be noted that the rules on conflicts of laws have to be rethought, from their present focus on conflicts between national legal orders to one on conflicts between transnational sectoral regimes and national legal orders. The immediately emerging question connected to that assumption is obvious: can we apply to such collisions the conflicts settlement rules that coordinate the interconnection between interacting national legal orders, or should we instead create new rules for deciding conflicts of legal orders involving transnational laws?

3.2. A new fundamental right in the new season of transnational law – the right to Internet access

Freedom of expression is strongly protected by all Western countries' constitutions as well as by charters and conventions on fundamental rights. Moreover, the importance of protecting free speech has been stressed several times in the case law of the European Court of Human Rights, the Court of Justice of the European Union and the US Supreme Court.

There is no doubt that in the current digital era it is on the World Wide Web that people find opportunities and chances to form, modify and express their ideas. Thus, having access to the Internet has become a

---

[110] A. Sajó, 'Book review: Christian Joerges, Inger-Johanne Sand, and Günther Teubner (eds), *Transnational Governance and Constitutionalism: International Studies in the Theory of Private Law* [and] Anne-Marie Slaughter, *A New World Order*', *International Journal of Constitutional Law*, 4 (2005), 697–705 at 702.

[111] See *ibid.* at 699.

prerequisite for people and organisations to form and express their opinions and creativity. Access to, and use of, the Internet strongly enhances freedom of speech. Indeed, in the offline world, the only way for an individual to circulate their ideas was either by standing on a box at Hyde Park Corner or accepting the mediation and filtering of media enterprises. This compulsory use of the traditional media business model has chilled and still chills individuals' freedom of speech. Now, the advent and development of the Internet have strongly marginalised the role of traditional media enterprises, which no longer constitute a *condicio sine qua non* for the enjoyment of freedom of speech. Thus, in the digital context individuals' creativity and innovation are capable of breaking the barriers present in the offline world and regain all their value. This is possible provided that a basic condition is met: access to the Internet must be guaranteed to anyone.

It is not surprising, therefore, that there has recently been a push by the United Nations to make Internet access a human right. The right to Internet access – also known as the right to broadband – has been increasingly perceived as acquiring the same relevance as the right to other public goods. The Internet has become vital in everyday life and positively affects the ability of people to communicate, work, manage finances, learn and generally participate in the collective life of our society.[112]

Finland was the first country to introduce a legal right to Internet access at constitutional level,[113] while Estonia in 2000 also passed a law stating that Internet access is a fundamental human right. Moreover, in a 2009 decision, the French Constitutional Court basically confirmed that the right to Internet access belongs to the category of fundamental rights.[114] Additionally, the Constitutional Chamber of the Supreme Court

---

[112] See A. Bridy, 'Graduated response and the turn to private ordering in online copyright enforcement', 89 *Oregon Law Review* 1 (2010), 81–132.

[113] In the *Yahoo!* case discussed above, as early as 2000, the right of access to cyberspace was at stake. See G. Teubner, 'Societal constitutionalism, alternative to state-centred constitutional theory?' in Joerges, Sand and Teubner, note 109 above, p. 4.

[114] France has taken into serious consideration the problem of online copyright. The first version of the HADOPI law was adopted in May 2009, creating an ad hoc administrative agency with the task of checking that Internet subscribers screen their Internet connections in order to prevent exchange of copyright material without agreement in advance by the copyright holders, and with the power to impose sanctions. The law is based on the 'three-strikes rule', or 'graduated response' – at the point of third infringement, either Internet access (with any service provider) is suspended for up to one year or the subscriber must implement security measures and pay penalty fees for non-compliance.

of Costa Rica declared Internet access to be essential for the exercise of fundamental rights.[115] In European Union law, Article 3*bis* of Directive 2009/140/EC, attaches great importance to the right to Internet access and expressly makes reference to the fundamental rights and freedoms of natural persons enshrined in the European Convention on Human Rights.

A few further comments on the right to Internet access are therefore necessary. First, this right could be identified as one of the first human rights belonging to the last generation of fundamental rights. It could be argued that this right emerged when it became clear that rights identified as fundamental in the digital era enjoy the same constitutional status as the traditional 'offline' freedoms. Second, merely identifying a right to Internet access as instrumental for other fundamental freedoms would not pay tribute to its essential role. Indeed, this right clearly represents a necessary precondition to the enjoyment of many constitutional freedoms in the digital era.[116] Third, as has been noted,[117] the development of this new constitutional right has called into question the dichotomy between negative and costless fundamental freedoms and costly social rights. This is a 'new-born' right that undisputedly ranks among fundamental rights. Moreover, protecting this right requires states to adopt specific policies aimed at ensuring its effective enjoyment by individuals and particularly to carry out extensive investments, especially in infrastructure. Last, but not least, since – as we have seen in the Internet governance constellation – a great role is played by private, multinational and extremely powerful companies, it becomes essential to go definitively beyond the limits fixed by the state action doctrine in order to grant protection to the 'right of

---

In June 2009 the French Constitutional Council found a portion of HADOPI unconstitutional in light of Article 11 of the Declaration of the Rights of Man and Citizen of 1789, as terminating individuals' Internet access affects their fundamental right to free expression; hence decisions depriving Internet access should be taken by a court after balancing the interests at stake, i.e. copyright protection and freedom of speech. The Court stated on freedom of speech that 'in the current state of the means of communication and given the generalized development of public online communication services and the importance of the latter for participation in democracy and the expression of ideas and opinions, this right implies freedom to access such services' (para. 12). On September 2009 the French Parliament amended the law (HADOPI 2, into force on 1 January 2010) authorising only courts to impose the sanction.

[115] See Supreme Court of Costa Rica, 20 July 2010.

[116] V. Zencovich, 'L'accesso alla rete come diritto fondamentale', presented at 'Il Diritto dell'Informazione tra Regole Antiche e Nuovi Media', Workshop in memory of Corso Bovio, Milan (2010).

[117] *Ibid.*

access to cyberspace' and also to other related, web-based, fundamental rights.[118]

In that light, the theory of the horizontal effect of fundamental rights has to be supported and, accordingly, the possibility to assert fundamental rights related to cyberspace not only against political bodies, but also against non-state actors.[119] On one hand there is no doubt that, as has been observed,[120] global governance structures for 'cyber law' operating outside international law have the advantage of empowering private actors with their scientific, technological and emancipatory resources without any previous, formal, government involvement.

But, on the other hand, it also true that lack of government involvement cannot mean either that those private entities should not be considered responsible for fundamental rights infringements, or that nation states are free of the protective obligations imposed upon them in order to combat threats to fundamental rights in areas remote from the state.[121]

It is exactly this, the one right scenario, in which constitutional law could rediscover its original roots in the new season of transnational law.

---

[118] P. Berman, 'Cyberspace and the state action debate: the cultural value of applying Constitutional norms to "private" regulation', 71 *University of Colorado Law Review* (2000), 1263–310.

[119] See Teubner, note 113 above, p. 7. See also J. Paust, 'Human rights responsibilities of private corporations', 35 *Vanderbilt Journal of Transnational Law* (2002), 801–25; and P. Muchlinski, 'Human rights and multi-nationals, is there a problem?', 77 *International Affairs* (2001), 31–48.

[120] J. von Bernstoff, 'The structural limitations of network governance: ICANN as a case in point' in Joerges, Sand and Teubner, note 109 above, p. 278.

[121] See Teubner, note 113 above.

Epilogue

Rethinking aloud

NEIL WALKER

1. Rethinking allowed

Any book that sets out to 'rethink' something as exhaustively 'thought-through' as law is asking for trouble. Is it not at best a vain hope, at worst a hubristic conceit, to set out to reconsider and reconstruct the intellectual foundations of a form of practical reason that has survived – and sometimes prospered – for thousands of years? This is not just a matter of age, of whatever sanctity we might attach to tradition or whatever value we might ascribe to accumulated wisdom. It is also because law is by its very nature past-oriented. When the first-year law student is introduced to the idea of legal authority, she is also introduced to a methodology that is intrinsically backward-looking. We attribute legal authority on the basis of some existing legal form – statute, constitution, code, custom, treaty, case precedent or whatever. And, as Kaarlo Tuori reminds us in his introductory essay, if we look beneath these legal surfaces there is a much deeper level of sedimented legal knowledge and culture that provides an implicit guide – or, more correctly, a set of cross-cutting indications – as to how we should organise the juridical world into different legal concepts, categories, doctrines, disciplines, orders and systems, and as to how we should frame, interpret and resolve legal problems. Beyond law's explicit past-directedness, then, there is a whole hinterland of assumptions and orientations that ground law's present even more firmly in its past practice and experience. We surely tamper with all of this at our peril.

But tamper with it we must; so runs the consistent and compelling message of this volume. Law in the transnational age confounds much of the received wisdom and settled authority of law in modernity. Old distinctions between public and private, national and international, constitutional and administrative, even norm-making and norm-applying, lose some of their sharpness in a new age of interlegality where different rules, orders, systems and institutions intermesh and overlap in a manner that, while far from inconceivable, was rarely and certainly less systematically *conceived* in the high modern age of 'black-box', mutually exclusive, sovereignties. This may result in the revision or reconstruction of existing legal discourses or doctrine along transnational lines, as in Alexander Somek's plea for a new, non-state-centred, cosmopolitan constitutionalism, or in Christian Joerges's reconceptualisation of private international law, or the conflict of laws, as a new law of conflicts. Or it may lead to the framing of entirely new fields, as in the Internet law analysed by Oreste Pollicino and Marco Bassini, or in the range of functionally specific, transnational, legal regimes such as *lex sportiva* discussed by Jan Smits.

But, of course, law cannot escape such a substantively rich past or methodologically insistent pastness so easily. All of the chapters in the volume, in fact, exhibit something of a Janus-faced quality. There is much reference to modern and pre-modern legal history as a key resource in reconstructing the present and blueprinting the future. Law's traditional nature, its long history of retrospective self-reference, has its inescapable say and leaves its indelible mark on this volume as, indeed, it does in the broader and burgeoning literature on law's new transnational pathways upon which this volume so richly draws. Yet if we are to avoid nostalgic Golden Ageism or head-in-the-sands denial we frankly have no option but to reconsider the foundational premises of contemporary legal ordering. Rethinking aloud would seem not merely to be *allowed*, so to speak, but even to be required. In endorsing that approach, and a volume that does much to explore it, let me simply make two brief reflections.

2. The legal scholar in the world

First, there is the question of the role of the legal scholar in all of this. It is one thing to say that we need to rethink legal thinking for a transnational age, but who precisely is or should be doing the rethinking, and what becomes or should become of that rethinking when it is done? Kaarlo Tuori draws a useful distinction here between first-order and second-order thinking in and about the law, indicating that the legal scholar straddles the two levels. Legal scholars are often commentators on first-order legislation or legal doctrine. Moreover, if they are eminent enough, or have been dead long enough, in most legal systems they can even supply a supplementary source of doctrinal authority. That is to say, they occasionally become an inside part of what it is they normally seek to appraise and influence from the outside. In addition, legal scholars, and in particular legal theorists and legal sociologists, act as second-order observers of the workings of the law. As interested spectators they tell us what is happening in the legal world, and how to make sense of it in social, political, economic, historical and, indeed, legal-systemic terms. It is here, however, that the new transnational law provides us with an interesting twist.

Now, normally, we think of second-order observation as having no effect, or certainly no direct effect, on that which is observed. But that is not always the case when we are concerned with the systemic or architectonic dimension of law. If we think of the glossators of medieval Roman law or the 'gentle civilizers' of modern international law,[1] for example, we see not just explanation and description, and so more than a mere passive recording of what is happening in the legal world. Instead, we observe a kind of active framing. In other words, the charting of the legal world from a particular disciplinary perspective in that legal world can have a constructive as well as a documentary function. It can be about creating as much as understanding, world-making as much as map-making. And from time to time therefore, the second-order chronicler of the legal world can write herself into that legal world, just as the first-order doctrinalist might. But what seems to be an occasional feature of our legal-systematising past is arguably a more insistent theme of the new transnational law. Much of the academic enterprise, say of global constitutionalism, or the new legal pluralism or, to take a particularly stylised example, global administrative law, is ontological as much as epistemological. On one hand, it seeks to explore and discover new trends in the legal environment and the law's incipient reactions to these trends. It tells us of the growth of ideas of proportionality, or the margin of appreciation, or the use of global indicators as the embryonic outline of a new category of normative proposition, or about new forms of experimental governance, or about 'nudging' and smart sanctions, or about new forms and contexts of notice and comment, or about original techniques of burden-sharing and trading in migration law or climate change law. On the other hand, it seeks to name, shape, massage, highlight, project and systematise these trends and so lend them provisional authority as part of the world's changing juridical furniture.

It seems that there are two sorts of danger, and two sorts of attendant responsibility, for the map-making and world-making legal scholar of

---

[1] See M. Koskenniemi, *The Gentle Civilizer of Nations: The Rise and Fall of International Law 1870–1960* (Cambridge: Cambridge University Press, 2001).

transnational law. One danger is simply that of irrelevance. The rethinker of legal thought may have no option but to engage in architectural work that involves a degree of forward projection, but she should avoid building castles in thin air. The new maps of the world must be discernible and plausible to the cultures of legal and political practice to which they talk, otherwise there is no practical point. There is nothing wrong with legal or any other scholars developing utopian blueprints – although legal scholars certainly possess no special qualification for such 'blue skies' thinking. But if they do so indulge the results should not be presented as maps of an emergent reality, otherwise they descend into hopeless or misleading fantasy. A second, and closely related, danger is that of arrogance, of false presumption. Transnational lawyers can indeed do vital map-making work, but it has to be understood as a process of engagement with the world, a suggestion building upon a pattern rather than an edict from on scholastic high. When Samantha Besson, for example, argues in her chapter for a certain type of understanding and development of the idea of human rights in the context of pluralist dialogue between apex courts, she is not, and should not be, telling it 'how it is' or saying where it is inexorably headed. Instead, she should see herself as engaged in a conversation of mutual persuasion and enlightenment with other academics but also, one would presume, with judges, national legislators, foreign office officials, international barristers, etc, about the direction in which an incipient trend might be persuaded to harden.

So the role of the legal scholar in all of this is that of a modest but important participant in a dialogue. This is the key sense, indeed, in which the rethinking in which we are bound to engage must be *aloud*. Part of the legal scholars' modesty, incidentally, should involve taking a hard look not only at whom they speak to and on what terms, but also at who gets to speak and how loudly *within* the academic community. The perspectivist approach developed by Tuori makes it clear that scholars with different disciplinary concerns will see the legal world in quite different ways through their particular prism of interests, values and sensibilities. And to these disciplinary fault-lines we should, of course, add other key dimensions of global difference, including the North–South divide. 'The mystery of global governance' can look very different from different positions within social and economic geography,[2] and it is clear that in transnational legal research (with the partial exception of

[2] D. Kennedy, ' "The mystery of global governance," ' 34 *Ohio Northern University Law Review* (2008), 827–60.

contemporary international law), as in so many other areas, the hegemony
of Western intellectuals in projecting their vision of the world remains
pronounced. In that regard, the present collection is certainly no worse
than most of its type; but candidly, we must concede that it is not much
better.[3]

3. Global law

A second concluding point I want to stress concerns the relationship
between the trends in transnational law that provide the general focus
of the volume's 'rethinking' efforts, and the particular question of the
development of some kind of globally unifying legal theme to overcome
what I have called 'the disorder of orders' in a world of increasingly
porous boundaries and overlapping jurisdictions.[4] Again, Kaarlo Tuori
makes some interesting observations in this direction, concluding that
it is not plausible to imagine the emergence of a new meta-principle
with the same kind of leading framing status previously held by the old
Westphalian principle of state sovereignty. Instead, he argues, the most
we can expect is the emergence of some kind of discursive consensus or
common ground, a tacit agreement to operate in the same general code
or register as a way of speaking and thinking 'Law' beyond the bounds of
different systems of 'laws'.

I share Tuori's scepticism about either the plausibility or the desirability
of a single, ruling meta-principle, but I believe more attention ought to be
paid to the different ways, short of the anointing of such a 'rule of rules',
in which we are coming to think about law again in world-encompassing
terms in a transnational age. If, as I have sought to do in other work, we
think of global law as one particular subset of transnational law and as
embracing *any endorsement of or commitment to the universal or otherwise
global-in-general warrant of some laws or some dimension of law*,[5] we can
in fact point to a number of contemporary trends in this direction. All of
these trends, as we shall see, emerge out of and reinforce a broader dialectic of legal universalism and particularism under conditions of globalisation.

---

[3] Although, as ever, Patrick Glenn's contribution is a model of subtle and inclusive awareness
of the diversity of global legal traditions and possibilities.
[4] N. Walker, 'Beyond boundary disputes and basic grids: mapping the global disorder of
normative orders', 6 *International Journal of Constitutional Law* (2008), 373–96.
[5] See my *Intimations of Global Law* (Nijmegen: Wolf Legal Publishing, forthcoming).

Global law, whether explicitly so-called or implicitly conceived, involves various different ways of imagining – and indeed *imaging* – a global aspect of law to 'contain' a world of legal variety. We may group these different ways of imagining into either convergence-promoting or divergence-accommodating approaches. The convergence-promoting approaches cover both structural and formal extensions of public international law as more than its conventional image of a transactional law between states. These are exemplified respectively by a UN-centred, institutional hierarchy sharpened through a use-of-force capacity not based on consent, and by a reconceptualisation of international law as a formally integrated world legal system complete with general principles, obligations *erga omnes, ius cogens*, etc. In both of these cases the prevailing juridical image is one of a pyramid. Within the convergence-promoting basket we also find a wide range of abstract-normative approaches, from general doctrines such as global human rights with persons rather than states as ultimate legal subjects, to pre-positive framing ideas – dimensions of legality rather than identifiable legal propositions – such as Klaus Gunther's universal code, the cosmopolitan perspective of Alexander Somek and others, or Gianluigi Palombella's global rule of law.[6] Here the defining image is of the container, either the over-container or umbrella of abstract doctrine or the under-container or vessel of pre-positive principle.

As to the divergence-accommodating perspective, this includes laterally coordinate approaches such as Christian Joerges's new law of conflicts and the plethora of new constitutional and other legal pluralisms. The image here is of links in a vertical chain permitting thin principles of connection between different legal orders, although, as Tuori reminds us, for the radical pluralists it is disputable whether the connecting mechanism has 'legal' in its DNA at all. Another divergence-accommodating approach has functionally specific regimes concerned with thematically circumscribed public goods in which the entire world is the relevant community of risk or fate, as is gradually and unevenly emergent in areas such as climate change, migration and nuclear non-proliferation. The image here is of the segment – the slice or section that presupposes a global whole but is concerned with only one part of that whole. In addition, and recalling the volume's much discussed theme of hybridity, there is a further divergence-accommodating approach to global law that involves mergers of existing legal fields into new hybrids or composite fields. I am thinking here of

---

[6] G. Palombella, 'The (re)constitution of the public' in C. MacAmhlaigh, C. Michelon and N. Walker (eds), *After Public Law* (Oxford: Oxford University Press, 2013), pp 286–310.

the so-called new 'law of peace'[7] or the new 'humanity's law',[8] both of which models involve a fresh mix of international criminal law, human rights law and other cognate elements to provide a new conception of global justice in the area of conflict resolution. I am also thinking of the new, global 'law of recognition',[9] vastly extended from the traditional state-centred international law of recognition to cover the dignitarian and participation dimensions of recognition for all active, contemporary, global constituencies – women, racial and religious minorities, etc. – previously denied them. Again, in all these areas, what is striking is the movement beyond the boundaries of international law as interstate law, and indeed constitutional law as intrapolity law, in search of a warrant that is genuinely global in its deep justification and in its jurisdictional reach. The image here is one of law as flow, as tributaries merging into a wider but still clearly embanked and so functionally segmented river.

A final group of global approaches to law also suggests a fluent movement, though here the idea of a common *historical* thread is key. Here, recalling Tuori's emphasis on legal discourse as a candidate for globality, we return to notions like global constitutional law or global administrative law, or Jeremy Waldron's new *ius gentium,* or the revived interest in the *ius commune.* Rather than hybrids, however, these are merely adaptations of a venerable legal discourse to the new global stage. These tend, moreover, to be highly open-ended, capable of being either convergence-promoting or divergence-accommodating, and so overlapping heavily with the approaches already mentioned. For example, global constitutionalism can focus on the convergence-promoting 'global constitution' of the UN, but equally on the thin intersystemic links of constitutional pluralism, or on Gunther Teubner's functionally segmented, 'societal constitutionalism'. Here the idea of global law reaches its limit of open texture, the common language as much a cue for disputation as the trace of a common code. It remains remarkable, however, that the common term of trade in this context of disputation remains law's potentially *global* warrant.

Two related points stand out from the catalogue of forms of global law as particularly significant for us. First, as with transnational law generally, the academic community – the map-makers and symbolic entrepreneurs

---

[7] C. Bell, *On The Law of Peace: Peace Agreements and the Lex Pacificatoria* (Oxford: Oxford University Press, 2008).

[8] R. Teitel, *Humanity's Law* (Oxford: Oxford University Press, 2011).

[9] E. Tourme-Jouannet, 'International law of recognition', 24 *European Journal of International Law* (2013), 667–90.

of the legal world – are implicated in the naming and framing. In some cases, as my definition suggested, the global law model is more about commitment than endorsement, projection than refinement, construction than reconstruction, and in these areas the academic community is particularly to the fore. In other cases, for example the structural and formal models, it is much more a question of the incremental extension and retailoring of existing practice, but even here the scholarly community is much involved in the work of persuasive adaptation.

Second, far from being rival candidate meta-principles, these different conceptions of global law, with their various images of pyramid, umbrella, vessel, chain, segment, flow and thread, stand in a complex relationship, one that is as much about complementarity as conflict. In all spheres of social and economic life, globalisation, with its unprecedented compression of time and space, creates and amplifies new, territorially unbounded commonalities and also new, territorially unbounded differences of interests, identities and values. Law is no exception. All of the global law models are a response to the ways in which transnational law unleashes and places in dynamic tension new forms of commonality and difference. As already noted, both divergence-accommodating approaches and convergence-promoting approaches set out to contain 'unruly' elements in the transnational mix, whether by refining or connecting the transnational fragments, or by advancing new forms of universal normative leverage. In so doing, they may supplement one another, but equally – as in the relationship between the new legal cosmopolitanism and the new legal pluralism, or between a single, post-international, global, legal order and globally segmented and fragmented regimes – they may challenge and provoke each other in a relationship of productive tension.

What this tells us, and what we must constantly bear in mind as we rethink legal rethinking, is that the academic exercise is never merely an *academic* exercise. Just as, on one hand, our models serve little practical purpose if they are purely utopian, on the other we must appreciate that such practical relevance as they have is always embedded within a deeper structure of social and economic relations and its associated contesting of values, interests, affinities and worldviews. We cannot be impervious to this deeper structure. And we cannot be innocent of its moving forces or general implications. Rather, we can only begin to rethink legal rethinking if we think hard about how we, and indeed the whole burgeoning world of transnational and global legal practice, are implicated in a larger set of fundamental changes in the world's steering mechanisms. Today, as ever, law and legal (re)thinking can only be *relatively* autonomous.

INDEX